Augusta Theodosia Drane

# The History of St. Dominic

Founder of the Friars Preachers

Augusta Theodosia Drane

**The History of St. Dominic**
*Founder of the Friars Preachers*

ISBN/EAN: 9783742814579

Manufactured in Europe, USA, Canada, Australia, Japa

Cover: Foto ©Thomas Meinert / pixelio.de

Manufactured and distributed by brebook publishing software
(www.brebook.com)

Augusta Theodosia Drane

**The History of St. Dominic**

ST. DOMINIC.

From the Print by GALLE.

# THE
# HISTORY OF ST. DOMINIC

### Founder of the Friars Preachers.

BY

## AUGUSTA THEODOSIA DRANE,

AUTHOR OF "THE HISTORY OF ST. CATHERINE OF SIENA AND HER COMPANIONS,"
"CHRISTIAN SCHOOLS AND SCHOLARS," ETC.

*WITH ILLUSTRATIONS.*

LONDON:
## LONGMANS, GREEN, AND CO.
AND NEW YORK: 15, EAST 16th STREET.

1891.

*Nihil obstat.*

FR. JOANNES PROCTER, O.P., S.T.L.
*(Censor deputatus).*


*Imprimatur.*

HENRICUS EDUARDUS,
*Cardinalis Archiepus.*


*Die 23tia Junii, 1891.*

# To the Memory

OF MANY DEAR FRIENDS DEPARTED,

WHO IN LIFE

SERVED GOD IN THE WHITE HABIT OF ST. DOMINIC,

AND WHOSE NAMES, IT IS HUMBLY HOPED,

ARE WRITTEN IN HEAVEN.

# ERRATA.

P. 16, line 7 from the bottom, for "profixiscens" read "proficiscens."

P. 28, *note*, line 2 from bottom, for "qui" read "quia."

P. 47, *note*, line 3 from bottom, for "able" read "about."

P. 65, *note*, for "Puy-Lamens" read "Puy-Laurens."

P. 82, *note*, for "Fratri" read "Fratris."

P. 121, line 4 from the bottom, for "wearing" read "weaving."

P. 130, *note*, for "en" read "im."

P. 213, line 5 from top, for "Blessed" read "Brother."

# PREFACE.

A COMPENDIUM of the Life of St. Dominic and of the history of his Order[1] was published by the present writer about thirty-four years ago. This volume having long been out of print, it has been thought desirable to supply its place with a more complete history of the Saint than it was possible to attempt within the limits of the former publication. In doing so, passages from the earlier biography have been freely reprinted whenever this was found convenient; nevertheless, such extensive corrections and enlargements have been introduced into the present volume as render it a new and distinct work.

The reader who enters on the study of the Life of St. Dominic, needs to be reminded of the period of history to which it belongs. It includes the fifty years which succeeded the martyrdom of St. Thomas of Canterbury, a time of much corruption and social disorder, during which we see the Church torn by schism and in deadly conflict with the secular power, but

[1] *The Life of St. Dominic, with a Sketch of the Dominican Order.* Burns and Lambert, 1857.

triumphant at last and asserting her supreme sway in the magnificent Pontificate of Innocent III. The men who left their stamp on the age were all characters of strong personality, whether for good or evil, and hence their lives present us with examples of heroic virtue mingled with others of appalling crime. The dominion of law was only beginning to be enforced on the turbulent society of modern Europe by powerful rulers, such as Henry II. of England, Philip Augustus of France, and the Emperor Frederic Barbarossa, themselves often responsible for deeds of violence as ruthless as any which they repressed. It may help us to realize the condition of Europe during the period of which our history treats, if we bear in mind that the birth of St. Dominic took place one year before the martyrdom of St. Thomas; that his life in the peaceful cloisters of Osma was passed at the time when Richard Cœur de Lion was warring in the Holy Land against the hosts of Saladin; that his apostolate in Languedoc coincides with that most miserable period of English history, the reign of King John and the Six Years' Interdict; and that the foundation of his Order took place in the same year that witnessed the signature of Magna Charta. It was emphatically a semi-barbarous age, replete indeed with great ideas, such as befitted the heroes of the Crusades, and the mail-clad champions of English liberty, but certainly not to be judged of by any modern standard, social or political.

When, therefore, in the early chapters of our history,

we find ourselves in presence of a war which exhibits the combatants on both sides as often practising cruelties most revolting to humanity, this need certainly cause no surprise. If, in the following pages, the details of these horrors have been but briefly alluded to, it has been from no sort of desire either to dissimulate their existence, or to defend their authors, for whom we plead only that they must be judged according to the ideas prevalent in their own time, not according to the maxims of a more civilized age. But in vindicating the saint himself from having had any share in these acts, we appeal, not to any such indulgent judgment, but to the plain truth of history. The closest and most critical examination of contemporary writers fails to elicit a single fact that can affix the stain of cruelty to the character of St. Dominic, and in the following pages we hope to have established the truth of this assertion in the mind of every candid reader.

In saying this, however, we are far from intending to represent the Saint as an advocate of religious toleration, a modern doctrine of which, as now understood, no trace is to be found in any religious body before the Edict of Nantes, and which in our own country received but partial application up to the date of Catholic Emancipation. To look for it in the thirteenth century would be an anachronism as great as to look, during the same period, for Parliamentary Government. St. Dominic during his whole career was the champion of truth, and, as such, the determined enemy of heresy. To deny this

A *

would be to rob him of one of his chief glories; but
to regard the assertion of this fact as equivalent to an
admission of his want of humanity, argues a certain
confusion of ideas, and the loss in some degree of the
sense of what is meant by religious truth. This result
has no doubt been produced in many minds by the
spread among us of modern liberal ideas, and we need
to be reminded that so far from the hatred of heresy
being opposed to true charity, it is a necessary part of
that love of souls which flows from the love of God.
The Saint who "studied only in the book of charity,"
who was "the lover of souls," because he was "the
friend of Jesus Christ," who is invoked as "the most
kind Father, Dominic," distinguished even among the
saints for his "matchless serenity," and for the tender
love that flowed from him as from "a well-spring of
sweetness," hated heresy out of the very fulness of his
love for souls; and the word VERITAS, which has
become the motto of his Order, was in his eyes but
another form of the yet sweeter word CHARITAS. This
truth, dimmed though it may have become in our own
age and country, is the real key to the character of
St. Dominic, and of all other Saints in whom this
enmity to that which opposes the truth is an integral
portion of their love of God; a Divine instinct, marking
their allegiance to His Supreme Sovereignty, and one
which can alone explain both their heroic labours in
defence of the faith, and the tears they wept over souls
perishing in error.

Although the authorities which exist for reconstruct- /
ing the history of St. Dominic are sufficiently abundant,
they do not always supply us with satisfactory information as to the chronology of his life, or the right
order of the events which they record. In these matters
hardly two writers exactly agree, and a modern compiler
can only do his best to harmonize their statements, and
choose between probabilities. All these authorities,
moreover, are not equally authentic, the more ancient
being, as a rule, the most trustworthy; whilst those
of the sixteenth and seventeenth centuries often admit
into their pages narratives which will not stand the test
of criticism. We proceed to name those most frequently
quoted in the following pages.

1. *Life of the Blessed Dominic, first Father of the FF.
Preachers.* This Life, written by Blessed Jordan of
Saxony, who succeeded St. Dominic in the government
of the Order, is printed by Echard and Quetif in the
first volume of their great work, entitled, *Scriptores
Ordinis Prædicatorum,* together with copious and valuable
annotations. It also appears in the collection of the
Bollandists (August. tom. 1). [It was written before the
year 1233, and is supplemented by an *Encyclical Letter,*
written after the translation of the Saint's body, and
giving an account of that ceremony]

2. *The Acts of Bologna,* consisting of the depositions
of nine of the brethren who were most familiar with
the Saint during his life, and whose evidence was taken
at the time of his canonization] These depositions

contain by far the most perfect portrait of the Saint that we possess, and the simplicity and sobriety of their language bespeak their truthfulness.

3. *The Acts of Toulouse*, drawn up before the canonization of the Saint, contain the testimonies of various persons, touching his virtues and miracles during his residence in Languedoc. All these persons were intimately acquainted with him, and gave evidence of what they had themselves witnessed. The letter of the Commissioners who received these depositions was signed by more than three hundred sworn witnesses.

4. *Life of the Blessed Dominic.* By Humbert de Romans, fifth General of the Order.

5. *Chronicle of the Order of Preachers.* By the same. Both written before 1254.

6. *Narrative of Sister Cecilia.* These five last authorities, all of great interest and value, are to be found printed in the Appendix to the first volume of the

7. *Annalium Ordinis Prædicatorum.* By Father Thomas Maria Mamachi, and others; a work of great research, in which are collected a vast number of original documents connected with the history of the Saint and of the Order.

8. *Life of the Blessed Dominic.* By Constantine de Medicis, bishop of Orvieto, 1242.

9. *Life of St. Dominic.* By Bartholomew of Trent, 1234. These are short biographies, but both of them contain some valuable matter elsewhere omitted. They are reprinted by the Bollandists.

10. *Vitæ Fratrum Ord. Præd.* This collection is sometimes attributed to Humbert de Romans,[2] but was really
compiled by Father Gerard de Frachet, to whom the
work was committed by Humbert after the Chapter of
1256. It consists of a collection of anecdotes, illustrative
of the early history of the Order, the second part being
devoted entirely to incidents belonging to the life of
St. Dominic. ·It is written in a style of devout simplicity, which possesses a great charm, and bears the
impress of truth on every page.

11. *Life of St. Dominic.* By Father Theodoric of
Apoldia. Father Theodoric was a German by birth,
Apoldia being a town not far from Weimar. He wrote
this Life by command of Munio de Zamora, seventh
General of the Order, about the year 1288. His work
is reprinted by the Bollandists, and though inferior in
point of style to that of Blessed Jordan, it is by far the
most full of all the ancient biographies.

Coming to a later date we have—

12. *Vitæ Patrum Ord. Præd.* By Father J. Flaminius
(Bologna, 1529).

13. *Annalium Sacri Ordinis Prædicatorum.* By Father
Thomas Malvenda (Naples, 1627). These works are full
of valuable information, but both are likewise open to the
charge of sometimes quoting from untrustworthy writers
whose statements they admit without sufficient criticism.

---

[2] The title *Blessed*, applied occasionally in the following pages to
Humbert de Romans and Alan de la Roche, is used only in compliance
with popular custom. Neither have been formally enrolled among the
*Beati* of the Order.

The same objection applies yet more strongly to the

14. *Vie du Glorieux Patriarche St. Dominique*, by Père Jean de Réchac (Paris, 1647), who repeats the most prodigious tales from uncertain authors with singular powers of credulity. Yet in spite of this defect his work is exceedingly valuable, both on account of its real research, and the information which it contains regarding the foundations of the Order in France, and the history of Prouille.

15. *Monumenta Conventus Tolosani Ord. Præd.* By Fr. John Jacob Percin (1693). This collection includes a chronicle drawn from the Life of St. Dominic by Bernard Guidonis, and other early writers, as well as a full account of the Albigenses, their errors, and the proceedings directed against them. It is an important authority for that portion of St. Dominic's life spent in Languedoc. The notices of the Albigenses which occur in the following pages are gathered partly from this source, and partly from the first volume of the second series of the *Études sur les temps primitifs de l'Ordre*, by Père Danzas, in which he devotes a considerable space to an examination of the doctrines and morals of the Cathari, and the history of the Crusade, to which those may refer who desire full information on the subject.

16. *Historia Generale di San Domenico e del Ordine suo.* By P. Ferdinand Castiglio (Venice, 1529). This learned and eloquent work was written in Spanish and translated into Italian by P. Timotheo Boltoni. In it the author has collected a vast amount of information, regarding

not only St. Dominic, but all the illustrious members of the Order who flourished up to the beginning of the sixteenth century.

17. *Della nobile e generosa progenie di San Domenico in Italia.* By Fr. Gio. Michele Pio. By the same author,

18. *Vite degli uomini illustri di S. Domenico* (Bologna, 1607). Both these works, but particularly the former, are invaluable authorities for tracing the history of the Italian foundations. The author has bestowed the most patient and conscientious labour in examining the MS. records preserved in the several convents, and in tracing the itinerary of the Saint in his different journeys through the north of Italy. He also furnishes us with an account of all the brethren of any celebrity who flourished in these convents, as well as in the provinces of France, Spain, and Germany, and he exhibits a care and judgment in the selection of his facts which is not always shared by writers of the same date.

19. *Vie de St. Dominique de Guzman.* Par R. P. A. Touron (Paris, 1639). Touron, it need not be said, enjoys a high reputation as an accurate and trustworthy historian, and his authority is therefore very great. When he fails it is certainly not on the side of over-credulity, and his disposition is generally to reject facts of a supernatural character rather than too freely to admit them. Whatever he does admit, therefore, we may feel sure has stood the test of close and severe investigation; and his history is rendered the more valuable by the very full references and quotations given for every statement.

20. *Vita del glorioso Patriarcha S. Domenica.* By Fr. Michel Angelo Nanni (Urbino, 1650).

21. *Vita di S. Domenico.* By Fr. Francesco Polidori (Rome, 1777). In the first of these Italian lives is collected every particular of any interest appertaining to the subject, without much exercise, however, of the critical faculty. The second is written with great judgment and accuracy, rejecting all narratives of doubtful character or authority.

22. *Les Dominicains dans l'Université de Paris.* Par l'Abbé Eugène Bernard (Paris, 1883).

23. *St. Bertrand de Garrigue, compagnon de St. Dominique.* Par l'Abbé J. P. Isnard (Valence, 1885).

24. *Notes pour servir à l'histoire de N. Dame de Prouille.*

26. *Histoire populaire de N. D. de Prouille.*

The great works of Echard and the Bollandists in their Annotations and Dissertations supply all that can be desired in the way of criticism in the use of the more ancient authorities, though the critics do not always agree in their respective conclusions. Echard has in addition attempted a chronological table of the events in St. Dominic's life, which has generally, though not invariably, been followed in the present work.

Among other writers who have treated of the life of St. Dominic, and whose works are occasionally referred to, are Vincent of Beauvais and Stephen of Salanhac, both of the Order of Preachers; together with the two historians, Peter de Vaulx-Cernay and William de Puy-

Laurens, who are regarded as the principal authorities for all that regards the history of the Crusade.

Certain inedited MSS. in the *Bibliotèque de la Ville* at Toulouse, contain the depositions made in the year 1245 and 1246 before the Dominicans Bernard de Caux and Jean de St. Pierre, and these have furnished some valuable facts as to the part taken by St. Dominic in the reconciliation of heretics.

For our illustrations we are endebted to the pencil of Mr. T. Sulman, whose drawings have been executed chiefly from photographs taken on the spots represented, or from the frescoes of Père Besson in the chapter-house of St. Sixtus. Three woodcuts are reproduced from the pages of the *Année Dominicaine*, through the obliging kindness of the editor of that Review.[3]

It only remains for us to express our grateful thanks to those kind friends whose generous assistance in the compilation and transcription of these pages has so greatly lightened the labours of the writer. May they find an abundant reward from the intercession of that loving Father in whose honour the work was undertaken, and to whom it is now offered as an homage of filial devotion.

A. T. D.

*St. Dominic's Convent, Stone.*
*April 14, 1891.*

---

[3] They are, the crucifix of St. Dominic, the convent of Calaroga, and the chasuble of St. Dominic.

# CONTENTS.

|  |  |  | PAGE |
|---|---|---|---|
| Chapter | I. | Childhood and University life. | 1 |
| „ | II. | The Subprior of Osma. | 12 |
| „ | III. | The Albigenses | 23 |
| „ | IV. | Beginning of the Apostolate | 37 |
| „ | V. | Prouille. | 49 |
| „ | VI. | Murder of the Legate. | 61 |
| „ | VII. | The Crusade | 73 |
| „ | VIII. | St. Dominic, the Apostle of Languedoc. | 87 |
| „ | IX. | St. Dominic, the Inquisitor | 106 |
| „ | X. | St. Dominic and the Holy Rosary | 120 |
| „ | XI. | Muret | 138 |
| „ | XII. | Foundation of the Order | 149 |
| „ | XIII. | Confirmation of the Order | 162 |
| „ | XIV. | Dispersion of the Brethren | 176 |
| „ | XV. | Return to Rome | 187 |
| „ | XVI. | St. Sixtus | 199 |
| „ | XVII. | Santa Sabina | 225 |
| „ | XVIII. | Blessed Reginald of Orleans | 247 |
| „ | XIX. | Portrait of St. Dominic | 254 |
| „ | XX. | Journey to Spain | 273 |
| „ | XXI. | St. Dominic in Spain | 281 |
| „ | XXII. | From Spain to Paris | 299 |
| „ | XXIII. | Paris University | 315 |
| „ | XXIV. | From Paris to Bologna | 334 |
| „ | XXV. | Reginald in Bologna | 341 |
| „ | XXVI. | Reginald in Paris | 356 |
| „ | XXVII. | St. Dominic in Bologna | 364 |
| „ | XXVIII. | St. Dominic's fifth visit to Rome | 379 |
| „ | XXIX. | First General Chapter. | 390 |
| „ | XXX. | Foundations in Italy | 407 |
| „ | XXXI. | Last visit to Rome, and Second General Chapter | 425 |
| „ | XXXII. | The Dominicans in England | 441 |
| „ | XXXIII. | Veni dilecte | 454 |
| „ | XXXIV. | Canonization of St. Dominic | 468 |

# ILLUSTRATIONS.

| | PAGE |
|---|---|
| Portrait of St. Dominic (from the print by Galle). *Frontispiece.* | |
| * Baptism of St. Dominic | 1 |
| St. Dominic disputing with the heretics (from a fresco by Simon Memmi) . . . . . . . *To face* 41 | |
| The Miracle of Fanjeaux, from the Ark of St. Dominic . *To face* 46 | |
| The Nuns of Prouille | 49 |
| West door of the Church of St. Gilles | 73 |
| Carcassonne | 87 |
| * St. Dominic at Muret | 138 |
| Crucifix of St. Dominic . . . . . . *To face* 146 | |
| * Vision of the holy Apostles | 162 |
| * Confirmation of the Rule | 171 |
| * Dispersion of the brethren | 176 |
| Tombstone of Simon de Montfort | 186 |
| Chapter House, St. Sixtus | 199 |
| Santa Sabina from the river | 224 |
| * St. Dominic led by the Angel | 246 |
| St. Dominic meditating on the Gospels (Fra Angelico) | 254 |
| The Alcazar of Segovia | 281 |
| The Convent of Calaroga . . . . *To face* 296 | |
| Rocamadour | 299 |
| Bell at Rocamadour | 305 |
| Cloisters of San Domenico, Bologna | 341 |
| Entrance to Santa Sabina | 379 |
| Piazza of San Domenico, Bologna | 390 |
| Church of San Domenico, Siena | 407 |
| St. Peter Martyr (Fra Angelico) | 425 |
| Seal of St. Dominic | 427 |
| Preaching Yard, Hereford | 441 |
| Seal of the Convent of Norwich | 447 |
| Scala Coeli | 454 |
| The Ark of St. Dominic . . . . *To face* 471 | |
| The Chasuble of St. Dominic . . . . *To face* 473 | |

The woodcuts marked * are from frescoes by Père Besson.

BAPTISM OF ST. DOMINIC.

# CHAPTER I.

### CHILDHOOD AND UNIVERSITY LIFE.

#### 1170—1195.

THE traveller who makes his way from the city of Osma to
the neighbouring town of Aranda in Old Castile, after crossing a barren and undulating plain of vast extent, finds himself
about half-way on his route at the entrance of a little village
which clusters at the foot of the mountains, whilst somewhat
higher up their slope may be seen a huge pile of buildings
easily to be recognized as those of a convent. Among them,
together with other more modern erections, there appears a
massive square tower of ancient date, surrounded by a court-
yard and a little flower garden. This is all which now
remains of the castle of the Guzmans, lords in the twelfth
century of the surrounding territory; and the village is none

B

other than "the fortunate Calaroga," destined to a happy immortality as the birthplace of the great Patriarch St. Dominic. In the large and handsome church attached to the convent, where a community of his religious daughters guard with their prayers what is now one of the holy places of Spain, is shown in front of the sanctuary a square space surrounded by a balustrade, on which a handsome monument has recently been erected. This, which is supposed to mark the exact site of his birth, is called the *Cuna*, and a crystal well has sprung up on the spot, the water of which is devoutly drunk by pilgrims.

There, then, in the year 1170, during the Pontificate of Alexander III., was born the most illustrious member of a family not the least noble among the grandees of Spain. There appears every probability that the ancestors of the Guzmans were of northern, not of Latin, extraction; and whilst some adduce proofs of their being originally Visigoths, others are not wanting who claim for them an Anglo-Saxon descent.[1] To whatever nation we may trace their remote ancestry, it is certain that the house of Guzman amply justified its claims to nobility both of rank and character. The records of the family preserve the memory of a long line of warriors and statesmen, whose names fill an honourable place in the history of their country. One of these was the gallant knight, Nugno de Guzman, who took part in the siege of Toledo, when that city was recovered from the Moors by Alphonsus VI. Of his two grandsons, the youngest was Don Felix Guzman, father to our saint, from whose elder brother, Alvar Diaz, descended the main branch of a family allied to many a noble house, and even to the royal blood of Castile. These alliances, and the privileges granted to the Guzmans by successive sovereigns, are set forth at length in the pages of more than one historian, and need not be repeated here. But the immediate ancestors of St. Dominic have a claim to our notice, on other and far higher grounds than the nobility of their pedigree. He was born of a family of saints. Felix

---

[1] See *Année Dominicaine*, August, 1889.

Guzman took in marriage Joanna of Aza,[2] belonging,
according to Castiglio, to a noble Castilian family, though
Père Jean de Réchac asserts her claim to be regarded as a
daughter of the ducal house of Brittany.  But, if authorities
differ as to the genealogy of Joanna, they one and all agree
in bearing testimony to her sanctity, and in our own time
she has been formally enrolled among the Blessed of the
Order.  Don Felix was not unworthy to be her husband, and
the household over which they ruled was so remarkable for
its piety and good order, that it was commonly said rather
to resemble that of a monastery than of a knightly castle.
Of their three sons, Antonio, the eldest, became a secular
priest, and, enamoured of holy poverty, distributed his
patrimony to the poor, and retired to a hospital, supposed
to have been that of St. Mary Magdalen, attached to the
neighbouring monastery of Silos, where he spent the remainder of his days humbly ministering to the sick. Manes,
the second son, also embraced the ecclesiastical state, and is
said by the historians of Silos to have taken the Benedictine
habit in the monastery of Gumiel d'Izan, a filiation from
Silos, which afterwards passed into the hands of the Cistercians.  At a later period, as we shall see, he became one of
the first members of the Order of Preachers.

By the dedication of both their sons to the service of the
sanctuary, Don Felix and his wife were left without an heir
to carry on the succession of their family, and desiring greatly
to obtain from heaven the gift of yet another son, Donna
Joanna resolved to present her petition to God through the
intercession of St. Dominic of Silos, a saint at that time
renowned throughout Spain by the fame of his miracles.

The monastery of Silos, which stands in the near vicinity
of Calaroga, was, at the time of which we write, a majestic
pile, the resort of pilgrims from every part of Spain; and
not only the shrine of the saint, but the very gates of
the monastery, were thickly covered with votive offerings,

---

[2] Aza is a small town not far from Aranda, on the southern bank of the
Douro.

specially with the chains of captives who had recovered
their liberty from slavery amongst the Moors by invoking
the saint of Silos.   Time has respected the ancient abbey,
which, though shorn of much of its former magnificence,
still contains his holy relics, preserved in a silver urn; and
together with them, are shown the chalice used by the
saint when celebrating Mass, his abbatial staff, and the
little cell where he breathed his last sigh.   The rugged
mountain road by which the abbey is approached is probably
the same as that traversed by Joanna, and the pilgrim may
still kneel on the spot where, seven centuries ago, she offered
her fervent prayers.   With the approbation of the abbot,
Joanna began a novena, spending not her days only, but her
nights also in the church, the hard pavement of which was
her only bed.   On the seventh day of the novena the saint
appeared to her, and declared to her that her prayers were
heard, and that she would become the mother of a son who
should be the light of the Church and the terror of heretics.
In gratitude she offered to the saint the child who was to be
given her through his intercession, and promised that in
memory of this favour he should bear the name of Dominic.
And it is added that before his birth she beheld her son in a
dream or vision, represented under the figure of a black and
white dog, holding in his mouth a torch which kindled and
illuminated the entire world.

The child thus obtained by prayer seemed marked even
from his cradle as specially chosen for the service of God.
The noble lady who held him at the font saw, as the water
was poured on his head, a brilliant star shining on his forehead, a circumstance which has been thought worthy of
notice in the Breviary Office for his feast—

> Stella micans in fronte parvuli
> Novum jubar præmonstrat sæculi.

Nor can we resist connecting this well-attested tradition
with the beautiful description of his appearance in after-life,
given by his spiritual daughter the Blessed Cecilia of Rome,
who tells us that " from his forehead, and between his brows,

there shone forth, as it were, a radiant light which filled men with respect and love."

We read also that whilst still an infant his father, Don Felix, with others of the household, beheld a swarm of bees settle on those lips, which were hereafter so eloquently to declare the Word of God; and at the same tender age, he was one day found by his nurse lying on the bare ground, though by what means he had left the cradle remained unexplained. The fact was remembered in after-years, as a token of that love of poverty and mortification which was to mark his future career, and to which Pope Gregory IX. refers in the Bull of his canonization, when he declares him to have waged a life-long war against all the delights of the flesh.[1] These and other prodigies disposed his parents to regard him as called to no ordinary destiny; and, as in the days of the Baptist, they said one to another, "What manner of child is this, think you? for the hand of the Lord is surely with him."

In fact, his conduct in those early years seemed to justify the presages which had been formed regarding him. It was his happiness to grow up in the atmosphere of a holy household, and to receive his first impressions from the teaching and example of a saintly mother, from whom he received two lessons which in after-years bore precious and abundant fruit. He learnt from her the habit of prayer and the habit of charity. Even when her son was almost an infant, Joanna was in the habit of carrying him with her to daily Mass, at which he assisted with precocious intelligence, in that parish church which still stands, poor and unpretending in its exterior, in much the same condition which it exhibited seven hundred years ago. And among the scanty notices preserved of her life is one which reveals her tender love of the poor, whose wants she relieved with so generous a hand as to deserve a special token of Divine approval. For having distributed in alms all the wine contained in a certain barrel, it was found miraculously refilled.

---

[1] "Sagittante delicias carnis."

These lessons were not thrown away on the heart of the little Dominic. Never was he seen to take part in the trifles common to his years. His recreation was to be taken to the church, where he would repeat the little prayers he had been taught by his mother, and listen with delight to the sacred psalmody. At an age when reason had not yet fully dawned he displayed a certain instinctive love of penance. The action reported of him when yet in his cradle was again and again repeated during his childhood, and he would often rise from his little bed and pass the night on the bare ground.[4] In the words of Blessed Jordan, "he seemed at once both young and old, for whilst the fewness of his years proclaimed him to be still a child, the sagacity of his demeanour and the steadiness of his character seemed rather to belong to one who had reached maturity."[5]

These dispositions filled the hearts of his parents with joy and thankfulness, and they considered how best to guard the treasure committed to their care, and to cultivate those seeds of Divine grace that had been so liberally sown in his soul. In those days it was the custom for the sons of noble families to receive their education, not in their own homes, but as pages in the household of some baron or ecclesiastic. This education generally began at the age of seven, and it was, therefore, quite in accordance with the manners of the times that at this age Dominic should leave his parents' roof and be placed under other care. The home which they chose for him, however, was no baronial castle, where he would have been trained in the hall and the tilt-yard, and taught the accomplishments of a perfect knight. Apparently by his mother's desire he was sent to the house of her brother, the archpriest of the church of Gumiel d'Izan, a town about twenty miles north-west of Calaroga, and the place of sepulture of the family of Guzman. Under the care of his uncle, a man of great prudence and piety, Dominic began his first studies, and prosecuted them with characteristic ardour. His whole time was divided between reading, prayer, and the service of the altar. Closely attached to his uncle's company, he followed all the offices of the Church, and took great delight in the ecclesiastical chant, the study of which in those days formed almost as essential a branch of liberal education as that of the Latin tongue or grammar. It was also his duty to serve at Mass, and to attend to the care of the sanctuary, and these duties he discharged as a labour of love, bearing himself with wonderful reverence in the presence of the Blessed Sacrament, sweeping the chapels, adorning the altars, and joyfully performing every humble office, whilst from time to time he recreated his soul by singing the hymns of the Church.[6]  As he was endowed with an excellent understanding, he made rapid progress in his studies, but did not on that account relax in his exercises of piety.  "If he prayed," says Réchac, "it was with ardour; if he studied it was with attention; if he sang he did so with fervour, and an angelic modesty; if he conversed it was with humility."  Specially was he observed to shun all that could tarnish the spotless purity of his soul, and in the words of Theodoric, "as a child of election, he guarded innocence, loved cleanness of heart, and preserved good discipline."  Thus seven more happy years passed away, some portion of which, it appears probable, was spent in the neighbouring monastic school of La Vigne, of the Order of Premontré, governed at that time by another of his uncles, Don Dominic Garcia d'Aza, whose tomb is still shown, and bears an inscription declaring him to have had "the incomparable honour of being the preceptor of St. Dominic, the founder of the Friars Preachers."

But at the age of fourteen it became necessary to consider what further steps should be taken to complete his education and fit him for his future career.  That a youth of his dispositions should make choice of the ecclesiastical state could hardly be matter of surprise, nor, in spite of their desire to perpetuate their family, did his parents place any

---

[6] The parish church of Gumiel still stands, and contains many memorials of the saint. The house occupied by his uncle is also shown, a few paces from the church.

obstacle in the way of his vocation.[7]  Desiring on the contrary to further it by every means in their power, they resolved on sending him to Palencia, the public schools of which city were at that time renowned throughout Spain for their excellence, though they did not obtain the privileges of a University till fifteen years later.[8]  There he followed the usual course of rhetoric and philosophy, not omitting several branches of natural science; but though he applied himself with diligence and success to the acquisition of humane letters, it was with yet greater eagerness that he entered on the study of theology and the Holy Scriptures. "Thirsting after these streams of living water," says Blessed Jordan, "they became sweeter than honey to his mouth." For the space of four years he gave himself up with such indefatigable ardour to the pursuit of sacred science, that he deprived himself of sleep, and spent the greater part of the night as well as of the day in study; and his memory was so retentive that it became a prodigious storehouse of heavenly maxims.  Nor was he content without reducing them to practice.  As Blessed Jordan beautifully remarks, "his was one of those blessed souls of whom the Gospels declare that they not only hear the Word of God, but keep it.  And as there are two ways of keeping the Word of God— and a double sanctuary, whereof one is the memory and the other the heart, so the Blessed Dominic was not satisfied with hearing and retaining the Divine Word, but let it penetrate deeply into his soul, until its fruits shone forth in works worthy of salvation."  He was intimately convinced that a knowledge of Divine Truth can never be fully

[7] There is some reason for supposing that Joanna had other children born after St. Dominic.  Flaminius speaks of two of his nephews who entered the Order of Preachers, and of a third who, at the age of fifteen, went to Rome to attend the Jubilee of 1200, and lived to return thither at the next Jubilee of 1300, making oath before the reigning Pontiff Boniface VIII. as to the fact of his former visit.  We also read of two other nephews who were present at the great battle against the Moors of Nava los Tolosas; but it is possible that by the name of nephews is to be understood a more distant kinsmanship.

[8] This University was afterwards incorporated with that of Salamanca by King Ferdinand III.

acquired by those who neglect to subjugate the flesh to the spirit; and with this view, for ten years, he never broke the rule he had imposed on himself, when entering the schools, of abstaining entirely from wine. We read also that he took no part in the amusements of his young companions, that he scrupulously avoided the company of women, and that, faithful to the habits of his childhood, he most often took his scanty slumbers on the ground, or even on the cold stones.[9] "It was a thing most marvellous and lovely to behold," says Theodoric of Apoldia, "this man, a boy in years, but a sage in wisdom; superior to the pleasures of his age he thirsted only after justice; and not to lose time, he preferred the bosom of his holy mother the Church, to the aimless and objectless life of the foolish world around him. The sacred repose of her tabernacles was his resting-place, his time was equally divided between prayer and study; and God rewarded the fervent love with which he kept His commandments, by bestowing on him such a spirit of wisdom and understanding, as made it easy for him to resolve the most deep and difficult questions." [10]

But among the virtues which he practised, two shone forth with special lustre, his angelic modesty and his tender compassion for the poor. He had early learnt that secret of the saints, which teaches them to place their innocence under the protection of the Queen of Virgins. From his childhood upwards, Dominic had showed himself her faithful client and servant. Some writers assure us that the devotion of the Rosary had already been revealed to him, and that he was in the habit of using it daily.[11] If this statement be held as doubtful, we have more authentic assurance of the singular love which he bore for the Angelic Salutation and the Our Father, "which latter prayer," says Bartholomew of Trent, "he never wearied of repeating." Nor did his application to study in any degree interrupt his practices of

---

[9] Theod. c. i. n. 18.

[10] *Ibid.*

[11] Réchac, who bases his assertion on the authority of Alan de la Roche.

devotion, which he very early reduced to rule, having, according to Flaminius, fixed times for prayer and meditation.[12]

He was just finishing his course of theology, when an opportunity occurred for manifesting that singular compassion for every form of suffering with which his heart overflowed. In the year 1191 the whole of Spain was desolated by a terrible famine, felt with peculiar severity in the provinces of Leon and Old Castile. The city of Palencia shared in the general misery, which the citizens showed but little disposition to relieve.

But their languid charity was shamed by the example of our young student. Not content with giving away everything he possessed in alms, Dominic, when his money was exhausted, sold his clothes, his furniture, and more precious than all beside, his very books, which as one writer tells us, were commented by his own hand, *manu suâ glossatos*,[13] and distributed the price to the starving multitudes. To estimate the cost of such a sacrifice, we must remember the rarity and value of manuscripts in the twelfth century. Yet when his companions expressed astonishment that he should thus deprive himself of the means of carrying on his studies, he replied in words preserved by one of his own followers, and treasured by after-writers as the first from his lips that have come down to posterity. " Would you have me study off these dead skins, when men were dying of hunger ? " [14]

So noble an example seems to have kindled the flame of charity in the hearts of those who witnessed it. The professors and students contributed generous alms, the citizens threw open their granaries ; and their united efforts soon relieved the most urgent needs of the sufferers.

A yet more heroic act of charity is recorded by all his biographers, and appears to belong to about the same date. Finding a poor woman in great distress on account of her son who had been taken captive by the Moors, Dominic, whose funds had been entirely exhausted during the time of

---

[12] " Orationes et contemplationes, quibus se totum statis horis dedebat."
[13] Stephen of Spain.        [14] *Ibid.*

the famine, desired her to sell him and release her son with the price; but needless to say, the generous proposal was not accepted. ✗

The example of such a life could hardly fail to make itself felt among his fellow-students. As those who knew him best assure us Dominic possessed in a very high degree that gift by which certain souls communicate themselves to others. " No one ever spoke with him without being better." No wonder, therefore, that many of his companions were drawn to God through his influence, and among them we are told was a young German student, Conrad d'Urach, who, touched by the Spirit of God, entered the Cistercian Order, of which he eventually became Abbot General. He was afterwards created a Cardinal and proved himself, as we shall see, a staunch friend and protector of the Order of Preachers.[16]

Dominic's course of studies at the University lasted ten years, of which six were devoted to the study of arts and four to theology. During this time he seems to have lost both his parents. The precise date of their death is not recorded, but we know that the bodies of both were interred in the church of the Cistercian monastery of Gumiel, whence in the year 1318 the remains of Blessed Joanna were transported to Penafiel, where the Infant Don John Emmanuel had founded a convent of Friars Preachers attached to his own castle. A magnificent monument was erected over her place of burial with an inscription which bears witness to her reputed sanctity: *Hic jacent ossa Sanctæ Joannæ uxoris D.D. Felicis de Guzman Patris B. Patriarchæ Dominici. Ejus pia memoriæ dicatum a filiis.*

[16] Malvenda, 1222, cc. 18, 19; Réchac, p. 44.

THE city of Osma, which in our own day scarcely exceeds the limits of a village, was in the twelfth century a place of no small importance, and was built upon the site of a yet more ancient Roman city, remains of which may still be seen occupying the summit of the hill on the sides of which the modern Osma stands. No picturesque beauty of any kind marks the neighbourhood; but rather a desolate severity, fitter to nurture its inhabitants in habits of labour and austerity than to prove a home of luxury or the arts. At the time to which our history belongs however, Osma, besides its importance as a frontier city, was about to become the centre of a noteworthy ecclesiastical reform. In 1194 its see was filled by Don Martin de Bazan, a prelate of eminent holiness and most zealous for the restoration of Church discipline. Following the plan then adopted in most European countries, to which moreover he was strongly urged by the recommendation of Pope Alexander III., he had engaged in the difficult task of converting the canons of his cathedral into Canons Regular, an arrangement by which they became subject to stricter ecclesiastical discipline and community life. In this labour he was greatly assisted by one whose name will ever have a peculiar interest to the children of St. Dominic—Don Diego de Azevedo, the first prior of the reformed chapter, who afterwards succeeded Don Martin in the episcopal see of Osma. Noble by birth, he was no less distinguished by the sanctity of his life. "Loving God above all things," says Theodoric, "he counted himself as nothing, and thought only how to gain the greatest number of souls to Christ." The name of Dominic and the reputation no less of his holiness than of his learning were naturally well known both to the bishop and to Diego, who determined to secure him, if possible, as a member of the new community, not doubting that his influence and example would powerfully assist their efforts at reform. In his twenty-fifth year, therefore,[1] Dominic received the habit of the Canons Regular, the white tunic and linen rochet, over which in choir a black mantle was also worn; and as he thus outwardly assumed the livery of religion, so did he clothe himself inwardly with the new man in Christ Jesus. Together with the Rule of St. Augustine he embraced all the observances of religious life; and the influence of his character was so soon felt and appreciated by his brethren, that though the youngest among them, he was shortly afterwards elected Subprior, an office which included the duties of archdeacon. In this position Dominic applied himself without delay to acquire the virtues proper to his state, that he might himself follow the way of perfection he was required to teach to others.

It was with this purpose, that choosing for his authority the pure wells of antiquity, he took for his text-book the *Conferences of Cassian;* not reading them alone, but entering into their very pith and savour, and learning from them the precious secrets of the spiritual life. The foundations of that life he placed in humility, omitting no means whereby

---

[1] Echard supposes that St. Dominic did not take the Canon's habit till the year 1198, when he would have been twenty-eight years of age, and imagines him to have spent the intervening years teaching at Palencia. This supposition rests on the single fact that the letter of Pope Innocent III. approving the reform at Osma, bears that date; whence it is argued, that he could not have received the habit at an earlier period. But though the reform then received its final approval, it is quite evident that it took several years fully to accomplish, St. Dominic probably bearing his part in the good work. Nor is there the smallest evidence of his having remained at Palencia after the expiration of his ten years of study. On the contrary, it is distinctly stated that, at the end of those ten years, by the *command of Diego,* he returned to the moderate use of wine. Diego therefore was at that time already his Superior.

he might ground himself in that queen of virtues. "In lowliness of heart he esteemed others better than himself: on the canons, his colleagues, he lavished every mark of veneration and respect, and regarding himself as the last of all, he showed himself ever ready to take the lowest place." [2] Blessed Jordan of Saxony has left us a beautiful picture of his manner of life at this period.

"Now it was," he says, "that he began to appear among his brethren like a bright burning torch, the first in holiness, the last in humility, spreading about him an odour of life which gave life and a perfume like the sweetness of summer days. Day and night he was in the church, praying as it were without ceasing. God gave him the grace to weep for sinners and for the afflicted; he bore their sorrows in an inner sanctuary of holy compassion, and so this loving compassion which pressed on his heart, flowed out and escaped in tears. It was his custom to spend the night in prayer, and to speak to God with his door shut. But often there might be heard the voice of his groans and sighs, which burst from him against his will. His one constant petition to God was for the gift of a true charity; for he was persuaded that he could not be truly a member of Christ unless he consecrated himself wholly to the work of gaining souls, following the example of Him, Who sacrificed Himself without reserve for our redemption." Theodoric tells us that these fervent prayers were accompanied by practices of penance so severe, that they had to be moderated by his superiors. "He macerated his body by fasts and prolonged abstinence, so as hardly to take what sufficed for the support of nature. He neither ate flesh-meat with the canons his brethren, nor refused it, but was accustomed to hide it in the food. In compassion for his weakness the venerable Bishop Diego obliged him to resume the use of wine from which he had abstained for ten years; but though he obeyed, he took it only in small quantities and largely diluted with water." [3] The long lapse of centuries has not effaced the memory of the saint whose presence once cast the perfume

<hr />

[2] Theodoric, 23.          [3] Ibid. 24.

of holiness over the cloisters of Osma. The stall he occupied
in the choir is still religiously shown, and as a mark of veneration is never occupied by any of the canons; and his cell is
likewise preserved, wherein it is said, may yet be discerned
traces of the blood shed in his nightly disciplines.

Some writers have attempted to prove that during the
period of his life at Osma, Dominic was engaged in a variety
of apostolic labours, and preached in many parts of Spain,
and even of France. Of this, however, there is no sufficient
evidence; on the contrary, the testimony of his earliest
biographers is express, that he was rarely seen outside the
walls of his monastery.[4] Nevertheless as the words above
quoted from Blessed Jordan abundantly testify, he was
already consumed by that noble passion for souls which
was to set its seal and impress on his after-career. " His
zeal for perishing souls," says Theodoric, " was a continual
and painful wound in his heart, for God had given to him
the gift of a perfect charity." Even at this early period,
we read that he had conceived the project of going one day
to preach the faith to the Cuman Tartars, then ravaging the
fold of Christ in Hungary and the neighbouring countries.
Diego, to whom in the confidence of friendship he revealed
his design, not only encouraged him, but even desired to
take part in the glorious enterprise. In the silence of the
cloister the Subprior of Osma was in fact being trained for
his future apostolate. And in this, as in so many other
respects, he resembled his great master and model, St. Paul,
who prepared in the deserts of Arabia to carry the Word of
God before the Gentiles,[5] and whose writings and example,
we know from certain evidence, he had early made his
favourite study.[6] Theodoric tells us that he was profoundly
versed in every part of the Sacred Scriptures, whether of the
Old or New Testament, but that his favourite portions were
the Gospel of St. Matthew and the Epistles of St. Paul,

---

[4] "Extra septa monasterii vix unquam comparuit " (Theod. 23).

[5] Galat. i. 17.

[6] "Epistolas Pauli multum studebat et eas fere corde tenus retinere "
(Theod. 195).

which he studied so constantly as to know them almost by
heart. Not only the doctrine, but the character of the great
Apostle touched a responsive chord within his soul : on that
model he seems to have shaped his whole idea of an apostolic
life ; and during those nine years of hidden communing with
God it cannot be doubted that precious seeds were sown
which needed but the Divine call to ripen into action. The
immediate circumstances which led the way to his entering
on a more active career did not seem of a kind from which
any vast results might have been anticipated.] In 1203, Don
Diego, who had succeeded to the bishopric of Osma a few
years previously, was selected by Alphonsus VIII., King of
Castile, to negotiate a marriage for his eldest son, as it is
commonly said, with a princess of Denmark. Considerable doubt, however, hangs over the accuracy of this statement. As a fact, neither Blessed Jordan, nor Theodoric of
Apoldia, make any mention whatever either of the princess
or of Denmark. The former says that the King desired a
marriage between his son Ferdinand and a certain noble lady
of the Marches, *quandam nobilem de Marchiis*. Theodoric omits
all reference to the marriage, and simply says that Diego
was sent as ambassador to the Marches on the King's affairs.
The precise locality indicated by these words is generally
acknowledged to be obscure. Bernard Guidonis, who lived
in the beginning of the fourteenth century, seems to have
been the first to suggest Denmark as thus signified, and
speaks of the travellers as in *Marchias, sive in Dacia profixiscens;* and this interpretation has been accepted by
several later writers. A much simpler and more probable
explanation, however, is offered by Père Jean de Réchac,
who suggests on the authority of a MS. history in the
Convent of St. James, of Paris, that the Marches were those
of Limousin ; in other words, the territory of the powerful
Hugh de Lusignan, who at that time reigned as Count de
la Marche, and whose alliance might suitably have been
sought by the Castilian monarch.[7] Diego chose for his

[7] The above explanation is accepted by Baillet, Fleury, and Touron.
Echard and the Bollandists examine the question and leave it undecided.

associate in the embassy thus imposed on him, his Subprior Dominic, between whom and himself there had grown up that perfect friendship which is based on an intimate sympathy, the links of which are made fast by union in God. They burned with the same zeal for the house of God, and the same ardent desire for the salvation of souls. And the Holy Spirit having filled both with His grace, He chose them for a ministry in which they suspected nothing of the designs of Divine Providence.[8]

They left Spain in the year 1203, and crossing the Pyrenees, entered Languedoc, then governed by the Counts of Toulouse, whose feudal sovereignty extended over the greater part of the Narbonnese provinces. It must be borne in mind how entirely the condition of the country differed, politically, from that existing in our own day. A large portion of the land we now call France, was then divided among a number of petty princedoms, independent in all save their feudal subjection to the crowns of France or Aragon. Toulouse, Foix, Beziers, and Cominges, were each governed by their own counts; the kings of Aragon were feudal sovereigns over considerable dominions at the mouth of the Rhone, whilst an immense territory, stretching from Normandy to the Western Pyrenees, was still subject to the English Crown.[9]

At the particular period to which our history belongs, these southern provinces were, from various causes, in a state of social disorder, which made a journey through the midst of them an undertaking of no little danger. Their rulers were generally engaged in petty wars one against another. " Armagnac, Cominges, Beziers, and Toulouse," says Michelet, " were never in agreement save when there was question of making war upon the Church." And he goes on to draw a frightful picture of the moral depravation both of princes and people. Moreover, these same provinces had been for many years wasted by the Manichean heretics,.

[8] Theod.
[9] In 1204 the greater part of this territory was wrested from King John, who retained only the provinces of Gascony and Guienne.

c

known in these parts by the name of Albigenses, who aimed equally at the overthrow of Christian faith and morals, and of all social order. Of them and of their history, we shall have more to say in future chapters, but it was on the occasion of this memorable journey that the character and extent of this terrible heresy first came under the notice of Diego and his companion. With their own eyes they beheld the fair plains of Languedoc through which they journeyed, reduced to the condition of a desert and covered with the ruins of churches and abbeys. Nor was the material desolation of the country the worst of its afflictions. Throughout many districts the faith had all but disappeared, the sacraments of the Church were despised and rejected, and a horrible corruption of manners everywhere prevailed. The zeal for God which filled both their hearts, kindled at the spectacle, and though the business on which they were then engaged, did not permit them at that time to undertake any apostolic labours, yet they received an impression which was never effaced, and which was strengthened by an incident that occurred at Toulouse, where they stopped for a night on their journey. This city was in fact the stronghold of the heretics, and from its bosom the infection had spread through all the surrounding provinces. The house where the travellers lodged was kept by a man belonging to the sect of the Albigenses; and when Dominic became aware of the fact, he resolved to attempt the rescue of at least this one soul. The time was short, but their conference was prolonged through the hours of the night; when morning dawned the winning eloquence of his unknown guest had conquered the obduracy of the heretic, and before they left his house he made his submission and was received back into the bosom of the Church. A troubadour of Picardy, who in the thirteenth century chose the history of St. Dominic as the subject of a poem, has not failed to seize on this incident as worthy of special record, and describes the conversion of the heretic in spirited words :

> Tantost s'ala agenouiller
> Devant lui et cria merci

Sire, je crois Dieu vous a chi
Envoié por moi amender.
Por cou je vous vuel creanter
Q'jamais en toute ma vie
Ne porsivrai le compagnie
De ceus ki sont contre le loy.
An cois, vivrai en droite foy,
Si com vous m'avez enseigné.[16]

"This," says Theodoric, "was the first sheaf which our saint gathered in the field of the Lord," a precious foretaste of the glorious harvest that was to follow, and, according to the historian, Bernard Guidonis, the saint from that moment conceived in his heart the project of founding an Order which should have for its object the salvation of souls by the ministry of preaching.

On reaching the end of their journey the two envoys were able to bring the negotiations to a happy issue, and returning to Castile, made known to the King the success of their mission. On the receipt of this intelligence they were once more despatched to the Marches, accompanied this time with a numerous retinue, and charged with the mission of conducting the young bride back with them to Spain. But on reaching her father's court, they found their embassy brought to an unexpected conclusion by the death of the princess after a short illness. "Death, the enemy of all men," says the troubadour poet already quoted, "death, who spares no one, neither old nor young, had not spared the young maiden, so young, so rich, and so beautiful." Thus released from their charge, the two envoys resolved before returning to Spain to make the pilgrimage to Rome. The object of the bishop in undertaking this journey was two-fold. He hoped in the first place to obtain leave from the Pope to resign his bishopric; and after that to carry out the plan long cherished by himself and his companion of preaching the faith to the heathen nations of the North.

Very few particulars have been preserved of this first visit of our saint to Rome, where the chair of St. Peter was then filled by Pope Innocent III. We only know that Diego's

[16] *Li Romans Saint Dominike.* Bibl. Nation. Fonds Français, 19531.

earnest entreaty for release was not granted, the Pope being
too well aware of his value to deprive the Church of so
zealous a pastor.   Nor did he show himself more favourable
to the bishop's other request, that he might be sent as a
missionary to the Cuman Tartars.   Whilst applauding his
generous intentions, Innocent required him to sacrifice the
wish that lay so close to his heart, and once more bow his
back to the burden of the episcopate.   "In these events,"
says Theodoric, "the wisdom of God had so directed all
things, that the pious desires of the bishop were granted,
not, indeed, in the manner he had sought, but according to
the good pleasure of the Lord; and Diego, by directing his
steps to return to Spain, carried with him the grace both of
obedience and charity."

In the course of this visit Brother Dominic became for
the first time known to the Pontiff and several of the
Cardinals, who quickly discerned the great qualities which
lay concealed under his modest exterior.   In particular, it
seems certain that the seeds were at this time laid of the
friendship which afterwards so closely united him with
the Cardinals Savelli and Ugolino, both of whom were
destined, as we shall see, to lend their powerful support to
the great work awaiting him in the future.

The two pilgrims made but a brief stay in Rome, but
before returning to Spain, they agreed to turn out of their
road to visit the great abbey of Citeaux, the mother-house
of the Cistercian Order, which at that time held the first
place in public esteem, and exercised a wide influence
throughout the Church.

They arrived at Citeaux in the spring of the year 1205,
and were received with the noble hospitality which formed
part of the Cistercian Rule.   Not to speak of the welcome
which would naturally be afforded to guests who bore so
plainly the character of servants of God, the apostolic spirit
with which both of them were animated, was one which just
then found a warm response at Citeaux. At this particular
time the Cistercian Order had been chosen by the Sovereign
Pontiff to bear the brunt of the struggle with the Albigenses;

and Arnold, Abbot of Citeaux, had been associated with other ecclesiastics whom Innocent appointed as his Legates for the purpose of taking such measures as might be necessary for checking the further spread of that heresy.

Diego and Dominic, therefore, were received with open arms, not merely as holy religious, but as apostolic men thirsting for a yet wider field in which they might labour for the salvation of souls. Yet in spite of the strong attraction with which he felt drawn to missionary labours, the sweet odour of monastic discipline which still flourished in full vigour within the walls of Citeaux, powerfully captivated the heart of Diego; and following the example which had been set some years previously by our own martyred prelate, St. Thomas of Canterbury, he begged and obtained permission to assume the Cistercian habit. Doubtless the failure of his deeply cherished plans had been no little pain to the Bishop of Osma, and his return to his diocese was a hard obedience. He was suffering under that thirst to strip himself of the world, which sometimes attacks the soul at the very time when it bows to the law that forces it back to the world's duties. Very willingly would he have remained at Citeaux, and begun his novitiate in that school of holy living; but as this could not be, he contented himself with taking the habit of the Order, and soliciting that he might carry some of the religious back with him to Spain, to learn from them their rule and manner of life.

Some authors represent St. Dominic also as having taken the Cistercian habit by way of devotion, while others affirm that he visited the Grande Chartreuse, and applying to be received there as a monk, was refused admission by the General of the Order, who dismissed him with the words, "Go, for thou art called to greater things." Of this latter statement we find no trace in any authentic history, but it is certain that the saint always retained a very special tie with the Cistercian brethren, and that his friendship with the Order was continued by his immediate followers.

Their stay at Citeaux does not appear to have been of any long duration, and at its close they set forth once more

on their homeward journey, accompanied by some of the
Cistercian brethren. Taking the route southwards, by the
banks of the Rhone, they reached Montpelier some time in
the summer of 1206.[11]   And there, as we shall frequently see,
they found the will of God awaiting them in unlooked-for
circumstances, which were destined clearly to reveal to our
saint his sublime and apostolic vocation.

[11] It must be borne in mind that the years at this time were reckoned
as beginning not in January, but in March. Their arrival at Montpelier,
therefore, took place in the same year as that in which they visited
Citeaux, although the latter event is given as happening in the year 1205,
on account of its occurring before the technical beginning of the year.
That their arrival at Montpelier was early in that summer is proved by
their presence at Montreal the same year on the feast of St. John the
Baptist.

# CHAPTER III.

BEFORE proceeding further in our history it will be necessary to present the reader with some account of the celebrated heresy, whose followers, under the various titles of Bulgarians, Patarins, Cathari, or Albigenses, waged an unceasing conflict with the Church, specially throughout the twelfth and thirteenth centuries. One and all, by whatever name they were known in popular parlance, were offshoots of that great sect of the Manicheans which from the earliest period of its existence had shown itself the most deadly enemy of the Church of Christ. Oriental in its origin, it had gradually worked its way from Bulgaria (where great numbers of a branch of the sect known as Paulicians had settled in the ninth century) up the valley of the Danube, into Swabia, whence its doctrines gradually spread into the north of Italy and the south of France.

As a fact, the Manicheans had no claim to be regarded as Christians in any sense. Their doctrines, to use the words of Père Danzas, "were the complete and radical negation of all Christian dogma." This assertion is fully in accordance with the judgment of certain Protestant historians, who, nevertheless, have undertaken to be their apologists. M. Schmidt, Lutheran Professor of the University of Strasburg, and the learned author of the *History of the Cathari or Albigenses*, frankly confesses that their teaching undermined the very foundations of Christianity. In fact, he says, " Catharism cannot even be called a Christian heresy." To this testimony we may add that of the very latest writer on the subject, also a Protestant. Mr. Henry Charles Lea, in his

*History of the Inquisition* (1888) says of the Albigensian heresy
that "it was based on a faith that can scarcely be called
Christian," and that "it threatened the permanent existence
of Christianity itself." The correctness of these statements
will not be called in question by those who have any real
acquaintance with the teaching of the sect. If its members,
for the purposes of concealment, made use of formulas in
which occur fragments of Catholic terminology, it was only
to clothe with them ideas and doctrines utterly subversive of
the Christian dogmas. They denied both the Unity and
Trinity of God, both the Divinity and Humanity of Jesus
Christ; they rejected the sacraments of the Church and her
Divine authority. To the fundamental article of the Christian
faith, which acknowledges one God, the Creator of all things,
visible and invisible, they opposed their belief in two co-
eternal principles, one, the good principle who was the
Creator of spirits, the other the principle of evil, who was
the Creator of matter, and whom they blasphemously identified with the God of the Old Testament, the inspiration of
which, it is needless to say, they rejected. If in words they
professed to believe in Father, Son, and Holy Ghost, these
terms by no means implied any admission of the doctrine of
the Holy Trinity. The Son and the Holy Ghost were, in
the Albigensian creed, angelic spirits, of whom the first-
named assumed only the appearance of mortal flesh. Their
belief in the essential evil of matter caused them to shrink
with abhorrence from the idea of the union of the Divine and
Human Nature in one Person. It equally caused their rejec-
tion of all the sacraments, in which the Church makes use
of material elements as sensible and efficacious signs of
invisible grace. These, in the eyes of the neo-Manicheans,
were diabolic inventions, and in the ceremony of initiation
the neophyte was required to renounce his Baptism, using
terms of execration in speaking of the baptismal water, or
holy chrism; and at the same time utterly to abjure the faith
of the Church of Rome. By a strictly logical consequence
of their theory on the creation of matter, they regarded the
Holy Eucharist with sentiments of peculiar horror, which

they manifested by most shocking profanations.[1]  But this
was not all.  Out of the dualism which may be regarded as
the central doctrine of the sect, they proceeded to draw
conclusions which struck at the root of all morality.  Evil of
all kind being inherent in matter created by the Evil
Principle, the soul of man created by the Good Spirit was
not to be held responsible for any deeds committed by the
body in which it had become accidentally imprisoned.  The
freedom of the will to choose between good and evil was
altogether denied; those who claimed to inflict punishment
for breaches of the laws of God and man, were denounced,
therefore, as impostors and tyrants; and thus all authority,
whether civil or ecclesiastical, which aimed at the repression
of crime, was systematically set at nought.  Nor were these
doctrines held in theory only; they were most rigorously
reduced to practice.  Whilst some, to deliver their souls
from the evil dominion of matter, held suicide to be not only
lawful but even meritorious, the larger number applied the
principle in a freer manner by permitting themselves every
kind of licence.  Their condemnation of the institution of
marriage, which formed a prominent article of their code,
struck at the root of all social morality; it destroyed the
very existence of the family, while at the same time it
imposed no restraint whatever upon the passions.  Their
theoretic contempt of authority issued in the practice of a
lawlessness which made the existence of the sect no less
dangerous to the State than it was hostile to the Church.
And inasmuch as nothing material could contribute to the
sanctification of the soul, it followed that churches, altars,
and images should be swept away as unworthy of the
votaries of a wholly spiritual worship.  In this enumeration
of the Albigensian doctrines we have purposely omitted
many blasphemous tenets held by them regarding the Sacred

---

[1] We learn from a letter by Conrad of Zähringen, who in 1219 was
Cardinal Bishop of Porto, and Legate in Languedoc, that the Albigenses
anticipated one of the worst excesses of the French Revolutionists, and six
centuries before the Goddess of Reason had been enthroned on the altar of
Notre Dame, a similar outrage had been committed in the Cathedral of
Toulouse (Danzas, *Etudes*, tom. ii. p. 265).

Humanity, as well as their shocking utterances concerning the Blessed Virgin and the saints. All the patriarchs and prophets of the Old Law were in their judgment lost souls, while they held St. John the Baptist in peculiar horror, and declared him to be one of the chief devils.

To what extent these principles were carried out, and with what success, we may have occasion to show hereafter; suffice it here to say that the condition of those districts which fell under the power of the Albigenses differed little from that of countries that had been ravaged by heathen barbarians. None of the externals of Christian worship were left in existence. "I have seen," wrote Stephen, Abbot of St. Geneviève, who was sent to Toulouse as envoy from the King of France, "I have seen churches burnt and ruined to their foundations; I have seen the dwellings of men changed into the dens of wild beasts."

But the Albigensian heresy was not merely subversive of existing institutions, it had its positive as well as its negative features. If all other rites were to be abolished, in their place was substituted the one pseudo-sacrament of the *Consolamentum*, which seems to have consisted in the imposition of hands, and recital of the *Pater noster* by one of the *perfect*. The word requires explanation, and introduces us to an important feature of the sect, its division, namely, into two grades, those of the simple *believers*, and of the fully initiated or *perfect*. The first class comprised the great body of members who were subject to few or no obligations, and for whom it sufficed that in the article of death they should receive the *Consolamentum*, which secured to the recipient eternal life without the necessity either of repentance or satisfaction. The second and much smaller class was that of the *perfect*, or fully initiated. These formed a kind of religious order, made profession of a rigid asceticism, abjured marriage,[2] and the use, not only of meat, but of eggs, cheese, and anything which had life. Whilst the supposed austerity of their lives secured for them the adulation of the multitude, there is ample evidence that it was practically but a cloak

[2] 1 Tim. iv. 3.

for licentiousness which from its very turpitude must escape popular exposure. The rigorism of their professions did but precipitate them into a lower depth of infamy. Nor will this appear surprising to any who are acquainted with that fatal law which again and again reveals itself in the history of false mysticism, the doom which seems to attach to every system of asceticism not based on Catholic teaching, in virtue of which those who in the spirit of pride would fain be supposed to lead the lives of angels, too commonly fall below the level of brutes.

The influence exercised by the *perfect* over the rest of the sect was all but unlimited. It could not be otherwise, when we remember that in their hands was supposed to rest exclusively the power of *consoling*, or, in other words, of securing the eternal salvation of the *believers*. "These unhappy men," says Stephen of Bourbon, a contemporary writer of great accuracy, "following the example of their master, Manes, who gave himself out to be the Paraclete, claim also for themselves the title of consolers. They pretend to give the Holy Spirit to a crowd of persons stained with every crime, on the sole condition that these persons should prostrate and adore them,[3] and receive from them the imposition of hands, exacting from them no kind of reparation either in act or promise, nor any sort of satisfaction."

If the perfect who formally engaged themselves to a life of extravagant austerity did not thereby escape from the infection of the most shocking disorders, it will not be difficult to conjecture what must have been the result of the Manichean doctrines on the multitude who were bound by no engagements at all, and whose prominent articles of belief effaced the very notions of sin and of moral responsibility. Without staining our pages with repulsive details, it is sufficient to say that the facts of history fully justify a

---

[3] This expression, which recurs continually in the documents of the time, is not supposed to imply religious worship properly so-called, but only certain marks of special veneration paid by the believers to the perfect. Its actual sense is, however, obscure.

contemporary writer who was perfectly well informed in the
matters of which he speaks, when he declares the actions
perpetrated by the followers of the Albigensian heresy to
have been too loathsome and horrible for description.[4]
Nevertheless the utmost difficulty was found in convicting
those accused of such crimes, for not only was it the custom
of the heretics to make use of evasions and sophisms under
examination, but there existed among them what we may
call the discipline of the secret, in virtue of which those
fully initiated, whether in the doctrine or practices of the
sect, were bound even to perjure themselves rather than to
reveal these secrets to the uninitiated.

The question naturally suggests itself how a sect, the
tendency of whose doctrines was destructive of all social
order, could successfully establish itself in a Christian
country, and obtain the support, if not the actual adhesion,
of many among its rulers. The chief reason will probably
be found in the grievous decay of manners which prevailed
in those provinces which were the principal seat of the
heresy. The people of Languedoc and Provence, descended
from Gallo-Roman ancestors, had nothing of the robustness
either of Franks or Normans. They boasted, indeed, of
their Roman refinement and superior culture, but it is
needless to remind the reader what was the character of
the later Imperial civilization. In its more modern form
it found expression in the licentious literature of the
troubadours, and in those famous tribunals presided over
by noble ladies, themselves adepts in the *gaie science*, who
did not blush to publish decrees in which the most ordinary
laws of decency and morality were set at defiance. It is
a significant fact that the Provençal troubadours never found
admittance in the Court of St. Louis, and that he permitted
none of his family to hold intercourse with them. Nor was
the chivalry of the Narbonnese provinces of better repute
than their literature. There, courage in the field and fidelity

[4] "Quæ ipsi faciunt in abscondito non est modo necesse in medium
proferre, qui sunt *fœtida et horribilia*" (Alberic Trium. Font. Gallic. Rer.
Scrip. Collection by Dom Martin Bouquet, t. xxi. p. 524).

to his plighted word were by no means necessary characteristics of the belted knight, nor did the want of these qualities earn for him any special mark of contempt. If elsewhere an extravagant adherence to the point of honour led to many grievous excesses, among too many of the nobles of Southern France, the virtue of honour was rather conspicuous by its absence. Worse than all and doubly fatal in its consequences, the prevailing vices of sloth and effeminacy had invaded the ranks of the clergy themselves. At a time when the northen dioceses of France were blest with a succession of saintly pastors whose vigilance was ever on the watch against false doctrine and evil customs, prelates like Raymund de Rabastens, Bishop of Toulouse, or Beranger, Archbishop of Narbonne, were bringing disgrace on their sacred dignity, and giving an example of every kind of disorder to the inferior clergy. Among these such laxity prevailed that the name of cleric was held in contempt, and ecclesiastics were ashamed to exhibit the tonsure or other marks of their calling. Again and again do we find the Roman Pontiffs bitterly complaining of these scandals, which they strove by all means to chastise and correct. Beranger, after repeated warnings, was finally deposed from his see by Pope Innocent III., whose tremendous denunciations of the luxury, the avarice, and the culpable negligence of the clergy may be read in his letters. Full fifty years previously St. Bernard had made the same complaints, and not only lamented that the faith should find among the clergy but few defenders (*paucitas defendentium*), but that certain priests and bishops should even be bought over to make disgraceful compacts with the heretics. The evil had not diminished with time, and at the beginning of the thirteenth century the faithful pastors in these infected provinces were largely outnumbered by those who betrayed their trust.

That a sect which avowedly defied the secular as well as the ecclesiastical authorities should find favour among the rulers of the country is a paradox to which, however, the political aspect of our own times would furnish a parallel.

Among men addicted to every licence the Manichean code of morals was acceptable enough, while there was every temptation to take part with the heretics when there was question of the spoliation of the Church. Whilst some, therefore, did not shrink from openly joining their ranks, a yet greater number contented themselves with secretly encouraging them, in the seeming persuasion that they could turn the general state of disorder and revolution to their own advantage without absolutely committing themselves as the partisans of heresy. Hence there arose among them a disloyal system of double-dealing and hypocrisy. Many of these Narbonnese nobles made it their practice, to use a common phrase, to run with the hare and to hunt with the hounds. Catholic Christianity was in those days too much the public law of Christendom for it to be altogether safe openly to disown the faith. When therefore Papal Legates or royal envoys expostulated with these men for their negligence in repressing the disorders of the heretics, their protestations of orthodoxy and their promises to see to the execution of the laws were officiously loud and prompt. Only when it came to the fulfilment of their pledges they had recourse to those shifts and evasions which exhibit them as masters in the art of equivocation. Thus princes like Raymund Roger, Count de Foix, were able to retain the name of Catholic while forming alliances of marriage with the heretics, and countenancing the *heretication*, as it was called, of their wives, sisters, and daughters. Yet their close connection with the sect did not prevent their withdrawing their protection, or even taking up arms against it whenever this suited their safety or their convenience. The double-sided bad faith thus displayed by the noble patrons of the Albigenses makes the task of the historian one of no small difficulty. The very men who appear at one time among their staunch supporters are to be found at another among the ranks of their opponents. In the case of Raymund V., Count of St. Gilles and Toulouse, for many years a prominent champion of the Albigenses, we may however infer that his change of policy was dictated by a sincere though tardy conviction of the dangerous tendency of the sect. In the year 1177 we find him writing to the Abbot and Chapter-General of Citeaux a letter in which he gives a picture of the condition of affairs which, coming from his pen, may safely be trusted as free from exaggeration. "This heresy," he writes, "has gained over even priests; churches are ruined and abandoned; the creation of man, the resurrection of the flesh, and every sacred mystery is rejected; Baptism is refused, Penance despised, and the Holy Eucharist held in abomination. Yet no one dreams of opposing these wretches. For myself I am ready to employ against them the sword that God has given me, but the forces at my command are not sufficient, as many of my nobles are themselves infected with these errors. I have recourse, therefore, to you for advice and your prayers. Spiritual arms are not enough; the temporal sword is also needed, and for this purpose I am resolved to appeal to the King of France that his presence may put an end to these abuses."

In the following year the Kings of France and England did actually undertake to proceed in person, and drive out the heretics from Toulouse and the surrounding provinces; but before unsheathing the temporal sword it was agreed at the urgent request of Pope Alexander III. to try the effect of gentler measures, and Papal Legates were appointed to visit the disturbed districts and to bring about, if possible, the return of the population into the bosom of the Church. The narrative of their labours, as given at length by Roger Hoveden, is sufficiently interesting; we will only briefly state that Peter Moran, the chief leader of the heretics, was received to penance, and sent to serve the sick at Jerusalem, while two false teachers, who after repeated tergiversations refused to confirm by oath their pretended recantation, were excommunicated and driven into exile; and these judicial sentences, not certainly extreme in their severity, were followed by the submission of great numbers of the heretics. Meanwhile the Count of Toulouse and the other feudal nobles solemnly swore in the presence of all the people to lend no support in future to the Albigenses, but to act in

concert with the ecclesiastical authorities in firmly repressing
their encroachments. How far these engagements were kept
we shall have occasion to show hereafter. But it is important
to notice that throughout the whole of these transactions, it
is from secular princes, the Count of Toulouse, and the Kings
of England and France, that the proposal comes to oppose
the Albigenses with the power of the sword. They are
roused to the necessity of action by the danger which
threatens society, the very foundations of which are being
sapped. Family ties are being destroyed by the condemnation of marriage. The moral law is set at nought, and
the rights of property are abolished. To carry on their war
of spoliation, the Albigensian leaders do not hesitate to
employ the armed bands of infamous brigands known as
Cottereaux [5] or Routiers, who lay waste churches, towns,
and villages, and commit sacrileges and profanations of the
most appalling kind. The secular rulers offer to use their
armed authority for the preservation and defence of society
from the attacks of these new barbarians, and themselves
appeal to the Church for aid and sanction. The action of
the Church is to suspend the uplifted sword, and to substitute
for armed repression the labours of her legates and envoys,
who succeed in reclaiming a great number of the heretics,
whilst the severest punishment decreed against those who
remain obstinate seems to have consisted of spiritual censures
and exile. Throughout this history it is abundantly manifest
that the action of the Church was on the side of mercy and

---

[5] The Cottereaux, known in history by a variety of other names, such
as Routiers, Basques, Aragonese, &c., were in reality soldiers of adventure,
the very off-scouring of society, made up of men of every rank, who for
one cause or another had lost all character, and hired themselves to such
princes as were not ashamed to employ their infamous services. It is
reckoned among one of the special atrocities of King John of England that
he took into his pay bands of these excommunicated ruffians, "abominable
Routiers," as Matthew Paris calls them, and let them loose on England,
after his compulsory signing of the Charter. They revenged themselves
by their crimes on society which had cast them forth out of its bosom,
and were close allies of the heretics. Raymund VI., Count of Toulouse,
was one of their chief protectors, and made use of them to pillage churches
and destroy monasteries.

moderation, and that the appeal to arms proceeded, in the first instance, from the secular rulers. The lawfulness of such an appeal was recognized by the rulers of the Church. The Third Council of Lateran, which was summoned by Pope Alexander III. in 1179, chiefly directed its canons against many abuses existing among the clergy; but it did not fail to take notice of the dangers threatened to society by the spread of the heresy which had established its head-quarters in the Narbonnese provinces. The terms in which it does so are worthy of notice as recognizing the lawfulness and necessity of seeking aid from the temporal power for the repression of a sect dangerous to the safety of society. The Cathari are anathematized together with their abettors and protectors, and with them are associated their sworn allies the Cottereaux, or brigands, who exist under various names, and ravage the unhappy provinces over which they roam. A terrible picture is drawn of their crimes and excesses, and the faithful are called on for the remission of their sins valiantly to oppose these monsters, and defend society from their assaults. Indulgences are granted to those who respond to this appeal, and the Church extends to them her protection "as to those who have taken up arms for the defence of the Holy Sepulchre." In this concluding canon of the Council, which recognizes the principle of an appeal to the secular arm, we see the germ of later action on the part of the Holy See; and the whole narrative throws important light on that great struggle between the Church and the Albigensian heresy which occupies so large a space in the history of the following century.

Admirably as the pacific measures hitherto adopted had been intended, they totally failed in their effects. The apparent submission of the heretics to the Papal Legates lasted as long as they remained in the country, and no longer; and the severer decrees of the Council found none to put them into execution. During the period from the death of Alexander III. in 1181 to the election of Innocent III. in 1198, no fewer than six Popes filled the chair of St. Peter, their deaths rapidly succeeding one another, and leaving no

D

time for the prosecution of any vigorous measures of government.   It was, moreover, a season of mourning for the whole
Church, for Saladin was making head against the Christians
in the Holy Land, and in 1187 came the fatal news which
thrilled the heart of Christendom with anguish, of the defeat
of Tiberias and the capture of Jerusalem.  Pope Urban III.
died of grief; his successor, Gregory VIII., survived his
election but six weeks.   In the universal consternation
troubles with the Albigenses claimed less attention, and
they took advantage of the truce thus obtained to strengthen
their position.  The accession of Innocent III. opened a
brighter chapter in the history of the Church, and in that
solicitude, which overlooked no portion of the flock confided
to his care, the alarming progress of the heretics both in
France and Italy did not escape his vigilant eye.   By this
time, Hurter assures us on the authority of Pope Innocent's
letters, that the heresy had infected nearly a thousand cities;
it had been openly embraced by the majority of the nobles
in the south of France, and even by some abbots and canons;
it was protected and connived at by many great feudal lords,
and was spreading rapidly in northern Italy.   Innocent
directed his first efforts to the reform of the Narbonnese
clergy, whose culpable neglect he never dissimulated.   His
letters exhibit him striving by all means to rouse the Bishops
of Languedoc and Provence from their fatal lethargy.   His
next thought was to provide for the refutation of heresy by
the preaching of the truth.   "Heresy," he delares,[6] "can
only be destroyed by solid instruction; it is by preaching the
truth that we sap the foundations of error."   In these words
we recognize the lightning glance which detected the real
remedy required.   The population sunk in gross ignorance
of the mysteries of faith, needed not merely envoys, but
apostles, and it was these that Innocent desired to supply.
His first appeal was to the Order of Citeaux, and in 1198
he confided to certain of their religious full powers for the
reform of the clergy and the conversion and reconciliation of
heretics by the ministry of preaching.   Their success was

[6] Serm. 2, *In Die Ciner.*

small, and in 1204 they were replaced by Peter of Castelnau and the monk Rodolph, to whom was afterwards added Arnold, Abbot of Citeaux. A glance over the narrative of their labours reveals to us the melancholy fact that the chief obstacles which opposed their progress came from the culpable negligence and even the open hostility of prelates, such as the Bishops of Beziers, Toulouse, Auch, and others —whom the chronicler hesitates not to designate as execrable and wicked men—*execrabiles et maligni.* Not a few of these incurred the well-merited sentence of deposition, others resigned to escape similar censures. But the struggle with laxity and corruption in every form was a disheartening task, and it needed the strong words of Innocent to dissuade the Legates from retiring from the field. In the scandalous lives led by too many of the clergy, the heretics found a ready retort to the exhortations addressed to them. " Begin by reforming your own clerks," they would say, " and when that is done you may preach to us." Moreover, the secular rulers of the country showed themselves once more to be the firm friends and protectors of the heretics. Raymund V., whom we have seen ranging himself at the close of his life on the side of the Church, had been succeeded in his dominions by his son Raymund VI., the child of an Albigensian mother, and himself deeply infected with the doctrines as well as with the contaminating practices of the sect. All the weight of his authority was put forth to favour and protect it, and it found its chief seat in his capital of Toulouse. Baffled and confounded in all their efforts, the Legates at length met at Montpelier to deliberate on what course to pursue. We are assured that they were unanimously of opinion that after drawing up a faithful report of their mission, and despatching it to the Sovereign Pontiff, they should renew their petition to be released from labours so painful and fruitless. But there is a well-known proverb that the moments of man's despair are the moments of God's Providence. " In those days," writes William de Puylaurens in his chronicle, " God had laid up in His Divine quiver two choice arrows. They were the Spaniards, Diego,

Bishop of Osma, and a religious named Dominic, canon of
the same Church, whose name was afterwards inscribed in
the catalogue of the saints." The two Spanish pilgrims
arrived at Montpelier at the very time when the Legates were
assembled there in consultation. This unforeseen com-
bination of events brought about in the decrees of God's
Providence a change in the whole aspect of affairs; in that
moment Languedoc received her true Apostle, fresh courage
was infused into the hearts of the Catholic leaders, and a
new chapter opened in the religious history of the country,
which for a full century previously had been overcast by so
dark a cloud.

# CHAPTER IV.

THE spot which had been chosen by the Legates for their conference was the village of Castelnau, which stood not far from the gates of Montpelier, on the road leading thence to the Spanish frontier. Peter of Castelnau was himself a member of the family to whom the territory belonged, and of whose protection they were therefore secure, whilst close at hand, on a hill overlooking the river Lez, which separates Castelnau from Montpelier, was the residence of the Bishop of Magnelone, whose see was some centuries later transferred to the latter city. Here, then, the Legates and other ecclesiastics were assembled, and had already begun their deliberations, when the arrival of the Spanish travellers was announced to them; and the news spread joy throughout the whole company present.

The reputation of the Bishop of Osma and of his Subprior, and the interest taken by both in the unhappy state of the country on the occasion of their previous visit, secured for them a hearty welcome from the Papal Legates, and an invitation to take part in their conference. Diego's episcopal character claimed for him special respect, and the Legates received him with every mark of honour, and asked his counsel, well knowing, says Blessed Jordan, "that he was a wise and holy man, and full of zeal for the faith." He began by inquiring into the customs of the Albigenses, and was informed that their teachers attracted disciples by their persuasive arts, and by a great exterior display of poverty and austerity. Moreover, as the Legates declared, one of

the greatest difficulties in dealing with the heretics was the
impossibility of convincing them that the truth of the
Christian faith rested not on the example of individuals,
but on the sure and infallible Word of God, as made known
by the teaching of the Church.   Diego glanced around him,
and was satisfied that one cause of the bad success of the
Legates lay in the manner of life which they adopted.   He
took notice that they were attended by a numerous suite of
followers, and were well equipped with horses and costly
apparel.   He did not, therefore, hesitate to declare to them
that the neglect of Evangelical poverty had in all probability
been at the root of their failure.   " It is not thus, my
brethren," he said, " that you must act.   The heretics
seduce simple souls by the pretence of poverty and mortification ; by presenting the contrary spectacle you will
scarcely edify them.   You will destroy their confidence, but
you will never touch their hearts.   Rather set one example
against the other; oppose their feigned sanctity by true
religion ; nothing but humility will ever triumph over
falsehood."

" Most excellent Father," said the Legates, " what would
you have us do ? "   " Do as I am about to do," replied
Diego, and, filled with the Spirit of God, he called together
his followers and commanded them to return to Spain with
all his equipage.   Then retaining Dominic as his sole companion, he declared his intention of remaining in the country
and devoting himself to the preaching of the faith.   Struck
by the words and still more by the example of the Bishop,
the Legates at once resolved to follow in the same track.
They dismissed their attendants and their baggage, and
reserving only the books necessary for the recital of the
Divine Office and for controversy, they henceforth travelled
on foot.   More than this, feeling the power of Diego's
character, they unanimously chose him to be their chief,
and declared their resolution in future to carry on their
labours under his direction.   These proceedings were at
once made known to the Pope, who, on hearing what
had taken place, did not hesitate to confirm their choice,

and to grant Diego the permission he had formerly refused him in the case of the Cumans; authorizing him to remain for two years in the French provinces, and devote himself to the preaching of the faith.

A new impulse was thus given to the enterprise on which the Catholics of Languedoc had embarked; with the apostolic life came a daily increase of the apostolic spirit. It was a very different thing to set about evangelizing a country encumbered with the pomp of a feudal retinue, and to traverse the same country on foot, with "neither purse nor scrip," as Diego was wont to send out his companions into the neighbouring towns and villages to preach the faith. Arnold of Citeaux had been obliged to return to his monastery, to attend the Chapter General of the Order, whence he promised to send fresh labourers to take part in the good work. There remained, therefore, together with Diego and Dominic, only the two other Legates, Rodolph and Peter of Castelnau. These, after the conference at Montpelier, all set out together towards Toulouse, stopping at different places on the road to preach and hold disputations with the heretics, as they were moved by the Spirit of God. We are assured that they made the journey barefoot, and trusted to God's Providence alone for their daily wants; and the effect of this new way of proceeding was soon evident in the success which attended their labours. Servian,[1] near Beziers, was the scene of their first success. Here, on a steep rock rising in the midst of a fertile plain, stood the ancient castle of Stephen, feudal lord of Servian, a vassal of the Viscount of Beziers, and like him, a zealous partisan of

---

[1] By most writers the name of this place is given as Carmain or Caraman, a town about five leagues from Toulouse. But Carmain is at least fifty leagues from Montpelier, whereas the locality in question was visited by the Legates on their road from Montpelier to Beziers. The text of Peter de Vaulx-Cernay as recently corrected by a writer in the *Année Dominicaine* (May, 1890) from a MS. of the thirteenth century in the National Library of Paris, runs thus: *Exeuntes autem a Montepessulano venerunt ad quoddam castrum nomine Cervianum.* Servian, here named, is only two leagues and a half from Beziers, and would naturally be visited by any one travelling to the latter city from Montpelier (See *Histoire de Languedoc*, t. vi. Edit. Privat.).

the heretics, two of whose principal leaders, Baldwin and
Thierry, dwelt there under his protection, and in this secure
refuge were able to propagate their pestilential doctrines
throughout the surrounding country. Servian had, in consequence, become one of the citadels of the Albigenses, and
in presenting themselves before its walls and challenging
a disputation with two such renowned heresiarchs, the
Catholic missioners were venturing on a step the very boldness of which was an augury of success. To refuse such a
challenge would have been an acknowledgment of weakness
that would have exposed the Albigensian teachers to
contempt. A public conference was therefore agreed upon,
and the discussion, which lasted eight days, resulted in so
marked a success on the part of the Catholics, that the
greater number of those who assisted at it declared themselves on the side of the truth, and insisted on expelling
Baldwin and Thierry from their territory; nor was the
authority of the castellan, Stephen, strong enough to prevent
them from carrying their purpose into effect. Moreover,
when the Legates continued their journey, taking the road
to Beziers, two thousand persons accompanied them out of
the town, escorting them on their way with every mark
of respect. Fours years later the Castle of Servian surrendered to the arms of Simon de Montfort, and Stephen,
abjuring his errors, solemnly engaged to hold no further
communication with the Albigensian leaders who had so
long enjoyed his protection.

At Beziers, where the Legates made their next station,
they gained but little fruit, for this unhappy city was the
head-quarters of the sect, whose leaders exercised great
power over the Catholic inhabitants; but at Carcassonne
they were more successful, preaching daily during a week,
and reconciling great numbers to the Church. Hitherto,
Dominic's part in these transactions has seemed to be a
secondary one: he has appeared before us rather as the
follower and companion of the Bishop of Osma, than as
the man whose name was to be for ever remembered in
future histories of the time as the chief champion of the

ST. DOMINIC DISPUTING WITH THE HERETICS.
*(from a fresco by Simon Memmi).*

*(To face p. 42.*

faith.   Few, probably, of those who witnessed these first openings of the campaign against the Albigenses, would have believed that the award of a deathless fame was to fall, not to the prelate whose prompt and commanding spirit had moved the Catholic missioners unanimously to choose him for their chief, but to one who followed in his train, known only as Brother Dominic, for he had laid aside even the title of Subprior, and took on him only an inferior part, as the subject and attendant of his bishop.   As soon, however, as the disputes with the heretics of which we have spoken, began to be held, his power and value were felt.   They were best evidenced by the bitter hatred which the heretics conceived against him.   The same sentiments had been so unequivocally evinced towards the Legate, Peter de Castelnau, that the others had persuaded him to withdraw for a time from the enterprise, in order not to exasperate those whom it was their object to conciliate.   The masterly eloquence and convincing arguments of Dominic, who time after time silenced his adversaries and conquered the obstinacy of vast numbers whom he won to the obedience of the Church, excited a no less vindictive feeling against him in the minds of those who might be confounded, but would never yield.   They spoke of him as their most dangerous enemy, and did not even conceal their resolve to take his life, whenever chance should give them the opportunity.   He treated such threats with absolute indifference.   The service of God was the only thing that he saw before him ; and whilst his days were spent in public disputations, his nights were consumed in interviews with those who secretly sought his counsel; or more frequently in those prayers, and tears, and strong intercessions with God for the souls of the people, which were more powerful arms in fighting the battles of the faith than were even the wisdom and eloquence of his words.

In the course pursued by the missionaries they were not unmindful of the principle laid down by Pope Innocent, that error can only be driven out by solid instruction in the truth.  For this purpose, besides daily preaching in the churches, they held frequent conferences in private houses, to' which they invited the heretics, and engaged them in disputation on the chief articles of the faith. One of these conferences was held at Verfeil, a place which then, as in the days of St. Bernard, was one of the chief strongholds of heresy, and the inhabitants of which turned a deaf ear to the exhortations of the Catholic preachers. Shaking the dust off their feet, therefore, they proceeded to the territory of Arzens, not far from Montreal, where an incident took place which is related by William of Puy-Laurens, and the memory of which is still carefully cherished. It was the feast of St. John the Baptist, a day then observed in France as a feast of obligation. But, as will be remembered, the heretics were accustomed to regard the Precursor of our Lord with peculiar detestation, and by way of marking their sentiments regarding him, and their contempt of the laws of the Church, the villagers of Arzens were occupied in reaping their corn. When Dominic beheld them thus engaged, he quitted his companions, and approaching the reapers, called on them to desist, threatening them, if they refused compliance, with some token of the wrath of God. Far from heeding his words, they laughed him to scorn, and one man, more violent than the rest, attacked the saint, and would have driven him out of the field with violence. But as he let fall his sickle, he beheld the ears of corn, as it were, filled with blood. Supposing himself to be wounded, he cried aloud to his comrades, but they, too, beheld their sheaves and their own hands also stained with blood. Struck by so strange a prodigy, they fell at the feet of the saint, confessed their fault, and implored him to make their peace with God. And following him to his companions at Montreal, they there, in his hands, abjured their heresy and were reconciled to the Church.[2]

Montreal is a town about three leagues to the west of Carcassonne, and here the missioners found ample field for

[2] This is reckoned as St. Dominic's first miracle in Languedoc. The spot known as the *Champ des Épis* is still shown about a league from Montreal, and at the request of the Master General of the Order, Père Larroca, a monument bearing a bas-relief of the event has recently been erected, which was blessed by the Bishop of Carcassonne on Rosary Sunday, 1888.

their labours. So thoroughly had the heretics estáblished
their power in this place that the Catholic church was
entirely deserted; and several communities of the *perfect*,
both men and women, lived there, having in their charge
a number of young girls whom they were preparing for
initiation. These communities were frequented indiscrimi-
nately by men and women, who practised the mysterious
rites of *adoration*, and among whom, we are assured by the
testimony of many who had taken part therein, the worst
disorders charged to the account of the heretics reigned
unchecked, and were encouraged by the example of the
castellan, Aymeric, and his too famous sister, Guirande.
Many of the most distinguished members of the sect
assembled on hearing of the arrival of the Legates, and
among others was Guilabert de Castres, who held high rank
among his fellows, and whose ordinary residence was at
Fanjeaux. Unceasing disputes between the Catholics and
heretics were held for the space of fifteen days, the controversy turning chiefly on the sanctity of the Church and
the doctrine of the Mass, which the Albigenses denied to have
been instituted by Jesus Christ. The disputations were held
in the presence of four judges, two knights, and two citizens,
who were accepted by the Albigenses, as being in no way
biassed in favour of the Catholic cause. In fact, as Peter de
Vaulx-Cernay observes, so deplorable was the condition to
which religion had been reduced, that to vindicate the
articles of the Catholic faith it became necessary to submit
to the arbitration of judges, themselves laymen, who were
too often weak in the faith, if not themselves suspected
of heresy. The dispute was carried on at great length, but
at its close the umpires, who perceived that the heretics
would in all probability be convicted of error, refused to
pass any judgment. Nevertheless, the conference resulted
in the conversion of many who were present at it. Nor was
this all. In the course of the disputation Dominic had
written down various quotations from the New Testament
in proof of his arguments, and giving the paper to one of the
heretics, prayed him to consider its contents attentively, and

not to shut his eyes to the truth if its perusal should bring conviction. That same evening, as the man sat over the fire with his companions, discussing the subjects of the day's disputation, he produced the document, which was read and re-read by all present. They found themselves unable to call in question testimonies drawn from those Scriptures which they themselves owned to be canonical, while at the same time they felt no disposition to accept the conclusions of their opponent. In this perplexity, one of their number proposed a new kind of test. Let them cast the writing into the fire; if the flames respected it, they would believe its contents; if it were consumed, they would take this as a triumphant proof in favour of their own opinions. The experiment was tried, and to the amazement of those who had proposed and consented to such a trial, the manuscript was cast forth from the flames, and remained altogether uninjured. One might have expected such a result to have been followed by the conversion of those who witnessed it, but this was far from being the case. The heretics, we are told, beheld and wondered, but agreed to keep the matter secret, lest, if it reached the ears of the Catholics, they should claim it as a token of victory. One man only, more noble-minded than the rest, was converted by what he saw, and made it known publicly. The narrative is inserted by Peter de Vaulx-Cernay, in his *History of the Albigenses*, on no less an authority than that of St. Dominic himself. "This event," he says, "took place at Montreal, as I heard from the lips of the holy man who gave the writing into the hands of the heretics."[3]

Montreal preserves many memorials of the presence of the blessed Dominic, who often returned thither to confirm its inhabitants in the faith; the pulpit in which he preached being still preserved as a precious relic. Yet more closely associated with this period of his life is the spot which was next visited by the missioners, and which was the scene of an occurrence very similar in its character to the one just narrated, though the two events must not be confounded

[3] Vallis Sern. *De Her. Albig.* c. 7, p. 78.

together. The town of Fanjeaux stands on the very summit
of a high conical hill overlooking a plain which stretches to
the foot of the Pyrenees. Its present appearance probably
differs but little from that which it bore on the day when
Dominic and his companions first entered within its walls,
passing under that ancient gateway, above which is now to
be seen a gilded statue of the Blessed Virgin. At the very
summit of the street stands the venerable parish church of
grand proportions, which so often echoed with the voice
of the saint; and near it may be seen the pool of water,
the *Fanum Jovis*, which gives its name to the town, a temple
of Jupiter having stood there in pagan times. Here then
the missioners preached for some days with considerable
fruit. The place was a stronghold of the heretics, whose
leaders challenged the Catholics to another public disputation. The challenge was accepted, and it was agreed that
each party should commit to writing the chief arguments in
support of their respective creeds. Among the writings of
the Catholics, that drawn up by Brother Dominic was
unanimously selected as the best; and on the day appointed
an unusual number of persons assembled to assist at the
disputation and witness the result. In fact this conference
appears to have been by far the most important and the
most numerously attended of any that had yet taken place.
We have the names of a considerable number, both men
and women, who took part in it; among whom were William
de Durfort, the territorial lord of Fanjeaux, and many noble
ladies. Indeed, it is said that of all the ladies of Montreal
one only had escaped the infection of heresy, namely, the
chatelaine Na-Cavaers, who shared with Durfort the
seigneurship of Fanjeaux. Guilabert de Castres had also
hastened his return to Fanjeaux, in order to assist his disciples and partisans, who were all of them distinguished by
their rank and influence. The judges were chosen equally
from both parties; and the conference was held in the house
of Raymund de Durfort, brother to William, and himself an
adherent of the Albigenses. The sectaries, finding themselves unable to answer the arguments of their opponents,

proposed to appeal to the judgment of God by the trial by fire. Some writers say that this was ordered by the arbiters. It does not appear whether or no they were aware of what had occurred at Montreal; but the proposal, which was fully in harmony with the customs of an age wherein the trial by ordeal had not yet become obsolete, was received with applause by all present, and a large fire was accordingly kindled on the stone hearth of the hall where they were assembled. The writings of the heretics were first cast into the flames and entirely consumed. Then the book containing Brother Dominic's defence of the Catholic faith was in like manner thrown into the fire and was cast forth immediately on touching the burning logs. "Not only did it remain uninjured," says Brother Jordan, "but before the eyes of all it was tossed out of the flames to a considerable distance. A second and third time it was thrown in, and each time sprang out as before, thus showing the truth of the orthodox faith and the sanctity of the writer." The ancient MS. Breviary of Prouille relates this event in words which are transcribed by Father Percin in his *History of the Province of Toulouse.* It is there stated that the book when tossed out of the fire " rested each time on a beam of wood, in which three deep holes may still be seen as a perpetual memorial of the miracle." This beam was formerly kept in the very hall where the incident took place, and where, in the following century, a church was erected by Charles le Bel, and attached to a convent of Friars Preachers. Père Jean de Réchac speaks of seeing it in this chapel, and describes the three holes as distinctly visible. On the suppression of the convent the beam was removed to the parish church of Fanjeaux, where it is still carefully preserved. The hearth-stone on which the fire was kindled was also kept under the altar of the same chapel; and here, on the feast of St. Dominic, the custom prevailed of substituting at the First Vespers, instead of the Responsary, *O spem miram*, that for the third Lesson at Matins, in which allusion is made to the well-attested miracle: *Verbum vitæ dum palam promitur,*

*surgunt hostes, liber conscribitur, fides extollitur. Ter in flammas libellus traditus, ter exivit illæsus penitus.*[4]

The conference at Fanjeaux, and the wonderful event with which it closed, brought conviction to the minds of many of those who assisted at it; but by far the greater number remained obstinate in their unbelief. Nevertheless, from this time Brother Dominic came to be regarded both by friends and enemies as foremost among the champions of the Catholic faith. Touron remarks that whereas the other missioners, whose number had now considerably increased, worked each one in the particular district assigned him either by the Legates or by the Bishop of Osma, Dominic seems to have had no such restriction, but to have been free to extend his labours wherever charity might guide him. In the course of these missionary journeys he made himself perfectly well acquainted with the condition of the country and of the evils which cried aloud for remedy. In particular he became aware of the special danger to which the daughters of the Catholics were exposed, through the artifices of the Albigenses and the culpable indifference of their own parents. Many of the Catholic gentry, reduced to ruin by the spoliation of their lands, did not hesitate for the bribe of a promised dowry to deliver their daughters into the hands of the sectaries to be by them nurtured and educated in heresy.

---

[4] In 1209, the goods of William de Durfort having been confiscated, the miraculous beam was taken from his house and deposited in the Convent of Prouille, where it remained until the foundation of the Convent of Fanjeaux. In 1346, the family of Durfort having regained possession of the forfeited territory, were desirous of consecrating the site of this celebrated miracle as a chapel dedicated to St. Dominic. They, therefore, sold the house for this purpose to Father Raymund de Durfort, a member of the same family, then Provincial of Toulouse, declaring that they did so "in consideration of the notable miracle worked by fire in that house, to the honour of the blessed Dominic, when he preached against heresy in that country." The chapel was accordingly erected, and many Indulgences were granted by the Sovereign Pontiffs to those who should visit it. This chapel was afterwards attached to the Dominican convent erected at Fanjeaux in 1350, and here the beam was preserved for many years. It was the custom to bring into this chapel the young maidens able to take the veil in the Convent of Prouille, that they might hear Mass and kiss the sacred relic, the greater portion of which is now carefully kept in the parish church of Fanjeaux.

The leaders of the Albigenses understood only too well what powerful instruments might then be fashioned for the propagation of their false doctrines. Indeed, it is remarkable how important a part was played by these proselytes. They found entrance into all families and exercised a powerful influence over many a Catholic household. From none indeed did the Albigenses receive more powerful support than from their female disciples, whom they were careful to recruit after the manner above described.

This abuse and its dangers, as insidious as they were alarming, did not escape the notice of the saint, and he rested not till he had provided a remedy. The plan suggested itself to him of founding a monastery for the express purpose of furnishing a retreat where young girls in danger of this kind of perversion might find a safe refuge, and where other women reclaimed from heresy might also be admitted and fully instructed in the faith. He conferred with Diego on this plan and received from him such warm encouragement, that both Blessed Jordan and Theodoric of Apoldia write as though the bishop had himself been the author of the scheme. This, however, is to be understood only as signifying that the proceedings of the missioners were naturally submitted to the approval of Diego as their recognized head, for the foundation of Prouille must be regarded as strictly the work of St. Dominic. This convent was in fact to become the real nursery of his Order, and the narrative of a foundation so interesting from every point of view in the history of our saint claims a chapter to itself.

THE NUNS OF PROUILLE.

# CHAPTER V.

## PROUILLE.[1]

### 1206.

In the plain that stretches from the foot of the hills on which
Fanjeaux is situated, lies the village of Prouille, where in the
thirteenth century stood a church dedicated to St. Martin,
together with an ancient chapel of our Lady, long the resort
of pilgrims, which Brother Dominic often visited in his
apostolic journeys, and wherein he loved to offer the Holy
Sacrifice. On the night of the 22nd of July, 1206, the saint,
according to his custom, had retired to a spot among the
hills overlooking the plain, in order that, after spending the
day in labouring for souls, he might devote the night hours
to communing with God. No doubt his heart was full to
overflowing with solicitude for the perishing souls among
whom he laboured, and the design with which God had
recently inspired him. The establishment of a monastery
such as he had in contemplation was no easy task for one a
stranger in the land, and wholly destitute of temporal means.

---

[1] Prouille is between Montreal and Fanjeaux, about a league from the
former, and a quarter of a league from the latter place.

E

In a country surrounded on all sides by those hostile to the faith, where should he find a site on which to erect his ark of refuge ?  Looking down on the plain below, he suddenly beheld a spectacle which seemed to give the answer to his doubts.  A globe of fire appeared in the air, and, after making several circuits, descended, and rested on the roof of our Lady's chapel.  The same prodigy was exhibited on the two following nights, and Dominic understood it to signify that the spot thus pointed out was the one chosen for his proposed foundation.  The convent, which was to receive into its shelter souls rescued from the snares of the enemy, was then, to be placed under the patronage of Our Lady of Prouille.  On inquiry he found that the land on which the chapel stood belonged to a noble dame whose family name was De Cavaers, the same who has been before mentioned as chatelaine of Fanjeaux, and enjoying the honourable dis-tinction of being the solitary lady of that neighbourhood who remained loyal to the Catholic faith.[2]  To her the saint made known what he had seen, and invited her to consecrate her territory to the service of God by consenting to the foundation on it of a monastery for women.  She yielded a joyful consent to the proposal, which received the hearty approval of Fulk, Bishop of Toulouse, to whom the co-patronage of the chapel belonged.  He not only gave his sanction to the undertaking, but furnished the foundation with such liberal alms, that in a short time the requisite buildings were erected, and the monastery sufficiently endowed for the support of a certain number of subjects.

While the work was in progress, Dominic continued to reside at Fanjeaux in a house which is still religiously preserved, and is called in the *patois* of the country the *Bourguet Sant Domenge.*  There may still be seen the chamber

---

[2] Dame Na Cavaers, foundress of Prouille, left a daughter and name-sake who inherited the lands, but unfortunately not the faith of her noble mother. Na Cavaers the younger was for many years in intimate relations with all the leaders of the sect, and even seems to have been admitted as a member. But wonderful to say, after forty years spent in error, she not only made her peace with the Church, but asked and received the holy habit of religion in the monastery of Prouille.

which gave him shelter, with its brick floor and ancient stone
hearth. Near this house rises a high rock, in a cavity of
which is a deep pool that is never stagnant, being fed from
some secret source. It bears the title of the water-stoup of
St. Dominic, and, according to the poetical tradition of the
place, sprang up on the spot so often watered by the tears
and sanctified by the prayers of the saint. Not far off a
little monument, surmounted by a cross, marks the spot
known as the *Segnadou*, or "the place where the saint saw
the sign,"[3] being that, whence as above related, he beheld
the flame descend from heaven upon the roof of our Lady's
chapel. This spot, as well as others which local tradition
associates with his name, is still visited by pilgrims who love
to pray on the scenes hallowed by his memory among these
mountain solitudes. A steep cleft in the rocks shows the
path he so often trod leading from Fanjeaux to Montreal,
and here it is said he once narrowly escaped falling into the
hands of assassins. The forest where he was wont to retire
for prayer and penance, with the old oaks under which he
loved to sit, are still pointed out; and half way between
Fanjeaux and Carcassonne is to be seen a fountain now
surmounted by his statue, where according to tradition he
often rested and took his scanty meal of dry bread, dipping
it in the waters of the fountain.

But perhaps the most interesting of the localities associated with his memory is the parish church of Fanjeaux
which even claims to have been served for a time by the saint
as parish priest. The pulpit in which he preached almost
daily during the time that he made his home in the village is
still reverently shown. Out of respect the floor of this pulpit
is now covered with boards, but we are assured it is the same
from which he so often announced the Word of God. On one
such occasion, after he had eloquently defended the faith
against the blasphemies of the Albigenses, an incident occurred
which we will relate almost in the words of Blessed Humbert.

---

[3] This monument, erected in 1860, stands on the site of a much more
ancient cross, which was placed there by the inhabitants of Fanjeaux in
1538, and which bore an inscription commemorative of the above event.

As the saint remained in the church to pray, according to his custom, he was accosted by nine women who threw themselves at his feet, saying, " Servant of God, come to our help. If what you preached to-day be true, our souls have long been blinded with error ; for those whom you style heretics, but whom we call *Bons Hommes*,[4] are the guides whom we have hitherto trusted with our whole hearts. But now we know not what to think. Have pity on us and pray to the Lord your God that He may make known to us in what faith we must live and die if we would be saved everlastingly. We cannot reply to your arguments, yet we dare not lightly condemn the teaching of our ministers. Resolve our doubts then, but we entreat you let it be in a way which may bring certain conviction to our souls."

Dominic recollected himself for a few moments in silent prayer, then he replied, " Have patience and fear nothing ; I believe that our Lord, Who wills not that any should perish, will show you manifestly who is the master whom you have hitherto served." Then he invited them to pray with him, and as they did so there appeared in the midst of them a monstrous and most hideous beast whose flaming eyes and frightful aspect filled them with terror. Springing into the air, it disappeared through the belfry of the church, leaving behind it a horrible stench. " This is the master you have served," said Dominic, "and whose likeness God has per- mitted you to behold that you might see and understand in what manner of slavery you have engaged by joining yourselves to these heretics."

Moved by the appalling sight, and with hearts already touched by Divine grace, the nine women entreated Dominic not to abandon them, but to receive them to some safe shelter, and direct them in the way of truth. The saint gave up to them the house he himself occupied, and spent that night, as was his frequent habit, in prayer among the hills. After carefully testing the sincerity of his new disciples, he not only received their abjuration, but agreed to admit them among the first members of the new community. History

[4] The title by which the " perfect " were commonly addressed.

has carefully preserved their names; they were Alaïde, Berengaria, Barberienne Jordan, Curtslana, Raymundine, Paperin, Riccarda, Guillelmine de Beaupuys, Raymundine Clarette, and Gentiana. Twenty-seven years later, Berengaria gave her testimony to the sanctity of St. Dominic, making oath before the commissioners of Toulouse as to the things she had seen and heard; and in this attestation she affirms having with her own eyes beheld the terrible spectacle above described as seen in the church of Fanjeaux. Another of the little company, whose name is not given, appears to have been possessed of considerable personal attractions, and in particular of a remarkably well-formed nose, which proved a source of temptation to her, and disposed her to return to the world. A grotesque accident, however, which befell the favourite feature and somewhat spoiled her beauty, seems to have cured her vanity and brought her to her senses. Confessing her fault to Brother Dominic, he confirmed her in her vocation, so that she never afterwards showed any signs of instability. To these nine were soon afterwards added two others, Catholics by birth and by education, of whom Guillemette de Fanjeaux, though the last comer, was chosen by Dominic to be the Prioress, an office she continued to fill for the space of nineteen years. The modest habitation which had been begun in the month of August, and which, poor as it was, was yet carefully adapted to the requirements of religious life, was completed early in November; and on the 22nd of this month, being the feast of St. Cecilia, 1206, the nuns took possession of their new abode. They were formally enclosed on the following feast of St. John the Evangelist, and thus was completed the foundation of the first convent of the Order. The community soon received a fresh increase by the admission of fifteen young girls, all rescued from the hands of the heretics, to whose instruction and guidance the saint devoted no small portion of his time.

An exact description of the spot so dear and sacred to every child of St. Dominic will not be unacceptable. It shall be given in the words of one to whom the scenes described have long been a familiar home. "Prouille is

situated in the department of Aude, between the Mediterranean and the Pyrenees. It lies in a vast and richly cultivated plain through which flow many crystal streams, their banks fringed with trees, specially willows. On the south it is shut in by a range of hills, still covered with the remains of vast forests, which once clothed them to the summit. Dotted here and there on its expanse appear farms and villages, with many a church tower rising to heaven through the clear and azure sky. Towards the east and west this plain stretches to a great extent, but it is bounded on the north by what are called the Black Mountains, the slopes of which in the time of St. Dominic were covered with thick forests." A little village, the houses of which were poor enough, and were for the most part built of mud, then clustered round the Church of St. Martin, long the resort of pilgrims; and the first abode of the nuns consisted of a few such mud cottages, which they continued to occupy until by gift or purchase they came into possession of larger territories. In this humble dwelling it was, then, that St. Dominic gathered his first religious, whom by the authority of the Bishop of Toulouse he clothed in the habit he had chosen for them, namely, a white tunic with a black mantle and veil. He gave them the Rule of St. Augustine, to which were added certain Constitutions drawn up by his own pen, in which was enjoined a strict observance of silence. Besides the hours devoted to prayer and the recital of the Divine Office, it was provided that a certain time should every day be given to manual work. The articles of a visitation of the convent held in 1340 by the Provincial of Toulouse show how much importance was attached by the saint to this salutary ordinance. "The procurators of the convent (we read) being asked how the sisters were provided with clothing, and if they had sufficient garments, and those of good and suitable materials, answered that every year there is delivered to them fifteen cwt. of clean, washed, and well-chosen wool, which wool they themselves spin and make up according to the ancient custom of the monastery, *and the express command of our Father St. Dominic*, who ordered that the nuns should

spin and sew in those hours when they were not employed
in the recitation of the Divine Office, in order the better to
avoid idleness, the cause of so many evils."[6]

Besides this manual work it was ordered that those who
had the capacity, should carefully apply themselves to the
study of psalmody, and a passage in the primitive Constitution names also "the study of letters" as fitly occupying a
certain portion of their time. An idea has very commonly
prevailed that the Convent of Prouille was founded as a
place of education for young girls, and considerable pains
has been taken by several learned writers to disprove this
error. The religious of Prouille, like all other communities
of the Second Order established later, were strictly contemplative and never undertook the work of education. Nevertheless, it is evident that being founded to receive those
rescued from heresy, means were provided for the careful
instruction of the inmates in the truths of faith, and as
amply appears from the annals of the monastery, the religious
who took no part in that work of teaching which so manifestly
belongs to the Order of Preachers, were trained to co-operate
in the salvation of souls by their penances and their prayers.

So singular an interest attaches to this nursery of the
Order of Preachers, and its foundation forms such an
important epoch in the life of our saint, that we shall make
no apology for tracing its history somewhat fully, the rather
that the documents we have to quote throw considerable
light on the actual position then held by St. Dominic, and
the nature of his work in Languedoc. So much of his
history has been presented to us in what is regarded by
many as a purely legendary form, that it is a satisfaction to
turn over the pages of formal documents indisputable in
their authenticity, and gather from them evidence corro-
borating many of the events above recorded.

First, then, as to the temporalities of Prouille. The
church had been granted to the use of the nuns from their
first foundation, but it was not until 1211 that they became
its actual proprietors. In that year Fulk, Bishop of Toulouse,

[6] *Visite de Prouille par le Provincial de Toulouse en 1340* (inedited).

with the consent of his Chapter, and at the request of Master
Dominic of Osma, gives and assigns the chapel of Our Lady
of Prouille to the religious women who shall be converted
by the preaching of those appointed to drive away heresy
out of the country.  He releases them from all pecuniary
obligations that might be claimed by the Chapter, and
grants them thirty paces of land surrounding the chapel.

Earlier than this is the document by which Beranger,
Archbishop of Narbonne, endows the monastery with lands
situated in his archdiocese.  In the April of 1207, only four
months after this foundation, he grants to the Prioress and
other religious women who have been recently converted to
the faith *by the exhortations and example of Brother Dominic, Canon
of Osma, and of his companions abiding at Fanjeaux in the Church
of Our Lady of Prouille*, the Church of St. Martin of Limoux,[7]
and the territory of Tax, contiguous to it, as a perpetual
possession which is accepted in their name by the Brothers
Dominic and William de Claret.  In this document we have
the first notice of the *companions* of St. Dominic, and of their
establishment at Prouille as a residence.  The William de
Claret here mentioned was a native of Pamiers, and offered
his services to the Bishop of Osma at the very commence-
ment of the mission.  Diego appointed him procurator to
the little company, and St. Dominic chose him to discharge
the same office for the community of Prouille, and to act as
their chaplain, though their spiritual care was afterwards
confided to Brother Noel of Prouille.

The "Brethren of Prouille" are also named in another
act dated in the same year 1207, in which Ermingarde de
Godeline and her husband, Sancho Gasc, dedicated not only
their goods, but their persons also, to God, the Blessed Mary,
and all the saints, to *the holy work of preaching, to Master Dominic
of Osma, and the brethren and sisters living at Prouille*.[8]  How many
of these brethren were established at Prouille in its early days

---

[7] According to the author of *Notre Dame de France*, vol. iii. p. 320, the
famous sanctuary of Notre Dame de Marceille, near Limoux, was also
granted to Prouille.

[8] Doat, t. 98, f. 3.

we do not know; it is probable that their numbers at first were small, possibly not exceeding the two whose names have been already given. But as time went on their ranks increased, and at a later date we find the community of the brethren amounting to as many as twenty-five priests besides lay-brothers.

Meanwhile the records of the monastery bear witness to its steady growth. A few years pass by, years of tumult and of bloodshed, but Prouille remains unaffected by the storm that rages round her walls. The ark of refuge floats securely on the surface of the troubled waters. The construction and enlargement of the monastery are carried on without intermission, while all the surrounding country is plunged in civil war; and in 1212, when armies are marching and counter-marching in the close neighbourhood, fresh acts of donation make mention of the "newly-erected abbey" and the "monastery recently constructed."⁹ The antique forms of some of these documents help us to realize the age to which they belong. Thus in 1212 Bernard de Barna makes over to Our Lady of Prouille and to the brethren and sisters living there, not only his goods moveable and immoveable, but his own person and that of his son. Needless to say this is to be understood in the feudal sense. He holds his lands henceforth, not as an independent proprietor, but as "the man" of the monastery. "Kneeling before you, Dominic, Canon of Osma," he continues, "with my hands in yours and receiving the kiss of peace, I pledge you my homage."¹⁰ Again, in another of these charters Peter, Castellan de Saissac, contracts a different kind of tie with the community. He disposes of his lands in favour of the brethren and sisters, adding, "and I, Peter de Saissac, make myself your brother, and if he so will, my heir shall do the same." The donation is accepted by the two brethren, Noel and William, in the name of the joint community. "We hereby receive you as a brother," they write at the foot of the contract, "and admit you to participation in all the prayers and good works that are here performed." That is to say,

⁹ Doat, t. 98, f. 8—10.　　　¹⁰ *Ibid* p 7.

that the donor becomes affiliated to the monastery not precisely as a religious, but as a kind of auxiliary, one of what were technically called the *frères donas*, whose numbers gradually increased with the increase of the lands and possessions of the monastery which were committed to their charge.

⤳ It will be seen, then, that two distinct communities were settled at Prouille, one of religious women and the other of brethren. The latter had for their use the Church of St. Martin, which separated the two divisions of the monastery. Père Réchac has given us an exact description of the building as it existed in the seventeenth century, and tells us of the quadrangle of the nuns with its central fountain, the stone cloisters with watch-towers at each of the four corners of the battlemented walls, with which, as time went on, the convent was surrounded, having fifteen other towers, their numbers corresponding to the mysteries of the holy Rosary. He describes how over the great gate of the monastery there stood an image of St. Dominic, stick in hand, while beneath it were engraved in antique Gothic characters the following lines:

> Ennemis de ma religion
> Ne troublez ce lieu sanctifié,
> Car autrement de mon bâton
> Très asprement vous frapperai.

The annals of the monastery record many instances of its singular preservation from perils of all kinds, due as was believed to his fatherly protection. Then, in 1309, fire broke out in the dormitory of the religious, who having invoked the aid of their holy patriarch, beheld a number of young children dressed in white, who extinguished the flames with their hands. This happened on the feast of St. Michael, and the grace was so generally attributed to angelic assistance that Père Adaubert, Provincial of Toulouse, ordained a daily commemoration of the Holy Angels to be made henceforth at Lauds and Vespers by way of perpetual thanksgiving. Needless to say that a very special devotion was always cherished by the religious of Prouille to their holy founder himself, whose chasuble, mantle, and scapular they preserved as precious relics, as well as a crucifix carved by his direction, which was kept in the chapel of the Rosary and was regarded as miraculous. This chapel was a place of great devotion. It was here that the novices used to assemble to recite our Lady's Office, and here it was said two of the sisters who were wont to resort hither to pray, were accustomed to see and converse with their guardian angels.

The community seems specially to have excelled in their admirable discharge of the duties of the choir. They recited it, says Père Réchac, in a manner suitable to the majesty of the place, without haste or precipitation, without the omission of a note or a syllable, the pauses carefully observed, and the chant kept up with perfect regularity. "Of this," he says, " I have myself been both an eye and ear witness, nor is it to be doubted that this perfect fidelity in the duties of the choir has been one of the special benedictions left by St. Dominic on these his eldest daughters." We will only add that to fervour in prayer they added an unbounded charity, as was shown by their daily distribution at the gate of the monastery of food, clothes, and medicine.

But it is time to close this subject, over which we have lingered out of loving reverence to the memory of a place sanctified by the labours and tears of our great saint, and so dear to his fatherly heart. ✝ The Prouille of St. Dominic exists no longer. The ancient monastery was entirely burnt down in 1715, and in 1790 the new convent raised upon its ruins was seized by the Revolutionary Government, the religious dispersed, and the convent itself sold to a speculator who levelled it to the ground and sold its stones as building materials. For more than fifty years nothing remained to mark the site but a few feet of crumbling wall, a portion of the ancient cloister.✝ But in our own days a new Prouille has arisen out of the ashes of the old, and on this very site a monastery of magnificent dimensions, raised through the munificence of a noble lady, has received within its walls a colony of Dominican nuns who can trace their religious

descent from the parent stock of the Prouille of St. Dominic.
Thus the lily garden of the Order has been planted afresh.
*Prulia*, or *Pruralilia*, as some old writers love to call it, still
lives to lift up holy hands for her unhappy country.    May
her prayers be abundantly heard as expressed in those words
which so often in old times resounded within her walls :

> O Salutaris hostia,
>   Spes unica fidelium,
> In te confidit Francia,
>   Da pacem, serva lilium.[11]

[11] An adaptation of the *O Salutaris*, used anciently in France in times
of public necessity.

# CHAPTER VI.

As soon as the community was happily settled at Prouille, Dominic left Fanjeaux, and rejoined Diego and the Legates at Pamiers, where Arnold of Citeaux soon after arrived, bringing with him twelve other abbots of his Order. Thus powerfully reinforced, the missioners prosecuted their labours with fresh vigour. At Montreal five hundred heretics abjured their errors, and the same success attended the preaching of the Catholics in other towns. Diego, therefore, thought the time a suitable one for revisiting his own diocese, from which he had now been absent for nearly three years. Before doing so, however, he agreed to return with the other missioners to Pamiers, where considerable numbers, both of Catholics and Albigenses, had assembled to assist at a great conference, which was to be held between their respective leaders. As Diego and his party approached the town, they were met and joyfully greeted by the Bishops of Toulouse and Conzerans, together with many of the clergy. The umpire chosen on this occasion was Arnold of Campranham, a secular priest of some learning, but who was known to favour the doctrines of the Albigenses. The conference took place in the house of Raymund Roger, Count de Foix, his wife, who had openly joined the heretics, being present at the discussions, as well as his two sisters, who belonged to the kindred sect of the Vaudois. These ladies were strongly inclined to take an active part in the proceedings, but received a salutary hint from Stephen, one of the Cistercian abbots assisting at the conference, who bade them listen in silence as more suitable to their sex.

"Go, madam," he said to the countess, "and attend to your spinning; it does not become you to take part in this debate." The conference resulted in the triumph of the Catholics, and not only did Arnold give judgment in their favour, but he himself renounced his errors in the hands of the Bishop of Osma, and thenceforward acted as a strenuous defender of the Catholic faith. His example was followed by many others, especially of the poorer classes, who made their submission with every sign of sincerity. This conference took place, according to Touron, in the July of 1207; and immediately on its close, Diego prepared to set out for Spain, his purpose being, after settling the affairs of the diocese, and collecting alms for the support of the missioners and the convent of Prouille, to return to Languedoc, and there resume his apostolic labours. Before leaving, he appointed Brother Dominic to be the head of the body of missioners, and named him Prior of Prouille, by which title we find him henceforth designated.

Dominic and his companions accompanied the bishop to the confines of the province, all journeying on foot, and preaching as they went. There the two friends who had been bound together by a tie so close, and of such long duration, parted in the confident hope of a speedy reunion. But the designs of God had otherwise ordained. Before the close of the year Diego departed to a better life, and was buried in his cathedral church of Osma, where his tomb is said to have been honoured by miracles. He was the first of a long line of great men with whom the founder of the Friars Preachers was united in bonds of no common friendship, nor was he the least worthy of the number. So holy and so stainless was his character that, as Blessed Jordan tells us, it won the admiration of the heretics themselves, who were wont to say that "it was impossible not to believe such a man predestined to eternal life, and that doubtless he had been sent among them that he might learn from them the way of salvation." It was his influence that had consolidated the scattered elements of the Catholic party into a firm and united body, and it seemed as though his death in a moment dissolved the tie that had bound them together. Many circumstances in fact, combined to break up the company which had hitherto acted in concert. Arnold of Citeaux was elected the General of his Order, and was necessarily obliged to return to the seat of its government. He was followed by the other Cistercian abbots, all of whom were recalled to their own convents. Peter of Castelnau had established himself in Provence, where Rodolph, the other Legate, prepared to join him, but died before reaching his destination; so that a few weeks after hearing of the death of Diego, Dominic found himself left to sustain the conflict for the faith almost single-handed.

There comes a crisis in the history of some souls, and especially of those chosen by God for special works, which seems designed to test and prove the strength that is in them. As the archer tries the firmness of his bow-string before delivering his shaft, so such souls are permitted in the darkness of desolation or the anguish of bereavement, to gather their strength to its true centre, and lean more utterly upon God. Not till then is manifested their full nobility, or the power of the grace which moves them. So, as we may conjecture, it was in the life-history of the Blessed Dominic. His hour of proof was that in which he stood *alone*, with the work to which God had called him still incomplete, while his fellow-labourers were all withdrawn, and he among the number in whose company for fourteen years he had enjoyed the rare happiness of a perfect friendship. He watched them depart one after another, the Spanish ecclesiastics to Spain, the Cistercians to their abbeys, but he remained firm and tranquil in the post where God had placed him. The sweetness of human consolation had been taken from him, but the Divine will, the law of his life, remained; and if men had hitherto regarded him only as following in the track marked out by another, they were now about to behold him revealed to the world in his true character as the founder of that great Religious Order which was to bear his name. "It was not to be," writes William de Puylaurens, "that the work of preaching, which had been begun so happily, should be

suffered to perish.    By Divine inspiration it was to be
carried on by preachers who should for ever bear that title
as their own.    For the Order of Preachers was about to
arise under the protection of the holy Bishop Fulk, of
Toulouse."

We have already more than once had occasion to mention
the name of this remarkable man, who had been appointed
to the bishopric of Toulouse in 1200, after the deposition of
Raymund de Rabastens.    His history, like his character,
was altogether extraordinary, exhibiting the energy of human
passion not laid aside, but transformed and sanctified by
Divine grace.    He had passed many years at the Courts of
Richard of England and Count Raymund V. of Toulouse,
where he was known, not merely as a man of the world, but
as a skilful troubadour.    His poetry, which still exists, is
praised by critics for the elegance of its conception, but if
we are to credit historians who gave currency to the popular
judgment regarding him, his life did not wholly escape from
the influence of the profligate society that surrounded him.
A sudden stroke of grace came to open his eyes to the
nothingness of the world, and to arouse him to nobler aspira-
tions.    " Were I condemned," he one day thought to himself,
" to lie for ever on the softest bed, how intolerable would
such a destiny be!    Yet if so, what will it be to endure the
everlasting torments?"    The shaft struck him to the heart,
and when once that fervent nature awoke to the conscious-
ness of the eternal truths, it could rest in no half turning
to God.    With the consent of his wife, he left the world and
entered the monastery of Toronet, in Provence, where in due
time he became abbot.    So entirely did he give himself up
to the service of God, and so remarkably did he display his
powers of government, that when he was chosen for the
difficult task of raising the Church of Toulouse from the
miserable condition into which it had been brought by the
misconduct of his predecessor, the appointment was received
with universal joy, and Peter of Castelnau, then lying on a
bed of sickness, lifted his hands in thanksgiving that so great
a happiness should be bestowed on that afflicted diocese.

The career of Fulk has been traced by the pen of William
de Puylaurens, who knew him well, and who, though the
chaplain of Raymund VII. of Toulouse, was not deterred
by any partiality for the princes whom he served from doing
justice to the prelate who showed himself so firm in resisting
their encroachments. He calls Fulk the venerable Father
chosen by God to repair the ruins of His Church laid waste
by heresy. He tells us that at the moment of his accession,
as he himself had often heard from the lips of the bishop,
the revenues of the see, once so rich and flourishing, did not
exceed ninety-six *sous*. He entered the diocese with no
greater equipage than four mules, which he brought from
his abbey. But he showed himself a vigilant pastor and an
eloquent preacher, and from the day of his installation the
Catholic cause in Toulouse showed signs of revival.

As we have seen, Fulk had very early recognized the
merits of Brother Dominic, and had given him his powerful
support in the foundation of Prouille. He equally proved
himself a firm friend in the present juncture, and throughout
the difficult time that was opening. Dark clouds, indeed,
just then hung over the horizon. Whatever success had
attended the labours of the missioners in the conversion of
individuals, and even of considerable numbers of the better
disposed among the heretics, it was far from being universal.
Encouraged by the example of their princes, the great
mass of the people showed themselves wholly indifferent
to the pacific measures hitherto exclusively employed to
reclaim them. To use the expression of the poet of the
Crusade,[1] "they cared no more for preaching than for a
rotten apple." On occasions indeed when the Legates hinted
at the possibility of interference on the part of the temporal

---

[1] William of Tudela was the author of the first part of the *Song of the
Crusade*, a poem in the Provençal language which is regarded as reliable
authority for the history of the war. The Song was continued by an
anonymous troubadour to whose statements the same credit does not
attach. The other contemporary authors on whom we chiefly depend
are Peter de Vaulx-Cernay and William de Puy-Lamens; the first a
Cistercian monk, the latter chaplain to Count Raymund VII., and a
singularly impartial writer.

F

power, as at Toulouse in 1204, a wonderful alacrity was
shown in expelling the Albigenses and meeting every
demand. But as soon as the danger was over all things
went on as before; until after ten years of these successive
and all but fruitless legations it became clearly apparent
that the evil was one which called for a severer remedy.
By none was the unsatisfactory result of these negotiations
more keenly felt than by Peter of Castelnau, who was
accustomed to say that religion would never again raise its
head in Languedoc till the soil had been watered by the
blood of a martyr, and it was his constant prayer that he
himself might be the victim. The special enmity of which
he was the object on the part of the Albigenses has been
sometimes attributed to the uncompromising severity of his
character. But it must be borne in mind that in his office
as Legate he was charged with the onerous duty, not merely
of preaching to the heretics, but of rebuking and pronouncing
censure on those who were the real authors of the existing
troubles. We have seen with what courage he had enforced
the authority of the Holy See against the slothful and
unfaithful pastors of the Church; and he showed no less
firmness in dealing with those who held and misused the
temporal power. Of these the one most conspicuous, both
by his rank and by the long tissue of his crimes and
treacheries, was Count Raymund VI. of Toulouse. He
showed no sympathy with the better dispositions evinced
by his father towards the close of his life; but from the day
of his accession acted as the avowed protector of the
Albigenses. Nor was this by any means his sole offence.
Through him the whole of the south of France was plunged
in petty wars, which he promoted for his own aggrandizement, taking into his pay large bands of the excommunicated
*Cottereaux* or *Routiers*, with whose aid he ravaged towns,
churches, and monasteries. It is necessary to remind
ourselves of the real condition of society in these lawless
centuries, left as it too often was at the mercy of ferocious
tyrants. Doubtless among the feudal rulers of the land many
were to be found who exhibited the true virtues of chivalry,

men who were the protectors of the Church, the champions
of the oppressed, the friends of the fatherless and the widow.
But others, and it may be feared the larger number, hardly
rose above the level of brigand chiefs. Their sole occupation
consisted in raids one upon another which do not deserve
the name of wars, and which were made the excuse for every
species of violence and rapine. In these intestine and bloody
quarrels the petty rulers of southern France were incessantly
engaged, and the *Cotteraux* found constant employment under
the banners of the rival chieftains.

No one even superficially acquainted with the history of
European Christendom can be ignorant how unceasing were
the efforts of the Popes to repress these evils. From the
gigantic wars between France and England down to the
ignoble strife that armed baron against baron, the voice of
the Sovereign Pontiff was always heard above the din of
battle pleading for peace. If the Church failed in putting an
end to war, she did her best to mitigate its atrocities. By the
Truce of God she did actually set limits to the violence of
the age. Under this title was understood the law by which
her councils forbade all men under the severest spiritual
censures to carry on any hostilities public or private during
certain specified seasons. These were, generally speaking, in
every week from Wednesday evening to Monday morning,
from the beginning of Advent to the octave of the Epiphany,
from the first day of Lent to the octave of Easter, and from
the Rogation Days to the octave of Pentecost. A number
of holy days differing in different parts were likewise included
in the Truce, and during all these times it was forbidden not
only to fight, but to lay waste lands and carry off cattle.
Churches and cemeteries were also placed under perpetual
protection, and it was declared to be a violation of the Truce
to kill or wound peasants engaged in agriculture, or helpless
women, or to destroy or injure the implements of husbandry.
Special officers with an armed force at their command were
appointed to guard the observance of this sacred law, the
infraction of which was regarded as an offence of the deepest
dye, and those found bold enough to violate its prescriptions

were held in universal reprobation. Nothing, perhaps, is
more extraordinary or more admirable in history than the
fact that such a law should not only be promulgated throughout Christendom, but that on the whole it should have been
observed, and it speaks volumes as to the beneficent influence
exercised by religion in those wild and troublous times.[1]

The Church then, and especially the Holy See, acted as
the universal peacemaker. The Legation sent into Languedoc by Innocent III. was far from being exclusively
directed against the heretical doctrines of the Albigenses.
One of its main objects was the pacification of the country
by the extinction of these miserable wars and the expulsion
of the *Routiers*. As we have said, Raymund VI. was one of
their chief protectors. " He had," says a contemporary writer,
" a wonderful liking for these men." His partiality for them
may perhaps be explained in the words of Michelet, who
after drawing a frightful picture of the excesses perpetrated
by the *Routiers*, particularly in the south of France, observes
that nevertheless "they were dear to the princes of the
country precisely on account of their impiety, which made
them indifferent to the censures of the Church."

It was then not merely as an abettor of heresy, but as
the promoter of bloody and unjust wars, and the protector
of excommunicated ruffians who lived only by crime and
violence, that Innocent III. addressed to the Count that
celebrated letter in which he enumerates his offences against
God and man, and calls on him to make reparation. " Would

---

[1] It is remarkable that at first the ecclesiastical authorities endeavoured
to abolish the custom of making war altogether and to establish what was
called "the *peace* of God." Needless to say the measure failed or success
by attempting too much, and about the middle of the eleventh century,
the *truce* of God was substituted for the peace, and men to whom fighting
was a kind of second nature were only required to restrict their hostilities
within certain limits. Henry II. of England, when resolved on establishing the reign of social order throughout his dominions, found no better
means of doing so than by copying this institution of the Church. He
proclaimed what he called "the King's peace," and the officers he
appointed to enforce it were known as "justices of the peace," phrases
still in use in our own day. For a full treatment of this interesting
subject, see Rohrbacher, *Histoire de l'Eglise*, vol. xiii. pp. 466—474.

that we could open your heart," he says, "and make you see the enormities you have committed! What pride has seized possession of you, that you will not keep peace with your neighbours, and that you break the laws of God by allying yourself with the enemies of the faith! . . . If you do not stand in fear of eternal punishment, at least fear that which is temporal: fear, lest by the hostilities you wage against your neighbour and the offence you offer to God by protecting heresy, you draw on yourself a double punishment. . . . Who are you, that you alone should refuse to make peace, in order that you may profit by these miserable divisions, whilst the King of Aragon and all the other most powerful lords of the country have at the entreaties of our Legates solemnly sworn to do so? Do you not blush to remember how often you have broken your oaths to drive the heretics out of your dominions? And was it not you who, laying waste the province of Arles with your hired bands, were entreated by our venerable brother the Bishop of Orange, to spare the monasteries and to suspend your ravages, if it were but during the holy season[3] and on feast-days. Then you took the bishop by the right hand, and swore on that hand, that you would have regard neither to the holy time nor to Sundays, and that you would spare neither consecrated places nor persons. And this oath, if we ought not rather to call it this profanation, you have observed better than your other oaths, taken in a lawful cause."[4]

This accumulation of outrages at last met with its well-merited punishment, and after repeated warnings and remonstrances the Legate pronounced against the Count sentence of excommunication. For the spiritual censure, Raymund cared little enough; but in the thirteenth century excommunication, by the common law of the Church, bore with it certain temporal penalties. At any moment the decree might go forth which would deprive him of his territories, and already a league was formed against him among certain of his barons who would joyfully have put such a sentence into execution. It was necessary therefore

[3] *i.e.* of the Truce.       [4] Epist. Innoc. III. t. x.

to temporize.  He invited the Legate to meet him at St.
Gilles, near the mouth of the Rhone, under the pretence of
seeking a sincere reconciliation with the Church.  Peter de
Castelnau accepted the invitation, and repaired to the place
appointed in company with one of his brother Legates.  But
it soon became apparent that nothing was further from
Raymund's intention than any kind of submission.  He
desired indeed to be relieved from his sentence, and threatened
the Legates with death if they attempted to leave the town
without giving him absolution.  But as to giving any pledges
that would bind his future conduct, he utterly refused to do
so.  He would neither make peace with his neighbours,
dismiss the *Routiers* from his employment, or withdraw his
protection from the Albigenses.  These were the three heads
to which the Legates reduced their demands, requiring not
only his acceptance of them, but some security that the
conditions would be observed.  As to oaths, too well did
they know what was their value in his eyes.  "A renegade
to his faith," says Peter de Vaulx-Cernay, "worse than an
infidel, and incapable of observing his oaths, he had already
sworn, and foresworn himself many times."  All negotiations
therefore failing, Peter de Castelnau boldly confronted the
tyrant, and reproached him with his crimes and perjuries.
Then, despising his threats, the two Legates left the town
accompanied by an escort given them by the civic magistrates.
That night they slept in a little inn by the shore of the
Rhone, and next morning, having said Mass and dismissed
their escort, they prepared to cross the river.  At that
moment two men approached them, one of whom, squire to
the Count of Toulouse, plunged a lance into the side of
Peter de Castelnau.  He fell to the ground mortally wounded,
exclaiming, "May God pardon you; as for me, I pardon
you!"  These words he repeated several times, adding as
he addressed his companions, "Keep the faith and serve
God's Church without fear and without negligence."  They
carried him into the poor wayside inn, where he lay raising
his hands and eyes to heaven, and from time to time praying
God to pardon his murderer.  "Towards cock-crow," says

the author of the *Song of the Crusade*, " he died after receiving
Holy Communion. His soul departed to God, and his body
was carried back to St. Gilles, and buried with lighted
candles and the chant of the *Kyrie eleison* sung by many
clerks."

The slaughter of an ambassador has in all times, and
among all peoples, been reckoned among the most heinous
of crimes. But as Rohrbacher observes, Peter of Castelnau
was the ambassador from the Head of the Church, despatched
to restore peace to a distracted country by exclusively
peaceful means. His murder was therefore an outrage on
the whole Christian world, and, according to what was then
the universally acknowledged law of Christendom, the author
of such a crime, as well as his accomplices and protectors,
forfeited all social rights, and was to be regarded as an
outlaw.

Nor could the death of the Legate be separated from the
cause in the defence of which he fell. Although the Count
of Toulouse had contrived to incur the censures of the
Church on many grounds, yet it was mainly by his protection
of the Albigenses and his connivance at their crimes, that
he, the Christian knight and noble, stood charged before
the chief tribunal of the Christian world. In judging the
question, we must regard it as it was then regarded by the
whole of Christendom, when the interests of the faith took
precedence of every other interest, and the abettor of heresy
stood convicted of the crime of *lèse-majesté* against God
Himself. The policy of the Holy See in dealing with the
Albigenses had hitherto been marked with nothing but
patience and moderation. As we have seen, it was by the
intervention of the Pope that the temporal sword had been
held for ten years from falling on the guilty provinces.
During that time, while apostolic missioners had sought the
conversion of the heretics by no other means than by preaching and disputation, the Legates of the Holy See had with
unwearied patience endeavoured to recall Count Raymund
to the obligations binding on him as sovereign of a Catholic
people. It was not until the murder of the Legate had

rendered all further compromise impossible that Pope Innocent consented to an appeal to arms. In the letter which he addressed to the knights and barons, the arch-bishops and bishops of Narbonne and the adjacent provinces, after enumerating the crimes of the Count of Toulouse, he declares that the time of endurance has passed, and that the censures long withheld must now fall on the author of so many offences. In other letters he called on the kings of France and England to forget their private quarrels and, girding on their swords, to march against the enemies of the faith. "Suffer not the Church to perish in this unhappy country," he writes, "but come to her assistance, and combat valiantly against these heretics, who are worse than the Saracens themselves."[5]

This appeal found a response in the hearts of those to whom it was addressed, a vast number of princes and nobles took up arms, and thus there opens before us the history of that bloody war which, while strictly speaking it forms no part of the life of St. Dominic, yet from its association with the cause to which he had devoted himself must first be briefly traced, before we can take up the thread of our narrative and follow him in his apostolic career.

[5] Innocent, Epist. 26—32.

WEST DOOR OF THE CHURCH OF ST. GILLES.

## CHAPTER VII.

### THE CRUSADE.

THE death of Peter de Castelnau took place in the February of 1208, and its effect, as we have seen, was to put an end to all hopes of temporizing. The crime of the Count of Toulouse was declared to be one which freed his subjects from their allegiance until such time as he should have made due reparation: and a new commission of bishops and abbots was appointed to preach the Crusade, and undertake the ecclesiastical government of the country. At its head was placed the Cardinal Legate, James Galba, commonly known as the Cardinal Milon, who lost no time in seeking an interview with Philip Augustus, King of France, and urging him to lead his forces in person against the Albigenses. The King excused himself on the plea that his own territories were endangered by the hostile attitude both of the Emperor and the King of England; nevertheless he gave permission

to all his vassals and subjects to take the Cross, engaging
that both he and his son would do the same as soon as the
safety of the kingdom was secured.    Active preparations
were accordingly set on foot, and Raymund, fairly alarmed,
himself had recourse to the King for counsel and protection.
But Philip gave him clearly to understand that his only
course lay in unconditional submission to the Holy See.
The Count therefore repaired to Rome for the purpose of
protesting his innocence of the murder of the Legate, and
obtaining for himself the best terms in his power.    He was
not unfavourably received, though as it happened, an
embassy of bishops from the Narbonnese provinces had
preceded him to Rome to make known to the Pope the
miserable state to which the country had been reduced by
the heretics and their supporters, and to implore his interference.

As regarded the Albigenses, it was felt that no further
indulgence was possible, but the Pope showed himself
willing to admit the Count to reconciliation with the Church
on certain conditions.    He was required, after making ample
reparation for his crimes, to deliver up seven strong places
in his dominions to persons appointed by the Holy See, as
a security for the fulfilment of his promises; and to submit
in every respect to the orders of the Legate.    These conditions he solemnly swore to observe, and returning to
France, he repaired to St. Gilles,[1] where the Legate, in
company with three archbishops and nineteen bishops were
to meet and receive him to absolution.

The proceedings which followed are singularly characteristic of the age, and make us clearly understand the
grounds on which Count Raymund stood charged as a public
criminal.    On the 18th of June, 1208, an altar was prepared
outside the western door of the Church of St. Gilles, whither,
in sight of an immense multitude, the Count was conducted;
and standing there barefoot, and with shoulders bare to the
waist, he swore on the Blessed Sacrament and holy relics,

---

[1] St. Gilles was the real capital of his hereditary dominions, and gave
its name to the family of the Counts of Toulouse.

henceforth to show himself a true son of Holy Church, and
to obey the Legate in all things that should be commanded
him.  This oath, which was in substance a public confession
of his crimes, ran as follows:

"I, Raymund, Count of Toulouse, do hereby swear to
obey the Pope and his Legate, in all the articles for which
I have been excommunicated, namely, that I have refused
to make peace; that I have not kept my oaths to expel the
heretics, but have always favoured them, and incurred
suspicion of heresy; that I have kept in my pay bands of
Routiers; that I have given public offices to the Jews; that
I have turned churches into fortresses; that I have driven
the Bishop of Carpentras from his see, have imprisoned the
Bishop of Vaison, and ill-treated his clergy and religious;
that I am suspected of the murder of Peter de Castelnau
of happy memory; that I have broken the holy Truce, and
disturbed the public peace on Sundays, and during the time
of Lent; that I have denied free passage by land and water
through my dominions to travellers, and have forced them
out of the beaten track;[2] that I have imposed oppressive
tolls on my subjects; that I have done violence to churches
and monasteries, and have troubled the peace of elections.
On all these articles I now swear obedience; and I moreover promise to enter into no alliance with the heretics, but
to bring them to justice; and if I violate these present oaths,
I consent that my seven strong castles shall all be forfeited;
that an interdict be pronounced on my dominions; and that
all my vassals be released from their oaths of fealty and
allegiance to me."

Sixteen of the Count's chief vassals stood by his side as
he gave these pledges, which they likewise bound themselves
to observe, adding some others on their own account.  They
promised, as became true knights, to guard the public roads,

[2] This was an offence of which the lawless tyrants of these times
frequently stand charged; and to understand its heinousness we must
bear in mind that the protection of unoffending travellers was one of the
duties demanded by the laws of chivalry from every belted knight; and
that the object aimed at was to force them into dangerous paths where
they could be more conveniently pillaged.

and not to ally themselves with brigands; whilst, should the
Count prove faithless to his engagements, they swore to lend
him no support, but to remain loyal to their oaths as became
true sons of Holy Church.

After these formalities the Cardinal Legate threw a stole
over the Count's neck, and taking the ends of it in his hands,
led him into the church, striking him with a rod on his bare
shoulders as they proceeded up to the high altar, where he
was absolved from all the censures he had incurred. The
crowds that had gathered in the church to witness the
ceremony were so great that Raymund, in returning, had to
make his way through the crypt, and in so doing, was obliged
to pass by the tomb of his murdered victim, Peter de
Castelnau. A few days later Cardinal Milon concluded
peace between the Count and a number of barons, with whom
he had persisted in waging war, and established a tribunal
for the just arbitration of their differences; and finally both
Raymund and his fast ally, the Count de Foix, swore on the
holy Gospels to aid and protect the forces of the Crusaders,
as long as they should remain in their territories.

The Catholic army had by this time assembled at Lyons,
and was now in full march for Languedoc. According to
some writers, it amounted to five hundred thousand men, but
this is probably an exaggeration. That the Crusaders were
very numerous is certain. "One would have thought," says
William of Tudela, "that all Provence was there." At their
head were many illustrious princes, prelates, and nobles;
such as the Duke of Burgundy, the Count de St. Pol, Simon,
Count de Montfort, the Archbishops of Rheims, Sens, and
Rouen, and many others of equal rank. But the historian
goes on to tell us, that the army itself was composed of very
heterogeneous materials. There were full twenty thousand
well armed knights, of whom fifteen thousand were despatched
by the King of France, and more than two hundred thousand
peasants; but these latter were but indifferently equipped,
and came partly as soldiers, to give their forty days of
military service, and partly to gain the Indulgence promised
to all those who should take the Cross. As they marched

they bore in their hands the pilgrim's staff, as a token that they were devoted to a sacred cause. But besides these there was, what the same historian calls "a ribald crowd," such as hangs on the skirts of every army: men whose sole object was pillage, and who were as ready to turn their hands against the Crusaders and the clergy themselves as against the enemy.

Among the Narbonnese nobles who had especially distinguished themselves as abettors of the Albigenses none was more conspicuous than the Viscount de Beziers, a near relative of the King of Aragon. He had done his utmost to dissuade Raymund from seeking reconciliation with the Church. Afterwards, constrained by the threatening aspect of affairs, he had himself reluctantly opened negotiations with the Legates; but finding their conditions too hard, he gathered all his vassals together, and, entrenching himself and his troops in the strong fortifications of Beziers and Carcassonne, resolved to hold out against the Crusaders until the King of Aragon should come to his assistance. The Crusaders therefore directed their first course towards Beziers. The Count of Toulouse was the feudal suzerain of the country, and the entrance of so vast an army into his dominions filled him with uneasiness. He therefore advanced to meet them; and, protesting that he was no longer to be regarded as an enemy to the Catholic cause, went so far as to receive the Cross from the hands of the Legate, and even offered to lead the army to the attack of Beziers. The inhabitants of that unhappy city, whether Catholics or Albigenses, had earned for themselves an infamous reputation by a long tissue of crimes. They had quite recently slaughtered one of their viscounts, before the high altar of St. Mary Magdalen's Church; and when Bernard the bishop bravely interfered to save the life of his sovereign, he was seized and cruelly beaten, after which his teeth were torn out by the brutal murderers. For the rest it is sufficient to say that the Albigensian code of morals largely prevailed amongst the citizens, and that besides being a stronghold of heresy, Beziers was regarded throughout the country as a real den of brigands. On

arriving before the walls, the chiefs of the Crusading army
despatched Reginald de Montpellier, bishop of Beziers, to offer
terms to the Catholic inhabitants, whom he invited to separate
from the company of the heretics and to leave the city, so as
not to be involved in the common ruin. But they not only
refused to do so, but confident in the strength of their
defences, mounted to the walls, and thence hurled defiance at
the besiegers. The heretics who accompanied them at the
same time discharged a shower of arrows, adding blasphemies
and outrageous acts, too shocking for transcription. It was
the 22nd of July, the feast of St. Mary Magdalen, whose
church had so shortly before been sacrilegiously profaned by
the murder of the viscount. The Crusading chiefs were still
holding counsel what means could be taken for the protection
of the Catholic inhabitants during the coming assault, when
the footmen of the army, enraged by these insults, rushed to
the attack without waiting for the orders of their commanders.
They were followed by the " ribald crowd," who were thirsting
for blood and plunder, and, scaling the walls, they poured
into the town, and commenced an indiscriminate massacre.
" No one was spared," says the poet of the Crusade, " neither
priests, women, nor children, the ribalds slaughtering them
before the very altars where they had taken refuge. Then
their leaders called out ' Fire l ' and, bringing lighted torches,
they set fire to the town from one end to the other." The
numbers slain in this horrible carnage is stated differently by
different writers. The Legate Arnold, in writing to the Pope,
sets it down as little under twenty thousand; but Peter de
Vaulx-Cernay estimates it at seven thousand, a more probable
calculation. It is asserted by one historian that St. Dominic
had joined the Crusaders after they passed the Rhone, and
that accompanying them to Beziers, he was present at the
sack of the town. According to the same authority, he
appeared in the streets with the crucifix in his hand, interceding for the lives of women and children, of the aged and
the infirm, who crowded to him for protection ; whilst Arnold
of Citeaux, on the other hand, is represented as encouraging
the soldiers to indiscriminate slaughter, in memorable words

which, whether truly or falsely reported, have found an unhappy notoriety.[3]

The fact of St. Dominic's presence on this occasion is, however, more than doubtful. Mamachi quotes the author in question, and gives the reference,[4] but without passing any opinion as to the correctness of the narrative, which is held of very questionable authenticity. We notice it here, however, as being among the rare passages in which the name of the saint occurs associated with any incident of the war; and the part thus attributed to him, even if we were to accept it as truly reported, is manifestly not unworthy the character of a man of God.

From Beziers the Crusaders marched to Carcassonne. The Viscount de Beziers, after making his escape with a considerable number of the inhabitants, had thrown himself into that strongly fortified town, where he made a resolute defence for fifteen days. At the end of that time the garrison surrendered, and the Crusaders formed themselves in possession of the whole country subject to the Viscount. A council was held for the purpose of electing a generalissimo of the army, who should also be invested with the sovereignty of the conquered territory. The person chosen was Simon, Earl of Leicester and Count de Montfort, a man no less illustrious by birth than by character. "Tall in stature, and powerfully made," says Peter de Vaulx-Cernay, "he had a countenance of singular beauty, and when armed *cap-à-pié*, he inspired courage by the very majesty of his appearance. Courteous and affable in his manners as he was resolute in action, he showed himself a true father to his followers: and at the siege of Carcassonne had saved the life of a wounded soldier at the risk of his own; bearing him out of the combat on his own shoulders to a place of safety." He had earned his great reputation as a warrior in the Holy Land, and shone amongst the nobles of the time as the very ideal of a

---

[3] "Cedite, cedite, novit Dominus qui sunt ejus."

[4] D'Andoque, in *Hist. Gallia Occitan*. The passage is likewise quoted by Father Percin in his history of the war, but Touron rejects the whole narrative as apocryphal, and denies St. Dominic's presence at Beziers at all.

Christian knight, chaste, valiant, loyal, and devout. " When once he had determined on an energetic course of action," says Hurter, " he was deterred by no fear of danger, for the habit of assisting daily at Mass and the Offices of the Church even in time of war inspired him with a calm and unshaken courage, the fruit of sincere confidence in God."[5]   Far from seeking any personal aggrandizement in entering on this campaign, he had joined the army of the Crusaders as a simple act of religion, with no other purpose than that of fulfilling his forty days of service, and gaining the Indulgence as a pilgrim: nor was it until charged by the Legate under obedience to assume the burden of command that he yielded a reluctant consent.  " The cause of God," he said, " must not be lost for want of a champion."

The news of his election to the chief command struck terror into the hearts of the enemy; a great number of towns and castles surrendered at once without striking a blow ; and could an available force have been kept in the field, there seems no doubt that the first successes of the Crusaders would have been speedily followed by the submission of the entire country.   Unfortunately, on the expiration of the forty days of feudal service, the immense armament which had encamped before Carcassonne melted away like snow. Jealousies, moreover, broke out among the commanders. The Duke of Burgundy and the Counts of Nevers and St. Pol considered it beneath their dignity to serve under the command of the Count de Montfort, who in the space of a few days found himself alone and all but abandoned, having with him no more than thirty knights and their followers.  But the inflexible constancy of the champion of God never gave way.  With the small force at his command he succeeded in reducing many strong places; but the successes of to-day were often enough lost on the morrow. Fresh pilgrims, it is true, came to take the place of those who departed, but as a general rule, they gave no more than their forty days of service.  Thus the number of the Crusaders was always fluctuating and their leader would find himself

[5] Hurter, *Hist. Innocent III.* l. 13.

one day at the head of twenty thousand men, and unable on the day following to gather more than a few hundreds to his standard. Among all his allies, none rendered him truer service than his heroic wife, Adela de Montmorency, who on one occasion accompanied by the Bishop of Carcassonne, brought him a reinforcement of fifteen thousand men. Their road lay through a wild and hostile country, and some of the soldiers becoming exhausted with fatigue, the Countess and the bishop dismounted from their horses, which they gave up to the service of their followers, themselves continuing the march on foot. In spite of every difficulty they succeeded in joining the Count who, with the timely aid thus afforded, was able to capture the strongly fortified town of Termes, within the walls of which Mass had not been said for thirty years.

Thus for five years the war rolled on with ever-changing fortunes. Its records supply us with few notices of any events in which St. Dominic took part, though Touron conjectures that he was often engaged in restoring Catholic worship in the towns captured by the Crusaders. In 1211, when the Count de Montfort visited Cahors, and there received the homage of William de Cardaillac, Bishop and Count of Cahors, we find among the signatures of the witnesses that of " Brother Dominic, canon of Osma and humble preacher." Father Percin informs us that after leaving Cahors the Count paid a visit to the neighbouring sanctuary of Roc Amadour, whither he was accompanied by the saint, to whom that place of pilgrimage was specially dear. This fact is given on the authority of the *History of the Church of Tulle*, which had some rights of patronage over Roc Amadour, and the historian adds that the blessed Father visited that sanctuary not once only, but many times during his life.

The act of homage above-mentioned is preserved in the archives of Carcassonne, and proves the presence of the saint among the forces of the Crusaders at least on that occasion. According to Touron, it was often enough needed for the repression of disorders prevalent among their ranks ; for his apostolic zeal found matter for its exercise no less in restraining the excesses of the Christian soldiers than in con-

G

verting the heretics. That he was bound in ties of close
friendship with the Count de Montfort is certain; and this
circumstance had its weight in determining the Count's
choice of Fanjeaux as the residence of his family during
the war. In that town, as we know, the saint fixed his
principal abode for several years, during which time a
constant tradition declares him to have exercised the office
of parish priest.⁰ And a strong fortress which stood near
the church, long remained, bearing the title of the *Chateau
de Montfort*, where the Count frequently withdrew during the
intervals of the war.

Meanwhile the part taken by Raymund of Toulouse was
one so involved in treachery and double-dealing as to render
it no easy task to unravel the narrative. Still wearing the
white cross on his breast, he confined his military operations
to supplying secret assistance to the heretics, with whom he
dared not openly take part. When, in 1211, five thousand
Catholic inhabitants of Toulouse, at the invitation of their
bishop, prepared to march to Lavaur, then besieged by the
forces of De Montfort, Count Raymund, after contriving to
throw into the town strong reinforcements, attempted by all
means in his power to prevent the men of Toulouse from
joining the Crusaders, or even supplying them with provisions. In like manner, while still openly professing
adhesion to the Catholic cause, he sent troops to act under
the orders of the Count de Foix, who treacherously surprised
and massacred a body of German pilgrims, who were marching to join the army of De Montfort. Meantime the pledges
given at St. Gilles remained unfulfilled. Neither the heretics
nor the *Routiers* were expelled from his territories; the oppressive tolls continued to be exacted, and the assassin of Peter
de Castelnau was retained in the service and favour of the
count, who often declared he was his only real friend.

Passing over many details in the confused history of this
memorable war, we shall briefly summarize those events

⁰ Fulk of Toulouse, in a Brief dated 1214, gives him the title of
chaplain, or rector of Fanjeaux: "Assensu Fratri Dominici *Capellani* de
Fano Jovis."

which bring us to the date at which it joins issue with that of St. Dominic. The treacheries of the Count of Toulouse became at length too apparent for further dissimulation; and a council of prelates assembled at Avignon in 1209, threatened him with fresh excommunication. Raymund, as before, appealed to the King of France and to the Pope, demanding to be allowed to clear himself from the charges brought against him. Innocent III. treated him with marked indulgence, and instructed the Legates to observe the utmost moderation in their proceedings. Indeed, the terms offered by them would have secured the Count in the possession of his territories on the condition of his observing the oaths which he had so solemnly and so repeatedly sworn; but as he persisted in refusing to do this, sentence of excommunication was once more pronounced against him in the April of the year 1211, and confirmed by the Pope's authority. Raymund at length threw off all disguise, and prepared for open hostilities. He repelled De Montfort from the walls of Toulouse, but sustained a bloody defeat at Castelnaudary. This victory of the Crusaders was followed by other successes; until at last Raymund found himself so hardly pressed as to be forced to take refuge with his brother-in-law, Peter, King of Aragon.

This prince, allied by marriage with more than one of the nobles of Languedoc, was naturally displeased by the presence of a hostile army in provinces many of which were fiefs of his own crown. He particularly resented the investiture of the Count de Montfort with the dominions of his nephew, the Viscount de Beziers. In 1212, therefore, he addressed to the Pope an appeal on behalf of the Count of Toulouse and his allies, whom he represented as having been unfairly treated. A fresh council was in consequence assembled at Lavaur in 1213, and its members were commissioned to examine into the statements of the King of Aragon, and report the result to the Pope. Their decision was that no terms could be granted to the Count of Toulouse, on account of his constant infidelity to every engagement; but that the other nobles in alliance with him might be received to reconciliation, on condition of their making due satisfaction. This decision was taken by the King of Aragon as implying a fixed purpose of crushing the Count of Toulouse, of whom he at once declared himself the protector. His representations appear to have produced some impression on the mind of the Pope, until deputies despatched from the Council of Lavaur made known to him the whole truth, and declared that the cause of Catholic Christianity would be lost in the Narbonnese provinces if the Count of Toulouse were left in possession of his dominions. Thus informed, Innocent commanded the King to desist from hostilities, and to conclude a truce with the Count De Montfort, pending the arrival of a Cardinal Legate, who should be empowered to bring the whole matter to a final settlement. But the command came too late. The King had already passed the Pyrenees, and having united his forces to those of the Counts of Toulouse, Foix, and Comminges, was entering Languedoc for the purpose of reinstating Raymund in his dominions by force of arms.

Here we will pause for the moment, for the events that followed are more directly associated with the history of St. Dominic, the thread of which must first be disentangled from that of the Crusade. In following the narrative of the war, it is most difficult to form any satisfactory judgment regarding its real character. In its chronicles are displayed by turns all the vices and all the virtues of the age. If at one time we are filled with admiration at examples of heroism and self-devotion on the part of the Crusading chief worthy of the best days of chivalry, at another we are simply appalled by the tales of blood and cruelty through which we have to wade. Even if some of these are to be rejected, as resting on insufficient authority, there seems no reasonable doubt that the war was in some sense one of extermination, and that whilst life and liberty were freely offered to such of the heretics as were willing to renounce their errors, those who refused to do so and who were taken in arms, were very commonly either burnt or put to the sword. It seems certain, indeed, that the capital sentence was reserved for

the "perfect," whose numbers bore a very small proportion
to those of the "believers." Rainier Sacconi, a contemporary writer, and who, after his conversion from heresy,
became a Friar Preacher, declares that throughout the whole
world they did not amount to four thousand. And this
statement is supported by the exact accounts which have
been preserved of the numbers of the "perfect" found in
the different towns which surrendered to the Crusaders; as,
at Minerva 140, at Montsegur 200, at Les Cassers 60.[7] To
these pardon was always offered on the condition of abjuration, whilst the simple believers were far more leniently dealt
with—only to the relapsed was no quarter given. But even
with these limitations, we shudder at the thought of all
which is involved in such statements. Nevertheless, in order
to form any just judgment of the case, we are bound to
remember two things. First, that we are reading a page
in the history of the thirteenth, and not of the nineteenth
century, and that the ferocity which characterized such
a method of warfare was not then condemned by public
opinion, as it would be in our own day. It would be unjust
to take any portion of history out of its proper framework,
and judge of it by the standard of humanity accepted in
a more civilized age. Death by burning, for example, so
repulsive to our modern sense, was a common punishment,
not reserved for obstinate heretics, but inflicted for a vast
number of other crimes. Nor was it by any means the most
terrible method of execution of which we find notice in contemporary history. Most readers will remember how the
archer who shot the fatal arrow which caused the death of
Richard Cœur de Lion, was flayed alive, a torturing mode
of death, of which, horrible to say, other examples are not
wanting. In fact, the cruelties with which the Crusaders
stand charged were only too much in accordance with the
manners of the times, and were equalled, if not surpassed,
by the proceedings of the heretics.

Secondly, it must be remembered who those were against
whom this war of extermination was directed. A vast sect

[7] Danzas, St. Raymond de Pennafort, tom. i. p. 444.

who for more than a century had been at work for the destruction, not of faith alone, but of the very foundations of society, and whose members, not content with propagating false doctrine, stand convicted of crimes so atrocious, that in any age and any country, they would be adjudged as capital. For upwards of a century, the authorities, whether secular or ecclesiastical, had exhibited a patient abstention from severity in dealing with these malefactors, which is the only fault chargeable against them, inasmuch as it permitted the pestilence to spread its poison unchecked. Thus, when at last the sword of justice was unsheathed, it had to deal its blows in no sparing measure. It is presumed that in any age a state of things may exist, the evil of which is so great and has attained such a head as to justify the extremest severity. If this be so, then most certainly the case of the Albigenses was one of this nature, and the severities of the Crusaders must be regarded less in the light of brutal massacres than of wholesale executions. That this was their actual character is apparent from the fact, which Rohrbacher states on the authority of a contemporary writer, that at the very outset of the war, this method of dealing with the enemy had been deliberately decreed by the chiefs of the Crusade. In some cases, and notably at Beziers, terrible excesses were committed in the heat of combat, but in general the proceedings which followed the capture of a town or fortress were carried out as judicial acts. And even in our own soft-mannered days, we have witnessed examples of such executions on a scale not greatly inferior to those of the thirteenth century. Public opinion did not shrink from sanctioning the slaughter of prisoners of war, whether belonging to the French Communists or the rebels of our Indian Empire. A stern necessity was in each instance held to justify such acts. Without presuming to decide on the correctness of such a judgment, we may yet plead that the same principle should be applied to the case under consideration, and that as much extenuation as was claimed by the authorities at Versailles or Calcutta, shall not be refused to De Montfort and his Crusaders.

CARCASSONNE.

## CHAPTER VIII.

### ST. DOMINIC, THE APOSTLE OF LANGUEDOC.

#### 1207—1215.

"After the return of the Bishop Diego to his diocese," says Blessed Humbert, "St. Dominic left almost alone with a few companions who were bound to him by no vow, during ten years[1] upheld the Catholic faith in different parts of Narbonne, specially at Carcassonne and Fanjeaux. He devoted himself entirely to the salvation of souls by the ministry of preaching, and he bore with a great heart a multitude of affronts, ignominies, and sufferings for the name of Jesus Christ."

This abridgment of the history of ten years is repeated

[1] This expression is not strictly correct, as the *ten* years can only be reckoned from the first arrival of Diego and St. Dominic in the country, and the saint's *solitary* labours in Languedoc did not begin till two years later.

in almost the same words by Theodoric of Apoldia, who adds : " During this time an intimate friendship sprang up between the illustrious Count de Montfort who fought against the heretics with the temporal sword, and Dominic the servant of God, who combated them with the sword of the Word of God." The same expression is used by the English historian Nicholas Trivet, who says that both these great men combated heresy, but in different ways : " one with the material sword, the other with the sword of the Spirit which is the Word of God."

The career, then, of the servant of God during these troublous years was exclusively that of an apostle. The few details preserved of his life at this period will disappoint any who look for stirring pictures of the Crusade. The powers entrusted to him by the Legates were, as we have seen, strictly limited to preaching and reconciling heretics ; and the too scanty records which we are able to gather together from contemporary writers, present him to us at this time as wholly engaged in apostolic labours. Some trait of humility and patience exhibited amid the insults of his enemies, a few words redolent of the spirit of prayer and trust in God, which have come down in the tradition of ages, or the record of miracles worked like those of the Master Whose steps he followed as he went up and down the hills of Narbonne, and among the towns and villages, preaching the faith and seeking for the sheep that were lost,—this is all we find. There is an evangelical sweetness of simplicity about these broken notices of his life which, coming in the midst of the troubled and bloody history of the period, sound like the rich notes of a thrush's song falling on the ear between the intervals of a thunderstorm, lost every now and then, and hushed by the angry roll of the elements, then sounding sweetly again in the stillness when the storm is over. Alone or attended by a single companion, he traversed every part of the country barefoot, going from village to village, and from town to town, preaching the faith and winning back souls to the flock of Christ. The records exist of official inquiries made some years after his death, as to the state of religion in the provinces he had found overrun by heresy : and from these we gather the most authentic testimony as to the wide extent of country which he thus visited, as well as of the success which attended his ministry. This success did not indeed often appear under the form which secures popular applause or makes much noise in the world. One by one individual souls were sought out and reconciled, and the examples of such conversions of which proofs have been preserved may be taken as furnishing indications of a far wider apostolate of which no trace now remains. To the power of the Word of God the saint added the yet more efficacious means of prayer and example. " With all the strength that was in him," says Theodoric, " he devoted himself day and night, by his prayers, his tears, his watching, fasting and labours, by his preaching in season and out of season, to spend himself for the salvation of souls, and to consummate his sacrifice by the glory of martyrdom. . . . Moreover, he crucified his flesh and mortified his members by excessive austerities, and his soul by continual sorrow and compassion for perishing sinners."

As we learn from Blessed Humbert, his ordinary residence at this time was at Carcassonne. Girt about with its battlements and towers, some of which owe their origin to the Visigoths and date as far back as the fifth century, Carcassonne still stands almost unchanged in aspect from the days when St. Dominic dwelt within its walls. Over that ancient bridge his feet must have passed times out of mind as he went forth on his errands of charity. Those narrow streets are the same he traversed daily, followed by scoffing bands who would show their hatred and contempt by throwing dirt on him, or spitting in his face, tying straws to his garments or pursuing him with shouts of derisive laughter. But he would pass through the midst of them with a tranquil and joyous aspect, giving thanks to God that he should be counted worthy to suffer affronts for the name of Christ. " Why do you not live at Toulouse, rather than at Carcassonne ? " he was asked by one who was aware of the treatment he received in the latter city, and who marvelled at his patient endurance. "I know many people at Toulouse," was his reply, "and they show me respect, but at Carcassonne every one is against me."

This enmity he earned not only by his defence of the faith against the attacks of the heretics, but by his fearless denunciation of their vices. "His words burnt like flaming torches," says Theodoric, "so that the heretics foamed against him in their rage, and often threatened him with death." "I am not worthy of martyrdom," was the only reply they could at such times draw from him.

Once he was warned of a party of heretics who lay in ambush in a certain place to assassinate him. He treated the information with his usual indifference, and passed by the place singing hymns with a joyful aspect. The heretics. amazed at his unshaken constancy, accosted him on their next meeting in their usual style. "And so thou dost not fear death? Tell us, what wouldst thou have done if thou hadst fallen into our hands?" Then the great and courageous spirit of Dominic spoke in a memorable reply: "I would have prayed you," he said, "not to have taken my life at a single blow, but little by little, cutting off each member of my body, one by one; and when you had done that, you should have plucked out my eyes, and then have left me so, to prolong my torments, and gain me a richer crown." It is said that this reply so confounded his enemies, that for some time afterwards they left him unmolested, being convinced that to persecute such a man was to give him the only con-solation he desired. The place of the intended attempt on his life is still shown, half-way between Prouille and Fan-jeaux, and its name "Al Sicari," in the dialect of the country, commemorates the event, and is marked by a cross called the "Croix de Sicari."

The zeal of the servant of God was, however, as far as possible removed from all bitterness. It welled up from a fountain of charity. To use the words of Blessed Jordan, "he strove with all his might to gain souls for Christ, and as many as he could; for there was in his heart a wonderful and almost incredible thirst for the salvation of all men.

Nor was he wanting in that love than which no man hath greater, that a man should lay down his life for his friends." And he proceeds to give as an example of this heroic charity, how on one occasion, having earnestly invited a heretic to return to the bosom of the Church, the man owned himself convinced, but added that, owing to his poverty, he was compelled to frequent the company of the heretics, on whom he depended for support. Then Dominic, having no alms at his command, offered to sell himself, and with the price to relieve the needs of this perishing soul, so that his temporal necessities should not stand in the way of his eternal salvation; and he would actually have done what he proposed if Providence had not supplied the requisite means in another way.[2]

The same lesson he enforced at a great conference appointed to be held with the heretics, to which one of the neighbouring bishops came, attended by a pompous retinue. This displeased the servant of God, and he hesitated not to offer his remonstrance. "My Father," he said, "it is not thus that we must act against this generation of pride. The enemies of the truth must be convinced by the example of humility and patience rather than by the pomp and grandeur of worldly show. Let us arm ourselves with prayer and humility, and so let us go barefooted against these Goliaths." The bishop complied with his wishes, and they all took off their shoes, and went to meet the heretics, singing psalms upon the way.[3] As they were not sure of their road, they applied to a man whom they met and believed to be a Catholic, but who was in truth a concealed and bitter heretic; and who offered to be their guide to the place of meeting, with no other design than that of embarrassing and annoying them. He led them, therefore, through a thorny wood, where the rough stones and briers tore their naked feet, and caused them to dye the ground with their blood. The bishop and his suite were a little disconcerted at this, but Dominic

[2] Jordan, 75.
[3] This event is not to be confused with the somewhat similar narrative recorded in chapter iv.

encouraged them to persevere. Joyous and patient as ever,
he exhorted his comrades to give thanks for their sufferings,
saying, "Trust in God, my beloved; the victory is surely
ours, since our sins are expiated in blood; is it not written,
'How beautiful are the feet of them who bring the gospel of
peace!'" Then, as was his custom, he entoned a joyful hymn,
and his fervour so moved the hearts of his companions, that
joining with him, they praised God for permitting them to
drink of these few drops from the chalice of suffering.
Touched by the example of such admirable patience, the
treacherous guide fell at the feet of the man of God, and
confessing the malice of his conduct, abjured his heresy.

Nor was this the only instance in which we find him
winning souls less by word than by example. Preaching,
even when accompanied by the display of miraculous power,
is not the only means, scarcely the most powerful, by which
the saints of God extend the kingdom of their Master. The
silent eloquence of a holy life has a larger apostolate than
the gifts of tongues or of healing; and we find some interesting records of the harvest of souls which were gathered
to the faith solely by the example of the servant of God.
There were living, near Toulouse, some noble ladies who had
been led to join the heretics, being seduced into this error
by the show of pretended austerity which their preachers
affected. Dominic, who had their conversion greatly at
heart, determined to preach there that Lent; and, going
thither with one companion, who is believed to have been
Bertrand of Garrigua, it chanced, by the providence of God,
that they were received to lodge in the house occupied by
these ladies. He remained there during the whole time of
his stay, and they saw with wonder the reality of that life of
penance which differed so widely from the empty professions
of the heretics. The soft beds which had been prepared for
them were never used, for Dominic and his companion slept
upon the ground. Their food was scarcely touched; until
Easter time they took only bread and water, and that in
scanty measure, whilst their nights were spent in prayer and
austerities, and their days in labours for God. Blessed

Humbert adds, that the saint and his companion begged these noble ladies to supply them with some garments of which they stood in need, which proved to be nothing else than coarse hair-shirts, charging them, however, to keep the matter secret.

So new and wonderful did this life seem to those who beheld it, that it opened their eyes to the truth of the faith by which it was inspired; and the whole household made their recantation in the hands of the saint before the time of his stay was ended. In after-days he was often accustomed to exhort his brethren to this, as the best method of preaching, reminding them that it was by good works, and by the outward habit, even more than by holy words, that we must let our light shine before men to the glory of God.

Often enough he conquered the hatred of his deadliest enemies by the very patience with which he bore their injuries. They might writhe under the terrific eloquence with which he denounced their vices, but in the end they could not resist the yet greater power of his charity. "Into the wide embrace of that charity," says Jordan, "he received all men, and as he loved all, so was he beloved by all." Indeed, if there was one feature in his character more marked than another, it was its singular loveableness. "He made it his business," says the same writer, "to rejoice with those that rejoiced, and to weep with those who wept, and wholly to pour himself out in pity for the afflicted, and love of his neighbour. All were, moreover, attracted by the fact that he never showed the least duplicity or pretence, whether in word or work, but always walked in the ways of simplicity." Something of this attractiveness was visible even in his exterior. "Unshaken in his firmness, he never betrayed any trouble save when touched by the sins or afflictions of others: and because a joyful heart makes the face cheerful, he displayed the placid peacefulness of his interior by a countenance that was always kind and joyous, for he was never known to yield to anger. Nor was the sweetness of his exterior thrown away on those with whom he conversed, for by it he easily won the love of all as soon as they looked on him."

Percin, in his *History of the Convent of Toulouse*, takes notice of one feature in the character of the saint, which seems to have escaped other writers, his fondness, namely, for children. Quoting from MSS. preserved in that convent, he tells us that the saint did not confine his ministrations to those of mature years ; but that he loved to instruct in the faith the children of the peasantry, teaching them how to make the sign of the Cross, and to recite the Lord's Prayer, the Angelic Salutation, and the Creed ; and exhorting them to obey their parents, and show respect to all men ; and this practice he likewise recommended to his followers. Peter Ranzi relates the same of St. Vincent Ferrer, and says that in this he did but follow the example of his holy Father, St. Dominic.

This singular holiness of life not only endeared him to all those among whom he was thrown, but led them earnestly to desire his promotion to the highest offices of the Church. Three times the episcopal dignity was offered to him, but he refused it with a kind of horror.[4] He was used to say he would rather go away by night with nothing but his staff than accept the burden of the episcopate. He could not however succeed in avoiding a temporary appointment as Grand Vicar to Guy, Bishop of Carcassonne, during the time that the latter was absent from his diocese preaching the Crusade, and gathering together fresh forces to join the army of the Count de Montfort. He held this charge during the Lent of the year 1213, during which time he resided in the episcopal palace, and discharged all the duties of the office, without however suffering them to interfere with his customary occupation of preaching. During this Lent we again find him spoken of as fasting on bread and water, and sleeping on the ground. " When Easter came," says his historian, " he seemed stronger and more vigorous than before, and of a better aspect."

Réchac says that he accepted the office of Grand Vicar at the prayers of the Chapter, and out of gratitude to the

---

[4] The three sees offered him, according to Theodoric, were those of Beziers, Conserans, and Cominges.

canons of the Cathedral of St. Nazaire among whom he ordinarily resided, and whose successors boast that he was once their dean. Traces of his residence were long preserved in various parts of the diocese, as at the monastery of Canons Regular at Ville Longue, about four leagues from Carcassonne, where he was wont to retire from time to time, rejoicing to find himself once more among his own religious brethren. Here for several centuries was kept as a precious relic one of his surplices, and so greatly was it prized that the canons refused all entreaties to surrender it to convents of the Friars Preachers. The custom prevailed at the vintage-time of steeping this surplice in the vine vats, in the belief that the wine so treated would never turn sour. Most of the anecdotes of this period which have been preserved by ancient writers are given without any attempt to fix either the precise date or the order in which they occurred. One event may, however, be assigned with certainty to the year 1211, as it took place just after open hostilities had broken out between Count Raymund and the Crusaders. It happened that the course of St. Dominic's apostolic wanderings had brought him to the banks of the river Garonne, not far from the spot where the Catholic army lay encamped under the walls of Toulouse. Whilst he was there, a band of English pilgrims also arrived in the neighbourhood. They were about forty in number, bound to the shrine of St. James of Compostella. In order to avoid the town, which lay under the Papal interdict, they took a boat to cross the river; but the boat, being small and overladen, was upset, and all those who were in it sank to the bottom. Dominic was praying in the church of St. Antony which stood near the scene of the accident, but the cries of the sufferers and of the soldiers who saw their danger roused him from his devotions. He came to the river's bank, but not one of the pilgrims was to be seen.

Prostrating on the ground with his arms in the form of a cross, and weeping bitterly, the saint prayed aloud, conjuring, and, as it were, bidding God in holy confidence to save His own pilgrims from death. Then rising, full of a lively faith, he drew near to the river's bank. "I command you," he

cried, " in the name of Jesus Christ, to come to the shore
alive and unhurt." Instantly the bodies rose to the surface,
and with the help of the soldiers, who flung them their shields
and lances, they all safely reached the bank, praising God
and His servant Dominic.

Gerard de Frachet relates this story on the authority of
an eye-witness, Peter de Salvaniaco, who was a soldier in the
army of the Count de Montfort, whom he calls " an old and
honourable man," and the manner in which, according to
him, the bodies of the pilgrims reappeared, sufficiently proved
that the event was not due to any natural cause. " They
rose above the waves," he says, " and *sat on the water* as
though it had been dry land, each one in the place where the
stream had carried him."

Among the pilgrims thus rescued was an Englishman
named Lawrence, who from that time joined himself to the
company of the blessed Dominic and became one of the first
brethren of his Order. Several other anecdotes are related
by the same writer and, unconnected as they are, we treasure
them as footprints left by the saint in his apostolic journeys.
In the same neighbourhood of Toulouse, it chanced one day
that he had several times to ford the river Ariege,[s] and as he
did so his books fell into the water. Nothing disturbed by
the accident, but praising God as was his custom when
suffering any mischance, the saint came to the house of a
good woman who was used to offer him hospitality, and who
held him in the greatest veneration on account of his sanctity.
When he told her of the loss of his books, she began to
lament over it, but he checked her sweetly, saying, " Grieve
not about it, good mother, for it behoves us to bear patiently
whatever God is pleased to ordain." On the third day afterwards, a fisherman going to fish at the spot where the books
had fallen, cast his hook into the water, and thought by the
weight that he had caught a large fish. Drawing out his
line, he found it fastened to the books, which were as
uninjured as if they had been carefully kept in a cupboard.

---

[s] Some say that it was the river Tarn near Toulouse, and others point
to a particular ford on the Fron, between Gaillac and Alby.

What rendered this the more wonderful was that the books were not wrapped in cloth or leather, or any covering that could have preserved them. He took them to the good woman, whose house was hard by, and who, full of joy, sent them to Toulouse, where the saint was then staying. On another occasion he was crossing the same river in a little boat, and being landed on the opposite shore, found he had no money to pay the boatman. The boatman insisted on his fare. "I am," said Dominic, "a follower of Jesus Christ. I carry neither gold nor silver. God will pay you the price of my passage." But the boatman, being angry, laid hold of his cloak, saying, "You will either leave your cloak with me, or pay me my money." Dominic, raising his eyes to heaven, recollected himself for a moment in prayer; then, looking on the ground, he showed the man a piece of silver which lay there, which Providence had sent, and said to him, "My brother, there is what you ask: take it, and suffer me to go my way."

Cardinal Ranieri Cappocci, who lived during the time of St. Dominic and was his intimate friend, preaching on his feast soon after his canonization, in the church of Santa Maria in Cosmedin, related the following fact which had come to his own knowledge. A certain religious chanced to be the companion of the saint on a journey of some days, but being of another country, and neither of them understanding the language of the other, they were unable to hold any conversation together. Desiring very much, however, to profit by the time he should spend in his society, this religious secretly prayed to God that for the three days they should be together, they might be intelligible to one another, each speaking in his own tongue, and this favour was granted until they reached their journey's end.

†In some of these narratives we begin to find notice of the *companions* who attended the blessed Dominic in his journeys and took part in his holy labours. Among these, the first place must be assigned to him on whom the biographers of the blessed patriarch confer the title, *par excellence*, of his

H

companion. "Bertrand of Garrigua," says Jordan, "was the companion of the blessed Dominic, one of the very first whom he met with in the country of the Albigenses." In fact Bertrand had been before him in that field of labour, having joined the company of Arnold of Citeaux and the other Legates before the arrival of the Bishop of Osma. Garrigua, from which place he derives his name, appears to have been a fief or farm, attached to the Cistercian abbey of Notre Dame de Bosquet, and to have formed part of the township of Bouchet, in the province of Comtat. From his youth Bertrand had become familiar with the terrible condition to which the country was reduced by the ravages of the heretics. It was at the head of an army of Albigenses that Raymund VI. in the year 1200, had overrun the country, directing his principal attack against monasteries and churches. The nuns of Bosquet had sought safety in flight, leaving the defence of their convent to their vassals. These however would have offered but a feeble resistance to the swarm of ruffians who surrounded the abbey and attempted to scale the walls, had not one of their number bethought him of overturning some beehives which stood on the battlements, and the exasperated bees issuing forth, fell on the besiegers, and did such execution on men and horses as speedily caused them to retire in confusion. Bertrand therefore had personal knowledge of the miseries which the Albigenses and their protectors had brought on the country. Brought up by the good nuns of Bosquet, he received an education which fitted him for Holy Orders; and he was no sooner ordained priest than he volunteered to join the mission conducted by the Cistercians. "He was," says Jordan, "a man of great sanctity and wonderful penance," and it would seem as though he had been chosen by Divine Providence to fill that place in the confidence of the blessed Dominic which was left vacant by the death of Diego. From the first day that they met a common sympathy in divine things knit their hearts together. Thus the ancient authors speak of Bertrand as "the beloved companion of Dominic," "the dearest associate in all his labours," "the sharer in his devotions and the imitator of his sanctity," and "the inseparable companion of his journeys."

Bertrand appears to have resided with Dominic at Carcassonne, and to have accompanied him wherever he went. "He followed him step by step," says Bernard Guidonis, "continually mortifying his flesh to glorify our Lord Jesus Christ. By his watchings, his fasts, and his other penances he succeeded so perfectly in imprinting on his own person the likeness of his beloved Father, that one might have said, seeing him pass by, 'Truly the disciple is like the master : there goes the very portrait of St. Dominic ! '"

His presence at Toulouse during the Lent which Dominic spent in that city has already been indicated. Another incident of their missionary life together is thus related by Jordan : " I have it from the lips of blessed Bertrand himself," he says, " that as he was one day journeying in the company of the blessed Father, a furious tempest broke over their heads and the country all around was deluged with rain. But Master Dominic made the sign of the Cross,[a] and the deluge of water retired before him. He and his companion were able to walk on in safety, beholding the thick clouds of rain falling to the ground before them at about the distance of three cubits, but without wetting so much as the hem of their garments."

The place where this prodigy took place is still pointed out between Montreal and Carcassonne, and is called "the field of the Oratory of St. Dominic." It derives this name from a little chapel which was erected in his honour on the spot, and which was held in great veneration by the country people, who believed that no rain ever fell within six paces of its walls, so that if a storm broke out they would betake themselves thither for shelter. This chapel having been destroyed in the time of the Revolution, the inhabitants of Montreal in 1868 erected on its ruins a monument bearing a figure of St. Dominic, with the following inscription engraved on the pedestal :

[a] Hence the allusion in the Office of St. Dominic, *Signo Crucis imber udit.*

*Here in the thirteenth century were miraculously preserved from a furious storm of rain, the glorious St. Dominic and his companion St. Bertrand of Garrigua.*

*St. Dominic and St. Bertrand of Garrigua, pray for us, and deliver us from tempests.*

A somewhat similar prodigy is related as happening on another occasion. Dominic and his companions being overtaken by a storm, their garments were completely soaked with rain. On reaching their destination, the others sat round the fire to dry their clothes, but he, according to his custom, repaired to the church to spend the night there in prayer. In the morning the clothes of his companions which had hung by the fire were still damp, whilst his were perfectly dry.

All writers agree in representing the blessed Bertrand as a man of rare sanctity, as tender in his charity towards others as he was pitiless to himself. "You might as well have tried to soften brass or marble," says one writer, "as to persuade him to spare himself." Gifted with angelic purity of heart, he regarded himself as the last of sinners, and was wont to weep day and night over the sins by which he feared to have offended God. The holy Father Dominic, to whom the innermost secrets of his heart were well known, judged that there was some excess in this, and enjoined him no longer to weep over his own sins, but over those of others. So powerful were the words of the saint, and so perfect the obedience of the humble disciple, that from that day he could no longer weep for his own miseries, even if he would have done so, whilst he shed abundant tears over those of others. Almost every day he celebrated Mass for the conversion of sinners, after whose salvation he sighed with the ardour that became a true son of St. Dominic. One of his brethren, Brother Benedict by name, questioned him in the intimacy of private friendship why he did not more often offer Mass for the souls in Purgatory. "Because," he replied, "the faithful departed are certain of eternal life, whilst the living are tossed about in continual danger of perishing." "But," continued Benedict, "supposing there were two beggars, one of whom had lost the use of all his members, whilst the other was in full possession of them, which of the two would you prefer to help?" "The one of them who was least able to help himself," replied Bertrand. "Well then," said Benedict, "that is the case of the departed. They have neither mouth with which to confess, nor hands to work, nor feet to go on pilgrimage; and they depend on us alone to assist them. Whereas sinners, so long as they live, have all these ways of helping themselves."

Bertrand, however, did not at once yield to the force of his friend's argument. But the night following there appeared to him the terrible figure of a departed soul who, with a great load of wood, seemed to press and torment him, waking him more than ten times that same night. When morning dawned, he called Benedict to him, and told him what had passed; thence religiously and with many tears going to the altar, he offered the Holy Sacrifice for the departed, and from that time forward did so very frequently.

It was, then, in company with this chosen associate and others of a kindred spirit who gradually gathered around him, that the blessed Dominic pursued his apostolic labours. Most of the anecdotes belonging to this time which have been above quoted, seem to have been selected by his biographers as exhibiting examples of his miraculous powers. But, as is truly remarked by Blessed Jordan, far more resplendent than his miracles themselves were the beauty of his soul and its spotless purity. These are what we would fain set before us in all their lovely reality when we meditate on his life, desiring, if it were possible, to summon before us that noble presence and to behold him as he lived and walked on earth and shed abroad the perfume of his sanctity. We desire to know him not merely as the great apostle and the wonder-worker of his age, but as he was known by the common people and in the intercourse of daily life. And in the depositions taken after his death, we gather some notices of his ordinary habits of life during the period of his residence in Languedoc, which, if less wonderful than the

narratives given above, are certainly not less interesting, and
have the value of an exceptional authenticity.  They come
from the lips of those who had borne him company on his
journeys, or who had sat with him at table, or given him
hospitality under their roofs.

Thus Raymund Gerald declares that he had often travelled
with him through the woods, and noticed how he used to
remain the last, and that when sought for he was often found
on his knees in prayer, notwithstanding the danger from
ravenous wolves, which had attacked many in those parts.
Several women who had entertained him in their houses
bore their united testimony to the wonderful abstemiousness
which he practised.  Wilhelmina Martina affirmed that she
had eaten with him more than two hundred times, but
though several kinds of food were prepared for him, they
never saw him take more than the quarter of a fish, or the
yolk of two eggs, with a single slice of bread.  If he drank
wine it was never more than one cup mingled with three
parts of water.  Even when ill he never slept in a bed,
and if others laid him there, he would presently leave it,
and prostrate on the ground.  Beceda, who afterwards
became a nun of Holy Cross, said that he had frequently
stayed in her house, and that she was very intimate with
him, and had never heard him speak an idle word.  She
had often found him lying thus on the ground as described
above, even when suffering from sickness; sometimes, out
of compassion, she would throw a covering over him, for she
took great care of him, but on her return she was sure to
find him as before, absorbed in prayer.  These good women
supplied him with some of his instruments of penance; and
Beceda adds the curious particular that she collected *cows'
tails*, out of which to spin hair-shirts for him and Don Fulk
of Toulouse.

But perhaps the most perfect picture is presented in
the deposition of William Peter, abbot of St. Paul's.  "The
blessed Dominic," he says, "was a true lover of souls,
and thirsted for their conversion.  He was so fervent in
preaching, that by day and by night, in church, in houses,

in the fields, and by the wayside, everywhere in short, he preached, and exhorted the brethren to preach, the Word of God. He was very sparing of himself in the matter of food, but always wished others to be supplied abundantly as far as their means allowed. Of all the men I ever knew, never have I seen one so humble, or who held the world in greater contempt. He received abuse, curses, and reproaches, not only with patience, but with joy, as though they were most precious gifts. No persecution troubled him: he went about secure and intrepid in the midst of danger, and never turned out of his way on account of fear. If on his journeys he was overcome with weariness, he would lie down by the roadside and take a scanty rest. Never did I know a man so given to prayer, or who so abounded in tears. Sometimes when in prayer he would cry out so loud as to be heard by others, and at such times would exclaim: 'O Lord, have mercy on this people! What will beome of sinners!' And so he would spend his nights without sleep, weeping and wailing over the sins of others, for as the Abbot of Bolbonne expressed it, 'The sins of others were a torment to him.' Often when he prayed the place where he knelt was found wet with his tears.

"Liberal and hospitable, he loved to share whatever he had with the poor, though none were poorer than he. He never wore but one tunic, and that was a patched one, and so far as the witness knew he never slept in a bed, but in the church, or if no church were at hand, he would lie on the floor or on some hard bench." To these testimonies were added those of many of the inhabitants of Fanjeaux with whom he so often dwelt, some of whom had been cured of fever by the touch of his hands, whilst all declared with one voice that never had they seen so holy or honourable a man, or one more wholly given tc the salvation of souls.[7]

---

[7] The above testimonies and others similar were sworn to before the Commissioners of Toulouse by more than three hundred witnesses. The letter of the commissioners is given by Echard, vol. i. p. 56, whence it has been copied by the Bollandists.

Here, then, is the portrait of the Apostle of Languedoc, as we can gather it from the lips of those who knew him in the intimacy of ordinary life; we see him, not bound by the ties of cloistered rule, but leading a wandering life, going about from town to town and from village to village on his Master's business, often with no better roof to shelter his head than the wild forest, the resort of wolves, and no softer bed than the roadside on which to sleep. Wherever he appears it is still as the lover of souls, embracing all men in the arms of his immense charity, becoming all things to all men, if by any means he might save some. No wonder that the memory of such a life should have struck its roots deep into the hearts of the people, and have left its stamp upon the traditions of the country. Accordingly, besides the records of that life which are to be found in the pages of historians, we find others preserved in the localities among which he dwelt, and from which six centuries, with all their changes, have not been able to efface them. In the chain of hills which extends from Toulouse to Carcassonne, may be seen the opening of a vast cavern, surrounded by huge rocks tossed about in wild confusion. The first shepherd whom you meet will tell you that this cavern is " the Grotto of St. Dominic," and that, according to unbroken tradition, it was here that in the midst of his gigantic labours he loved from time to time to take refuge. But it was with him as with his Divine Master, when He too retired into the wilderness to rest awhile. Thither also the multitudes followed him, and he could not refuse to break to them the bread of life. Climb down to the mouth of the cavern with your guide, and he will show you a projecting platform of rock which still bears the title of "St. Dominic's Pulpit," for it was thence that he was accustomed to preach the Word of God to the villagers who gathered round him in these new catacombs. Here it was, perhaps, that he first explained to them the mysteries of the Holy Rosary; no doubt these rocky vaults have resounded often enough to the tones of his voice, as in their company he recited the Angelic Salutation; and here among the tortuous windings of the caverns which extend far into the heart of the mountains, the simple peasants who surrounded him are said more than once to have escaped from the hands of the heretics who endeavoured to surprise them.

We have now to follow him in the exercise of other duties which appertained to his apostolic office no less than the preaching of the Word. He had not only to *instruct*, but to *reconcile* heretics, and in doing this, to blend the ministry of justice with that of mercy. In what spirit and in what manner did he discharge this ministry? To this question we shall endeavour to reply in the following chapter, and whilst doing so we will keep before our eyes the portrait which has been sketched by the eye-witnesses of his life in the foregoing pages.

# CHAPTER IX.

IT is the constant tradition of the Order that St. Dominic was the first Inquisitor, a tradition confirmed by the words used by Pope Sixtus V. in his Bull for the canonization of St. Peter Martyr.[1] Accepting the tradition as authentic, its precise signification remains open to inquiry. The question is involved in great obscurity in the absence of all documents showing when, or in what terms the office was conferred, or in what its duties precisely consisted.

These points form the matter of a lengthy controversy between the Dominican author, Echard, on the one hand, and the Bollandists on the other, in which the former seeks to establish the fact that prior to the Council of Lateran, in 1215, the office of Inquisitor did not even exist, and that whatever office was held by St. Dominic previous to that date, it did not bear the title of Inquisitor, was limited to the *reconciliation* of heretics, and had nothing whatever to do with their *punishment*. The Bollandists admit the fact that the *title* of Inquisitor was of later date, but maintain that the office was in existence, and that it included the punishment as well as the reconciliation of heretics.

To state the case as briefly as we can, it appears admitted by both parties that prior to the Council of Lateran St. Dominic held and received certain powers in virtue of a commission given him by the Papal Legates; that this commission empowered him to reconcile heretics and to

[1] "Is enim præclarus Ordinis Prædicatorum alumnus imitatione accensus Beati Patris Dominici, ut ille perpetuis et concionibus et disputationum congressibus officisque Inquisitionis quod ei primum prædecessores nostri Innocentius Tertius et Honorius Tertius commiserant contra hereticos mirabiliter se gessit."

impose on them canonical. penances; but that he did not
then bear the title of Inquisitor.  And the question at issue
seems to be, was this office identical in fact though not in
name with that of Inquisitor; did its powers include the
capital punishment of heretics, and were these latter powers
ever exercised by the saint ?

Echard not only affirms that it was not, but declares
furthermore as an indisputable fact that up to the year
1209, when the Crusade may be said to have begun, *there is
no record of any Albigensian heretic being taken or condemned to
death.*  After that date executions took place frequently
enough, but these executions were, as he maintains, carried
out exclusively by the leaders of the Crusading army, who
neither asked nor required the consent of the saint to any
of their judicial proceedings.  The question therefore narrows
itself to the part taken by St. Dominic between the years
1209 and 1215, at which latter date his apostolic labours in
Languedoc may be said to have terminated.  The silence
of Blessed Jordan must not be taken as absolutely conclusive evidence on any subject, as he undoubtedly omits from
his history many things which one would naturally have
expected to have found noticed.  Still it has its weight in
our argument, the more so as we find one expression in it
in which he sums up the character of the saint's labours
during this precise period, as exclusively apostolic.  " During
the time that the Crusaders were in the country," he says,
" the blessed Dominic continued there, diligently preaching
the Word of God until the death of the Count de Montfort."
Limiting ourselves to certain facts, and carefully excluding
inferences and suppositions, it may confidently be affirmed
that no scrap of evidence can be produced to show that the
saint either took part in the condemnation of heretics, or
possessed any power to do so.  No document giving him
such powers can be quoted; no single example of his
exercising them can be adduced.  The Bollandists " infer "
and they " gather," but not one historic fact are they able to
bring in support of a theory which the universal silence of
historians would in itself be powerful to disprove.  More

than this, such inferences to carry any weight must hold together. Now, if we ask from whom did St. Dominic receive these powers, the reply is, that they were *probably* included in the commission granted to him by the Legates in 1206. Clearly, however, the Legates could not delegate to another larger powers than they themselves possessed, and in the Brief of Innocent III., which defines these powers, no mention of the capital punishment of heretics occurs. Neither, as we have seen, were any capital punishments inflicted until 1209, that is, for fully five years after the Legates entered on their mission; and when this was done, it was the act, not of any ecclesiastical tribunal, but of the chiefs of the Crusaders. From the fact of no executions taking place during the five years during which the ecclesiastical authorities alone were engaged against the heretics, the natural inference is that they possessed no powers to inflict these punishments, and if so, they certainly could not delegate such powers to others. Moreover, to be rigorously exact, we may remark that Pope Sixtus V. speaks of St. Dominic as appointed Inquisitor—not by any Legate, but by the two Popes, Innocent III. and Honorius III., the latter of whom did not begin to reign till the year 1216.

This expression seems to confirm the opinion of many writers, including Echard himself, that St. Dominic's appointment as Inquisitor cannot be dated earlier than the Council of Lateran,[2] in which case it is needless to say that the whole superstructure of his supposed acts as Inquisitor *prior to that date* falls to the ground.

In point of fact, however, a confusion has very generally been made between two things wholly distinct, and belonging to different orders of jurisdiction; the judicial powers for

---

[2] We may add that it is in one of the decrees of that Council that we find the first creation of such an office; that, namely, wherein every bishop is required to appoint three men of good character who shall assist him in visiting those parts of his diocese infested by the heretics, that they may seek them out and bring them to justice. In this we see the germ of the office of Inquisitor, though the title is not used. But, be it remembered, the date of this Council is 1215, the very date when St. Dominic's active labours in Languedoc came to an end (See Rohrbacher, vol. xvii. p. 422).

judging and condemning impenitent heretics and those found
guilty of capital crimes, and the assignment of canonical
penances to those who were reconciled to the Church.   The
former powers belonged to the secular arm, and were exercised by the chiefs and leaders of the Crusade; the latter
were a portion of the penitentiary discipline of the Church,
and belonged of right to the bishop, or to persons expressly
delegated by him, or by the Legates of the Holy See.   The
assignment of these canonical penances formed a portion of
the *ministry of reconciliation*, not of *condemnation*, and the fact
that the saint was invested with the power so to assign them
cannot be accepted as any kind of proof that he possessed
or exercised other powers of a totally different character.
Yet it is remarkable that all the writers, whether friendly or
adverse, who are most solicitous to establish the fact of his
being an Inquisitor, alike rest their arguments on certain
documents which prove nothing more than that he absolved
heretics and admitted them to such penances.   These documents we will proceed to quote, and then give the conclusions
which historians of very opposite shades of opinion have
drawn from them.

   The first is without date, but is believed to belong to the
year 1207 or 1208.   It runs as follows:

   " To all the faithful in Christ to whom these presents may
come, Brother Dominic, canon of Osma, wishes health in
the Lord.   By the authority of the Lord Abbot of Citeaux,
who has committed to us this office, we have reconciled to
the Church the bearer of these presents, Ponce Roger, converted by the grace of God from heresy to the faith; and we
order, in virtue of the oath which he has taken to us, that
during three Sundays or feast-days he shall go to the
entrance of the village, bare to the waist, and be struck
with rods by the priest.   We also order him to abstain for
ever from flesh, eggs, cheese, and all which comes from flesh,
except at Easter, Pentecost, and Christmas, when he shall
eat some to protest against his former errors.   He shall keep
three Lents each year, fasting and abstaining from fish, and
three days in each week he shall fast, and abstain from fish,

oil, and wine, unless from bodily infirmity or the heat of the
weather he shall be dispensed. He shall dress in religious
habit, as well in the form as in the colour, to the ends of
which shall be hung two little crosses. Every day, if
possible, he shall hear Mass, and he shall go to Vespers on
festival-days. Seven times a day he shall recite ten *Pater
nosters*, and he shall say twenty in the middle of the night.
He shall observe chastity, and once a month he shall, in the
morning, present this paper to the chaplain of the village of
Céré. We desire this chaplain to have great care that his
penitent lead a holy life, and observe all we have said until
the Lord Legate shall otherwise ordain. If he neglect to do
so through contempt, we will that he be excommunicated as
perjured and heretic, and be separated from the society of
the faithful.''

To this document is appended the waxen seal of St.
Dominic, representing the Lamb of God, bearing the Cross,
surrounded by the words, *Jhesu Christi, et prædicationis.* The
severity of the penalties here assigned must be measured by
the ideas and practice of the thirteenth, and not of the nineteenth century. Public flagellation was a penance then
very commonly enjoined on those whose crimes had caused
public scandal. The penance performed by Henry II. of
England, after the murder of St. Thomas, is commonly
regarded as something strange and exceptional, whereas
those who are at all familiar with original authorities are
aware that other examples of the same punishment as
adjudged to public misdoers, and those often of the highest
rank, are common enough both in English and foreign
history. We have seen the Count of Toulouse himself
obliged to perform this humiliating *amende honorable* before
he could be absolved from the guilt incurred by the murder
of the Legate. So also the fasts and abstinences enjoined on
Ponce Roger were by no means so much out of proportion to
those generally observed by the faithful, as they would be
in our own day; and they certainly did not overpass the
ordinary rule of many religious orders. In any case it
must be borne in mind that the penance was not one of

private selection, but adjudged according to the existing penitential discipline then in force.

The second document is also without date, but the mention of the " Lord Cardinal " shows that it must have been issued after the arrival in the country of Cardinal Milon.

" To all the faithful in Christ to whom these presents may come, Brother Dominic, canon of Osma, the humble minister of preaching, wishes health and charity in the Lord. We make known to your discretion that we have permitted Raymund William de Hauterive Pelaganira to receive into his house of Toulouse, to live there after the ordinary life, William Huguecion, whom he has declared to us to have hitherto worn the habit of the heretics. We permit this until such time as it shall be otherwise ordered either to him or to me by the Lord Cardinal; and this shall not in any way turn to his dishonour or prejudice."

Of Ponce Roger, who is named in the first of these documents, nothing is positively known, save that he belonged to Treville, a town a few leagues distant from Prouille, and that he had been admitted among the ranks of the *perfect*. The severity of the penances imposed on him leads us to infer that there were particular and aggravating circumstances connected with his case, for, as we shall presently see, other examples are recorded in which far milder sentences are given. But the point to which for the moment we would draw attention is the fact that these documents are the sole evidence, produced both by friends and enemies in proof that St. Dominic exercised the office of Inquisitor. We will listen first to Malvenda, the historian of the Order, and one zealous for all that redounds to the honour of its holy founder. After distinctly claiming for him the title of the first Inquisitor, he says:[3] " As regards the time when this office of Inquisitor begun to be exercised by St. Dominic, our own authors and others differ; but all agree that it was before the confirmation of the Order,[4] at the time when St. Dominic was preaching against the Albigensian heretics in the province of Toulouse, *which*

---

[3] P. 122.  [4] Echard, as we have seen, does not admit this.

*seems to be clear from the old forms for the reconciliation of heretics
of which St. Dominic made use.* . . . These forms are those
which he was accustomed to use either in reconciling
heretics to the Church, or imposing on them salutary
penances, or performing other duties which belonged to
the office of Inquisitor. Out of many such documents these
two only have escaped the ravages of time," and he proceeds
to give those above quoted. In the opinion of Malvenda,
then, these diplomas are to be taken as sufficient proof that
St. Dominic at that time held the office of Inquisitor. But
if so that office *as then exercised* had for its only object the
reconciling of heretics, and the receiving them to penance,
for no word appears in them bearing reference to any severer
kind of punishment. That they should be adduced as
evidence that the saint took part in the *execution* of heretics,
whether by burning or otherwise, is simply incomprehensible; the parties named in them appear, not as condemned
criminals, but as absolved penitents; their object is entirely
one of reconciliation.

Yet the use made of these documents by the Calvinist
historian of the Inquisition, Philip de Lymborch, is to attempt
to prove not only that St. Dominic was an Inquisitor, but the
*founder of the Inquisition ;* in order to bring home to his account
all the supposed cruelties with which that tribunal stands
charged. For this purpose he quotes a certain Louis de
Param, who wrote a treatise on the subject, about the end
of the sixteenth century, and who affirms that St. Dominic
proposed the institution of the Inquisition in France to the
Legates, and that he was appointed to the office of Inquisitor
*after the Council of Lateran,* by letters pontifical, "which letters
some authors declare to have seen." It may just be remarked
that if St. Dominic was only appointed Inquisitor in France
after the Council of Lateran in 1215, he had a very short
time in which to exercise that office against the Albigenses,
as shortly after the close of the Council he left Languedoc
and established himself in Rome. During the ten previous
years, which cover the whole period of his active apostolate
among the Albigenses, he would, according to this theory,

have held no such office at all, and his Inquisitorial cruelties therefore could have had no existence. This is but one of many instances in which the evidence of the witnesses does not agree. Lymborch himself appears aware of the unsatisfactory nature of the testimony, for after quoting the statement of Louis de Param, he adds: " However that may be, it is well known that Dominic was a bloody and cruel man," and in proof of this assertion he cites the canonical penance assigned by him to the heretic Ponce Roger.

Evidently, therefore, this was the severest act which it was in the power of this writer to bring forward as having been exercised by the saint in his character of Inquisitor. Had there been a single word in any authentic history by which it could even have been implied that he was connected with more sanguinary proceedings, we may take it for granted that the passage would not have been overlooked. Could it —we will not say have been *proved*—but only made the ground of specious surmise, that St. Dominic had ever delivered one heretic to the flames, who can doubt that the authority would have been produced and made the most of by those whose object it is to exhibit him in the character of a " bloody and cruel man "? As it is, the fact that the two diplomas above quoted are claimed both by friends and enemies, as furnishing the only proofs that St. Dominic was an Inquisitor at all, justifies us in using these same documents to show in what that office as exercised by him really consisted. No one can fail to be struck by the fact that in the history of our saint every single action recorded of him in connection with the heretics partakes of the nature of mercy. The inference from such a fact is that no proceedings of a different character are to be imputed to him, and that whatever was the title of the office he held, its duties were strictly limited to the ministry of reconciliation, under which head the assignment of canonical penances must of course be included.

These penances varied in severity according to the requirements of each case. It is a principle in logic that we must not judge of the whole by a part, nor must a single

I

example be taken as a fair evidence of a whole body of
administrative acts. Nevertheless the penance assigned to
Ponce Roger has in all probability been often enough so
used. It reappears in every Life of St. Dominic, and
standing alone, has doubtless conveyed to the minds of
many a reader the impression that this was the ordinary
treatment which the penitents of the saint had to expect at
his hands. But such a supposition would go far to disprove
itself. No doubt many things were possible in the thirteenth
century which would be impossible in our own, but we can
imagine no state of society in which hundreds, or it may be
thousands of persons could be living under the same conditions as the luckless Ponce Roger. Happily no such
conclusion is forced upon us. In the first place, a broad
distinction was always drawn between the two classes of
heretics, namely, the *perfect*, and the *believers*, to the former
of whom much severer penalties were adjudged than to the
latter. Even in the wholesale proceedings of the Crusaders
it appears certain that the capital punishment was inflicted
only on the impenitent members of the first class, whose
numbers were comparatively insignificant. Another distinction reserved severer measures for the *relapsed*. Nor
must the important fact be forgotten that it was not solely
as *heretics*, that is, as the holders of false doctrine, that the
Albigenses were proceeded against, but as the enemies of
the public peace, and the perpetrators of enormous crimes.[5]
Whilst the execution of such criminals when impenitent
was clearly justifiable as a judicial act, it is equally clear
that the penances assigned to the more heinous offenders
on their submission and reconciliation would be in propor-

[5] Echard takes note of this (p. 9, note 5), where, speaking of the
execution of heretics which took place after the taking of towns by
the Crusaders, he says that "they caused to be burnt many obstinate
heretics, or *those guilty of more grievous crimes*," but that "this was done by
the leaders of the Crusade, and in these things Dominic does not appear."
The particular here related is an important one, and is entirely overlooked
by those who would simply represent the Albigenses as innocent persons
suffering persecution for conscience' sake. Such executions belonged
manifestly to the administration of the secular law, which could in no
way fall under the saint's jurisdiction.

tion to their guilt. This will explain the severity of the penance assigned to Ponce Roger, who was of the number of the *perfect*. For there is abundant evidence from authorities hitherto inedited that the ordinary penances imposed on the simple *believers* who were reconciled were of a far milder character. Certain depositions made in Languedoc before the Dominican Inquisitor, Bernard de Caux, and others, in the years 1243—1246, are preserved in MS. in the Public Library of Toulouse, and throw valuable lights on this subject. Thus at Le Mas les Saintes Puelles, Na Segura, wife of William Vitalis, a witness on oath, says that when she was a girl of ten years old she was clothed as a heretic and lived as such for five years, and then she gave it up. . . . The Blessed Dominic reconciled the witness from heresy. The Bishop of Toulouse gave her *two crosses to wear*, and many days she did not wear the crosses, and sometimes she wore them covered. In this case we see St. Dominic absolving the penitent and the canonical penance assigned by the bishop.

In other cases, however, we find the penance assigned by the saint. Thus at Fanjeaux, Arnalda of Tremac makes oath that in 1206 she was reconciled by Brother Dominic, who gave her as a penance to wear two crosses in front until she married; and the witness adds that she wore them for a year and then took a husband. Wilhelmina Martina, also of Fanjeaux, went to confession to Brother Dominic, and had as a penance from him to wear two crosses in front for two years, and during that time to abstain from flesh-meat except on Christmas Day, Easter, and Pentecost, which penance she fulfilled, and had letters from Brother Dominic concerning the said penance.

Other examples are given both of men and women in which the precise penance assigned is not named, but in several of these cases we note the expression that the witness "did not adore," *i.e.*, did not take part in any acts of heretical worship, whence it may be concluded that a lighter description of penance would be imposed. One man, Ponce Marcelli, deposed to having lived with the heretics as

a boy at Fanjeaux, at which time he "adored" several times.
What penance was assigned him on his reconciliation does
not appear, but his treatment at the hands of Brother
Dominic cannot have been very severe, as by his own choice
he joined himself to the saint, and lived in his company for
twelve years afterwards.

From these extracts we gather several important facts.
All heretics on their reconciliation were not assigned
penances on the same scale as that of Ponce Roger. The
penances were in proportion to the degree of guilt incurred.
There was a distinction drawn between those who were made
heretics by others as children, and those who embraced heresy
of their own accord; between those who returned to the bosom
of Holy Church and persevered, and those who relapsed
after reconciliation; between those who merely frequented
the company of heretics, and those who wore their dress and
took part in their rites.  The penances imposed by Dominic
were similar in kind to those assigned by the Bishop and by
the Abbots of St. Papoul and Ville Longue, whence we gather
that whether severe or lenient they were given in accordance
with the existing Penitentiary Code, which was simply
*administered* by the confessors, who had no power of arbitrary
punishment. To the large number no severer penalty was
assigned—will it be believed?—than the wearing of two
crosses for a certain period, and the Inquisitorial surveillance
cannot have been so formidable in its strictness, as the
penitents were evidently able to evade or neglect the fulfilment of their penance, without, as it would seem, thereby
incurring much risk.

But before concluding this subject we must notice one
event in the life of our saint, in itself of considerable interest,
and to which the Bollandists appeal as affording evidence
that he did possess the power of inflicting capital punishment. It is thus related by Theodoric of Apoldia: " Some
heretics having been taken and convicted in the country of
Toulouse, were given over to secular judgment because they
refused to return to the faith, and were condemned to the
flames. Dominic looked at one of them with a heart to

which were revealed the secrets of God, and said to the officers of the court, ' Put that man aside, and beware lest he suffer harm.' Then turning to the heretic, he said with great sweetness, ' My son, I know you must have time, but at length the day will come when you will be good and holy.' Wonderful to relate this man remained for twenty years longer in the blindness of heresy, till at length touched by the grace of God he renounced his errors, and died in the habit of the Friar Preachers with the reputation of sanctity."

Theodoric does not give the date of this event, but we learn from Vincent of Beauvais that it took place after the siege of Lavaur in 1261, and that the name of the released heretic was Raymund de Grossi. It is the one solitary occasion in which we find the name of Dominic in any way associated with an act of judicial severity, and as will be noticed, his part therein is not to condemn, but to release. But the Bollandists argue that his power to release implies that he possessed, and had been exercising, the power to condemn, and that he appears in this anecdote in the character of the judge by whom the sentence of death had been pronounced. To this conclusion we demur, first, because it is distinctly said that these heretics had been condemned by the *secular* judgment, and secondly, because if St. Dominic were really acting as judge on this occasion, his release of Raymund de Grossi would have been an unwarrantable act. The prisoner was not a penitent; on the contrary, he was obstinate in his errors ; and for a judge, administering the law, to have released such a criminal in such a manner would have been a manifest breach of justice. We can only regard the saint as acting on this occasion by a supernatural inspiration and in the spirit of prophecy, the credit which he enjoyed among the Catholic leaders disposing them to defer to his wishes as to a command.

But it may be added, how is Dominic's presence on this occasion to be explained, if we are correct in asserting that he took no part in the capital punishment of heretics ? This brings us to the last point connected with this subject which calls for explanation, and the explanation is a very

simple one.    Besides the reconciliation of those who submitted, he had, as the minister of mercy, to discharge
another duty in what was called the *convincing* [6] of those who
did not submit.    No heretic, however guilty, or however
obstinate, was ever condemned without every effort being
made to win him from his errors and to gain his repentance.
This office was frequently discharged by the saint, as we
gather from Blessed Jordan, who tells us both that his labours
were often crowned with wonderful success, and that he
resolutely insisted on no sentence being carried out until all
means had been tried by which the conversion of a prisoner
could be effected.    That this office of " convincing " the
heretics was entirely distinct from that of " convicting " them
must be apparent to all; nor can the one be supposed to
imply the other, unless we confuse the action of a gaol
chaplain, when he strives to move a condemned murderer to
contrition with that of a judge who has passed his sentence.
It was in this capacity that St. Dominic seems to have been
present at the execution of. Lavaur, wherein he appears
attending the unhappy criminals even in their last moments,
and exercising on behalf of one of their number an extraordinary act of clemency.

This was certainly not the only occasion on which he
discharged such duties, though no precise record exists of
other examples.    Réchac appears to think that an incident
which occurred in the neighbourhood of Toulouse took place
while the saint was engaged in " convincing " an obstinate
heretic, though the narrative, as related by Castiglio, makes
mention only of his holding a disputation with this man, and
says nothing to imply that he was a condemned prisoner.
Having spent the greater part of the night in these labours,
he withdrew at length and went to the nearest church in
company with a certain Cistercian lay-brother, desiring to
perform his accustomed devotions.    They found the doors
closed, and not being willing to give up their purpose, they
knelt outside and there began their prayers.    But they
had not remained there many minutes before they found

* Not convicting.

themselves transported within the church and kneeling
before the high altar, the doors remaining closed as before.
When day dawned, the people gathering together found the
man of God in the church, and brought a number of sick and
possessed persons for him to cure. The sick he healed,
invoking over them the Holy Name; then taking a stole, he
threw it first over his shoulders, as though vesting for Mass,
and then placing it on the neck of those possessed, he bade
the devil go forth in the name of God, and the sufferers were
immediately relieved.

The conclusion then to be drawn from the whole matter
is that the labours of the holy patriarch among the heretics
of Languedoc were exclusively those of an apostle. It
matters little if the office which he held were or were not
identical with that which afterwards bore the name of
Inquisitor. The fact, if it be a fact, in no way contradicts
the other fact established by all historic evidence, that his
mission, and that of his immediate followers, was entirely one
of mercy and reconciliation, and bore on every part of it the
broad seal of a supernatural charity.[7] He wept, he prayed,
he did penance for the sins of the people. To convert these
he would have shed his blood, or sold himself into slavery.
No single act is recorded of his ten years' life among them
which was not an act of love and self-devotion; for their
curses he returned blessings, rejoicing to suffer contumely
for the Name of Jesus. The two poles of his spiritual life
were charity and humility. They appear again and again in
every anecdote of his apostolic career. "A certain cleric,"
says Theodoric, "listening to his admirable preaching and
the wonderful power with which he explained the Holy

---

[7] This assertion is supported by an authority which cannot certainly
be suspected of any undue favour towards Inquisitors or the Inquisition.
In the report on the character of that tribunal, which was presented to the
Spanish Cortes in 1812, and which was followed by its suppression, there
occur these remarkable words: "The *early* Inquisitors encountered heresy
with no other arms than those of prayer, patience, and instruction; *and
this remark applies more particularly to St. Dominic.*" Such a testimony could
only have been rendered by such witnesses on the strength of incontro-
vertible evidence.

Scriptures, could not refrain from asking him in what book he had studied to find matter so sublime. ' My son,' replied the saint, ' I have studied chiefly in the book of charity, it is there that we learn all things.' Filled with that sacred fire he went about towns and cities and villages, preaching everywhere the Word of God, visiting the poor, consoling the afflicted, and healing the sick. . . . The tenderness with which his heart overflowed made him all charity to his neighbour, all compassion for the unfortunate. Everything had the power of touching his heart, but it was, above all, the sins of men which consumed him with grief and pity. So that when he approached any town or village and beheld it from afar, he would melt with tears as he thought of the misery of its inhabitants ! "

Such was the spirit and such were the ministrations of the first Inquisitor; nor in his discharge of that office shall we discover a single trait that is out of harmony with his character as the Apostle of Languedoc.

# CHAPTER X.

## ST. DOMINIC AND THE HOLY ROSARY.

BEFORE proceeding further in the history of St. Dominic, we must speak of him in connection with that great and precious devotion which, according to the universal Catholic tradition, he was the first to institute and propagate, thus bestowing on the faithful to the end of time a special claim to their veneration and gratitude.

For that it was through his hands that the Blessed Virgin delivered to us her children the devotion of the Holy Rosary, is the firm and constant tradition of the Church, supported by a weight of authority which can hardly be called in question without temerity. Nevertheless it cannot be presented with those precise details of time and circumstance which are demanded in a narrative of historic facts. To use the words of one who has devoted extraordinary care and diligence to the critical examination of the whole subject,[1] " The Rosary has no history, and will probably never have one." Like so many other of the more exquisite of God's gifts to men, like the life of her by whose virginal hands it was bestowed, the early history of this devotion is shrouded in silence and reserve.

> When nature tries her finest touch,
> Wearing her vernal wreath,
> Mark ye how close she veils her round,
> Not to be traced by sight or sound,
> Nor soiled by ruder breath ?

[1] R. Père Antoine Danzas, in the exhaustive chapter on the Rosary which is to be found in the fourth volume of his *Études sur les temps primitifs de l'Ordre de St. Dominique.*

*Who ever saw the earliest rose*
*First open her sweet breast;*
Or when the summer's sun goes down,
The first soft star in evening's crown
Light up her gleaming crest ? [2]

So was it with the " earliest rose" in our Lady's beautiful
garland.   We have no *historic* notice of that sublime moment
when the servant of God received, as we believe from our
Blessed Lady herself, the command to preach her Psalter,
and to make known to the world that form of prayer which
thenceforth was to become, alike among rich and poor,
the badge of Catholic devotion.   Hence critics are not
wanting who have called in question the fact itself, and have
thus endeavoured to rob the holy patriarch St. Dominic of
one of his chief glories.   Our limits necessarily forbid us
to do more than acknowledge the existence of this hostile
criticism, and then briefly state the arguments by which
the ablest writers on the subject have agreed in repelling it.
    First, then, as to the tradition itself.   The form in which
it has come down to us will best be stated in the words of
P. Cornelius de Snecka, a disciple of Blessed Alan de la
Roche, who in one of his sermons on the Confraternity of
the Holy Rosary, speaks as follows: " We read that at the
time when he was preaching to the Albigenses, St. Dominic
at first obtained but scanty success: and that one day,
complaining of this in pious prayer to our Blessed Lady,
she deigned to reply to him, saying: ' Wonder not that
until now you have obtained so little fruit by your labours;
you have spent them on a barren soil, not yet watered
with the dew of Divine grace.   When God willed to renew
the face of the earth, He began by sending down on it the
fertilizing rain of the Angelic Salutation.   Therefore *preach
my Psalter*, composed of 150 Angelic Salutations and 15 Our
Fathers, and you will obtain an abundant harvest.'   The
servant of God in consequence began to preach this devotion
and make it known to the people, and from that time he

-----

[2] *Christian Year.*  Fourth Sunday in Lent.

won an immense harvest of souls."[3]    In this narrative it
will be observed that there is no mention either as to the
time or place of the revelation.    Muret, Roc Amadour, the
sanctuary of Notre Dame de Puy, and that of Prouille, are
respectively named by various authors, the claims of the
latter place being those most strongly supported by the
tradition of the Order.    But beyond tradition we have
nothing to guide us.    Nothing is to be found in the writings
of the saint's earliest biographers bearing reference to the
origin of the Rosary, a fact which would tell very strongly
against the authenticity of the legend, did we not know how
incomplete on matters of equal interest and importance are
the histories which they have left.    None of these writers
appear even to have aimed at producing anything approaching to an exact history of the holy patriarch.    They content themselves with gathering together certain incidents in
his life, without much regard to chronology, omitting all
allusion to many historical events of undoubted authenticity
which we should have supposed must have found a place
in any carefully compiled biography.    Their silence, therefore, on the subject of the institution by him of the Holy
Rosary cannot be taken as evidence against its truth,
however gladly we should have welcomed their testimony
in its favour.    The doubt that has been cast over the real
origin of the Rosary has arisen less from this silence of the
early historians than from the circumstances which followed
its first propagation by St. Dominic and his immediate
followers.    However powerfully it was preached by them,
and however widely it was disseminated during the early
days of the Dominican Order, it shared the fate of all pious
institutions during that period of general religious declension
under which the whole Church groaned in the fifteenth
century, and for a considerable time fell, at least partially,
into oblivion and neglect.    It was revived towards the end
of that century through the exertions of the celebrated
Dominican, Blessed Alan de la Roche, a Breton by birth,

[3] Mag. Corn. de Sneckis, Sermones xxi. super Conf. de Serto Rosaceo,
Serm. x. fol. 29.

who preached from the years 1473 to 1475,[4] since whose time its use has never been discontinued, every succeeding century witnessing some fresh increase both in its popularity with the faithful and the favour with which it has been regarded by the Sovereign Pontiffs. But the fact of its temporary neglect, and its subsequent revival by Blessed Alan, has been made the ground on which is based a theory, upheld by certain critics, that Alan was himself the author of the devotion. And the Bollandist writer, Father Cuyper, in a dissertation attached by him to the Life of St. Dominic, offers for our choice one of two suppositions—either that the Rosary existed as a devotion long before the time of St. Dominic, or that it never existed at all until the time of Blessed Alan. And in either of these cases St. Dominic is equally denied to be its author.

The reply to this dilemma, therefore, has to be reduced to two heads. We have to show first that the Rosary had no existence in the centuries preceding that in which it was preached by St. Dominic; and secondly, that we have such incontestable proofs of its existence and very general propagation in the years immediately succeeding, as will entirely dispose of the theory which would represent Blessed Alan as the originator, rather than the restorer of the devotion. Now with regard to the supposed antiquity of the Holy Rosary, when we examine the evidence brought in proof of this view, we find it to consist in the fact, that from very early times the faithful were in the habit of repeating a certain number of *Pater nosters* which they counted on knotted cords or strings of beads, whence these beads themselves were commonly called *Pater nosters*. In no country was this custom more general than in England. In 1040 we have the example of the Countess Godiva of Coventry, who bequeathed to the monastery which she there founded a chain of pearls and precious stones, whereon she was accustomed to count her prayers ; and two centuries earlier we find an English Council

---

[4] The very short time during which Alan's public ministry lasted renders it still more improbable that he should have been able in that time to spread the new devotion throughout Christendom (See Père Danzas, vol. iv. p. 341, and note).

directing that "seven belts of *Pater nosters* " should be recited
for a person deceased. In England, too, as in other countries,
these instruments of popular devotion were sold in great
numbers, so as to give a name to the locality where the
vendors of these goods congregated. Hence the title of
Paternoster Row, which still survives in London.   In Paris
there were no fewer than three corporations of artisans exclusively employed in the manufacture of such objects, and
the same industry was carried on in Rome and other capitals.
These facts, which can be illustrated by many examples, are
undisputed, but they prove nothing whatever to the purpose,
for it must be evident to every reader that the recital of
any number of *Pater nosters*, even if counted upon beads, is
not the devotion of the Rosary.   The utmost that can be
said is, that in this method of reciting prayers we see what
Père Danzas calls a certain *prelude* to the use of the Rosary,
a method, that is, which having already obtained currency
among the faithful, was the more easily adapted to the new
devotion. Two things are absent from these ancient practices
of piety which are essential to the Holy Rosary, the recital
of a fixed number of Hail Marys, and the accompanying
meditations upon the Life of our Lord.   Now laying aside
a multitude of other arguments and illustrations which bear
upon the subject, we may content ourselves with one statement, the accuracy of which will stand the closest investigation.   Prior to the century from which the devotion to the
Holy Rosary, properly so-called, dates its origin, the *Angelic
Salutation was not in general use as a popular devotion.*[5]   Isolated

---

[5] According to Mabillon (Præf. *Acta Sanct.* sæc. v. n. 120), one of
the earliest notices of the use of the Hail Mary occurs in the works of
St. Peter Damian, who speaks of a certain cleric who was used to recite
it as far as the words *in mulieribus*.   The Cistercian lay-brethren were
also enjoined to recite the *Ave Maria*, together with the *Pater* and the
Creed (Inst. Dist. 14, c. 2), but this rule does not appear to have been
made until early in the thirteenth century.   Father Bridgett however, in
his *Dowry of Mary*, has collected a number of examples showing that
though nowhere enjoined by episcopal authority before 1196, the prayer was
certainly used by many pious persons during the previous century.   The
solitary place in which it was introduced into the Liturgy before the
thirteenth century was in the Offertory of the Mass of the Fourth Sunday
in Advent (See Dr. Rock, *Church of our Fathers*, vol. iii. pp. 315—319).

examples, and those by no means rare ones, are no doubt
to be cited, but it cannot be said to have been universally
on the lips of the faithful as a familiar prayer. Yet more
remarkable is the fact that it was precisely in the lifetime
of St. Dominic, that we find the recital of the Angelic Salutation first becoming popular, and its use by the faithful
encouraged and enjoined by the pastors of the Church. In
1196, only a few years before St. Dominic quitted the cloisters
of Osma to enter on his apostolic career, Eudes, bishop of
Paris, published a decree, wherein he desires that the clergy
should frequently exhort the faithful to join the recitation
of the *Ave Maria* to that of the *Pater noster* and the Creed in
their daily prayers. And in 1246, we find an ordonnance
made by the Dean of the church of Rouen, couched in
similar terms. This decree was confirmed in the Synod of
Sens, held in the same year. The fifty years between these
two dates covers the missionary portion of St. Dominic's
life, and the first propagation of the Rosary by himself and
his first disciples, and forms the precise period in which the
Hail Mary came into general and popular use. "After that
date," says Mabillon,[6] "the use of the Angelic Salutation
became universal," and he adds many proofs from authentic
documents showing that anterior to that period the *Pater*
and *Credo* alone formed the ordinary devotion of the faithful.

We may content ourselves with the establishment of this
fact as sufficient to disprove the theory of the *antiquity* of the
devotion, for manifestly where there was no Hail Mary there
could be no Rosary. But before passing to consider the
second head of the indictment, it may be well to point out
the peculiar fitness and suitability of the choice made by
St. Dominic of this particular prayer in the devotion which
he used as his great weapon of defence against the heretics.
The *Pater noster*, that divinest of all prayers, and to which
he himself had so great and peculiar a devotion that, as
Castiglio says, "he never wearied of repeating it," had been
put by the Albigenses to profane and superstitious use,
and had been made the exterior form for bestowing their

[6] Praef. *Act. Sanct. Ord. Ben.* saec. v. n. 121.

pseudo-sacrament, the *Consolamentum*. Foremost among their pernicious errors was a denial of the Incarnation, nor did the heretics shrink from propagating doctrines concerning the Blessed Virgin and her Divine Maternity, to which, out of reverence for her sacred name, we can do no more than allude. The introduction of the Hail Mary, therefore, as a popular devotion, not substituted for the *Pater*, but rather linked thereto, a devotion in which she is invoked as the "Mother of God," and which thereby roots in the heart the doctrine of the Incarnation, and the association with this vocal prayer of meditations on the Life of our Divine Lord which present to the minds of the faithful a compendium of the Gospel, was a method of restoring the orthodox faith through the instrumentality of daily prayer, the admirable fitness of which will commend itself to every thoughtful reader. We do not pause to inquire whether the preaching of the Rosary spread the more universal use of the Hail Mary, or whether it was the increasing love and popularity of that prayer which moved the holy patriarch to adopt it. The fact remains, and is sufficient for the present purpose, that the period assigned by tradition as that of the origin of the Holy Rosary exactly synchronizes with the date before which the Hail Mary as a popular devotion was not in general use.

We have now to consider the second theory advanced by the critics, who would have us consider Blessed Alan, and not St. Dominic, as the first institutor of the Rosary. We have already spoken of the temporary neglect into which the devotion fell during the fourteenth century. If this neglect had been total, a certain degree of plausibility would have attached to the representation that its revival at the beginning of the fifteenth century was not a revival, but an institution. But this is far from being the case, in proof of which we have first, the positive assertions both of Blessed Alan and the Sovereign Pontiff at that time reigning, and secondly, the stubborn evidence of facts. In producing this evidence, we must press on our readers that though at the distance of five centuries it may be difficult for us to satisfy

ourselves how far the Holy Rosary had, or had not, fallen
into oblivion, the question could have been involved in no
obscurity at all to those living at the time. Not only do we
possess in the authentic writings of Blessed Alan repeated
assurances that the devotion of the Rosary first instituted
by St. Dominic was by him only revived, but we have the
testimony of not a few weighty and contemporary authorities
to the same effect. The first formal revival of the Rosary
may be accredited to the University of Cologne, where, in
the year 1475, the very year of Alan's death, James Sprenger,
prior of the Dominican Convent of that city, established
anew the Confraternity of the Holy Rosary. A notice of this
event has been left by the pen of no less a personage than
Thomas à Kempis, who in his Chronicle of the Monastery of
St. Agnes has these words: "In 1475, the University of
Cologne witnessed the foundation of a Confraternity of the
Rosary by doctors in sacred letters belonging to the Order
of St. Dominic, or rather this Confraternity was only renewed,
*for we read that it was preached by the holy Father St. Dominic,
although for a time it had fallen into neglect.*"[7]  In the year
following, Alexander, bishop of Forli, and Legate of the
Holy See, granted to this Confraternity certain Indulgences,
and declares almost in the same terms, that the Confraternity
was rather renewed than instituted, inasmuch as we read
in various histories that the devotion had been originally
preached by St. Dominic, and since his time had been
partially neglected, *fere neglecta.*  Precisely similar statements
are made by the contemporary Sovereign Pontiffs. Thus,
in 1479, Sixtus IV. speaks of the Rosary as a devotion
"formerly in use among the faithful of various countries."
In 1491, Innocent VIII. reproduces the terms used in the
Bull of Sixtus IV., and applies to the devotion the name of
the Rosary; and in 1494, Alexander VI. granting fresh
Indulgences to the devotion, declares that by the merits of

---

[7] *Chron. S. Agnet.* p. 96. This passage is quoted both by Benedict XIV.
in his work on *The Canonization of the Saints,* and by Mabillon, Præf. *Act.
Sanct. Ord. Ben.* sæc. v. n. 128. Trithemius, also, expresses himself in
the same terms as Thomas à Kempis.

St. Dominic who preached the Rosary in former years, " the whole world was preserved from imminent ruin."

These Pontiffs did not issue their decrees at a time when the facts of the case had fallen into oblivion. The subject was one of which, as contemporaries, they were perfectly well able to judge; and, moreover, they had at their command documents and histories, many of which there can be little doubt have since perished. Writers must certainly be regarded as worthy of credit who speak on their own knowledge as to the existence or decay of any practice in the period immediately antecedent to their own, nor can such testimony be considered as merely vague or traditionary.

But conjoined to their evidence, we possess abundance of historical facts which corroborate their statement. Our limits forbid the citation of more than a few of those which belong to the thirteenth and fourteenth centuries, and are therefore anterior to the time of Blessed Alan. Thus the great Beguinage of Ghent, which was from the first placed under the direction of the Friars Preachers, possessed statutes not later in date than 1234, in which each Beguine is required to recite daily "three coronas forming what is called the Psalter of the Blessed Virgin:" and this recitation was to be accompanied by meditation on the Mysteries of the Life of our Lord.[8] The rule of the Beguines was still observed in full vigour in the year 1471, at which date Blessed Alan, then lector in the Dominican convent of Ghent, was able to cite the example of these religious women, who for nearly two hundred years had recited our Lady's Psalter in lieu of the Canonical Office.

In 1243, Brother John de Mailly drew up a collection of saints' lives in which he tells us, that at that date, it was

---

[8] The Bollandists have attempted to escape from the powerful evidence furnished by these statutes by declaring that the ancient rule was retouched in more modern times. Mamachi admits the fact, but proves in reply (1) that the alterations referred to were made in the year 1354, more than a century before the birth of Blessed Alan, and (2) that they in no way regarded the recitation of our Lady's Psalter (Mamachi, *Annales Ord. Præd.* pp. 327—353).

J

the custom with many holy women to recite the Angelic Salutation one hundred and fifty times, and that this devotion was called the Psalter of the Blessed Virgin, the number of Hail Marys corresponding to the number of the Psalms of David. Bartholomew of Trent, a contemporary of Blessed Jordan of Saxony, also speaks of the same devotion, and relates an anecdote of one religious named Sister Eulalia, who, being very devout to the Blessed Virgin, recited every day one hundred and fifty Angelic Salutations in her honour, to whom our Lady deigned to appear and declare how acceptable this practice was to her, specially when the words *Dominus tecum* were pronounced slowly and devoutly. In consequence of this instruction, Eulalia from this time reduced the number of her prayers from one hundred and fifty to fifty, but was more careful in her manner of reciting them. Again at Lille, in the collegiate church of St. Peter, is still preserved an ancient volume in parchment, bearing the date 1231, which is the register of a confraternity called the *Treille*. In it are inscribed the names of several pious ladies, who contributed, instead of offerings of money or lights, spiritual donations consisting of so many Psalters of our Lady. If this phrase is not judged sufficiently precise, let us compare it with what we are told of the devotion in practice among the Dominican nuns at Toes, in Switzerland, who recited "three times fifty *Ave Marias* under the title of the Psalter of the Blessed Virgin, counting their prayers on the beads of a chaplet which they held in their hands, and meditating at the same time on the Mysteries of the Life and Death of our Lord."

This most exact description of the Rosary is taken from a MS. of great interest and undoubted authenticity belonging to the collection of the late Mgr. Greith, Bishop of St. Gall. It is considered to belong to the year 1454, and though this date is later than the examples already cited, it is certainly anterior to the time when Blessed Alan began to preach.[9]

It clearly appears, therefore, that however much the devotion of the Holy Rosary may have fallen into partial

[9] Greith, *Die deutsche Mystik en Prediger Orden*, p. 402.

neglect, its disuse between the time of St. Dominic and that of Blessed Alan was by no means universal. In England, indeed, we are able to affirm with the utmost certainty that the use of this devotion was never laid aside, but existed with undiminished popularity all through the thirteenth and fourteenth centuries. In the wills of various personages belonging to that period, we find bequests of richly ornamented beads or *Pater nosters*. The learned author of the *Pietas Mariana Britannica* gives the inventory of a jeweller's shop in 1381, which includes " four sets of *Pater nosters* of coral, six sets of *Aves* of geet, with *Pater nosters* of silver-gilt ; thirty-eight sets of *Aves* of geet, with gawdees or beads of silver-gilt," &c. And this notice is the more significant, as the title of *Ave* bestowed on some of these devout objects shows that the prayers said on them included not merely the *Pater* but the Hail Mary. But the most indubitable proofs that the real Rosary of our Lady, as we now recite it, was generally used in England before Blessed Alan's revival of the devotion in other countries, are to be drawn from the statutes of many hospitals, colleges, and other pious foundations of the fourteenth and the fifteenth centuries, in which the founders enjoin on the members of their several fraternities the recitation of our Lady's Psalter. Chief among these are the statutes of Eton College, founded by Henry VI. in the year 1440, in which he requires his scholars to say daily " the complete Psalter of the Blessed Virgin, containing a *Credo*, fifteen *Paters*, and one hundred and fifty *Ave Marias*." To evidence so conclusive as this, it would appear unnecessary to add other examples ; we will therefore do no more than allude to the two famous monuments which existed in the church of St. James in Paris prior to the French Revolution, one of which was the tombstone of the lord of Villepierre, whose effigy was sculptured between that of his wife and his mother, the latter of whom was represented holding in her joined hands a rosary composed of fifteen decades, each separated by a larger bead representing the *Pater noster*. This tomb was of the fourteenth century. In the same church was to be seen a magnificent monument

of brass, bearing the date 1355, and erected over the
remains of Humbert, Dauphin of Viennois, who resigned
his sovereignty to enter the Order of Friars Preachers. He
was afterwards raised to the patriarchate of Alexandria, and
was represented in his religious habit, over which appeared
the pallium. Around his effigy were smaller figures of
Dominican friars, holding in their hands rosaries or chaplets,
composed of fifty beads, without reckoning the *Paters*. Both
this brass and the above-named tombstone were destroyed
by the Vandals of the eighteenth century, but fortunately an
exact representation of both is engraved by Mamachi. Thus
to the facts of history we may add the testimony of sacred
art, and we may say also that of sacred poetry, for as poetry
we may rank the words of Albert the Great, who, in his work
*De laudibus B. Mariæ*, compares the Blessed Virgin to " the
Rose of Jericho blossoming with one hundred and fifty
petals," in which we cannot avoid recognizing an allusion
to her as Queen of the Holy Rosary.

It is not without a particular interest that we come on
facts connecting the revived devotion of the Rosary with
that reform of the Dominican Order which took place in
the beginning of the fifteenth century. It would seem as
if the fortunes of the Order were so indissolubly linked with
those of the Rosary, that, as they declined together, so
it was together that they flourished anew. Such indeed is
the opinion expressed by P. Monroy, Master-General of
the Order, who, in a circular dated 1671, declares that " the
Rosary is the most beautiful flower of the Order. When
that flower begins to fade, the charm and splendour of our
Institute likewise disappears, . . . but when it revives it
draws down upon us the plenteous dew of heaven." And
this opinion seems borne out by facts. The Reform which
was inaugurated in Lombardy at the end of the fourteenth
century by Blessed John Dominic, was promoted at the same
time in Germany by Father Conrad Gross, who died in
1426, and P. Jonchheere attributes to this great man the
restoration of the Rosary simultaneously with that of regular
observance.

Three of the Blessed of the Order, all of whom are more or less associated with the history of the Reform, are specially named as clients of the Holy Rosary. Of Blessed Clara of Gambacorta, whose community was the very focus of the Reform in Italy, we read that when a child of twelve years old she was accustomed to gather together girls of her own age, and kneeling down with them, devoutly to recite the Rosary. Blessed Clara died in 1419, when Alan must have been still a child, and could not clearly have derived her knowledge of the devotion from him. Again, Blessed John of Licci, who was born in the year 1446, and was one of the pillars of the Reform, placed in the convent which he founded in Sicily a beautiful marble image of Our Lady of the Rosary. And lastly, of the Blessed Anthony Neyrot, who was martyred at Tunis in the year 1460, and who was a member of the Reformed Convent of St. Mark at Florence, it is said that he died grasping in his hands the Rosary and the Crucifix.

The facts hitherto quoted may be taken as sufficient to prove the two points which at starting we undertook to establish, namely, that the real Rosary did not exist before the time of St. Dominic, and that it was widely known and practised before its revival by Blessed Alan. But have we no historic fact to present to the reader which associate it absolutely with St. Dominic himself? Not to speak of the Bull of Pope Clement VIII., published in 1602, in which he restores to the Order of Preachers the Church of St. Sixtus, and declares that it was in that church that the Confraternity of the Rosary was first erected in Rome by St. Dominic himself; not to speak of the frequent and positive assertions made both by Flaminius and Malvenda, as to the fact of the saint having preached the devotion in Rome and elsewhere, and thereby effected many wonderful conversions, there exists one document of undoubted authenticity, which we have reserved as the last link in our chain of evidence, and which proves beyond dispute that at least one Confraternity of the Holy Rosary was established by St. Dominic. The document referred to is the will and testament of a certain Anthony Sers, who in the year 1221 makes various dispositions in favour of the Confraternity of the Holy Rosary, *founded at Palencia by the good Dominic Guzman*, "of which Confraternity," says the testator, "I am a member." He desires that the brethren of the Confraternity should be gathered together at certain times to pray for his soul, and that in return for this act of charity, and to discharge the expenses of the candles borne by them, thirty-eight *maravedis* and three measures of wheat should be distributed amongst them. The foundation of this Confraternity must have taken place at the time that the holy patriarch visited Spain in 1218 or 1219, which will be noted in its proper place.

Having spoken thus far of the evidence of facts, we have now to say a word on the evidence of tradition, a tradition which claims from us no ordinary degree of respect, being that of the Church herself, resting on the supreme authority of the Holy See. This authority can be adduced, not merely in support of the belief that the devotion of the Rosary took its origin in the time of St. Dominic, and was first propagated by him and his immediate followers, but it declares him in no vague terms to have been the first to institute the devotion, and to have received it from the hands of the Blessed Virgin herself. If we are justified in recognizing St. Dominic to have been the first Inquisitor, less from any historic proofs of the fact than from the tradition of the Order, confirmed by the words of Pope Sixtus V., much more are we bound to accept this other tradition concerning the origin of the Rosary, which is world-wide in its extent, and has been sanctioned by the authority of no less than *thirteen* Sovereign Pontiffs. Such a tradition can hardly be assailed without temerity, for it would imply the most culpable disrespect to these illustrious Pastors of the Church to suppose that they would commit themselves to a precise affirmation of the fact without such examination of the evidence in support of it as would be satisfactory to the most stubborn of critics. It would be safe for us to take this as granted, but, as it happens, we have irrefragable proofs of the careful investigation bestowed by them upon the matter. In 1724, Benedict XIII. being then seated in the Chair of St. Peter, petitions were addressed to him on the part of the secular clergy, praying that in the Office of the feast of the Holy Rosary, which had been inserted in the Roman Breviary in 1716 by authority of Pope Clement XI., the Lessons for the second nocturn, narrating the history of the devotion, should be substituted for those hitherto in use. Now the Lessons thus petitioned for contained an explicit statement that the Rosary was instituted by St. Dominic inspired by the Blessed Virgin, and before granting the request the Pope directed that the matter should be submitted to the Congregation of Rites, and that the Lessons in question should be carefully examined. The Promoter of the Faith was at that time no less a personage than Prospero Lambertini, afterwards Pope Benedict XIV., a man whose learning and authority on such matters have never been surpassed. In our own days his *votum* on the subject has been brought to light,[10] and in it he appears as the warm advocate of the tradition in question, the truth of which he carefully investigates, and demonstrates by irresistible arguments. In consequence his conclusions were adopted, and the Lessons asserting the tradition were accepted and inserted in the Breviary. Yet, wonderful to say, Father Cuyper, the author of the dissertation which appears in the Bollandists, declares himself not satisfied with the evidence afforded by these Lessons and their approval by the Holy See. In his opinion they are not based on any ancient testimony, and have no sufficient authority. It is charitable to believe that he wrote in ignorance of the illustrious authority by whom they had been examined. His remarks, however, did not escape the notice of Lambertini, who being then Archbishop of Bologna, in his great work on the Canonization of Saints, and again in his treatise *De Festo Rosario*, reaffirms his vindication of St. Dominic as the author of the Rosary, and declares the tradition which had been examined by him to rest upon the most solid basis, *Validissimo fundamento*. After stating that the learned collections published by the Bollandists had been

---

[10] It was published in the *Analecta Juris Pontif.* Fourth Series, liv. 31, in 1860.

carefully consulted by him, he concludes one of his dissertations with the following words : " You ask if St. Dominic was
really the institutor of the Rosary, you declare yourselves
perplexed and full of doubt upon the subject. But what
account do you make of the decisions of so many Sovereign
Pontiffs—of Leo X., of Pius V., of Gregory XIII., of
Sixtus V., of Clement VIII., of Alexander VII., of Innocent XI., of Clement XI., of Innocent XIII., of Benedict XIII., and of many others, who are all unanimous in
declaring the Rosary to have been instituted by St. Dominic
himself?" To this list we can now add the names of Pius IX.
and Leo XIII. Our limits will not allow us to do more than
acknowledge the testimony that they have borne to the fact
in question, but we cannot conclude without at least quoting
the words of him who has perhaps done more than all his
predecessors to extend the use of the Holy Rosary, and to
multiply its privileges. When, in 1883, Pope Leo XIII.,
addressing himself to the Bishops of the Universal Church,
commanded for the first time the observance of the Month of
the Rosary, he made use of the following memorable words,
in which he sums up the history of the devotion : " None of
you, venerable brethren, are ignorant what woes and afflictions were caused to the Church of Christ towards the end of
the twelfth century by the Albigensian heretics, who, born of
the sect of the later Manichæans, filled the south of France
and other parts of Europe with most pernicious errors.
Carrying everywhere the terror of their arms, they sought
to extend their power by fire and sword. Then, as you
know, God in His mercy raised up against His enemies
a man of eminent sanctity, the Father and Founder of the
Dominican Order. This man, great by the integrity of his
doctrine, by the example of his virtues, and by his apostolic
labours, undertook the magnificent task of defending the
Catholic Church, not by force, nor by arms, but by the sole
power of that prayer *which he was the first to make known under
the title of the Holy Rosary*, and which was propagated far and
wide by him and by his disciples. Enlightened from on high,
he understood that this prayer would be the most powerful

weapon for overcoming the enemies of the Church and defeating their impiety. And the event proved that he was right. For, in fact, the use of this prayer having been spread and practised according to the instruction and institution of St. Dominic, piety, faith, and concord once more flourished. The enterprizes of the heretics failed, and their power gradually decayed; a vast number of souls returned to the true faith, and the fury of the impious was vanquished by the arms of the Catholics, who repelled force by force."

Comment on these words is as needless as it would be unbecoming. Rome has spoken, the cause is decided, and in presence of the authoritative decisions of so long a line of august Pontiffs, all captious criticism must henceforth be put to silence.

ST. DOMINIC AT MURET.

---

# CHAPTER XI.

## MURET.

### 1213.

WE once more return to the public history of the time, and resume our narrative at a moment when the fortunes of the Catholic cause seemed gravely imperilled by the decision that had been taken by the King of Aragon on behalf of Count Raymund and his allies. He had entered Languedoc at the head of a powerful army, and speedily made himself master of many strong places. He was now directing his march towards Toulouse, where, at the head of all the confederates who espoused the cause of the Count, he reckoned on being in a position to dictate his own terms to the Catholic chieftains. At this critical moment, De Montfort found himself deprived of the support of the French King, on which he had confidently reckoned. The league lately formed between the Emperor of Germany and the King of England obliged Philip Augustus to defend himself against their joint attack, and for the moment rendered it impossible for him to give any assistance to the Crusaders.

Their position indeed seemed but gloomy, for their forces were far outnumbered by those of the King of Aragon. A lay-brother of the Cistercians, who watched the progress of the war with painful interest, went in company with Stephen de Metz, another religious of the same Order, to consult Dominic at this juncture, well knowing that God often revealed to him the secrets of coming events. "Will these evils ever have an end, Master Dominic?" asked the afflicted Brother. He repeated his question many times, but Dominic remained silent. At length he replied: "There will be a time when the malice of the men of Toulouse will have its end, but it is far away; and there will be much blood shed first, and a king will die in battle." Brother Stephen and the Cistercian interpreted this prediction to allude to Prince Louis of France, the son of Philip Augustus, who had joined the army of the Crusaders in the previous February. "No," replied Dominic, "it will not touch the King of France: it is another king whose thread of life will be cut in the course of this war." This prophecy was very shortly to be accomplished, and Dominic himself was destined to be present on the spot where the decisive struggle took place which witnessed its fulfilment.

Very shortly after uttering the prediction, he left Carcassonne on the return of the bishop, intending to join the Congress of the Catholic prelates, which was to be held at Muret. On the road thither he passed through the city of Castres, where the body of the Spanish Martyr, St. Vincent, was preserved for the veneration of the faithful. It was the custom of Brother Dominic during his journeys to visit the holy shrines and places of pilgrimage that lay in his way, and the local traditions of many such spots, such as the great sanctuary of Our Lady at Puy and Notre Dame de Drèche near Albi, bear witness to his frequent presence there. But none was dearer to him than Castres, where he loved to pray by the tomb of his illustrious countryman, the martyr-deacon of Valencia. The town of Castres was one of those with the lordship of which the Count de Montfort had early been invested. The ancient chapel, wherein were preserved the relics of the martyr, had in former years been very irregularly served; but De Montfort, at the instance of St. Dominic, founded prebends for twelve secular canons, to whom was committed the charge of the chapel. He appointed as dean or prior of these canons one Matthew, a native of his own territory of Montfort L'Amaury, under whose government Castres recovered its former prosperity; and pilgrims resorting thither in great numbers, Dominic frequently came there, not only to satisfy his own devotion, but to break to the multitude the Bread of Life. It is said that a crucifix preserved in this chapel once spoke to him, and encouraged him to bear with constancy the contumelies to which he was exposed. On the present occasion, after having said Mass, he withdrew to a retired part of the church to make his thanksgiving, and meditating on the words: "The Lord shall feed him with the Bread of Life and immortality, and give him the Water of Wisdom to drink," he was wrapt in extasy and remained so for a good space. Meantime the prior, Father Matthew, and the other canons, were expecting him to join them in the refectory: and after waiting some time, the prior despatched a messenger to call him and warn him that the hour was late. The messenger, whose name was Sicard Sabbatier, found him raised from the ground in extasy and wholly absorbed in the things of God. Full of wonder and admiration, he hastened back to the prior to relate what he had seen, and Matthew accompanying him to the church beheld the same spectacle, and dared not disturb the sublime contemplation of the saint. Reverently kneeling near him therefore, they waited for awhile until he gently descended to the ground, when they saw him prostrate before the altar, as though to give thanks for the Divine favours which had been granted to him in prayer. The two canons were profoundly moved by this spectacle: but when the holy Father became aware of their presence and knew how long he had kept them waiting for their dinner, he was covered with confusion; and in return for their charitable patience, promised to Matthew, and to all those who should receive him with similar kindness, that God would not fail to give them the Bread of Life and the Water of Wisdom. This event decided Matthew's vocation. Shortly afterwards he resigned his office of prior, and entreated permission to follow Brother Dominic and to share his labours. The saint joyfully accepted this new disciple, repeating as he did so the words which from that time became his customary form of blessing to those who offered to join his company or who bestowed any charity upon him: *Det vobis Dominus panem vitæ et aquam cæli.* This story is related both by Stephen of Salagnac and Bernard Guidonis, the latter of whom was Prior of Castres, and tells us that Sicard Sabbatier joined the Order of Preachers, and became later on founder of the convent of Castres. After this incident Dominic returned to Fanjeaux, and there joined the Count de Montfort for the purpose of proceeding with him to Muret.

This fortress was one of great strategical value, both from its near neighbourhood to Toulouse, and from the fact of its commanding a bridge over the Garonne. In the year 1212, this bridge had been partially burnt by the forces of the Count of Toulouse, on which occasion De Montfort displayed a singular example of chivalrous heroism. Arriving on the banks of the river, he and his horsemen swam across the stream and reached the castle in safety. A few foot-soldiers who were left behind attempted to cross the bridge, but finding it too much injured to bear their weight, they were obliged to encamp on the further bank, where they were assailed by a furious tempest and in imminent danger of being attacked by the enemy. When De Montfort perceived this, he declared his intention of returning to bear them company. In vain was it represented to him that the larger portion of his troops were now secure, that only a few foot-soldiers remained on the other side of the river, now so frightfully swollen by the torrent of rain that it could not be crossed without danger. "What!" was his reply, "would you have me abandon the pilgrims of Christ left there unprotected while I remain safe within these walls! God may do with me as He may see fit, but I shall rejoin

them and share their danger." And recrossing the river
at the peril of his life, he remained with the soldiers, until
having repaired the bridge, he was able to lead them all
safely into the castle.

It was at Fanjeaux, about eight leagues distant, that he
now received the intelligence of the King of Aragon's appearance under the walls of Muret at the head of a hundred
thousand, or as others more probably state, of forty thousand
men. The Catholic chieftain was taken by surprise, for
only a few weeks previously he had been invited by the
King to a friendly conference, and owing to the negotiations
then pending with Rome, he was so little prepared for active
hostilities that he had with him no more than eight hundred
horse and a thousand foot-soldiers with whom to march to
the relief of the besieged. But Muret was far too important
a stronghold to abandon to its fate. By several bold and
successful sorties the garrison had inflicted considerable
loss on the forces of Count Raymund, and it was at his
suggestion that the King had directed all his strength to the
reduction of the place. On hearing of his approach, De
Montfort at once prepared to hasten to the rescue, regardless
of the entreaties of his wife and the remonstrances of some
of his followers, who represented that to oppose the army
of the King with so contemptible a force was little short of
madness. But his resolution remained unchanged. "A
good army," he said, "consists not in the number, but in
the valour of its soldiers." He set forth therefore without
delay, stopping on his road at the Cistercian monastery of
Bolbonne in order to recommend himself and his undertaking to the prayers of the monks. Entering the church
he laid his sword on the altar, and remained there for some
time in prayer: then taking back the weapon, as now no
longer his, but God's, he proceeded to Saverdun and there
spent the night in confession and preparation for death.
His pious example was followed by his companions, and on
the following morning they all heard Mass and communicated, as men who were about to offer their lives in sacrifice
for the cause of God.

De Montfort had been joined at Bolbonne by the Legate
and a number of bishops and abbots, among whom was Fulk
of Toulouse, who, together with St. Dominic, accompanied
him to Muret, in the hope of being able even yet to negotiate
terms of peace.   The army reached Muret and crossed the
bridge leading to the town without opposition from the
enemy, who were well content to see their opponents caught,
as they supposed, in a trap, whence they could not issue
without falling into their hands.   A messenger despatched
to the King by the Bishop of Toulouse demanding a safe
conduct for the prelates who wished to propose an accommodation, brought back for answer that no safe conduct
would be granted to those who came in company of an
armed force.   Nothing discouraged by this repulse, the
bishop made a second attempt to obtain at least a truce
to hostilities.   The answer sent by the King was couched
in terms of contempt.   " For the sake of four or five rascals
whom the bishops had brought with them it was not worth
while to grant a conference."   But they determined on yet
another effort, and very early in the morning sent word that
they would wait on the King barefoot, and lay before him
proposals for peace.   They were preparing to execute this
design when a body of troops attacked the gates, for the
King had ordered an advance without even deigning a reply
to the last message.

This attack was repulsed, but was followed by a storm
of stones and arrows directed on the quarters which were
occupied by the prelates.   " You see," said the Count, "that
your efforts avail nothing : the time for negotiation is past,
and nothing is left but to combat even unto death."   He
therefore descended into the town, and mustering his scanty
forces made the necessary dispositions for a sally.   The
infantry were left to strengthen the garrison, and at the
head of his eight hundred cavaliers the Count prepared to
face the enemy.   " Have you reckoned the number of the
King's troops ? " asked one of his followers.   " It is not my
custom," was his reply, " to count either my own soldiers
or those of the enemy : if God be with us we shall be strong

enough." But before the little band of devoted men left the walls of Muret, there was witnessed one of those scenes so characteristic of the ages of faith. Mass was celebrated in the church of St. James by the Bishop of Uzès, and when he turned to give the blessing, De Montfort knelt before him, clad in armour, saying: " I offer my life and my blood for God and His Church." Then the swords and shields of the combatants were solemnly blessed, and when this ceremony was over, and the horsemen were gathered together waiting for the word of command, Fulk, clad in pontifical vestments, appeared, bearing in his hands a relic of the true Cross, with which to bless the soldiers. Immediately every man flung himself from his horse and presented himself on his knees to kiss the sacred relic. But the Bishop of Comminges fearing to delay the march of the troops, took the relic from the hands of Fulk, and mounting a little eminence, blessed with it the whole army, bidding them go forth in God's name to victory or to martyrdom. " The Crusaders had already confessed," says the historian, " they now embraced and asked pardon one of another, and this done they re-mounted their horses, and rode out of the gates." Whilst the ecclesiastics returned to the church to pray, De Montfort marshalled his men on a level space of ground outside the walls and divided them into three companies. On perceiving this, the King of Aragon left his entrenchments, and at the head of his magnificent cavalry reckoned on easily crushing the contemptible force opposed to him. Obeying the orders of their commander, the Crusaders made a feigned move-ment of retreat, which deceived the enemy, and drew from them insulting cries of joy: when suddenly, De Montfort gave the word of command, and his horsemen, turning rein, dashed right on the ranks of their opponents with the im-petuosity of a mountain torrent. Swift as lightning they broke through the troops who opposed their onward course, scattering them before their horses' hoofs with amazing energy, nor did they draw bridle till they reached the centre of the army where the King himself was stationed surrounded by the flower of his nobles. The shock was so violent that in the words of the younger Raymund, who beheld the battle from the neighbouring hill, "the sound of the clash of arms resembled that which is heard when a troop of woodcutters cut down with their axes the oaks of the forest."[1] The King was one of the first to fall, and his fate decided the fortune of the day. Terrified by the shock of that tremendous charge, the main body fell into confusion; and De Montfort, following up his first advantage, directed a few soldiers whom he held in reserve, to attack the enemy's flank. This completed the rout of the army. The Counts of Foix Comminges, and Toulouse, had been the first to seek safety in flight, and their example was speedily followed by the Spaniards. The voice and example of their chieftain might yet have rallied them, but that was wanting: Peter of Aragon lay dead on the field, and Dominic's prophecy had found its fulfilment.

Whilst the cavalry of the two armies were thus engaged, the infantry of the allies had made a fierce attack on the defences of the town. But De Montfort, returning from his pursuit of the fugitives, fell on the rear of the assailants, who offered but a faint resistance. Great numbers were cut to pieces, or surrendered as prisoners; others fled to their boats, and escaping to Toulouse, carried with them the tidings of their disastrous defeat. The whole conflict had not lasted more than three hours, but the victory of the Crusaders was complete. More than twenty thousand of the enemy are said to have perished, whilst we are assured by all authorities that of the Catholic army only one knight and eight soldiers were slain.

When De Montfort and his knights rode forth to battle, the prelates and other ecclesiastics returned into the church, and gathered before the altar to pray for the success of their arms. Prostrate on the ground, which they watered with their tears, they poured out their souls in prayer to God. Bernard Guidonis, who wrote in the following century, when the memory of these events was fresh in the memory of the people, does not forget to notice what part was taken by the

[1] William de Puy Laurens, c. 22.

K

ecclesiastics in the deeds of that memorable day. "Going
into the church," he says, "they prayed, raising their hearts
to heaven and beseeching God for His servants who were
exposed to death for His sake, with such great groans and
cries, that it seemed not as if they prayed, but rather howled."
But from this agonizing suspense they were roused by the
shouts of the populace. The cry of victory sounded in their
ears; they hastened to the walls, and beheld the plain
covered with the flying companies of the heretics. Some
plunged into the waters of the Garonne, and perished in
their armour: others trampled their own comrades to death
in the confusion of their flight. Of all the immense multitude
which a few hours before had been encamped before the walls
of Muret, not a single man remained.

Where, meanwhile, was St. Dominic himself, during the
memorable battle whose issue was to exercise so marked an
influence on his future career? Some authors represent him
as remaining in the church of St. James with the prelates;
but many historians of the Order declare that he appeared on
the castle walls, or (as others say) on the battlefield itself,
holding aloft the crucifix and animating the courage of the
soldiers. A shower of arrows was discharged by the enemy
at the sacred emblem which he displayed, some of which
pierced the wood of the cross, without, however, touching
the figure of our Lord. This crucifix is still preserved in
the church of St. Sernin, at Toulouse, whither it was
removed from the house of the Inquisition in 1791. Its
appearance is most ancient, exhibiting three or four holes
made by the arrows, the shafts of some of them still
sticking in the wood.[2]

---

[2] Fastened at the foot of the crucifix is a silver plate bearing the
following inscription:

*Soux le coduc del brave Conté de Montfort, general de la guerra, mareschales
eran Guy de Levis, Lambé Turi, Pey Voicin, e Oto Niort, e fray Domeng ab la
Sancta Crou.*

*Hæc ex originali Chartularis seculi 13, quo nobilitas harum familiarum probata
fuit Montpelii per Dominum Nicolaum Tamisier, regium pro nobilitate commis-
sarium, 8. Oct. 1647 (Monumenta Conv. Tolo. Ord. Præd., Sec. i. p. 10. F.M.T.
pos. 1695).*

ST. DOMINIC'S CRUCIFIX.

[To fac: p. 146.

As the Count de Montfort rode over the victorious field, he checked his horse at the trampled and bleeding body of the King of Aragon.   De Montfort had some of the failings, but all the virtues of his order: he was cast in the heroic type of Christian chivalry.   Descending from his horse, he kissed the body with tears, and gave orders for its honourable interment as became a gallant enemy: then, returning bare-foot to Muret, he went first to the church to return thanks to God, and gave the horse and armour with which he had fought to the poor.   It was a true picture of the ages of faith.

We need scarcely be surprised that so wonderful a victory was looked on as miraculous and accounted to be the fruit of prayer.   De Montfort himself ever so regarded it, and attributing his success, under God, to the intercession of St. Dominic, lost no opportunity of testifying his love and gratitude.   The chapel of our Lady in the church of St. James at Muret, was built by him as a memorial of the victory in the course of the same year.   It is supposed to have been the first chapel ever dedicated to the Holy Rosary, and in it was placed a picture representing the Blessed Virgin giving the rosary to St. Dominic, who holds in his right hand the crucifix pierced by three arrows, whilst on the other side of our Lady kneel Simon de Montfort and Fulk of Toulouse. Tradition has always claimed the victory of Muret as one of the first triumphs of the Holy Rosary, and we are led to infer that the devotion was first generally propagated about this time.

The battle of Muret was fought on the 13th of September, 1213, and proved a fatal blow to the cause of the Count of Toulouse.   De Montfort followed up his victory by making himself master of Limousin, Perigord, and the adjacent pro-vinces: and in the December of the year following, a Council assembled at Montpelier invested him with the sovereignty of the conquered territories.   This act of the Council was submitted to the approval of the Pope, who in that spirit of justice and moderation which is observable in all his dealings with the Count of Toulouse, decreed that De Montfort should

indeed be invested for the present with the conquered territories, but that Raymund should be allowed a right of appeal
before the General Council about to be assembled at Rome.

Twice again does Dominic's name occur associated with
the busy scenes of De Montfort's history. He was called on
to baptize his daughter, afterwards a nun in the convent of
St. Anthony at Paris, and to celebrate the marriage of his
son Almeric with the daughter of the Dauphin of Vienne.
But a new chapter in the life of the saint was about to open,
carrying him far from the distractions of courts and camps.
The shifting chances of the war, guided by the hand of
Providence, were opening to him, after long waiting, a
way to that design long secretly cherished in his heart.
The clouds which until now had hung over the horizon,
had risen at last; and when Toulouse at length opened
her gates, and the storm of combat for a time was lulled,
Dominic, in his forty-sixth year, prepared to lay the foundation of that Order which was to bear his name to future
generations as long as the world and the Church should last.

# CHAPTER XII.

POLITICAL events did not permit St. Dominic to enter Toulouse immediately after the victory of the Crusaders recorded in the last chapter. Withdrawing from the army at the very moment of its triumph, he returned to Carcassonne, where he spent several months entirely engaged in apostolic labours. His preaching won many conversions among some of those very citizens who had formerly hooted him through their streets and pelted him with mud, but who now came to ask his forgiveness, and seek reconciliation with the Church. The troubadour of Picardy, in his metrical Life of St. Dominic, has not failed to notice this incident, which he relates in graphic style, as an example of the singular patience and humility of the saint in dealing with the heretics. One man (he says) was deeply touched with repentance, and coming to the saint, " Sir," he said, " I well remember that I once cast filth in your face out of scorn and malice, and I also fastened an old dish-clout to your dress, to make game of you." When the holy man heard this he began to sigh. " Ah! Lord God!" he said, " I have not done deeds good enough to deserve martyrdom." He is also said to have had the happiness at this time of reconciling an apostate bishop who had pursued him with the most inveterate malice, and had been wont contemptuously to scoff at the devotion of the Holy Rosary. His eyes were opened to see his error by a terrible vision, in which he seemed to find himself plunged into thick mire from which there was no way of escape. Raising his eyes, he saw above him the forms of our Lady

and the blessed Dominic, who let down to him a chain made
of a hundred and fifty links, fifteen of which were of gold;
and laying hold of this he found himself safely drawn to dry
land.   Touched to the heart, he not only sought the saint
and recanted his pernicious errors, but for the remainder
of his life continued faithful in the daily recitation of the
Rosary.[1]

It was not until the summer of the year 1214 that
Dominic found himself free to return to Toulouse, where
it was his purpose, in company with the disciples who had
gathered round him in his apostolic journeys, to lay the
foundations of his religious community.   He was joyfully
received both by Fulk and the Count de Montfort, but
neither of these distinguished persons were destined to be
the immediate co-operators with him in the foundation of
the Order.   Peter Cellani, an opulent citizen of Toulouse,
and another of the same rank, known to us only under the
name of Thomas (but whom some suppose to have been his
brother), presented themselves to him shortly after his arrival
at Toulouse, and placed themselves and all they had at his
disposal.   Peter Cellani offered his own house, a large and
commodious building near the gate of Narbonne, for the use
of the saint and his companions.   They were but six in all,
and in after-years Peter was accustomed to boast that he
had not been received into the Order, but that it might
rather be said that he had received the Order into his own
house.   With these six followers, whom he clothed in the
habit of the Canons Regular which he himself always wore,
the saint accordingly began a life of poverty and prayer
under the rules of religious discipline.   "From the time
when they first took up their residence in Toulouse," says
Malvenda, "the blessed Dominic, and all those who had
joined his company, began to conform themselves to religious
rules, and to perfect themselves more and more in the practice
of humility."  Great indeed was the change which thus passed
over his life.   Eleven years had rolled away since the Subprior of Osma had exchanged the calm life of religious

[1] Flaminius, quoted by Malvenda, c. 29.

retirement which he had led up to his thirty-third year, for one of apostolic labour : and during this period he had been wholly separated from all which, to the heart of the true religious, makes up the nameless sweetness of the cloister.   The monastic silence, the choral office, the charm of regular and community life, all these he had sacrificed at the call of God, in order to wage a hand to hand conflict with vice and unbelief on a foreign soil, and among an ungrateful people.   Too often he had been thrown in contact with scenes of violence and bloodshed revolting to humanity, and had suffered "the contradiction of sinners" against himself with an unalterable virtue which won for him the title of the "Rose of Patience."   Few can estimate the costliness of such a sacrifice to a soul attuned, as his was, to the sublimest secrets of contemplation.   And now the time seemed come when all that he had renounced was to be given back to him even to the hundred-fold.

What a joy to be once more within the walls of a religious house; to see around him devoted souls, disciples, and children with whom he might resume all those exercises of regular life from which he had so long been exiled !   The narrow cell which he occupied in that house was for centuries jealously preserved, a sacred spot indeed which had been sanctified by his prayers and watered by his blood. Père Réchac, who visited it in the seventeenth century, when it had been turned into a chapel, describes the altar above which was to be seen a picture of the saint, engaged in his nightly exercises of prayer and penance, and beside it a little niche painted in antique style with the instruments of the Passion, which was held to have been the actual oratory of the saint.[2]   Here was preserved the crucifix he was said to have held at the battle of Muret, with other precious memorials of his presence; and the whole chamber, says

---

[2] The house of Peter Cellani was afterwards made over to the Fathers of the Inquisition.   It still stands, being now used as a college, and the chamber of St. Dominic continued to be shown within it so late as the year 1772.

the same writer, was so redolent of devotion, that no one could kneel there with his heart unmoved.

But sweet as must have been this brief interval of devout repose, the heart of the saint was not satisfied. He had long conceived in his mind the idea of a religious Order which should be trained to labour for the salvation of souls by means of a ministration of the Divine Word, based on a profound knowledge of sacred science. The whole future scope of the Friars Preachers was in the mind of Dominic at the moment of its first foundation. That it was so, is evinced by the first step taken by him after assembling these six brethren in the house of Peter Cellani. He explained to them the extent and nature of his design; and showed them that, in order to carry it out, and fit themselves to become teachers of the truth, they must first be learners. There was then in Toulouse a celebrated doctor of theology named Alexander, whose lectures were greatly admired and frequented. To him Dominic resolved to entrust his little company. One morning Alexander had risen very early, and was in his room engaged in study when he was overcome by an unusual and irresistible inclination to sleep. His book dropped from his hand, and he sank into a profound slumber. As he slept he seemed to see before him seven stars, at first small and scarcely visible, but which increased in size and brightness, till they enlightened the whole world. As day broke, he started from his dream, and hastened to the school where he was to deliver his usual lecture. Scarcely had he entered the room, when Dominic and his six companions presented themselves before him. Malvenda remarks on the singular humility with which, in order to encourage his companions, the blessed Father offered himself as a disciple, although he was well known to be profoundly versed in sacred science, as had been repeatedly proved in his controversies with the heretics. All were clad alike in the white habit and surplice of the Augustinian Canons, and they announced themselves as poor Brothers who were about to preach the Gospel of Christ to the faithful and the heretics of Toulouse, and who desired first

of all to profit by his instructions. Alexander understood
that he saw before him the seven stars of his morning
dream; and many years after, when the Order had indeed
fulfilled the destiny predicted, and had covered Europe with
the fame of its learning, he himself being then at the English
Court, related the whole circumstance to Brother Arnulf de
Bethune, and boasted with pardonable pride of having been
the first Master of the Friars Preachers.

These first steps of the brethren were marked by the
Bishop Fulk of Toulouse with unmixed satisfaction. The
piety and fervour displayed by them, and their exact following
in the footprints of Brother Dominic, for whom he had ever
entertained a peculiar reverence, determined him to give
the infant Order the support of his powerful protection. With
the consent of his chapter he assigned the sixth part of the
tithes of his diocese for their support and the purchase of
the books necessary for their studies. The document in
which he makes this grant will not be without its interest:
"In the Name of our Lord Jesus Christ. We make known
to all present and to come, that we Fulk, by the grace of God
the humble minister of the see of Toulouse, desiring to
extirpate heresy, to expel vice, to teach the rule of faith,
and recall men to a holy life, appoint as preachers throughout our diocese Brother Dominic and his companions, who
propose to go on foot, as becomes religious, according to
evangelical poverty, and to preach the word of evangelical
truth. And because the workman is worthy of his hire, and
we are bound not to muzzle the mouth of the ox who treadeth
out the corn, and because those who preach the Gospel
shall live by the Gospel, we desire that, whilst preaching
through the diocese, the necessary means of support be
administered to them from the revenues of the diocese.
Wherefore, with the consent of the chapter of the church
of St. Stephen, and of all the clergy of our diocese, we assign
in perpetuity to the aforesaid preachers, and to others who,
being moved by zeal for God and love for the salvation of
souls, shall employ themselves in the like work of preaching,
the sixth part of the tenths destined for the building and

ornamenting all the parochial churches subject to our government, in order that they may provide themselves with habits, and whatsoever may be necessary to them when they shall be sick, or be in need of rest. If anything remain over at the year's end, let them give it back, that it may be applied to the adornment of the said parish churches, or the relief of the poor, according as the bishop shall see fit. For inasmuch as it is established by law, that a certain part of the tithes shall always be assigned to the poor, it cannot be doubted that we are entitled to assign a certain portion thereof to those who voluntarily follow evangelical poverty for the love of Christ, labouring to enrich the world by their example and heavenly doctrine; and thus we shall satisfy our duty of freely scattering and dividing, both by ourselves and by means of others, spiritual things to those from whom we receive temporal things. Given in the year of the Word Incarnate, 1215, in the reign of Philip, King of France, the principality of Toulouse being held by the Count de Mont-fort."

Neither was De Montfort wanting in liberality towards the young Order. He had already made many grants to the house of Prouille, and in this year we find him making over the castle and lands of Casseignoul to the use of Dominic and his companions. He moreover, addressed a letter to the seneschals of Carcassonne and other cities in his dominions, commanding them "to defend the houses and goods of our most dear Brother Dominic, as though they were our own."

In the September of the same year, Bishop Fulk of Toulouse set out for Rome to attend the approaching Council of the Lateran, and Dominic accompanied him, leaving Bertrand of Garrigua at the head of the little community of Toulouse. Long years had passed since his last visit to the capital of Christendom in company with Diego of Azevedo; and the work, the plan of which had even then dawned on his mind, was only now developing into actual existence. A higher strength than that derived from any human enthusiasm must have been in his soul, or he might well have been daunted as coming for the second time within sight of the Eternal City, he looked back on the forty-five years of his life, so full of patient labour, but which to human seeming had been blessed with so little fruit.  Yet it was with no failing courage that he now prepared himself for his gigantic task; whilst all the materials he had as yet gathered for the struggle were the six unknown and unlettered companions whom he had left at Toulouse.

Innocent III, still filled the Papal Chair, and the Council of Lateran formed almost the closing scene of a pontificate which must be held as one of the greatest ever given to the Church.  On the 11th of November, 1215, five hundred bishops, and above eight hundred abbots and priors, with the ambassadors of every European sovereign, met in that ancient and magnificent church, the mother-church of Rome and of the world.  Few Councils, save that of Trent, have a greater claim on our veneration, for in it were defined some of the sublimest articles of the Christian faith.  In the first canon were set forth in precise and lucid terms all those doctrines assailed by the Manichean heretics; such as the Unity of God, Who was declared to be the Creator of all things whether spiritual or corporal; the Incarnation of the Second Person of the Holy Trinity; and the nature of the Church and of the Sacraments, specially of the Holy Eucharist. Among the canons of discipline was one laying upon all the faithful the obligation of yearly Confession and Communion, which has remained in force until our own time, and which, while it attests the lamentable decay from primitive fervour which could have rendered such a decree necessary, placed a secure barrier against further relaxation.  Very stringent regulations were also made for the visitation of dioceses, the reform of the clergy, and the extirpation of heresy, the bishops being charged to appoint certain officers who should assist them in seeking out heretics and bringing them to canonical punishment.  In fact, the singular energy displayed by this celebrated Council, and the very nature of its decrees, are a sufficient proof of the state in which the world and the Church were then found.  There was everywhere

a decay and a falling off.  Old institutions were waxing
effete, and had lost their power; whilst indications were
everywhere visible of an extraordinary activity and restless-
ness of mind, which was constantly breaking out into
disorder for want of channels into which it might be safely
guided.   Europe had taken some centuries to struggle
through the barbarism which had fallen on her after the
breaking up of the Roman Empire.   As the waters of that
great deluge subsided, life came back by degrees to the
submerged world, and just at this period was quickening into
a vitality which, in the succeeding century, was manifested
in a luxuriance of growth.   It was one of those junctures in
the world's history, when God is wont to raise up great men
who lay their hands on the human elements of confusion,
and fashion them into shape.   And among these is to be
reckoned the founder of the Friars Preachers.

His reception by the Fathers of the Council, and by the
Pope himself, was cordial and flattering.   Met as they were,
in a great measure, to discuss the questions which had arisen
out of the state of the French provinces, Dominic's name,
and the part he had taken during the last ten years, were
not unknown and unappreciated by them.   Before the formal
opening of the Council, Pope Innocent granted him an
Apostolic Brief, by which he received the convent of Prouille
under the protection of the Pontifical See, and confirmed the
grants made to it.   But when the plan for the foundation of
the new Order was laid before him, its novelty and the vastness of its design startled him.   As yet the Church possessed
only the more ancient forms of monasticism, with some
institutes of later creation, which had, however, but a
limited object, or a merely local influence; for the Friars
Minor, though they preceded the Preachers by several years,
could not as yet be said to have been formally established
as a religious Order.   Dominic's idea included a much wider
field than had been as yet attempted by any of the more
modern founders. As has been already said, he had conceived
the design of an Order devoted to the work of preaching and
teaching, and which for that purpose should apply itself to

the study of sacred letters, with the express object of the salvation of souls. But preaching and teaching had hitherto been considered the peculiar functions of the episcopate, and one of the decrees of this very Council of Lateran, after enumerating the evils flowing from the neglect or inability of the bishops in respect to those offices, empowers them to choose fit and proper persons in each diocese to discharge the "holy exercise of preaching" in their stead. This decree, however, in nowise contemplated the establishment of any body of persons exercising the office in any other way than as deputies to the bishop, and the plan was, therefore, one full of novelty. It seemed to encroach on the privileges of the episcopate, and its boldness appeared dangerous at a moment when men's minds were so powerfully agitated. The troubles of the Waldenses were fresh in the mind of the Pontiff; for that sect had grown out of the simple abuse of the office of preaching, usurped by men without learning or authority. The Church, in short, was jealous of innovation, and had just ruled in the Council then sitting, that no more new Orders should be introduced or allowed. In the face of this fresh regulation, it required no small degree of boldness and confidence to present the scheme of a new foundation for approbation, and to persevere in the request, for in spite of the warm recommendations of the Bishop of Toulouse, who bore witness to the great need of apostolic men to preach the Word of God in the afflicted provinces of France, and of the extraordinary merits of Brother Dominic, the Pope showed no disposition to favour the design laid before him. A second application proved equally unsuccessful, but the saint did not lose heart. He looked not to man but to God for an answer to his petition, and spent his days visiting the relics of the saints and his nights in prayer and penance.

It pleased God to make known His will to Innocent in a vision of the night, wherein he seemed to see the Lateran Basilica about to fall, but supported on the shoulders of St. Dominic. Four years before a similar vision had been granted to him, when St. Francis of Assisi had visited Rome to solicit the Pope's approbation of his infant Order; and by this coincidence the Pontiff understood that in the designs of God these two men had been raised up to repair the ruin caused in the Church by vice and heresy, and to support her by their doctrine and example. ⟩The cause was gained, and sending for the bishop and for Brother Dominic, he made known to them the joyful news that their petition was granted.

Nevertheless the language of the Council was too strong to be entirely evaded; it was as follows: ⟨In order that the too great diversity of religious Orders be not a cause of confusion in the Church of God, we strictly prohibit that any one do for the future form any new Order; whoever desires to become a religious, let him do so in one of those already approved. In like manner, if any one desire to found a new religious house, let him be careful that it observe the rule and constitutions of one of the approved Orders." Not, therefore, to act in positive contradiction to a principle so recently and distinctly laid down, Innocent, whilst commending the zeal of the servant of God, and assuring him of his approval of the design, desired him to return to France, that, in concert with his companions, he might choose one out of the ancient rules which should seem to them the best fitted for their purpose. When the selection was made he was to return to Rome, in order to receive from the Apostolic See the necessary confirmation.

Besides this encouragement and promise of future protection, Innocent was the first who bestowed on the Order the name which it has ever since borne. The circumstances under which he did so were a little singular, and have been preserved with unusual exactness. Shortly after granting the above favourable answer to the prayer of Dominic, he had occasion to write to him on some matters connected with the subject, and desired one of his secretaries to despatch the necessary orders. When the note was finished, the secretary asked to whom it should be addressed. "To Brother Dominic and his companions," he replied; then, after a moment's pause, he added, "No, do not write that;

let it be, 'To Brother Dominic and those who preach with him in the country of Toulouse;'" then, stopping him yet a third time, he said, "Write thus, *To Master Dominic and the Brothers Preachers.*" This title, though not at first formally given by his successor Honorius in the Bulls of confirmation, was, as we shall see, afterwards adopted, and has always continued to be used.

The object of his visit to Rome was now fully accomplished; yet Dominic did not return to Languedoc until the spring of the following year. The Council still sat, and it is probable that he was present at the deliberations held at its conclusion concerning the future government of the Narbonnese provinces. After hearing the whole cause pleaded at great length, Innocent gave sentence that Raymund VI. should be adjudged to have forfeited his dominions but was to be allowed a suitable revenue; whilst his wife, sister to the late King of Aragon, should be secured in the peaceable possession of her dowry. The provinces which had been wrested from the Count by the arms of the Crusaders were to remain in the possession of the Count de Montfort, who had already been conditionally invested with their sovereignty: but those not yet conquered were erected into the marquisate of Provence, and placed under the guardianship of persons appointed by the Holy See, who should hold them in trust for the younger Raymund, and make them over to him when he came of age, if by that time he should have shown himself worthy. This decision was far from being satisfactory to the two Raymunds, who before leaving Rome did not conceal their intention of attempting to re-possess themselves of the conquered provinces by force of arms, a design they were not slow in carrying into practice, and thus the fair fields of Languedoc were once more plunged in the horrors of civil war.[3]

[3] Much confusion has arisen from the fact that the anonymous continuator of the *Chanson de la Croisade* has turned the history of the Council into a veritable romance, placing on the lips of the chief actors, and notably of Pope Innocent, speeches wholly imaginary, and attributing to the latter words and sentiments inconsistent with his actual conduct. A

But St. Dominic's connection with this portion of the civil history of his time was now nearly concluded; henceforth he was to belong not to Languedoc or to France alone, but to the world.   He remained in Rome until the conclusion of the Council, and during this time made his first acquaintance with the holy patriarch St. Francis, under the following circumstances. One night being in prayer in the Basilica of St. Peter he saw the figure of our Lord in the air above his head, holding three arrows in His hand, with which He seemed about to strike the world in punishment of its enormous wickedness.   Then the Blessed Virgin prostrated herself before Him, and presented to Him two men whose zeal should convert sinners and appease His irritated justice. One of these men he recognized as himself; the other was wholly unknown to him.   The next day, entering a church to pray, he saw the stranger of his vision, dressed in the rough habit of a poor beggar; it was Francis of Assisi, and recognizing him as his companion and brother in the work to which both were called by God, he ran to him, and, embracing him with tears, exclaimed, " You are my comrade, you will go with me; let us keep together, and nothing shall prevail against us."   This was the beginning of a friendship which lasted during the remainder of their lives.   From that time they had but one heart and one soul in God; and though their Orders remained separate and distinct, each fulfilling the work assigned to it by Divine Providence, yet a link of fraternal charity ever bound them together: " brought forth together," in the words of Blessed Humbert, " by our holy mother the Church," they felt that " God had destined them from all eternity to the same work, even the salvation of souls."

We read, in the Life of St. Francis, that St. Angelus, the Carmelite, who was shortly afterwards martyred in the island

translation of the *song* written in Provencal prose more than a century later has been accepted by many modern writers as an authentic chronicle; and thus the fancies of the poet have been gravely quoted as sober history.

of Sicily, was also in Rome at this time, having come thither on his way from Jerusalem.

Being one day in the church of St. John Lateran, he there met the two holy patriarchs, Dominic and Francis, and the latter, filled with the spirit of prophecy, said aloud to his companion: "Behold Angelus of Jerusalem, a man angelic in very truth, who is soon to become a martyr of Jesus Christ!" and prostrating on the ground with deep humility he devoutly kissed the feet of the blessed Angelus. Then they all mutually embraced one another, and going forth together out of the church they met a leper of noble rank, who recommending himself to their prayers was presently cured. It is added that the three saints spent the remainder of that day and the following night in each other's company, spending the whole time in prayer and Divine discourses. St. Angelus is likewise said to have preached in the Lateran in the presence of the two founders, predicting their future greatness and the extension of their Orders.[4]

---

[4] The authenticity of this narrative is questioned by the Bollandists, and though related with many additional particulars in the Life of St. Angelus, it is assigned by the Carmelite authorities to a later date. Some Franciscan writers also place the meeting of Dominic and Francis in the following year, when both were again present in Rome for the confirmation of their respective Orders, but the Dominican authorities are generally agreed in giving it as occurring during this visit.

L

VISION OF THE HOLY APOSTLES.

# CHAPTER XIII.

## CONFIRMATION OF THE ORDER.

### 1216, 1217.

THE Council of Lateran broke up at the end of November, 1215, and soon afterwards Dominic, in company with the Bishop of Toulouse, set out to return to France. On their road thither they stopped at several cities of northern Italy, specially Siena, where they were received with great honour, and according to the Chronicle of Nanno Donati, overtures were made to the saint by the magistrates of the city, who desired that he should establish some of his disciples among them. This was at the time impossible, and the holy Father was anxious to lose no time in rejoining his brethren at Toulouse. During his absence their numbers had increased from six to sixteen, and the mutual joy of their meeting can be well imagined. The saint explained to them the result of his petition to the Holy See, and the necessity which now lay on them to make choice of a Rule. For this purpose he appointed a meeting of all the brethren, to be held at Prouille, where the brothers William de Claret and Noel, who took care of the nuns, were already awaiting them. ✓ Thither, in the month of April, they all repaired, and assembling in the little chapel of our Lady, after earnest prayer and invocation of the Holy Spirit, they agreed to choose the Rule of St. Augustine, under which the holy founder himself had lived ever since he had worn the habit of a Canon Regular, and which they had all observed during their residence at Toulouse. It was the better fitted for their purpose by its very simplicity, which rendered it capable of nearly any development which the peculiar objects of their Institute might require. In choosing it, Dominic fulfilled the obligation imposed on him by the Pope, while at the same time he was left free to add Constitutions of his own to the general principles of religious life laid down by St. Augustine. ✓

He was not the first who had made a similar use of this Rule. If we compare the plan of St. Dominic with that of St. Norbert, who had preceded him by nearly a century, we shall find a very striking similarity between them. St. Norbert's Rule was a reformation of that of the Regular Canons. In its design he departed from the ordinary line of the more ancient forms of monasticism, and set before him as his object active missionary labours for the salvation of souls. His work was preaching. He himself preached over all the provinces of France and Flanders, and obtained faculties from Pope Gelasius II. authorizing him to preach wherever he might think proper. But whatever similarity was to be found existing between the two Institutes, they were called to fill a different place in the Church of God. Religious Orders, we must never forget, are the result of Divine vocation, not the mere creations of human intelligence; and those vocations they accomplish in an infinite variety of ways, which human intelligence could never have planned or executed; they are like the varieties of plants and animals in nature, whose mingled similarities and distinctions, multiplied in a thousand forms, attest the authorship of an infinite Creator.

The founder of the Friars Preachers was well acquainted with both the Premonstratensian and the Cistercian Rules, and freely borrowed from them both whatever he found suitable for his purpose; but the idea which had existed in his mind from the very first was distinct from either. His plan was three-fold. The first and primary object of the Order was labour for the salvation of souls; but in setting this before him as his principal aim, he was unwilling to abandon anything of the religious character which attached to the elder Institutes of the Church. The whole of his design is expressed in that passage of the Constitutions where it is said that "the Order of Preachers was principally and essentially designed for preaching and teaching, in order thereby to communicate to others the fruits of contemplation, and to procure the salvation of souls." Dominic well knew that to sanctify others, the teachers should first be sanctified themselves, and he was content to follow the guidance of antiquity in choosing the means of that sanctification the fruits of which were to be imparted to the world.

He therefore included in his Rule all the essential characteristics of monastic life; the abstinence from meat, and the long fast from Holy Cross until Easter; the observance of silence at the times and in the places appointed; the daily chapter; the strict law of poverty, and the rigorous practice of penance. At the same time a certain freedom and expansiveness were mingled with the strictness of its discipline, which enabled it to bend and mould itself so as to meet its great and primary purpose, the salvation of souls. In the Constitutions of the Order, accordingly, we find, mixed with the usual enactments of regular discipline, certain powers of dispensation, to be used when a literal and unbending adherence to the letter of the Rule would embarrass and impede the brethren in their more active duties. There are also express Constitutions, both for the ordering of their own studies, and

the regulation of such schools as they might open for
the teaching of others ; so that all their active and apostolic
undertakings, instead of being departures from the Rule,
should be provided for in it, and partake of its own
spirit and discipline. We may therefore consider contemplation, apostolic labour for souls, and the especial cultivation
of theological science, as the three objects which Dominic
sought to unite and to provide for in the Constitutions of
his Order.

We must now proceed to give a brief account of the
brethren who joined with the saint in the deliberations
held at Prouille, and who must be regarded as the founda-
tion-stones of the Order. Of Bertrand of Garrigua, the
saint's beloved companion, and Matthew of France, the
former prior of Castres, something has been said already;
both enjoyed the peculiar confidence of the holy founder,
and were afterwards charged by him with important undertakings. The two brethren, William de Claret, of Pamiers,
and Noel, a native of Prouille, have also been named as
residing at the latter place, where they had the direction
of the nuns. The first of these had been a missioner among
the Albigenses in the time of Diego of Azevedo, by whom he
was employed to superintend the temporal affairs of the little
company. After wearing the habit of the Friars Preachers
for twenty years, he left the Order and joined the Cistercians,
being, it is said, dissatisfied with the law of absolute poverty,
which by that time had been enjoined. Not content with
this, he even tried to use his influence with the nuns to
induce them to follow his example, an attempt which proved
altogether without success. Of Brother Noel we know but
little, except that he was one of the saint's first companions,
and that he was unhappily drowned in the river Blan, when
on a journey to Limoux.

Suero Gomez was a Portuguese of noble birth, who left
the royal Court to join the army of De Montfort against the
Albigenses. He was one of those who witnessed the deliverance of the fourteen English pilgrims, and who, having
assisted in bringing them to shore, shortly afterwards passed

to the company of Dominic; he is said to have been distinguished for many virtues, and was the founder of the Order in Portugal. Michael de Fabra, a Spaniard of noble blood, was the first lecturer on theology in the Order, and held that office in the convent of St. James, at Paris. He was also a celebrated preacher, and accompanied King James of Aragon in his expedition against Majorca. "So great was the esteem had of him," says Michael Pio, "that during the fifteen months that the siege lasted nothing was done in the camp, either by soldiers or captains, save what was by him ordered." Such was the reverence in which he was held, that after the conquest of the island he was looked on as its father and ruler, and his name was always invoked next after God and the Blessed Virgin. Divers stories of his apparitions and supernatural assistance to the Christian soldiers are to be found; and the Moors were themselves accustomed to say, that it was the Blessed Virgin. and Brother Michael, not the Spaniards, who conquered the island.

Another Michael, called De Uzero, was afterwards sent by Dominic to establish the Order in Spain. Brother Dominic, called sometimes the little, on account of his stature, or by others, Dominic the second (and confused by some writers with Dominic of Segovia,[1] or the third), had also been one of the holy patriarch's first companions in the missions of Toulouse. "He was," says his historian, "little of body, but powerful of soul, and of great sanctity." He, too, was a wonderful preacher, and cleared the Court of King Ferdinand, "as it were, in a moment," of all buffoons, flatterers, and other evil company.

Next comes Lawrence, the Englishman. He was one of the pilgrims whom Dominic saved from drowning, as before related, and by many is called the Blessed Lawrence, a title

---

[1] Many authors tell us, that "Dominic the little" was the first Provincial of Lombardy, and afterwards of Spain; and that he was likewise called "Dominic of Segovia." It is clear, however, from the account of Michael Pio, that the two Dominics were distinct persons, and that Dominic of Segovia, the Provincial of Lombardy, was *not* the same as the early companion of the holy patriarch of his Order.

he seems to have deserved by his sanctity and his gifts of prophecy and miracles. Then there was Stephen of Metz, a Belgian, "a man of rare abstinence, the frequent mace-rator of his own body, and of burning zeal for the eternal salvation of his neighbour;" and John of Navarre, whom St. Dominic had brought with him from Rome to Toulouse, and there given the habit. He it was to whom St. Dominic gave the celebrated lesson on holy poverty, which we shall notice in its proper place. "He was then imperfect," says his biographer, "but he afterwards made many journeys with St. Dominic, and by familiar conversation with him learnt how to be a saint, which indeed he became." He was one of those who gave his evidence on the canonization of the holy Father. Peter of Madrid accompanied Suero Gomez into Portugal, but afterwards, journeying into Castile, became the founder of several convents in that kingdom. The two citizens of Toulouse, Peter Cellani and Thomas, have already been mentioned. Oderic of Normandy had been a Crusader, and becoming a lay-brother, accompanied Matthew of France to Paris, where he was known and reverenced for his "perfection of sanctity." Lastly, there was Manes Guzman, St. Dominic's own brother, "a man of great contemplation, zealous for souls, and illustrious for sanctity." He had a great gift of preaching, although his attraction was wholly to contemplation. Michael Pio gives us his character in a few expressive words: "Above all things he loved quiet and solitude, taking most delight in a contemplative life, in which he made marvellous profit; and in living alone with God and himself, rather than with others. He had the government of the nuns who were established at Madrid. Sincerity and simplicity shone in him above all things; and many miracles declared to the world how dear he was to heaven." Of those named above, Bertrand of Garrigua and Manes Guzman are numbered among the Blessed of the Order.

As soon as the little Council of Prouille had concluded its deliberations, Dominic returned to Toulouse. There fresh demonstrations of the friendship of Fulk awaited him.

With the consent of his Chapter he made him the grant of three churches: St. Romain, at Toulouse, and two others; one at Pamiers, and another, dedicated to our Lady, near Puy-Laurens. These in time had each a convent attached to them; but that of St. Romain was begun immediately, for Peter Cellani's house was no longer adapted to their increased numbers. A very humble cloister was therefore built contiguous to the church, and over it were placed the cells of the brethren, "which were arranged," says Blessed Jordan, "for the purposes of study and religious retirement." This was the first regular house of the Order; it was poor enough, and soon completed, and the little community removed into it in the summer of 1216.

As soon as the brethren were established in their new convent, Dominic prepared to return to Rome, to report to the Sovereign Pontiff the decision which had been taken, and to obtain from him a formal confirmation of the Order and its Rule. But before doing this he gave a proof of his disinterestedness, and of that love of poverty which he so greatly prized, by making over to the nuns of Prouille all the lands which had been granted by various benefactors to himself and his brethren. It was even with reluctance that he retained the revenues recently given for the support of the community by Fulk of Toulouse; but the prudence of doing so was pressed on him by the bishop; and the obligation of absolute poverty, which was afterwards made a law of the Order, had not as yet been introduced into the Constitutions. Before taking leave of the brethren he made them an earnest and touching address, in which, says Flaminius, he charged them to keep to the old paths and the traditions of the holy Fathers, by adhering to which they would be preserved from the danger of falling into heresy, or any kind of error. Then appointing Bertrand of Garrigua, as before, to govern the community in his absence, he once more set out for Rome, about the feast of St. John. Baptist, 1216.

It was in the course of his journey to Rome that Dominic received the intelligence of the death of Pope Innocent III.,

which took place at Perugia on the 16th of July, 1216, and
of the election as his successor of Cardinal Savelli, who took
the title of Honorius III.   The news exceedingly afflicted
the saint, not only because the deceased Pontiff had shown
himself a sure and faithful friend, but because of the loss
sustained by the Church which he had so wisely and powerfully governed.   It was, moreover, no small anxiety to have
to treat for the confirmation of an unknown and untried
Institute with a new Pontiff, of whose sentiments Dominic
was wholly ignorant.   Nevertheless he continued his journey,
and arriving at the Roman capital in the month of September,
found the Pope still absent at Perugia, which caused some
further delay.   During the interval the saint lived a poor
and obscure life, begging his bread from door to door during
the day, and at night having no other lodging than the
churches.   Many difficulties seemed to oppose the success
of his undertaking, for the Pontiff was engaged in various
important and troublesome negotiations, and his Court was
full of dissensions.   Dominic, however, took refuge in prayer
and patience, and in his long night watches commended the
cause he had at heart before many a holy shrine.   But
the spot that was dearest to him above all was the ancient
Vatican Basilica.   There night after night he invoked the
aid of St. Peter, the Prince of the Apostles, and of the
glorious St. Paul, his own especial patron; and whilst thus
praying he was granted a vision well fitted to strengthen and
encourage him during this time of suspense.   For the two
great Apostles appearing to him as he prayed, St. Peter
bestowed on him a staff, and St. Paul a book, addressing
him in these memorable words: " Go and preach, for to this
ministry thou art called; " and as they disappeared from his
sight, he seemed to behold his brethren going forth two and
two throughout the whole world, preaching the Word of God
to all nations.

Great, indeed, was the joy which filled his heart at such
an assurance of the Divine approval.   He knew full well
that if God were with him no human opposition would avail
against him, and felt that the sublime vocation of himself

and his brethren had now received a seal from heaven. Some writers add that the Holy Spirit was at the same time seen to rest on his head in the form of a fiery tongue, and others that he was thenceforth specially confirmed in grace, and freed from many temptations. It is certain that he regarded what had passed as a most precious token of favour, and in memory of it, he ever afterwards carried with him, says Flaminius, whether at home or abroad, a staff, together with the Book of the Gospels and St. Paul's Epistles, the study of which he constantly urged on his brethren.[2]

The confidence of the saint at length obtained its merited reward. Towards the end of the year Pope Honorius returned to Rome, and two Bulls confirming the new Order were issued by him on the 23rd of December, 1216.

The first of these Bulls is of considerable length; it grants a variety of privileges and immunities to the brethren, and confirms the Order in the possession of all the lands, churches, and revenues with which it had been endowed by Fulk and other benefactors. The second Bull is much shorter, and appears to have been intended that the brethren might carry a copy of it with them in their apostolic journeys to present to the bishops through whose dioceses they might pass, thus furnishing them with testimonials of due authority.[3]

"Honorius, Bishop, servant of the servants of God, to our dear son, Dominic, prior of St. Romain, of Toulouse, and to your brethren who have made, or shall make, profession of regular life, health and the apostolic benediction. We, considering that the brethren of your Order will be the champions of the faith and true light of the world, do confirm the Order in all its lands and possessions present

---

[2] The staff he was accustomed to use was still preserved at the convent of Bologna when Père Réchac wrote his history.

[3] In the Chapter of Strasburg, 1296, it was ordained that this second Bull should be carried by all religious sent on a journey as an authentic proof of their apostolic mission.

and to come ; and we take the Order itself, with all its goods
and rights, under our protection and government.

"Given at Sta. Sabina, at Rome, on the 11th of the
kalends of January, this first year of our Pontificate.

"HONORIUS."

CONFIRMATION OF THE RULE.

The church of Sta. Sabina, whence these Bulls were
issued, adjoined what was then the palace of the Savelli
family and the residence of the reigning Pontiff. Both of
them were granted on the same day, but in neither of them
did the new Order receive the title of *Preachers*, which had
been bestowed on it by Innocent III. The manner in which
this omission was rectified is thus related by Thomas of
Cantimpré, the disciple of Albert the Great. "Pope
Honorius, when publishing the two Bulls, in which he
granted the confirmation of the Order, did not make use
of the title of Brothers Preachers, but desired that the
inscription should be written on the back of the folded

patent, 'To Master Dominic and the Preaching Brothers.'
But instead of this the notary wrote, 'To the Brothers
Preachers.' The Pope, reading over the document before
signing it, asked of the notary why he had altered the words.
'Because,' replied the notary, 'the word *Preacher*, signifies
both the act and the office, whereas that of *Preaching* implies
indeed the act, but does not denote the office, and your
Holiness has thought fit to commit to them both the act and
the office.' The Pope approved this explanation and desired
that the title should stand so amended, and thenceforth the
Order, thus solemnly confirmed, became universally known
under the title of the Order of Friars Preachers."

Meanwhile, the saint's daily life during the period of his
stay in Rome, was anything but an idle one. Not only did
he preach almost daily in one or other of the churches, but
he took part in many works of charity, both spiritual and
corporal. Outside the walls of the city there resided at that
time certain recluses, commonly called *Murate*, from their
habitation. They lived a sort of eremitical life, each
in a poor little cell, separate one from the other, in which
they were enclosed, never leaving them ; being moved to this
singular life by a particular spirit of mortification and solitude. Almost every morning, after celebrating Mass and
reciting the Divine Office, Dominic went to visit them,
conversing with them on holy subjects, and exhorting them
to perseverance. He was also accustomed to administer to
them the Sacraments of Penance and the Holy Eucharist,
and was, in short, what would be now called their director.

During this visit he also formed ties of close intimacy
with several distinguished persons then residing at the
Roman capital, who afterwards became, in various ways,
associated with the history of the Order. He had, indeed,
that aptitude for friendship, which is to be found in those
who, possessing large and deep sympathies, have also the
special power of communicating themselves to others. Hence
the history of his life is embellished with the records of many
dear and noble friendships, which, once formed, lasted even
until death.

Among those whose acquaintance he at this time made, was Ugolini Conti, Cardinal Bishop of Ostia, and afterwards successor to Honorius, under the title of Gregory IX. He was already the friend and protector of St. Francis and the Friars Minors, and now for the first time made acquaintance with the founder of the Friars Preachers. He was advanced in age, but a man of warm and enthusiastic feelings, who ever accounted the close personal ties which united him to these two great men, as among the greatest privileges of his life. At his house, Dominic also met another younger friend, William de Montferrat, who was spending Easter with the Cardinal. The charm of the saint's intercourse, which we are assured was of a very peculiar and winning kind, so captivated him that he resolved to take the habit of the new Order. He has left the account of the whole matter in his own words. " It is now about sixteen years," he says, " since I went to Rome to spend Lent there; and the present Pope, who was then Bishop of Ostia, received me into his house. At that time Brother Dominic, the founder and first Master General of the Order of Preachers, was at the Roman Court, and often visited my lord of Ostia. This gave me an opportunity of knowing him; his conversation pleased me, and I began to love him. Many a time did we speak together of the eternal salvation of our own souls, and those of all men. I never spoke to a man of equal perfection, or one so wholly taken up with the salvation of mankind, although indeed I have had intercourse with many very holy religious. I therefore determined to join him, as one of his disciples, after I had studied theology at the university of Paris for two years, and it was so agreed between us; and also, that after he had established the future discipline of his brethren, we should go together to convert, first, the pagans of Persia or of Greece, and then those who live in the southern countries." [4]

We gather from these words how entirely the saint had opened his whole heart to the writer, to whom he not only made known the burning zeal for the salvation of souls with

[4] *Acts of Bologna.*

which he was consumed, but confided that cherished desire
which had been shared long ago with Diego of Azevedo, and
never laid aside, that he might one day be suffered to labour
for the conversion of heathen nations.   His great heart was
inflamed with an ardour which knew no limits so long as
there were souls to save.   Réchac enumerates four distinct
occasions on which this desire of his was formally expressed,
and gives us to understand that the idea of offering himself
to preach to the Saracens and unbelievers of the East, had
been inspired at this time by the preparations then actually
going on at Rome for the promotion of a fresh Crusade.
For Innocent III. had before his death equipped a fleet to
proceed to the Holy Land, the prosecution of this undertaking having been urgently pressed by the late Council,
and the whole matter had engaged the serious attention
of Honorius from the first moment of his accession.   Very
probably, therefore, the plans discussed between the two
friends were connected with the memory of that land towards
which all Christians still turned with love unspeakable, and
which they would have given their heart's best blood to
redeem from the hands of the infidel.   Doubtless the soul
of St. Dominic took fire with the hope that he and his
children should one day take part in the glorious enterprize,
and we can imagine the charm which such vast and glowing
thoughts, clothed in the eloquence which was all his own,
must have exerted over the minds of those who listened to
him.   He endeavoured also to persuade Bartholomew of
Clusa, archdeacon of Mascon and canon of Chartres, one
of his own penitents, to enter the new Order, for he clearly
discerned that such was God's vocation to his soul.   Bartholomew, however, turned a deaf ear to all he said, and Dominic
predicted that many things would befall him in consequence
of his resistance to grace, which things, he himself assures
us, did really afterwards happen to him ; but what they were
does not appear.

On the reception of the Bulls of Confirmation, the saint
at once prepared to return to St. Romain, but before doing
so he took one step of great importance and significance.

He had, of course, made the religious vows many years before, when he was professed as a Canon Regular at Osma ; but he was now about to establish among his brethren a rule of life which addèd far stricter monastic obligations to those embraced by the Canons. But whilst about to impose these on others, he desired first to bind himself to their observance, and before leaving Rome, therefore, with the consent of Honorius, he made his solemn profession as the first Friar Preacher, in the hands of the Sovereign Pontiff.

DISPERSION OF THE BRETHREN.

———•———

## CHAPTER XIV.

### DISPERSION OF THE BRETHREN.

#### 1217, 1218.

IT was not until the May of 1217 that Dominic was able
to return to Toulouse, where he found his brethren established in their new convent of St. Romain, to which they had
removed in the October of the previous year. The joy of
reunion was somewhat qualified on the part of the brethren
when they learned that it was the resolution of the saint very
speedily to disperse the little community which was but just
gathered together. He made known this intention to his
followers almost immediately on his arrival at Toulouse,
where, after addressing them a fervent exhortation on
the rule of life to which they were about by their
profession to pledge themselves, he plainly declared his

intention of sending them forth in companies of twos and threes, in order that they might plant the foundations of their Order in other parts. The plan seemed the height of imprudence; all joined in blaming it and endeavouring to dissuade him from it. But Dominic was inexorable; the vision which he had seen beside the Tomb of the Apostles was fresh in his eye ; their voices yet sounded in his ear. Fulk of Toulouse, De Montfort, the Archbishop of Narbonne, and even his own companions, urged him to pause, but nothing would stir him from his purpose. "My lords and fathers," he said, "do not oppose me, for I know very well what I am about." He felt that the vocation of his children was not to one place, but for all nations; not for themselves alone, but for the Church and the world. "The seed," he said, "will fructify if it is sown; it will but moulder if you hoard it up." Some little time he gave them to consider if they would submit to his determination, with the alternative of withdrawing from the Order. But his followers had too profound a veneration for his person and character to oppose their judgments to his, and soon yielded the point. The event showed how entirely his resolution had been guided by the Spirit of God.

Meanwhile in the preparation which he made for this dispersion of his children, he showed how great was his anxiety for the preservation among them of the observance and spirit of their Rule. The convent of Toulouse he designed to be the model which was to be followed in all later foundations, and he therefore made several regulations to render it more perfect in its arrangements. He thought it well that the brethren should from time to time meet together for mutual counsel and encouragement. For this purpose he caused two large additional rooms to be built, one for containing the habits of the community, the other for the brethren to assemble in; for until now, like the Cistercians, they had no rooms but their cells and the refectory. These two additions to their little convent added materially to the comfort of those who were to be left to inhabit it, and were welcome proofs of the watchful thoughtfulness of their Father.

M

He was very earnest in enjoining the strict observance of that part of St. Austin's Rule which forbids all private appropriation of the smallest article, and prohibited the use of the words "mine" and "thine," as contrary to holy poverty. Even in the church itself he desired that the spirit of poverty should never be forgotten; and though he constantly insisted on its being kept a mirror of cleanliness, yet he forbade all elegancies and curiosities, and even ordered that the sacred vestments should not be made of silk. As to the cells of the brethren, the poverty he enjoined was absolute: a little cane bedstead and a miserable bench were the only furniture he allowed. They had no doors, in order that the Superior might always be able to see the brethren as he passed along; the dormitory resembled, as closely as possible, that of a hospital.

But besides these regulations for the exterior of community life, he at the same time applied himself to such interior training of his disciples as should best fit them for the apostolic duties of their sublime vocation. He failed not to impress on his followers the necessity that the members of an Order of Preachers should apply with ardour to sacred letters, and exhorted them above all to steep themselves in the study both of the Old and New Testament. At the same time, well knowing that learning alone does but foster the pride that puffeth up, he was no less earnest in bidding them unite prayer and meditation to the pursuit of science, that digesting in prayer what they had learnt from study, they might be the better able to communicate its fruit to others. And to this end he willed that wherever any convent of the Order should be founded in time to come, special attention should be given to the choral recitation of the Divine Office, the celebration of which he would have always accompanied by the chant and sacred ceremonies.

Flaminius, in the very interesting account which he gives of these early beginnings of the Order at Toulouse, adds that the holy Father, whilst devoting himself to the spiritual training of his children, failed not to impose on himself an altogether new rule of life, to which he faithfully adhered even until death. He would not be merely the teacher, but the exemplar of those into whose hands he was about to entrust the foundation of his Order in distant countries; and whilst seeking to form them to that ideal of religious life which should henceforth mark the true Friar Preacher, he desired himself to be the first to lead the way. And to this he was the more urged by the words of Pope Honorius, in a patent addressed to the prior and community of St. Romain, which the saint had brought with him from Rome, together. with the Bull of Confirmation. In this document the Pontiff, after giving thanks to God, the Author of all grace, for inspiring the brethren with their generous design, welcomes them as labourers in the field of the Lord, and champions of the faith, who shall hereafter win glorious victories for the salvation of souls by the apostolic ministry of preaching. But he reminds them that this can only be done by those who, burning with the fire of charity, spread abroad the good odour of holiness, that so, commending themselves as true and faithful servants of God, they may freely distribute to others the talents which they have received.[1]

The manner in which the saint began from this time to order his life was rigorous indeed. Whether in or out of the convent, he never broke the rule of abstinence from meat, and kept an almost continual fast. He chose for himself the worst accommodation and the poorest habit in the house, and never allowed himself the luxury of a bed. After Compline it was his custom to watch in prayer before the Blessed Sacrament until Matins, at which he assisted with extraordinary devotion, often going from one side of the choir to the other and animating the brethren to chant with fervour. When the Office was ended, he remained alone in the church for a considerable time longer, praying and offering to God the sacrifice of bloody disciplines; and when at last he gave his body a little repose, it was taken either on the bare ground, at the foot of the altar, or on a plank, or something equally austere and incommodious. Even then he slept but little, and the brethren who occupied the

[1] Réchac, p. 302.

cells nearest to the place of his repose, were often awakened
by his sighs and tears, and the strong crying with which he
poured out his soul to God in prayer for the salvation of
souls.   At home or abroad he strictly kept the rule of silence
which he would have observed by others, and even when he
spoke, he was never known to utter an idle word, observing
the law which he never wearied to impress on his brethren,
that the tongue of the religious should never be used save
to speak either *to* God or *of* God.   And yet to all this
austerity of life he united a tranquil cheerfulness which won
the hearts of all men, for his countenance was always serene
and gay, as that of one to whom the practice of penance
brings no bitterness, but rather sweetness unspeakable.
Under the guidance of a master who presented in his own
life a model of the perfection which he taught with his lips,
it is no wonder that the novices of St. Romain made rapid
progress, and that in these days of early fervour the example
of their holy Father was closely followed by many of those
who were formed under his personal direction.

It was whilst thus engaged in the training of his disciples,
that the saint had a vision which foretold to him the
approaching death of the Count de Montfort.   He seemed
to see an immense tree, in whose branches a great quantity
of birds had taken refuge; the tree was luxuriant and
beautiful, and spread out its arms over the earth: suddenly
it fell, and the birds all took flight, and Dominic was given
to understand that this represented the fall of him who had
been known in a special manner as the protector and " father
of the poor."   This was accomplished in the following year,
when the two Raymunds having regained possession of
Toulouse, the Count de Montfort fell at the siege of that city.
It is probable that his knowledge of the approaching return
of war hastened Dominic in the execution of his designs.
He accordingly fixed the approaching feast of the Assumption for the assembling of all the brethren at Notre Dame
de Prouille that they might there pronounce their solemn
vows before leaving for their respective missions.[2]

[2] John of Navarre in his deposition, which forms part of the Acts of

On the appointed day, the little company all met to keep the festival with an unusual solemnity in the church of their mother-house of Prouille. It was a deeply touching spectacle to all present, and to Dominic himself one of profound and singular emotion. Great numbers of persons from the surrounding country, who knew the circumstances which had gathered the brethren together, came to witness the ceremony of the day; among them was De Montfort himself, and several prelates, all anxious to ascertain the final determination of St. Dominic as to the destination of his little flock. It was he himself who offered the Holy Sacrifice, and who, still habited in the sacred vestments, preached to the assembled audience in language some of which is still preserved to us. Its severity compels us to draw conclusions little favourable to the people of Languedoc. "Now for many years past," he said, "have I sounded the truths of the Gospel in your ears, by my preaching, my entreaties, and my prayers, and with tears in my eyes. But, as they are wont to say in my country, the stick must be used when blessings are of no avail. Lo! princes and rulers will raise all the kingdoms of this world against you; and woe be unto you! they will kill many by the sword, and lay the lands desolate, and overthrow the walls of your cities, and all of you will be reduced to slavery; and so you will come to see, that where blessings avail not, the stick will avail." These dismal announcements were too truly fulfilled; and they indicate that the evils under which the unhappy country had so long laboured had produced an effect which not even the ten years' labour of an apostle had been able to counteract: it was a solemn farewell which framed itself into words of prophetic warning. He then

Bologna, declares that he himself received the habit from the hands of Brother Dominic on the feast of St. Augustine, 1215, and made his vows on the same feast at the convent of St. Romain, as we may suppose, a year later. This declaration is in no way inconsistent with the fact as narrated above, that the subsequent profession of all the brethren took place at the convent of Prouille on the feast of the Assumption, 1217, a fact which rests on the authority of the MS. of Prouille, and is accepted by Echard. Percin, and other writers as a statement of undoubted accuracy.

turned to his own brethren, and reminded them of the first
origin of their Order, the end for which it was instituted, and
the duties to which they stood pledged. Above all, he
exhorted them to confidence in God, and a great and un-
flinching courage, always to prepare for wider fields of
labour, and to be ready to serve the Church, in whatever
way they might be called to work for the conversion of
sinners, heretics, or infidels. His words had an extraordinary effect on those who listened ; any lingering feelings
of dissatisfaction they might have felt were dispelled by
this appeal to the heroism of their nature. Like soldiers
harangued by a favourite leader on the battlefield, they
all seemed kindled with a spark of his own chivalrous ardour,
and were impatient to be led on to the enterprize which
awaited them.

When Dominic had concluded his address, the brethren
knelt before him, and made their solemn vows in his hands,
for until then they had been bound to him by no other tie
than their own will. The nuns of Prouille, in like manner,
all made their profession on the same day, adding the fourth
vow of enclosure.[3] When this ceremony was over, he
declared to each of them the quarter to which they were
destined. The two Fathers, who had until then had the
direction of the convent of Prouille, were to remain there as
before, whilst Peter Cellani and Thomas of Toulouse were
to continue at St. Romain. A large section of his little
company were appointed for the establishment of the Order
in Paris, where flourished the most famous university then
existing; and from the first it entered into the designs of
the holy founder to plant colonies of his brethren in the chief
seats of learning throughout Christendom. No fewer than
seven brethren were therefore set apart for the foundation at
Paris; Manes, the saint's own brother, Michael de Fabra, and
the lay-brother Oderic, were the first despatched, and they
were followed a few weeks later by Bertrand of Garrigua,
Matthew of France, John of Navarre, and Lawrence of
England. Matthew of France was appointed to be the head

[3] Percin.

of this little company, but associated with him in the responsible task of founding the convent was Brother Bertrand, "in whom," says Mamachi, "Dominic had perfect confidence on account of his rare virtue." Indeed, according to this writer, Bertrand alone was charged with the foundation, but it is evident from the words of Blessed Jordan that he only acted conjointly with Matthew, and on his withdrawal from Paris the following year the latter remained Superior of the little company.[4] The four Spaniards, Michael Uzero, Dominic of Segovia, Suero Gomez, and Peter of Madrid, were to be sent to Spain, the saint reserving Stephen of Metz for his own companion to return with him to Rome.

Before they separated to their several destinations, Dominic determined to provide for the future government of the Order in case of his death or removal, for as we have seen, he still cherished the secret design of himself departing for the countries of the infidels, and finding perhaps a martyr's crown among them. He therefore desired them to make a canonical election among themselves of some one who should govern the Order in his absence, or in case of his death. Their choice fell on Matthew of France, who received the title of *Abbot*, a designation never continued in the Order; after his death the brethren were content with the title of *Master* for him who held the chief authority, whilst the other Superiors were called priors and subpriors, names chosen as best befitting the humility of their state. This election being finished, Dominic committed the Bull of Confirmation to the keeping of the new abbot, that it might be solemnly published in the capital of France, and gave them a parting exhortation to keep their vows, and be diligent in founding convents, preaching God's Word, and following their studies; and so dismissed them with his blessing.

One of them, and one only, showed signs of reluctance to obey. It was John of Navarre, who had strongly shared in the sentiments of those ecclesiastics who condemned the holy patriarch for imprudence. He ventured, before departing,

[4] Jordan, apud Echard, t. i. p. 16; Mamachi, *Ann.* lib. 2, 366, 367.

to ask for a little money for his expenses on the way. The request seemed reasonable; but Dominic clearly discerned the secret feelings of distrust and discontent which prompted it. He sharply reproved him, and set before him the example of the disciples whom their Lord sent forth, "having neither scrip nor purse;" then, quickly exchanging severity for the paternal tenderness which was more natural to him, he threw himself at the feet of the Brother, and with tears in his eyes besought him to lay aside his cowardly fears, and to arm himself with a generous trust in God's Providence. "Go in confidence, my son," he said, "for nothing is wanting to those who trust in God." But John still continuing stubborn in his view, and unconvinced of the practicability of travelling two hundred miles without funds, Dominic desired them to give him twelve pence, and then dismissed him.

We are told that some Cistercians who were present expressed their surprise in no measured terms, that he should send out these ignorant, unlettered boys to preach and teach. Dominic bore the officious remarks with the equanimity which he never failed to exhibit on such occasions. "What is it you say, my Brothers," he replied with his accustomed sweetness; "are you not a little like the Pharisees? I know, nay I am certain, that these 'boys' of mine will go and return in safety, and that they will bring back with them great fruit of souls."

Thomas of Cantimpré, relating this anecdote on the authority of Flaminius, remarks that it was indeed a matter worthy of all admiration that in the beginning of the Order, such great things should have been wrought by a few inexperienced youths, many of them delicately nurtured in the world, who going forth as sheep among wolves, escaped the perils which beset their innocence and did the work of apostolic men. He attributes the success which attended their labours and their own preservation in the midst of a perverse and evil generation to the singular devotion cherished by them towards the Blessed Virgin, the peculiar Patroness of the Order, under whose maternal protection they were defended from the assaults of temptation. And he goes on to quote the authority of one who, having heard the confessions of more than a hundred brethren in the early days of the Order, declared that out of that number no less than seventy had kept their baptismal innocence unstained.

One by one then the little companies departed, and by the middle of September the saint found himself left with only three companions at the convent of St. Romain. But the numbers of the community were soon increased by the reception of fresh members, among whom were Poncio Samatan, afterwards founder of the convent of Bayonne, Raymund Fulgaria, or De Felgar, a Narbonnese noble who became successor to Fulk in the bishopric of Toulouse, Arnold of Toulouse, first prior of Lyons, and the Blessed Romeo of Livia, afterwards fifth provincial of Provence. The saint himself was preparing to depart on his return to Rome when a dispute which arose between the brethren of the convent and the procurators of the bishop's court, and which bore reference to the portion of tithes which had been granted to the community by the bishop, gave occasion for him to give another token of his magnificent disinterested-ness. He speedily settled the difficulty by executing a deed in accordance with the views of the procurators, regarding it as a thing hateful to God and man that charity should be wounded for filthy lucre's sake. This document is dated September 11, 1217, only two days before Raymund of Toulouse, by stratagem, regained possession of his ancient capital.

From this time there will be but few occasions for return-ing to the history of those provinces which had been the scenes of the saint's earliest labours, and had witnessed the foundation of his Order. The future course of his life will lead us forward into other countries; the bright star which had risen in Spain, and spent its long meridian in France, was to shed its setting splendour on the fields of Italy. For a time indeed, events seemed to threaten the overthrow of the Catholic cause in Languedoc, and the ultimate triumph of the heretics and their supporters. On the resumption of

hostilities, victory declared itself for the two Raymunds, father
and son, who succeeded in stripping the Count de Montfort
of the greater part of the provinces with which he had been
invested; and in 1218, urged to a last effort for their recovery,
he laid siege to Toulouse with a force wholly unequal to the
enterprize. It was sunrise on the 25th of June, when word was
brought him of an ambuscade of the enemy. He received
the message with tranquillity; and arming himself with his
usual composure, he went to hear Mass before going to the
field.   Another despatch arrived in the middle of the ceremony; they had attacked his machines of war, would he not
hasten to their defence?   " Leave me!" was his reply,
" I stir not till I have seen the Sacrament of my redemption!"
Yet once again another messenger rushed into the church;
the troops could hold out no longer; he would surely come
to their aid.   He turned to the speaker with a stern and
melancholy air: " I will not go," he said, " till I have seen
my Saviour."   He knew his last hour was at hand; the
sadness of deep disappointment was in his heart, but he
surely made that day a solemn offering and resignation to
God of the life whose human hopes had failed.   When the
priest elevated the Sacred Host, De Montfort knelt and
uttered the words, *Nunc dimittis.*   Then he went out to the
scene of combat.   His presence had its wonted effect on
his followers, as well as on his enemies.   The men of Toulouse
fled back to the city, pursued by the victorious Crusaders;
but a stone from the wall struck their gallant leader to the
ground; and smiting his breast with his hand, he expired,
recommending his soul to God, and with the name of Mary
on his lips.

His remains were honourably laid to rest in the cathedral
of Carcassonne, whence they were afterwards removed to
his own territory of Montfort d'Amaury, [near Paris; but
his original tombstone may still be seen at Carcassonne,
recalling the memory of one whose character presents us
with as fair an example of Christian chivalry as we shall
find portrayed on the page of history. Even Raymund VII.
himself was forced to bear witness to his merits.   " Often,"

TOMBSTONE OF SIMON
DE MONTFORT.

writes his chaplain, William de Puy-Laurens, "have I heard the last Count of Toulouse, although his deadly enemy, speak in praise of the courage, the fidelity, and the magnanimity of the Count de Montfort, and declare him to have possessed every quality that belonged to a great prince."

His friendship towards the Order of Friars Preachers survived in his family. One of his daughters, Amice, or, as the Italians sweetly name her, Amicitia, the wife of the Seigneur de Joigny, bore so peculiar a love to the children of Dominic that she used all her endeavours to induce her only son to take the habit. He, however, followed the army of St. Louis to the Holy Land; but whilst detained in the island of Cyprus, he was taken with a mortal sickness, and on his death-bed, remembering his mother's prayers, he sent for the friars, and received the habit from their hands. When the tidings were brought her, she gave thanks to God, and on the death of her husband resolved to enter the Order herself. She was constantly repeating the words, "If I cannot be a Friar Preacher, I will at least be one of their sisters;" and she succeeded, after much opposition, in founding the convent of Montargis, where she herself took the habit, and died in the odour of sanctity about the year 1235.

The warlike struggle continued to rage under varying fortunes for ten years after the death of De Montfort, whose son, Amaury,[5] unable to resist the arms of Raymund VII., resigned his rights over the county of Toulouse to King Louis VIII. For a time the triumph of the house of St. Gilles

[5] De Montfort left four sons, the youngest of whom was Simon, Earl of Leicester, so well known in English history.

seemed complete, and under its restored rule the Friars Preachers of St. Romain had much to suffer. Count Raymund VII. followed close in the footsteps of his father, and far from repressing the violence of the heretics, showed himself their constant protector. But a term was put to his tyranny in 1226, when all the nobles of the disputed provinces, as by a common impulse, made their voluntary submission to the French crown.

Two years later the authority of the young King St. Louis IX. was firmly established by the treaty of Paris, and Raymund, finding all further resistance useless, sought reconciliation with the Church, and repaired to Paris to fulfil the required conditions. There standing in the porch of Notre Dame, barefoot and bareheaded, and in the humiliating garb of a penitent, he swore to observe the terms of the treaty, one clause of which required him to give his only daughter in marriage to the King's brother, Alphonsus, who, on receiving the hand of the bride, was to be declared the heir to her father's territories. Then being absolved from excommunication, he was dubbed knight by the young King, a dignity which up till then he had, as an excommunicated rebel, been deemed unworthy to receive. At the same time Toulouse was relieved from interdict, and the heretics being driven out of the city, the Catholic worship became once more established within its walls. In compliance with one of the articles of the treaty of peace, a university was established at Toulouse, and Count Raymund had to contribute a large annual sum towards the maintenance of its professors of theology, canon law, and arts. The foundation of this university was decreed for the express purpose of supplying sound Catholic teaching at the very head-quarters of heresy. From this time the power of the Albigenses and their supporters was broken, and though the entire extinction of the heresy was only gradually obtained, yet the restoration of religion throughout the country so long laid waste by their sacrilegious hands, may be said to date from its submission to the crown of France.

# CHAPTER XV.

RETURN TO ROME.

1217.

In the October of 1217, Dominic bade farewell to St. Romain,. and set out on his return to Rome, accompanied by Stephen of Metz. None of his early biographers have preserved any particulars of this journey, over which there hangs a certain obscurity. Nevertheless, a careful study of local tradition enables us to follow his course with tolerable certainty, and makes it apparent that on leaving Toulouse he bent his steps northwards. We find him first at Pamiers, where the Count de Montfort and the newly-appointed Cardinal Legate had met to confer on the altered aspect of affairs caused by the recent successes of the two Raymunds. After urging on them the necessity of adopting vigorous measures for the recovery of Toulouse, and recommending to their joint protection the two communities of Prouille and St. Romain, the saint continued his course towards Paris. According to the archives of the cathedral of Puy, he visited that famous sanctuary on his road, and prepared the way for a foundation afterwards made there in the year 1221. It is probable that he more than once paid his devotions at Puy, and some writers suppose that it was there that our Lady revealed to him the devotion of the Holy Rosary. From Puy he continued his journey to Clermont, and there so touched the hearts of the people by his preaching that they conjured him to stay with them, offering him more than one site for a convent. The saint promised to send them brethren as soon as he should be able to do so, and a foundation was accordingly made there about three years later.

Clermont preserved the memory of this visit with the utmost
jealousy, and an ancient inscription over the door of the
chapter-room claimed for this house the honour of being
the fourth in the whole Order, though this was certainly
inaccurate. ✝ Reaching Paris, the saint found the seven
brethren recently despatched thither suffering great discouragement. Both during their journey, and on their first arrival
in the capital, they had met with difficulties and obstacles of
all kinds. It was Laurence the Englishman who cheered
his companions, and animated them to persevere at a moment
when they were half-tempted to abandon their enterprize.
We read in his Life that as they drew near the city full of
doubt and anxiety, God, willing to encourage them, revealed
to his servant Laurence, all that should afterwards befall
them there; the abundant favours He would bestow on the
convent which they should found, and the many stars of
learning and sanctity which should arise within its walls.
Making known this revelation to his brethren, they received
it in faith, out of the great opinion they had of his sanctity,
and joyfully entered the city, where in due time all his
predictions were fulfilled. Nevertheless, their first experiences
were hard and difficult. They were all strangers in Paris
with the exception of Matthew of France, who had formerly
studied at the university; and being entirely without means,
they had to beg their bread for daily support. At first they
occupied a little house situated between the bishop's palace
and the Hotel Dieu, a locality which enabled them the
more easily to frequent the schools, and to render the bishop
such assistance in the ministry of preaching as he might
require of them. At the end of ten months passed in extreme
distress, John de Barastre, dean of St. Quentin, an Englishman
by birth, and one of the King's chaplains, being struck
by their piety, the eloquence of their preaching, and their
patient endurance of so much poverty, was moved to befriend
them. He had some years previously founded a hospital
for pilgrims which stood on Mount St. Geneviève, to which
was attached a chapel dedicated to St. James. This chapel
was often visited by the brethren, and their modest and devout

aspect attracting the notice of the dean, an acquaintance began which soon ripened into friendship; and he ended by making over to them, with the consent of his colleagues, the church and hospital which was thenceforth to be known as the Dominican convent of St. James.

If St. Dominic really visited Paris in 1217, it must have been for the purpose of consoling and encouraging his brethren in their early days of depression; the visit must have been of very short duration, and no particulars regarding it have been preserved. The first place where we find any certain evidence of his presence after leaving Pamiers is Metz, the registers of which city declare him to have arrived there in company with Stephen of Metz in the latter part of 1217. He was warmly received by the citizens, who flocked to hear his preaching, several asking and receiving from his hands the habit of the Order. An image of our Blessed Lady in one of the churches, before which he was accustomed to pray, was long held by them in great veneration; it obtained the title of "The Virgin of St. Dominic," and on the foundation in the city of a convent of the Order, it was transported thither and placed in the dormitory of the religious. Yielding to the pressing solicitations of the citizens, Dominic consented to leave Stephen of Metz among them for the purpose of founding this convent; a design which the latter was prevented from executing by his early death, though it was afterwards carried out by his fellow-citizen, Guerric of Metz. † The saint himself continued his journey, passing through Germany and Switzerland. Having crossed the Alps, he directed his steps towards Venice, visiting Milan, Padua, and finally Brescia, on his way. At Milan he was hospitably entertained by the canons of St. Nazzaro, who received him as one of themselves, he and his companion still wearing the habit of the Canons Regular. At Padua his preaching attracted crowds of the citizens, who earnestly besought him to give them a colony of his brethren. Unable at that time to comply with their request, he promised to satisfy them as soon as he could, and passed on to Venice, which he entered together

with four companions, Gregory, Henry, Albert, and Otho,[1]
whose names indicate them to have joined him either in
Metz or in Germany.    The fact that the first visit of the
saint to Venice took place in 1217, is proved by ancient
records, preserved in the convent of SS. John and Paul, and
sent to Rome by the Fathers of that convent.   " In the year
1217," they say, " the holy Father Dominic came to Venice
with a few other brethren, and received from the Republic
the oratory then dedicated to St. Daniel, but which after his
canonization was called the chapel of St. Dominic."    The
circumstances which led to his obtaining the grant of this
chapel are related by Castiglio, who, however, assigns them
the date of 1221, to which date undoubtedly belongs the real
foundation of the convent.   " There was," he says, " at that
time in Venice, a little church or hermitage, dedicated to
St. Daniel, which the Doge Giacomo Tiepolo, beheld in a
dream adorned with a multitude of most lovely flowers,
blossoming there as in a garden.   As he stood and gazed
with wonder at their beauty, he saw a company of angels
descend, carrying thuribles in their hands, and passing in and
out among the flowers, they swung their censers to and fro,
thus adding to the exquisite perfume.   Presently there came
into the garden a flight of snow-white doves, having on their
heads crosses of gold, and as he was still beholding these
things with great delight, he heard a voice which declared
to him that it was God's will to be served in that place by
a community of white-robed preachers.   Awaking from his
dream the Doge assembled the Signoria, and made known to
them what he had seen, and all with common consent agreed
to bestow the church with grounds adjoining on Brother
Dominic, that a convent of his Order might there be
founded."   Here then arose a few years later the great
convent of SS. John and Paul, remains of the ancient fabric
being preserved in a portion of the building called the
novitiate.   So great was the love which the Doge bore to
this foundation that he chose it for the place of his sepulture,
and before his death gave orders that in memory of the

----

[1] *Prog.* p. 309.

above event, there might be painted on his tomb the representation of a flower-garden, wherein should appear the angels with their thuribles and the doves with their golden crosses.[2] Malvenda considers it probable that it was at this time also that the saint sent brethren to Spalatro in Dalmatio, the convent in which place was certainly founded not later than 1218, by a religious whose name was Gregory, and who is supposed to have been the same already mentioned as having accompanied St. Dominic to Venice.

┤During this journey Dominic followed the same rule which he observed in the course of all his apostolic wanderings. They were always made on foot, he and his companions depending on charity for their support, and preaching in all the places through which they passed./ Malvenda remarks on the wonderful recollection which was exhibited in his exterior as he travelled along, stick in hand, with his bundle on his shoulders, and absorbed in God. As soon as he was out of the towns or villages he would stop and take off his shoes, performing the rest of his journey barefoot, however rough and bad the roads might be. If a sharp stone or thorn entered his feet, he would turn to his companions with that cheerful and joyous air which was so peculiar to him, and say, "This is penance," and such kind of sufferings were a peculiar pleasure to him. Coming once to a place covered with sharp flints, he said to his companion, "Ah! miserable wretch that I was, I was once obliged to put on my shoes in passing this spot." "Why so?" said the Brother. "Because it had rained so much," replied Dominic. He would never let his companions carry his bundle or his shoes, though they often begged him to suffer them to do so. When he looked down from the heights which they were descending, over any country or city which

---

[2] *Prog.* p 307. In notices of the foundations of convents in Italy, we frequently find a discrepancy of dates similar to that which appears above. The fact is easily explained. The ancient conventual records from which Father Michael Pio has collected so many interesting particulars, often assign as the date of their foundation that of the first visit paid by the saint to their city, this being in general only a prelude to an actual foundation made some time later.

N

they were about to enter, he would pause, and look earnestly at it, often weeping as he thought of the miseries men suffered there, and of the offences they committed against God.   Then, as he pursued his journey and drew nearer, he would put on his shoes, and, kneeling down, would pray that his sins might not draw down on them the chastise-ment of heaven.   The prayer that he was accustomed to use at such time is preserved in the MS. of Prouille, and runs as follows: " O Lord, in Thy goodness regard not my sins, but withhold Thine anger from these people among whom I come; punish them not, neither destroy them for my iniquities."[3]

There was in his character a singular mixture of that joyous cheerfulness so invariably to be found in a high and chivalrous mind, with a tender melancholy which had in it nothing morose, but rather flowed from profound reverence for the purity of God, the outrages against Whom, as they hourly came before him, were felt with an exquisite sensi-bility.   He seldom looked about him, and never when in towns or other places where he was not alone.   His eyes were generally cast down, and he never seemed to notice anything curious or remarkable on the way.   If he had to pass a river he would make the sign of the Cross, and then enter it without hesitation, and was always the first to ford it.   If it rained, or any other discomfort disturbed him on the road, he praised and blessed God, singing in a loud voice his favourite hymn, the *Ave Maris Stella*, or the *Veni Creator*.   More than once at his word the rain ceased, and the swollen rivers were passed without difficulty.

He constantly kept the fasts and abstinences of his Rule, and the silence prescribed by the Constitutions until after Prime; and this silence he insisted on being also observed by the others; though, as regarded the fasts and abstinences, he was indulgent in dispensing with them for the brethren whilst they were travelling; requiring them to eat twice a day, an indulgence he never extended to himself.   Then, as they went along, he would beguile the way with talking of

[3] Percin, *Mon. Con. Tol.* p. 5.

the things of God, or he instructed his companions in points of spiritual doctrine, or read to them; and this kind of teaching he enjoined on the other brethren when travelling with younger companions. Sometimes, however, he would say, "Go on before, and let us think a little of our Divine Lord." This was the signal that he wished to be left to silent meditation. Then remaining behind to escape observation, he would very soon begin to pray aloud, with tears and sighs, losing all thought of the road he was following or the possible presence of others. Sometimes they had to turn back and search for him, and would find him kneeling in some thicket or lonely place without seeming to fear wolves or other dangers. The dread of personal danger indeed formed no part of Dominic's character. His courage, though always passive, was essentially heroic. Over and over again he had been exposed to the assaults of his enemies, and warned of their intentions against his life; but such things never so much as made him change his road and alter the plan of his journey in any particular. He always treated the subject with silent indifference. When his prayers were ended, his brethren, who often watched him on such occasions, would see him take out his favourite book of the Gospels, and, first making the sign of the Cross, pursue his road, reading and meditating to himself. However long and fatiguing was the day's journey, it never prevented him from saying Mass every morning whenever there was a church to be found, and most frequently he would not merely say, but sing it, for he was one who never spared his voice or strength in the Divine Offices. We are constantly reminded of the heartiness of the royal psalmist, in the character left us of Dominic's devotion. " I will sing to the Lord with all my strength," was the language of David; "I will sing to the Lord as long as I have any being." And Dominic had no indulgence for any indolence or self-sparing in the praises of God. He always rendered Him the sacrifice, not of his heart only, but of his lips; and called on all his companions to do the same, for he felt it a good and joyful thing to praise the Lord.

In this matter his wonderful bodily constitution was no little assistance to the fervour of his soul. He never felt that fatigue, or indisposition, or other little ailments and difficulties could be an excuse for doing less for God. Therefore when he stopped for the night at some religious house, which he always preferred doing when it was possible, he never failed to join them in the singing of Matins, and he gave it as his reason for choosing to stop at a convent, in preference to other lodgings which he might have accepted, saying, "We shall be able to sing Matins to-night." At such times he generally chose the office of waking the others.

His invariable custom of making his first visit to the church has been religiously preserved in the Order. Blessed Humbert, commenting on the text, *Et intravit Jesus in templum Dei*, observes, "Hence has arisen the custom for the religious on arriving at any convent always first to visit the oratory, and many do the same thing in towns or villages through which they pass."[4]

His passing visits to the convents, whether of his own or of other Orders, were always full of profit to their inmates. They made the most of the few hours of his stay, and Dominic never thought of pleading for the privilege of a weary traveller. If the convent were under his own government, his first act was to call together the religious, and make them a discourse on spiritual things for "a good space," and then if any were suffering from temptations, melancholy, or any kind of trouble, he was never tired of comforting and advising them till he had restored to them the joy of their souls. Very often these little visits were so delightful to the religious who entertained him, that on his leaving them in the morning, they would accompany him on his way to enjoy a little more of his discourse; for the fascination of his conversation was universally felt to be irresistible. But if there were no such houses to receive him, he left the choice of the night's lodging to his comrades, and was all the better pleased if it chanced to be incom-

4 Hum. in cap. i. in Const. Ord. Præd.

modious, only making it a rule, before entering, to spend
some time in the nearest church. When people of high rank
entertained him, he would first quench his thirst at some
fountain, lest he should be tempted to exceed religious
modesty at table, and so give occasion of scandal, a prudence
which, in a man of such austerity of life, gives us a singular
idea of his humility. Even when ill, he would eat roots and
fruit rather than touch the delicacies of their tables, and
adhering to the rule he had observed when canon of Osma,
he never touched meat.

Thus journeying, he would stop and preach at all the
towns and villages in his way; what kind of preaching this
was we can easily guess. "With all his strength," says
Blessed Jordan, "and with the most fervent zeal, he sought
to gain souls to Christ without any exception, and as many
as he could, and this zeal was marvellously, in a way not to
be believed, rooted in his very heart." His favourite way of
recommending to man the truths of God, was the sweetness
of persuasion, and yet, as his parting address to the people
of Languedoc shows us, he knew (according to his own
expression) "how to use the stick." Finally, to cite once
more the words of the writer just quoted, "Wherever he was,
whether on the road with his companions, or in the house
with the guests or the family of his host, or among great
men, princes or prelates, he always spoke to edification, and
was wont to give examples and stories whereby the souls of
those who heard him were excited to the love of Jesus Christ,
and to contempt of the world. Everywhere, both in word
and deed, he made himself known as a truly evangelical
man." The same testimony was borne by those who were
examined on his canonization: "Wherever he was," they
said, "whether at home or on a journey, he ever spoke *of*
God or *to* God, and it was his desire that this practice should
be introduced into the Constitutions of his Order."[5]

---

[5] "(Prædicatores) qui accepta benedictione exeuntes ubique . . . sicut
viri Evangelici sui sequentes vestigia Salvatoris, *cum Deo, vel de Deo*, secum
vel cum proximis utiliter loquendo, vitabant suspiciosi comitatis familiar-
itam " (Cons. FF. Præd. Dist. ii. c. xli. De Prædicatores).

Such is the picture left us by his brethren and companions of the habits observed by the servant of God in the course of those apostolic journeys in which the remaining years of his life were for the most part spent.    We must now resume the thread of his story, which at the close of the year 1217 finds him once more within the walls of Rome.

CHAPTER HOUSE, ST. SIXTUS.

# CHAPTER XVI.

## ST. SIXTUS.

### 1218.

DOMINIC was received at Rome with renewed evidences of affection and favour from Pope Honorius, who showed every disposition to forward the design with which he had returned thither, namely, the foundation at Rome of a convent of his Order. The church granted to him by the Pontiff for this purpose was chosen by himself; it was one already full of ancient and traditionary interest, which its connection with the rise of the Dominican Order has certainly not lessened. There is a long road that stretches out of Rome, following the course of the ancient Via Appia, which, deserted as it now is by human habitation, you may trace by its abandoned churches and its ruined tombs. In the old days of Rome, it was the patrician quarter of the city; the palace of, the

Cæsars looks down upon it, and by its side stand the vast ruins of Caracalla's baths, with the green meadows covering the site of the Circus Maximus. This circumstance of its being formerly the place of popular and favourite resort, accounts for the abundance of Christian remains which mingle with the relics of a pagan age, and share their interest and their decay. For here were formerly the houses of many of noble and some of royal birth; and when their owners confessed the faith, and died martyrs for Christ, the veneration of the early Church consecrated those dwellings as churches, to be perpetual monuments of names which had else been forgotten. But in time the population of Rome gathered more and more to the northern side of the Cælian Hill, and the Via Appia has long been left to a solitude which harmonizes well enough with its original destination, for it was the Roman street of tombs. There, mixed with the ruined towers and melancholy pagan memorials of death, where the wild plants festoon themselves in such rich luxuriance, and the green lizards enjoy an unmolested home, stand these deserted Christian churches, never open now, save on the one or two days when the Stations are kept there, and crowds flock thither to pray at shrines and altars which at other times are left in the uninterrupted silence of neglect. Among these is one dedicated to St. Sixtus, Pope and Martyr, and the tomb of five others, Popes and Martyrs. Attached to this church were certain buildings erected by Innocent III., with the intention of gathering together within their walls a number of religious women then living in Rome under no regular discipline. It had been part of his plan to confide the care of these religious to the English Canons of Sempringham, known as Gilbertines, whose Rule was drawn up with a view to their undertaking the direction of communities of nuns. Difficulties, however, had stood in the way of realizing the plan, and the Gilbertines had not shown much promptitude in answering the Holy Father's appeal. Neither had their care of the church of St. Sixtus been at all satisfactory, so that Honorius III., early in the year 1218, addressed them a letter requiring them at once to send a sufficient number of brethren to undertake the proposed work, and serve the church in a becoming manner, or in case of their failing to do so, to be prepared to resign it into the hands of other religious. As the canons still delayed, the affair ended by the Pope relieving them altogether of the care of the church, which he made over to St. Dominic, with the design of entrusting to him and to his brethren the work originally intended for the Gilbertines.[1]

His first care was to reduce the house to a conventual form, and to enlarge it so as to be capable of receiving a considerable number of brethren. To do this he was obliged to solicit the alms of the faithful, which were indeed abundantly supplied; the Pope himself liberally contributing to a work in which he felt no common interest. Meanwhile, Dominic laboured at his usual office of preaching. We have the authority of Pope Clement VIII.[2] for asserting that the first Confraternity of the Rosary ever erected in Rome was that established by St. Dominic himself, in the church of St. Sixtus, where for many years was preserved the pulpit from which he preached the devotion, and thereby, according to Flaminius and Malvenda, obtained a number of striking conversions. We are assured that many of the Cardinals were enrolled in the Confraternity, and that the reputation of the saint spread far and wide, attracting many to become his disciples. Various influences paved the way for the success and rapid development of the Orders founded by St. Dominic and St. Francis. They, indeed, and the work which they set on foot were wanted by their age: the world was restlessly heaving with the excitement of new feelings, which stirred men with emotions they neither understood nor knew how to use. We need not therefore wonder at the

---

[1] From the date of the letters of Honorius, it is evident that the church of St. Sixtus was not formally withdrawn from the Gilbertines till the end of the year 1219—so that up to that time, it can only have been held *conditionally* by St. Dominic and his brethren (See Reg. Hon. III. ann. ii. and iv.).

[2] In a Bull given by Réchac, p. 344, and by Nanni, p. 207.

enthusiasm with which they flung themselves into the ranks of the two leaders whom God had sent them. For, after all, great men are not merely the exponents of their own views or sentiments. Be they saints, or heroes, or poets, their greatness consists in this, that they have incarnated some principle which lies hidden in the hearts of their fellow-men. All have felt it; they alone have expressed and given it life: and so when the word is spoken which brings it forth to the world, all men recognize it as their own; they need no further teaching and training in this thought, for unconsciously to themselves they have been growing into it all their lives; and the devotion with which they follow the call of him who guides them is, perhaps, the strongest sentiment of which human nature is susceptible; made up not merely of admiration, or loyalty, or enthusiasm, but in addition to all these, of that gratitude which a soul feels towards that greater and stronger soul whose sympathy has set its own prisoned thoughts at liberty, and given them the power and the freedom to act. Then, like some pent-up and angry waters, that have long vexed and chafed themselves into foam, and beaten aimlessly against the wall that kept them in, when the free passage is made, how impetuously they rush forth! At first agitated and confused, but gathering majesty as they flow, till the torrent becomes a river, and the river swells into a broad sea, the dash of whose long united waves no barrier can resist. This is what we call a popular movement. Europe has seen such things often enough, as well for good as for evil; but she never saw one more universal or more extraordinary than the first burst into existence of the mendicant Orders. That of St. Francis was earliest in point of time, and the first Chapter of his Order saw him in the midst of five thousand of his brethren. But the fields were white with the harvest, and the Friars Minor were not to be the only gatherers of it. In three months Dominic had assembled round him at Rome more than a hundred religious with whom to begin his new foundation. His convent of St. Sixtus had to be even yet more enlarged; and here he began to carry out

the entire observance of that rule of life which was first
established at St. Romain.

Faithful, however, to the principle he had laid down at
Prouille, that the " grain must be scattered and not hoarded
up," Dominic, as he witnessed the rapid increase of the
brethren, rejoiced at the thought of yet further extending
their labours. Nor was he long in choosing the site of his
next foundation. After the Universities of Paris and Oxford,
that of Bologna was most highly in esteem, and the eagle
eye of the great patriarch had from the first discerned the
importance of planting convents of the brethren in all these
seats of learning. The wisdom which guided him in this
decision was fully justified by the result, for in a very few
years after the death of St. Dominic, the Friars Preachers
had become a great teaching power in all the universities
of Europe, whose most illustrious members daily recruited
the ranks of the new Order.

✝ Bologna, therefore, was selected as the site of the next
foundation, the city which boasted to be at once the home
of liberty and learning. " The two grand features of the
Bolognese character," says Eustace, " are the love of liberty
and the love of knowledge, and they are expressed on their
standard, in the centre of which blazes in golden letters the
word ' Libertas,' while ' Bononia docet ' waves in embroidery
down the sides."

As usual, when the work to be accomplished was one of
unusual importance, Dominic called to his aid his faithful
companion, Bertrand of Garrigua, who by reason of the very
confidence that was placed in him, found himself constantly
called on to change his place of residence and face the
difficulties of some new undertaking. He was accordingly
summoned from Paris, and after a brief stay at Prouille,
reached Rome, in company with John of Navarre and
Lawrence of England, in the month of January, 1218.
Retaining Lawrence at St. Sixtus, the saint despatched
the two brethren, Bertrand and John, to Bologna, where
they were soon after joined by Michael of Uzero and
Dominic of Segovia, who had returned from Spain, where

their efforts to establish themselves had proved unsuccessful.
These were shortly followed by two others, Richard and
Christian, together with a lay-brother named Peter, all of
whom had recently entered the Order, Richard being
appointed prior of the new community.  The preaching
of the friars soon attracted attention: they are said to
have been the first religious who had ever been heard to
preach publicly in Bologna, and the admiration inspired
by their eloquence was increased when it was understood
that they were disciples of that Brother Dominic whose
fame had by this time spread through every city in Italy.
Two houses were soon given to them, together with a
neighbouring church called Santa Maria della Mascarella.
Their first care was to arrange their dwelling in a conventual
form; for in the early foundation of the Order this was
regarded as an indispensable condition for carrying out their
Rule, even when the community numbered no more than four
or five persons.  As well as they could therefore, considering
the confined space which was at their disposal, they made a
dormitory and refectory, with other necessary offices; their
cells were so small that they were not more than seven feet
long, and four feet two inches wide, so that they could
scarce contain a hard and narrow bed and a few other of
necessary furniture; but they were more content with this
poor habitation than if they had possessed the largest and
most magnificent palace.  Here they led "a life of angels;"
and "so wonderful was their regular observance, and their
continual and fervent prayer; so extraordinary their poverty
in eating, in their beds and clothes, and all such things, that
never had the like been seen before in that city."[3]

The example of such a life attracted some to join them,
among whom was Tancred, afterwards prior of St. Sixtus,
who was called to the Order in a singular manner.  He
was a German, and a courtier of the Emperor Frederick II.
Being at Bologna when the first brethren arrived there,
he was one day made sensible of a singular and powerful
impression on his soul, urging him to reflect on the great

[3] *Prog.* p. 75.

question of eternity in a manner wholly new to him. Disturbed and agitated, he prayed to the Blessed Virgin for direction; and in the night she appeared to him, saying these words: "Go to my household." He awoke in doubt as to their meaning, but in a second dream there appeared to him two men dressed in the habit of the Order, the elder of whom addressed him, saying, "Thou hast asked of Mary to be directed in the way of salvation: come with us, and thou shalt find it." In the morning he begged his host to direct him to the nearest church, that he might hear Mass. As he entered, the first figure he met was that of the old man he had seen in his vision; the church was, in fact, Santa Maria in Mascarella, and the friar was none other than the prior Richard. Tancred's mind was soon made up as to his future course; and, abruptly severing his engagements with the Court, he proceeded to Rome, where he took the habit.[4]

But in spite of the adhesion of a few disciples and the favourable reception at first given to them by the citizens, the brethren did not make much progress, and suffered many affronts and discouragements till the end of the year, when, as we shall see, a fresh impulse was given to their enterprize by the arrival among them of Reginald of Orleans.

In Spain, Brother Peter, of Medina, had succeeded in founding a convent at Madrid, concerning which no particulars have been preserved. Two of his companions, as we have seen, rejoined Dominic at Rome, but the third, Suero Gomez, went on to his native country of Portugal, where he became known to the Infanta Donna Sancha, who gave him a little oratory on Monte Sagro, about six miles from Alanquez, dedicated to Santa Maria *ad Nives*. Here he built a miserably poor convent, or rather hermitage, formed of stones and straw cemented together with mud, "according to the manner of those first days of fervour in the Order."

---

[4] Tancred of Germany is not to be confused with Tancred Tancredi, of Siena, who received the habit in 1220 from the hands of St. Dominic. Marchese, in his *Diario Domenicano*, and some other writers, suppose that there was but one religious of the name, and attempt to blend together in one biography the incidents related of two distinct persons.

He lived in this singular dwelling alone for some time, but
very soon numbers of all ranks flocked to him to receive the
habit from his hands; and "though they were so many, and
of such character and nobility as might have done honour to
any Order in the Church, yet did he not abate one iota in the
rigours which he had learnt from his holy master, and which
were established as laws in the Constitutions." Every day
he preached in the city, which soon became renowned for
its sanctity of manners. He was a true son of Dominic,
"thinking only how to sow the Divine Word, and caring
nothing for his own body;" and so, little by little, the
mud hermitage was frequented as a place of pilgrimage,
and the crowds who thronged there to see and hear one
whom they reckoned to be rather an angel or apostle than
a common man, compelled him to enlarge his dwelling in
order to receive them, so that in the following year, when
Dominic himself visited the spot, he found a spacious and
well-ordered convent, the mother-house of the Order in
Portugal. Suero was in every way a remarkable man: his
adherence to the Rule, even in the minutest particular, was
almost a proverb. In 1220, when he went to Bologna to
attend the first General Chapter, he performed the whole
journey on foot, carrying only a stick and his breviary, and
so begged his way the entire distance. He became afterwards the first Provincial of Spain.

During the early struggles of these distant foundations,
and whilst the walls of the convent of St. Sixtus were rising
above the ground, St. Dominic was busy at Rome, forming
a spiritual edifice out of the hearts of those whom he won
by the power of his eloquence. And as though to make him
and his exalted mission better known to men, God was
pleased at this time to confirm his teaching and authority
by many and notable miracles. The first of these was on
the occasion of an accident which happened during the
erection of the convent. A mason whilst excavating under
part of the building was buried under a mass of falling
earth. The brethren ran to the spot, too late to save him,
but Dominic commanded them to dig him out, whilst he

betook himself to prayer. When the earth was removed the man arose alive and unhurt. This miracle, however much it confirmed the faith of his own followers, was little known or talked of beyond the walls of his convent; but it was followed by another of more public notoriety. Dominic was accustomed at this time to preach in the church of St. Mark, where he was listened to with enthusiasm by crowds of all ranks who flocked to hear him. Among them one of his most constant auditors was a certain Roman widow, Gutadona, or Tuta di Buvalischi; and one day, rather than miss the preaching, she came to St. Mark's, having left her only son at home dangerously ill. She returned to her house to find him dead. When the first anguish of her grief was over, she felt an extraordinary hope rise within her that by the mercy of God, and the prayers of His servant Dominic, her child might yet be restored to her. She therefore determined to go at once to St. Sixtus; and firm in her faith she set out on foot, whilst her women servants carried the cold and lifeless body of the boy behind her. St. Sixtus was not yet enclosed, on account of the unfinished state of the convent, and she therefore entered the gates without difficulty, and found Dominic at the door of the chapter-house, a small building standing separate from the church and convent. Kneeling at his feet, she silently laid the dead body before him, whilst her tears and sobs of anguish told the rest. Dominic, touched with compassion, turned aside for a few moments, and prayed; then, coming back, he made the sign of the Cross over the child, and taking him by the hand, raised him, and gave him back to his mother, alive and well.

This miracle was witnessed by the brethren, Tancred, Sisto, Gregory, Otho, Albert, and Henry, who afterwards gave their evidence in the process of canonization. Dominic strictly charged the mother to keep the fact a secret, but she disobeyed him, as the woman of Judea had before disobeyed One greater than *him*. Her joy was too abundant, and out of its abundance her heart and lips were busy, and so the whole story was quickly spread through

Rome, and reached the ears of Honorius, who ordered it to
be publicly announced in the pulpits of the city. Dominic's
sensitive humility was deeply hurt: he hastened to the
Pontiff, and implored him to countermand his order. "Otherwise, Holy Father," he said, "I shall be compelled to fly
from hence, and cross the sea to preach to the Saracens; for
I cannot stay longer here." The Pope, however, forbade
him to depart: he was obliged to remain and receive what
is ever the most painful portion of the saints, the public
honour and veneration of the populace.

Great and little, old and young, nobles and beggars,
"they followed him about" (to use the words of contem-
poraneous authors) "wherever he went, as though he were
an angel, reputing those happy who could come near enough
to touch him, and cutting off pieces of his habit to keep as
relics." This cutting of his habit went on at such a pace
as to give the good Father the appearance of a beggar, for
the jagged and ragged skirt scarcely reached below his knee.
His brethren on one occasion endeavoured somewhat harshly
to check some of those who crowded round him, but Dominic's
kind heart was hurt when he saw the sorrowful and disappointed looks of the poor people. "Let them alone," he
said; "we have no right to hinder their devotion." A
memorial of these circumstances may still be seen in that
same church of St. Mark spoken of above. Once a year,
on the festival of its patron saint, there is an exhibition in
that church of saintly treasures, which few sanctuaries can
rival and none surpass. There, amid the relics of apostles
and martyrs in jewelled and crystal shrines and elaborate
carvings, you may see, enclosed in a golden reliquary, a little
piece of torn and faded serge. Priests are there holding up
these precious objects one by one for the veneration of the
kneeling crowd, and they hold this also for you to look at
and to kiss, whilst they proclaim aloud, "This is part of the
habit of the glorious patriarch St. Dominic, who, in the first
year of his coming to Rome, was wont to preach in this
church." And fancy is quick to suggest that this precious
morsel may be one of those so unceremoniously torn from

him by the crowds who flocked about him on that very spot.

Other miracles are related as having occurred about the same time, though the precise date of each is not recorded.

Among the "Murate," mentioned in a former page, and whom he still continued to visit and direct, there were some who lived a life of extraordinary mortification, and were entirely enclosed in little cells built in the walls, so as that none could enter or communicate with their inhabitants; food and other necessaries being given to them through a window. One of these recluses was a woman named Buona, who lived in a tower near the gate of St. John Lateran; another, Lucy, in a little cell behind the church of St. Anastasia. Both of them suffered from incurable and most terrible diseases, brought on by the severity of their mode of life. One day, after Dominic had administered the Sacrament of Penance and the Holy Eucharist to Buona through her little window, and exhorted her to patience under her dreadful sufferings, he blessed her with the sign of the Cross, and went away; but at the same instant she found herself perfectly cured. Lucy was likewise restored in a similar manner, as Brother Bertrand, who was present on the occasion, attested.

But among all these miraculous events none are more interesting than the two visits of the angels to the refectory of St. Sixtus, the latter of which is still daily commemorated in every Dominican convent. The first of these events is related by Vincent of Beauvais, who tells us that one day the brethren sent out into the city to beg having returned empty-handed, Giacomo del Miele, who filled the office of procurator, came to the holy Father to represent the case, saying that there was absolutely nothing to set before the brethren, then forty in number, save a few dry crusts. Dominic, full of joy and holy confidence, commanded him to assemble the religious in the refectory and distribute to them what he had. In those days the most sumptuous fare ever partaken of by the brethren consisted of a little bread, with some vegetables, and occasionally a few fishes; but on

o

this occasion even these scanty provisions were wanting. Nevertheless the brethren sat down to table, and were preparing to content themselves with their crusts, when two beautiful youths entered the refectory, carrying in the folds of their garments fresh loaves, which they distributed in silence, beginning at the upper table, where St. Dominic was seated. The brethren at first imagined that they must have been the servants of some rich noble of the city who had sent them this timely alms, but the two youths suddenly disappearing, they concluded that they were angels in a human form, sent by their Heavenly Father to provide for them in their need.[5]

The second occurrence of a like nature shall be related in the words of an eye-witness: "When the friars were still living near the church of St. Sixtus, and were about one hundred in number, on a certain day the blessed Dominic commanded Brother John of Calabria and Brother Albert of Rome to go into the city to beg alms. They did so without success from the morning even till the third hour of the day. Therefore they returned to the convent, and they were already hard by the church of St. Anastasia, when they were met by a certain woman who had a great devotion to the Order; and seeing that they had nothing with them, she gave them a loaf, 'For I would not,' she said, 'that you should go back quite empty-handed.' As they went on a little further they met a man who asked them very importunately for charity. They excused themselves, saying they had nothing themselves; but the man only begged the more earnestly. Then they said one to another, 'What can we do with only one loaf? Let us give it to him for the love of God.' So they gave him the loaf, and immediately they lost sight of him. Now, when they were come to the convent, the blessed Father, to whom the Holy Spirit had meanwhile revealed all that had passed, came out to meet them, saying to them with a joyful air: 'Children, have you nothing?' They replied, 'No, Father;' and they told him all that had happened, and how they had given the loaf

[5] Vincent of Beauvais, *Spec. Hist.* lib. 30. cap. 72.

to the poor man. Then said he, 'It was an angel of the Lord: the Lord will know how to provide for His own: let us go and pray.' Thereupon he entered the church, and, having come out again after a little space, he bade the brethren call the community to the refectory. They replied to him, saying: 'But, holy Father, how is it you would have us call them, seeing that there is nothing to give them to eat?' And they purposely delayed obeying the order which they had received. Therefore the blessed Father caused Brother Roger, the cellarer, to be summoned, and commanded him to assemble the brethren to dinner, for the Lord would provide for their wants. Then they prepared the tables, and placed the cups, and at a given signal all the community entered the refectory. The blessed Father gave the benediction, and every one being seated, Brother Henry, the Roman, began to read. Meanwhile the blessed Dominic was praying, his hands being joined together on the table; and, lo! suddenly, even as he had promised them by the inspiration of the Holy Ghost, two beautiful young men, ministers of the Divine Providence, appeared in the midst of the refectory, carrying loaves in two white cloths, which hung from their shoulders before and behind. They began to distribute the bread, beginning at the lower rows, one at the right hand, and the other at the left, placing before each Brother one whole loaf of admirable beauty. Then, when they were come to the blessed Dominic, and had in like manner placed an entire loaf before him, they bowed their heads, and disappeared, without any one knowing, even to this day, whence they came or whither they went.

"And the blessed Dominic said to his brethren: 'My brethren, eat the bread which the Lord has sent you.' Then he told the servers to pour out some wine. But they replied, 'Holy Father, there is none.' Then the blessed Dominic, full of the spirit of prophecy, said to them: 'Go to the vessel, and pour out to the brethren the wine which the Lord has sent them.' They went there, and found, indeed, that the vessel was filled up to the brim with an excellent wine, which they hastened to bring. And Dominic

said, 'Drink, my brethren, of the wine which the Lord has
sent you.' They ate, therefore, and drank as much as they
desired, both that day, and the next, and the day after that.
But after the meal of the third day, he caused them to give
what remained of the bread and wine to the poor, and would
not allow that any more of it should be kept in the house.
During these three days no one went to seek alms, because
God had sent them bread and wine in abundance. Then
the blessed Father made a beautiful discourse to his brethren,
warning them never to distrust the Divine goodness, even
in time of greatest want. Brother Tancred, the prior of
the convent, Brother Odo of Rome, and Brother Henry,
of the same place, Brother Lawrence of England, Brother
John of Rome, and many others, were present at this
miracle, which they related to Sister Cecilia, and to the
other Sisters, who were then still living at the monastery of
Santa Maria on the other side of the Tiber; and they even
brought to them some of the bread and wine, which they
preserved for a long time as relics."[6]

The name of Brother Albert, who is mentioned in the
above narrative as one of those sent out to beg, occurs in
another story belonging to this time, together with that of
a certain Brother Gregory, "a man of great beauty and
of perfect grace."

One day, Dominic being full of the Holy Spirit, was
holding Chapter, and was observed by all present to be very
sad. According to Gerard de Frachet, he had spent the
previous night watching in prayer in the Catacombs, where
he seems to have received a revelation of coming events.
"Children," he said, "know that within three days, two of
you now present will lose the life of your bodies, and two
others that of their souls." Within the time described, the
two brothers, Albert and Gregory, died. Gregory was the
first to return to our Lord, having devoutly received all
the sacraments. On the third day after, Brother Albert,
having also received the sacraments, departed from this
darksome prison to the palace of heaven. And at the same

* Narrative of Sister Cecilia.

time, two others, whose names are not given, returned to the world.

Of the other brethren named above as present when the angels appeared, Tancred and Lawrence are already known to the reader. Blessed Henry was a Roman by birth, and had entered the Order against the earnest remonstrances of his family. As they expressed their determination to carry him back by force if he would not return of his own will, Dominic sent him out of Rome with some companions by the Via Nomentana. His relations followed the party as far as the banks of the Anio. Seeing there was no way of escape, Henry raised his heart to God and invoked His help through the merits of His servant Dominic, and the waters of the stream suddenly swelled into a torrent so deep and rapid that the horses of the pursuers were unable to pass. After this he was suffered to return undisturbed to St. Sixtus.[7]

We said that the circumstances of the angels' visit to the refectory of St. Sixtus, is still daily commemorated in the houses of the Order. And it is so; for from this time the custom was adopted of beginning to serve the lowest tables first, and so going up to the table of the prior; a custom which was afterwards made a law of the Order, being introduced into the Constitutions.

It will be observed that in the narrative as given above Brother Roger is named as discharging the office of procurator. This is explained by the fact that Giacomo del Miele, who usually filled that office, was at this time attacked by a sickness, which increased so rapidly that he received Extreme Unction and was warned by the physician to prepare for death. The brethren were greatly afflicted, for he was a man of singular ability for his office, and much beloved. Dominic was overcome by the tears of his children; desiring them all to leave the cell, he shut the door, and like Elias when he raised the Sunamite's son, extended himself on the almost lifeless body of the dying man, and earnestly invoked the Divine mercy and assistance. Then, taking him by the hand, Giacomo arose entirely recovered, and Dominic,

[7] Narrative of Sister Cecilia.

opening the door of the cell, delivered him to his companions
who awaited the result outside, and who knew not how to
contain and express their joy. Giacomo was able at once to
resume the duties of his office, and himself narrated the
circumstances of his cure to Vincent of Beauvais, by whom
it is recorded.

St. Antoninus mentions a third occasion when the
brethren, having little or nothing to eat, St. Dominic, as he
sat at table, commanded the small portion of bread that was
in the house to be brought to him, and having given his
blessing, it multiplied so as to satisfy them all, leaving
sufficient also for another day. Nor do these appear to be
by any means the only instances in which the saint
miraculously supplied the wants of his children, to all of
which allusions are made in the words of the Office:

> Panis oblatus cœlitus
> Fratrum supplet inopiam.

The great opinion which Pope Honorius had conceived
both of the sanctity and wisdom of St. Dominic, increased as
it was by the fame of these events, led him to place in his
hands a matter as important in character as it was difficult
in execution.

Some mention has already been made of the design
entertained by Pope Innocent III. of appropriating the
church of St. Sixtus to a number of religious women then
living in Rome without enclosure, some even in the private
houses of their relations. The plan of collecting them
together under regular discipline had been found fraught
with difficulty, and had failed; even the Papal authority,
aided by the power and genius of such a man as Innocent,
had been unable to overcome the wilfulness and prejudice
which opposed so wise a project. Honorius, who no less
than his predecessors ardently desired to see it carried
out, resolved to commit the management of the whole affair
to Dominic. He could not refuse to accept the charge, but
aware of the complicated obstacles which lay in the way, he
made it a condition that three other persons of high authority

might be united with him in a business which, he probably felt, was far harder than the foundation of many convents, namely, the reform of relaxation, and the union under one head and into one body of a number of individuals who owned no common interest or authority.

These religious had for a considerable time been badly governed; perhaps, we should rather say, they had not been governed at all. They claimed exemption from the ordinary rules, were members of powerful families, and their relatives, among whom many of them lived, urged them on to resist every encroachment on their liberty as an act of tyranny. And indeed, in the then existing state of things, they could not be said to be absolutely compelled to obedience; the matter was one rather demanding address than authority. But if ever man possessed the art of persuasion it was the blessed Dominic, of whom it is said, " None could ever resist him," or rather persuasion with him was not an art, but nature. It was the effect of that admirable union of patience, prudence, and firmness, tempered with the charm of a sweet and tranquil gaiety, which gave so wonderful a magic to his intercourse; and his powers were never more severely tested than on this occasion. The coadjutors given him by the Pope were the Cardinals Ugolino, bishop of Ostia, the venerable friend of St. Francis; Stephen of Fossa Nuova; and Nicholas, bishop of Tusculum. The very first steps which the cautious commissioners took raised a storm of obloquy. The Cardinals had enough to do to quiet the nuns, and bring them to listen to the Pope's proposals. But those who held out had a strong party in their favour. The gossip of Rome was on their side; and there was a tempest of busy angry tongues all declaiming against tyranny and aggression, and talking great things about innovation on an ancient custom. " And truly," says Castiglio, with a touch of Spanish humour, " the custom was so very ancient, that it could scarce keep its legs. Moreover," he adds, "we know well, that for relaxation and liberty there will always be ten thousand persons ready to do great things, but for virtue not one willing to stir a step." However, as we have said, the nuns had the popular clamour on their side, and they used their advantage with considerable address. They had but to receive visitors all day long, and keep up the excitement of their friends by perpetual talking, and the Pope and Cardinals would be held at bay.

The most refractory of these religious were some who were living at that time in the monastery of Santa Maria in Trastevere, in which was kept a celebrated picture of our Blessed Lady, said to have been painted by St. Luke. This picture was a particular favourite with the Roman people. According to the current tradition it had been brought to Rome, many centuries before, from Constantinople, and was the same that had been borne processionally by St. Gregory in the time of the plague, on that Easter Day when the words of the *Regina Cæli* were first heard, sung in the air by the voices of the angelic choirs. This picture had for several centuries been kept in the church of Santa Maria in Trastevere, then belonging to a community of Benedictine nuns, whence an attempt had been made by Pope Sergius III. to transfer it to the palace of the Lateran. He himself is said to have carried it thither, placing it near the celebrated picture of our Divine Lord now preserved in the *Sancta Sanctorum*, but which was at that time kept in the Lateran. This removal of the venerable picture from Santa Maria was not made without strong protest on the part of the nuns. "But," says the ancient legend, "the following night by a stupendous and incomprehensible prodigy, the picture was by Divine power carried back to the spot whence it had been taken the evening before." The Pope, hearing what had happened, came himself to the convent to inquire into the fact, and satisfying himself by ocular demonstration that the holy image had indeed been restored to its original resting-place, he did not venture again to remove it.[8]

This wonderful event added much to the fame of the picture and the veneration with which it was regarded, and its possession contributed not a little to increase the power

[8] *La Vierge Acheropita, dei SS. Domenico e Sisto a Roma*, Fr. G. Berthier, pp. 53, 54.

and popularity of the nuns of Santa Maria. Without it they determined never to stir, and there seemed great difficulties in the way of again removing it. Dominic's plan was simply to carry out that previously conceived by Pope Innocent, and collect all the nuns of the different convents that had no regular discipline, as well as the others living out of enclosure, into one community, to whom he proposed giving up his own convent of St. Sixtus, which had been originally intended for the purpose. Pope Honorius, to whom he submitted the proposal, not only approved of it, but to render it more easy of execution, offered to assign to him and his brethren one half of his own family palace adjoining the church of Santa Sabina on the Aventine Hill. This offer was gratefully accepted, and by order of the Pope the ancient church was itself divided by a wall into two parts, one of which he reserved for the Papal functions, whilst the other was given up to the use of the religious.[9]

The necessary alterations were at once set on foot, and the saint was careful to give the buildings assigned to the use of his community the same arrangements which had been adopted at St. Sixtus and St. Romain. These being completed, the brethren removed thither with their scanty possessions, including the books necessary for their studies, and St. Sixtus was left vacant for the occupation of the nuns. But much had yet to be done before Dominic could obtain their consent to remove thither. His first proposal resulted in failure; the very mention of enclosure and community life was received by a very intelligible declaration that they would be controlled neither by him, the Cardinals, nor the Pope. But Dominic was not so easily daunted. He used all the skill and address of manner with which God had endowed him, and on his second visit found means to win over the abbess Eugenia del Gora, and after her all the community with one solitary exception. There were, however, conditions proposed and accepted. These were that they must be suffered to carry their picture with them to

---

[9] This division continued until the time of Sixtus V., who took down the intermediate wall, and gave the whole church to the friars.

St. Sixtus, and should it come back to the Trastevere of itself, as in the days of Pope Sergius, that they should be held free to come back after it. Dominic consented; but, saving this clause, he induced them to profess obedience in all else to himself; and they having done so, he gave them as their first trial a prohibition to leave their convent in order to visit any of their friends or relatives, assuring them that in a very short time St. Sixtus should be ready to receive them.

After this it seemed as though the affair were pretty well settled; "but," to use the words of Polidori, "the instability of human nature, and especially of the female sex, easy to be moved by whatsoever wind may blow, very soon made the contrary to appear." The wise regulation which Dominic had made was evaded, and the vituperating tongues of friends and relations were busier than ever. There were no terms too strong to use in denouncing the proposed migration to St. Sixtus. It would be the destruction of an ancient and honourable monastery; they were about blindly to put themselves under an intolerable yoke of obedience, and to whom? —to a *new man*, a "*frate*," whose Order nobody had ever heard of before—a scoundrel (*ribaldo*), as some were pleased to term him; they must certainly have been bewitched.

The nuns began to think so too, and many repented of their too hasty promise. Whilst this new disturbance was going on, Dominic was relating the success of his mission to the Cardinals. But the fresh disorders which had arisen were revealed to him by the Holy Spirit even at the moment that they occurred. He resolved to let the excitement exhaust itself a little before taking any new measure; and a day or two afterwards proceeded to the convent, where, having said Mass, he assembled all the religious in Chapter, and addressed them at considerable length. He concluded with these words: "I well know, my daughters, that you have repented of the promise you gave me, and now desire to withdraw your feet from the ways of God. Therefore, let those among you who are truly and spontaneously willing to go to St. Sixtus make their profession over again in my hands." The eloquence of his address, heightened by that strange and wonderful charm of manner to which all who knew him bear witness, whilst none can describe it, was victorious. The abbess, Eugenia del Gora, instantly renewed her profession (with the same condition respecting the picture), and her example was followed by the whole community. Dominic was well satisfied with their sincerity; nevertheless he thought it well to add one precaution against further relapse. It was a simple one, and consisted of taking the keys of the gate into his own custody, and appointing some of his own lay-brothers to be porters, with orders to provide the nuns with all necessaries, but to prevent their seeing or speaking with relatives or any other person whatsoever.

On Ash Wednesday, which fell that year on the 28th of February, the Cardinals assembled at St. Sixtus, whither the abbess and her nuns also proceeded in solemn procession. They met in the little chapter-house before mentioned, where Dominic raised to life the widow's child. The abbess solemnly surrendered all office and authority into the hands of Dominic and his brethren; whilst they, on their part, with the Cardinals, proceeded to treat concerning the rights, government, and revenues of the new convent. Whilst thus engaged, the business of the assembly was suddenly interrupted by an incident which is best told in the language of Sister Cecilia, an eye-witness: "Whilst the blessed Dominic was seated with the Cardinals, the abbess and her nuns being present, behold! a man entered, tearing his hair and uttering loud cries. Being asked the cause, he replied, 'The nephew of my lord Stephen has just fallen from his horse, and is killed!' Now the young man was called Napoleon.[10] His uncle, hearing him named, sank fainting on the breast of the blessed Dominic. They supported him; the blessed Dominic rose, and threw holy water on him; then, leaving him in the arms of the others, he ran to the spot where

---

[10] Napoleon Orsini. Since this time, says Abbé Curé, in his annotated translation of Theodoric of Apoldia, it has been the custom for the princes of the house of Orsini to name their eldest sons, *Dominic Napoleon*.

the body of the young man was lying, bruised and horribly mangled. He ordered them immediately to remove it to another room, and keep it there. Then he desired Brother Tancred and the other brethren to prepare everything for Mass. The blessed Dominic, the Cardinals, friars, the abbess, and all the nuns, then went to the place where the altar was, and the blessed Dominic celebrated the Holy Sacrifice with an abundance of tears.

" But when he came to the Elevation of our Lord's Body, and held It on high between his hands, as is the custom, he himself was raised a palm above the ground, all beholding the same, and being filled with great wonder at the sight. Mass being finished, he returned to the body of the dead man; he and the Cardinals, the abbess, the nuns, and all the people who were present; and when he was come, he arranged the limbs one after another with his holy hand, then prostrated himself on the ground, praying and weeping. Thrice he touched the face and limbs of the deceased, to put them in their place, and thrice he prostrated himself. When he was risen for the third time, standing on the side where the head was, he made the sign of the Cross; then, with his hands extended towards heaven, and his body raised more than a palm above the ground, he cried with a loud voice, saying, ' O young man, Napoleon, in the name of our Lord Jesus Christ, I say unto thee, Arise.' Immediately, in the sight of all those who had been drawn together by so marvellous a spectacle, the young man arose alive and unhurt, and said to the blessed Dominic, ' Father, give me to eat;' and the blessed Dominic gave him to eat and to drink, and committed him, joyful and without sign of hurt, to the Cardinal, his uncle."[11] There is a wonderful grandeur in this simple narrative. We realize at once the alarm and emotion of the bystanders, and the supernatural calm and tranquillity of the saint, who was acting under the Spirit of God. Never, perhaps, was any miracle better attested, or more accurately described; and, as we shall hereafter see, it bore abundant fruits.

[11] Narrative of Sister Cecilia.

The Cardinal testified his gratitude by making over to the convent of St. Sixtus the revenues of a certain benefice which he enjoyed in England, to which Malvenda, quoting from a MS. in the Vatican library, gives the name of Bara-burgh, and says the donation was worth the annual sum of three hundred gold florins.[12]

Needless to say, any hesitation which may have remained in the minds of the nuns, disappeared after witnessing with their own eyes so marvellous a proof of the power and sanctity of him to whom they had given their obedience.

Four days later, on the first Sunday in Lent, they took possession of their convent. They were forty-four in all, including a few seculars, and some religious of other convents. The first who spontaneously threw herself at Dominic's feet, and begged the habit of his Order, was the same Sister Cecilia whose narrative has just been quoted. She was then but seventeen, of the house of Cesarini, and distinguished for the great qualities of her soul even more than for the nobility of her birth. Meagre as is the account left us concerning her, her character is sufficiently evidenced in the little which is preserved. She had a soul large enough to appreciate that of Dominic. Child as she was, she had been quick to realize, and value at their true worth, the qualities of that mind which had brought into order the tempestuous and disorganized elements of the community of the Trastevere. Then she became an eye-witness of that great miracle which we have just related in her own beautiful language, and the admiration which she had already felt for him was raised to a devotion as fervent as it was lasting. Dominic communicated to her the most hidden secrets of his heart; and the narrative which she has left, so noble and touching in its biblical simplicity, shows that she was not

[12] The chapter-house which was the scene of this celebrated event stands as in the days of St. Dominic, and a few years since was adorned by paintings representing the chief incidents in the life of the saint, by Père Hyacinth Besson, then prior of Santa Sabina. The three largest of the paintings depict the raising to life of the mason, the widow's son, and the young Napoleon, which all took place within, or closely adjacent to, its walls.

unworthy of such a confidence. Her example was followed by the other nuns; all received the habit of the new Order, and took the vow of enclosure.

Dominic waited until nightfall before he ventured to remove the picture so often named; he feared lest some excitement and disturbance might be caused by this being done in broad day, for the people of the city felt a jealous unwillingness to suffer it to depart. However, at midnight, accompanied by the two Cardinals, Nicholas and Stephen, and many other persons, all barefoot and carrying torches, he conducted it in solemn procession to St. Sixtus, where the nuns awaited its approach with similar marks of respect. It did not return; and its quiet domestication in the new house completed the settlement of the nuns.

The success with which the saint had brought to a close this difficult and important business did not fail to excite the rage of the great enemy of souls. On the Sunday following that which had witnessed the profession of the nuns, Dominic was preaching in their church to a crowded audience, when a possessed woman who was present began to create a disturbance with her cries. " Ah, wretch!" exclaimed the evil spirit, speaking by her tongue, " I had four of these women in my power, and thou hast wrested them all from me!" Dominic imposed silence on the evil one, threatening if he did not obey to cast him out of the unfortunate woman whom he possessed. " That thou shalt not and canst not do," was the reply, " for we are seven who have taken up our abode here, and we will never come forth." But the saint, making the sign of the Cross, commanded them in the name of Jesus Christ to leave their victim, and never more to molest her. Immediately she was seen to bring up a quantity of blood, which flowed from her mouth and nose; whilst at the same time she cast forth what seemed like burning coals; after which the demons left her lying half dead. But Dominic desired that she should be carried to a neighbouring house, where she presently revived; and as soon as his preaching was ended the saint visited her, and gave her salutary instructions, bidding her return thanks to God for her merciful deliverance. Full of gratitude, she implored to be admitted into the community of St. Sixtus, and Dominic granting her request, gave her the habit of the Order four days later, and bestowed on her the name of Amata or Amy. The community was soon afterwards joined by twenty-one nuns from various other houses, including Sister Blanche and seven companions whom Dominic summoned from Prouille, to assist in training the new religious in regular discipline. Four of these afterwards returned to Prouille; but Sister Blanche and two others remained at Rome; and thus was formed the second house of religious women living under the Rule of St. Dominic.[13]

[13] In process of time the neighbourhood of St. Sixtus becoming infected with malaria, the nuns were forced to abandon the convent, and St. Pius V. granted them a site within the walls, on the hill called Magnanopoli, where they built a sumptuous church and convent, now known by the title of SS. Domenico e Sisto. It is still occupied by a community descended from that of St. Sixtus, and within its walls is preserved with the utmost veneration the miraculous picture of our Lady.

SANTA SABINA FROM THE RIVER.

## CHAPTER XVII.

### SANTA SABINA.

IT is said that all lives have their chapter of poetry; if so, the poem of Dominic's life is now opening before us. No period of his history is at once so rich in legendary beauty, and so full of ample and delightful details, as that of his residence at Santa Sabina—the church which, as we have already said, had been granted to him and his brethren by Pope Honorius when they abandoned St. Sixtus to the nuns of the Trastevere. It was attached to the palace of the Savelli, of which family Honorius was a member; and we are told that the change of residence was particularly welcome to the friars, inasmuch as the neighbourhood was at that time more thickly populated than that of St. Sixtus, and the church was one of popular resort. This character has long since departed from it; and the tide of population, retreating every year further and further to the west, has left the Aventine Hill once more to its silent and solitary beauty. Built on the brow of that hill, as it rises abruptly above the

Tiber, the convent of Santa Sabina stands between the ancient and modern city. On one side it looks over a long vista of churches and palaces, until the golden glow of the horizon above Monte Mario is cut by the clear sharp outline of that wonderful dome which rises over the tomb of the Apostles. Turn but your head, and you gaze over a different world. Heaped all about in fantastic confusion, may be seen gigantic arches with the ruins of walls and watch-towers standing among the vineyards; and beyond them is the wide Campagna stretching like a sea into the dim horizon, spanned by the long lines of the aqueducts, that seem as though they reached the very base of those distant mountains which stand round the Eternal City as "the hills stand about Jerusalem."

The Aventine is said on the authority of Virgil[1] to derive its name from the birds of prey who resorted there in days of old, and built their nests in the ample forests with which it was then clothed. It was now to become the home, not of eagles or vultures, but of a white-robed multitude, successive generations of whom should be nurtured here, as in a nest of holy living. It has its Christian as well as its classic associations. The church of Santa Sabina which crowns its summit stands on the site of a house once occupied by the holy martyr whose name it bears. It was a favourite sanctuary of St. Gregory the Great, who often preached within its walls, and is said there to have first instituted the singing of the litanies.[2] The church is regarded as one of the holy places of Rome; and here on Ash Wednesday is held the first Station of Lent, when the barefooted brethren of the *Sacconi*, all of noble birth, in company with the devout of both sexes, may be seen toiling up the sandy road to keep the *Caput Jejunii* in this time-honoured sanctuary. Two paths lead down from Santa Sabina to the

---

[1] Lustrat Aventini Montem . . .
Dirarum nidis domus opportuna volucrum.
(Æn. lib. viii. 231, 235.)

[2] The practice of singing the Litany of the Saints on St. Mark's day is said to have been instituted by St. Gregory. Seven processions, starting from seven of the Roman churches singing litanies as they went, met in the church of St. Mary Major.

P

valley below.   One descends abruptly to the Tiber, the other winds down a gentler declivity, planted thick with almond-trees, till it reaches the valley separating the Aventine and the Palatine Hills.   This was the road so often trodden by the blessed Dominic as he passed to and fro in his daily visits from Santa Sabina to St. Sixtus.   " No pathway exists," says Père Lacordaire, " which so faithfully preserves the traces of his footsteps."   Day after day for more than six months he climbed down these slopes, and took his road through this valley, passing on his way that other ancient church of St. Anastasia, near to which, it will be re-membered, dwelt those pious recluses to whom his visits of charity brought such timely consolation.

To those then who are familiar with the history of the holy patriarch, every footstep of the Aventine is fragrant with his memory.   But above all do the church and convent of Santa Sabina preserve that memory in all its freshness. The aspect of both, as now existing, differs much from that which they presented in the days of St. Dominic; neverthe-less many portions of the building belong to his time. Among these is the refectory, where, out of reverence to his memory, the place in which he formerly sat has never been occupied by another.   A part of the dormitory is also certainly identical with that which he arranged for the reception of his brethren, and in it one cell, now turned into a chapel, is preserved with the utmost veneration as formerly occupied by the saint.   The proportions of this cell are exactly the same as those of St. Romain, and here is preserved the so-called portrait of St. Dominic painted by Bozzani, which however has no claim to be regarded as a *vera effigies*, though it very probably reproduced his traditionary likeness.   In the antechamber is to be seen a picture of the three saints, Dominic, Francis, and Angelus, who are believed to have met here and to have spent one entire night conferring together on the things of God, a fact commemorated by an inscription.[3]   Possibly also the severe

---

[3] *Attende, advena, hic olim sanctissimi viri, Dominicus, Franciscus, Angelus Carmelita in divinis colloquiis, vigilas pernoctaverunt.*

and devout cloisters, surrounding the quadrangle with its ancient well, are the same which once re-echoed with the footsteps of the saint, and not far from the entrance stands the orange-tree planted by his hands, the leaves and fruit of which are distributed to devout pilgrims. Père Réchac also mentions a peach-tree in the convent garden, which was held by constant tradition to have been planted by the saint, and which after the lapse of four centuries still flourished in spite of the custom which prevailed of cutting branches from it to distribute among the crowds who flocked thither every Ash Wednesday.

The church itself underwent a process of restoration and adornment during the Pontificate of Sixtus V., which has effaced many of its ancient features. Nevertheless, within these same walls took place more than one event of memorable interest, of which we shall presently have to speak. Here, according to Malvenda, St. Dominic constantly preached the devotion of the Holy Rosary, the Confraternity having been transferred hither from St. Sixtus after the removal of the brethren.[4]

Here, too, lying on the stone pavement, he passed the hours of his night-watches, and offered to God his "inexpressible penances." We look at the roof of the ancient apse, where appears a representation of the Lamb of God, surrounded by twelve sheep, and standing on a little green hill whence flow streams of living water, and wonder whether that mystic picture ever met the eyes of the blessed Dominic, reminding him of the green pastures and running waters of eternal life. Here, at any rate, he prayed, he preached, and shed around the sweet perfume of sanctity; so we will leave to archæologists the task of distinguishing with exactitude the changes which have passed over this holy sanctuary since the days of our saint, and content ourselves with the memories which no such changes can ever banish from the spot.

One of the most interesting of these is connected with the vocation to the Order of two brothers, destined to

[4] Malvenda, cap. xxviii. p. 221.

be numbered among its brightest ornaments. They were Hyacinth and Ceslaus, nephews to Ivo Odrowatz, the Polish bishop of Cracow, both of them canons of his cathedral and men of singular virtue. They had come to Rome in company with the bishop on a pilgrimage of devotion, and all three had been present at St. Sixtus and had witnessed the raising to life of the young Napoleon. When by means of Cardinal Ugolino they afterwards became personally acquainted with the blessed Dominic, the deep impression made on their minds by that event was increased by his saintly conversation. Ivo urged him to send some of his brethren to the northern countries, but the difficulty of the language seemed to offer obstacles to this plan; and Dominic therefore suggested that the best way of carrying out his wishes would be if some of his own followers would take the habit.

A few days after this Hyacinth and Ceslaus, with two others, Henry of Moravia, and Herman, a noble German, presented themselves at Santa Sabina, and, throwing themselves at the feet of the saint, begged to be allowed to enter the Order. Their offer was joyfully accepted, and they received the habit in the chapter-room, over the door of which still appears an inscription commemorating the event. Their progress was as rapid as it was extraordinary. Doubtless, in that time of early fervour, the growth of souls planted in a very atmosphere of sanctity was quicker and more vigorous than now; and we are led to exclaim, "There were giants in those days," when we find these novices, within six months after their first admission, ready to return to their own country to be the founders and propagators of the Order. They travelled back with the Bishop of Cracow, preaching as they went. Separation, that law of the Dominican Institute, was the lot that awaited them also. Hyacinth and Ceslaus pursued their way to the north, where they divided the land between them. Ceslaus planted the Order in Bohemia, whilst the apostolate of Hyacinth extended over Russia, Sweden, Norway, Prussia, and the northern nations of Asia. It is considered as probable that he also visited Scotland. Dominic's old dream of a mission to the

Cumans became realized in the labours of this the greatest of his sons, and in him the Order of Friars Preachers took possession of half the known world.

Both brothers have been raised to the altars of the Church and are known in the Order as St. Hyacinth and the Blessed Ceslaus. Henry proceeded to Styria and Austria, and founded many convents, especially that of Vienna. An account of singular beauty is left of his death. He fell sick in the convent of Wratislavia; and finding his last hour draw near, he fixed his eyes on a crucifix before him, and sang sweetly while he had strength. After a little space he was silent, yet smiled, and put his hands together, and showed in his eyes and his whole face a great and inexplicable joy. Then, after a brief time, he spake, and said, "The demons are come, and would fain disturb and trouble my faith, but I believe in God the Father, and the Son, and the Holy Ghost;" and with these words on his lips he gently expired. Herman, the fourth of this society, was left at Friesach to govern a convent founded in that place. He was a man of extraordinary devotion, though of small learning. In consequence of his simplicity and ignorance he was often despised and ridiculed by his companions; and, seeking comfort from God in prayer, he obtained the gift of so much understanding of the Holy Scriptures that, without study of any kind, he was enabled to preach not only in German, but also in Latin, with extraordinary eloquence and success.

The residence of the saint at Santa Sabina at a time when the quarters assigned to the use of himself and his brethren formed a portion of the Pontifical palace, gave occasion for his being charged by Honorius with an office of considerable importance. He was, it is said, much distressed at seeing the servants of the Cardinals and others who frequented the palace, idling about the antechambers, playing games of chance, whilst their masters were engaged in the business of the Church; and he suggested to the Pope whether some means could not be devised for the better employment of their time, by the appointment of some one who might explain to them the Holy Scriptures or give them other useful instructions. The Pope, agreeing with his views, instituted the office of Master of the Sacred Palace, and bade him enter on it by delivering explanations of the Epistles of St. Paul, not only to the humble audience whose spiritual wants he had sought to supply, but to the Court and Cardinals. The saint obeyed, and his wonderful eloquence and knowledge of the Holy Scriptures attracted crowds of disciples. John of Colonna, who was almost a contemporary of the saint, in his book *De Viris Illustribus*, tells us of the vast numbers who gathered to hear the Word of God from his lips. He says that he explained the Epistles of St. Paul in the public schools, and that his pulpit was surrounded both by scholars and prelates, all of whom gave him the name of " Master." He discharged, in fact, two offices, distinct in themselves though often afterwards held by the same person ; he taught the family of the Pontiff, as Master of the Sacred Palace, and lectured on theology as *Lector* of the Palace, and out of this latter office it is supposed by some that the university of Rome took its rise. The Mastership of the Sacred Palace continues to our own day, being always held by a member of the Dominican Order. Its duties are considerable, and include among other things the censorship of books published in Rome.[5]

Besides delivering these lectures, the saint preached almost daily in one or other of the churches of the city, and often in the basilica of St. Peter's, neither his bodily powers nor the marvellous richness of his mental resources ever seeming capable of exhaustion.

But the object which occupied the chief attention of Dominic from the moment of his first establishment at Santa Sabina, was the training of those disciples who flocked into the Order in ever increasing numbers. Before all other works he held in importance the religious formation of the brethren.

[5] The institution of this office is sometimes referred to an earlier visit of the saint to Rome ; but if the circumstances of the saint's residence at this time within the Pope's own palace are taken into consideration, the probability of its belonging to this period will become apparent.

Nor while applying himself to their interior training did he neglect those exterior means so powerful in religious education. The Friars Preachers were to sacrifice all comfort and all human ties for the work of God: they were to endure poverty, humiliation, and detachment of heart in their most painful forms; but one thing they were not to sacrifice, and that was the character of religious and the habits of regular observance. Whilst they begged their bread, and lived on alms, the first thing on which those alms were expended was the rude and imperfect conversion of their poor dwellings into a religious shape. In their deep and living humility they acknowledged that they were powerless to retain the religious spirit, made up as it is of prayer and recollection and continual self-restraint, without certain external helps and hindrances. Every part of the Dominican Rule and Constitutions breathes of this principle; whilst the salvation of souls is ever placed before us as the end and object of the Order, the formation of the religious man himself is provided for by regulations of the most astonishing minuteness; and as a part, and an essential part, of these, is included the beautiful ordering of the religious house.

This necessary connection between the outward form and the inward spirit is nowhere stated in express terms, for there was not much talk about theories and general principles among men in the middle ages; yet, unconsciously to themselves, they ever acted under a deep prevailing sense of this sacramental character of our being. They believed that not in soul alone, but also in body, the whole nature was to be made subject to Christ; and with the simplicity of antique wisdom, they condescended to provide for this by making laws, not only for their work and their prayer, but even for their houses and their dress. The religious man was ever to be surrounded by an atmosphere redolent of sanctity; he was to reflect a light of holiness cast on him by the very walls of his dwelling. Nothing, therefore, was neglected by which they could be invested with this peculiar character. They were the mould in which souls were insensibly to receive a shape that separated them from the world. The amateurs of ecclesiastical architecture tell us that, in its purest form, no ornament will ever be found introduced for ornament's sake; there was always a use and significance in the most fanciful and grotesque of those elaborate designs. And so in the conventual house, common and necessary things were not exchanged for what was fanciful or extraordinary; but a religious form and colouring was given to the whole. Thus the man who was being trained to the life of religion was placed where he saw nothing that did not harmonize with that one idea. His refectory was as unlike as possible to a dining-room; it was as much a room to pray in, as to eat in. There, ranged in a single row behind the simple wooden tables that stood on either hand, sat the same white-robed figures beside whom he stood in the choir, and with an air scarcely less modest and devout. At the top was the prior's seat; there were neither pictures nor ornaments on the wall, only a large crucifix above that seat, to which all were to bow on entering; for even in hours of relaxation the religious man was to be mindful of the sufferings of his Lord. There was no talking or jesting as in the feasting of the world, for the refectory was a place of inviolable silence; but from a little pulpit one of the brethren read aloud (as we have seen Brother Henry represented doing in the scene at St. Sixtus), that, to use the words of the Rule of St. Austin, "whilst the body was refreshed, the soul also might have its proper food." The house was to be poor and simple, having "no curiosities or notable superfluities, such as sculpture, pavements, and the like, save in the church," where some degree of ornament was allowed to do reverence to the Presence of God. The dormitory too had its own character: the cells were all alike in size and arrangement, for here all were equal. They were separate, that every one might be silent and alone with God; yet partly open, that the watchful eye of the Superior might never be shut out. Even the dormitory passage itself had something holy; for it was ordained, that "to promote piety and devotion to the Blessed Virgin, the especial Patroness of the Order, an altar with her image should be erected in the dormitory of every convent," and here the lamp was kept burning through the night. Each of these places had its own sweet tradition. Angels, as we have seen, have before now served in the Dominican refectories; and the dormitories have been blessed no less than the choir with the sweet presence of our Lady, who through those open doors has given her benediction to the sleeping brethren, and sprinkled them with her maternal hand. Such houses were as the gate of heaven. All about them were holy sentences, preaching from the walls; poverty reigned everywhere, but clad in the beauty and majesty of that spirit of *order*, which has been fitly termed "the music of the eye." All things were in common, and common things were made to speak of God; yet there was neither gloom nor melancholy, but rather a glad and cheerful aspect, tempered by the pervading tone of silence and recollection; so that the beholder might well exclaim, "How good and joyful a thing it is for brethren to dwell together in unity!"

The life of a saint like St. Dominic is not made up alone of journeys and foundations and the dates of his birth and death; his living soul is to be found in the Rule, the most striking features of which were the impression of his own hand: and it is not a little remarkable that, together with that free and pliable spirit which is one of its distinguishing characters, there should be this invariable adhesion to the externals of monastic and community life. The same rule was observed in all the foundations of the Order, and this of course by the particular direction of its founder; a fact which reveals more of his mind and feeling than whole volumes of commentary. It exhibits him to us in that mixed character of contemplation and action, the union of which is the basis of the Dominican life: we see him at once, "the Jacob of preaching and the Israel of contemplation;" and we see also what in his eyes constituted the essentials of such a life, and the indispensable means for attaining it.

"The Christian perfection which he taught," to use the admirable words of Castiglio, "consisted primarily indeed in the love of God and of our neighbour; but secondarily and accidentally in that silence and solitude, and in those fasts, mortifications, disciplines, and ceremonies, which are the instruments whereby we reach that high and most excellent end." It would seem indeed as if these "ceremonies" he speaks of formed no insignificant part of Dominic's great idea of spiritual training. We read of his " diligent training of the nuns in the rules and ceremonies;" and again, St. Hyacinth is said to have become a perfect master in " all the ordinances and ceremonies of the Order during his short novitiate."

From the beginning of the Order both the Mass and the Divine Office were daily chanted to note.[6] The Office was to be sung sweetly and devoutly, but in order not too greatly to impede the active duties of the brethren the recitation was also to be brief and succinct. It was to be accompanied by certain inclinations and prostrations carefully prescribed in the Rule. These prescriptions may be traced partly to that deep sagacity on the part of the holy founder which perceived how large an influence is exerted over the inner man by the subjugation of his external nature, and partly to his own characteristic love of order. Whilst wholly free from the narrowness of mere formalism, his soul yet delighted in that harmony which is a chief element of perfection: it was as though his eagle eye had gazed on the ordering of the heavenly courts, and, drawing from the image pictured on his soul, he strove to reflect something of their beauty in his convent choirs. And so, perhaps, those bowings and pros-trations of the white-robed ranks, which, when exactly performed, give so unearthly and beautiful an appearance to the worship of a religious choir, may, at the same time as it harmonized the souls of the worshippers into recol-lection, have been intended to recall and symbolize those scenes on which doubtless his own spiritual vision had so often rested, and the repeated foldings of those many wings and the casting of the golden crowns upon the ground.

[6] " Matutinam et Missam omnesque horas canonicas quotidie cantabunt solemniter et distincte" (Theodoric of Apoldia, cited by Père Danzas, vol. i. p. 160).

† But in addition to the government and training of his own brethren, the saint found himself charged with the yet more difficult task of establishing regular discipline in the community of St. Sixtus, among whose members there existed long habits of negligence and relaxation which had to be eradicated before the spirit of fervour and observance could be planted in their stead. These two undertakings, carried on at the same time, called for a genius of government which few have ever possessed in a more remarkable degree than the blessed Dominic. But within his soul there lay vast resources, and a certain fulness of spiritual light which never failed to guide him in the direction of others; and in addition he possessed that which no mean authority has declared to contain the secret of true genius, namely, the power of taking pains. How hard and how difficult was the work he had to accomplish at St. Sixtus may be judged from the unwearied assiduity with which he applied himself to it. Every day he visited the nuns, instructing them in the minutest particulars of their Rule, as well as in the principles of the spiritual life. Sometimes he would gather them together in the garden attached to the convent, and sitting with them there by the side of a little stream which ran through the grounds, would discourse on the things of God. On one such occasion the Sisters were alarmed by the sudden appearance among them of a strange and hideous reptile, and were preparing to fly in terror when Dominic, recognizing the wiles of the enemy who sought to disturb their conference, bade them fear nothing; and making the sign of the Cross, commanded the monster to depart, whereupon it plunged into the waters of the stream and disappeared from sight. Most often, however, he came in the evening when the labours of the day were over, at which times he brought some of his companions with him and spoke with the Sisters at the grating in the church.

Even here sometimes the spiritual instruction was interrupted by strange disturbances on the part of the evil one, to whose malice nothing could be more hateful than the work on which the holy Father was engaged. Many indeed are

the examples of such exhibitions of infernal malice that are
recorded in the life of St. Dominic, and in all of them there
is a distinctive character.   Never do we find one instance in
which Satan was permitted the least power to vex or trouble
him.   Never was he suffered to do him bodily harm, or to
assault him with grievous temptations.   The enemy appears
to us always baffled and contemptible, as in the power of
one who is his master, the very Michael among the saints.
Yet, though always petty, and as it were ridiculous, he
ceased not in his efforts to thwart and disturb him, and
chiefly directed his malice against the friars and the Sisters
of St. Sixtus, grievously trying them by perpetual distractions,
as though he hoped thereby at least to diminish something
of the fervour of their devotions.   Such attempts, however,
proved altogether fruitless, for the patient labours of the
blessed Dominic were crowned with complete success.
Enclosure and the observance of a holy rule, explained
by the lips and illustrated by the example of a saint, ere
long transformed the once undisciplined inmates of the
Trastevere into mirrors of sanctity and grace.

We have spoken of the assaults directed against the
saint by the great enemy of souls, as, generally speaking,
contemptible in character.   Once, however, he was permitted to make a serious attempt against Dominic's life.
One night, as the saint was praying in the church of
Santa Sabina, a huge stone was hurled at him by an
invisible hand from the upper part of the roof, which all but
grazed his head, and even tore his hood, but falling without
further injury to the saint, was buried deep in the ground
beside him.   The noise was so loud that it awoke several of
the friars, who came in haste to the spot to inquire the
cause; they found the fragments of the broken pavement,
and the stone lying where it fell, but Dominic was kneeling
quietly in prayer, and seemed as if unconscious of what had
happened.

Another story is told as follows: "The servant of God,
who had neither bed nor cell of his own, had publicly
commanded his children in Chapter, that in order that they

might wake the more promptly, to rise to Matins, they should retire to bed at a certain hour, in which he was strictly obeyed. Now, as he himself abode before the Lord in the church, the devil appeared before him in the form of one of the brethren, and though it was past the prohibited time, yet did he remain in the church with an air of particular devotion and modesty. Wherefore the saint, judging it to be one of the friars, went softly up to him, and desired him to go to his cell, and sleep with the others. And the pretended friar inclined his head, in sign of humble obedience, and went as he was bid; but on each of the two following nights, he returned at the same hour and in the same manner. The second time, the man of God rose very gently (although, indeed, he had reason to be somewhat angry, seeing he had during the day reminded all of the observance of that which had been enjoined), and again desired him to go away. He went; but, as we have said, returned yet a third time. Then it seemed to the saint that the disobedience and pertinacity of this Brother was too great, and he reproved him for the same with some severity; whereat the devil (who desired nothing else save to disturb his prayer and move him to break the silence) gave a loud laugh, and, leaping high into the air, he said, ' At least I have made you break the silence, and moved you to wrath ! ' But he calmly replied, ' Not so, for I have power to dispense, neither is it blameworthy wrath when I utter reproofs to evil-doers.' And the demon, being so answered, was obliged to fly."

On another occasion, as the blessed Father was by night walking through the convent of Santa Sabina,[7] guarding his flock with the vigilance of a good shepherd, he met the enemy in the dormitory, going about like a lion seeking whom he might devour; and recognizing him, he said, " Thou evil beast, what doest thou here ? " " I do my office," replied the demon, "and attend to my gains." " And what gains dost thou make in the dormitory ? " asked the saint.

[7] Bernard Guidonis relates this incident as happening, not at Santa Sabina, but at Bologna.

" Gain enough," returned the demon. " I disquiet the friars
in many ways ; for first I take the sleep away from those
who desire to sleep in order that they may rise promptly for
Matins; and then I give an excessive heaviness to others,
so that when the bell sounds, either from weariness or
idleness they do not rise; or, if they rise and go to choir,
it is unwillingly, and they say their Office without devotion."
Then the saint took him to the church, and said, " And what
dost thou gain here ? " " Much," answered the devil; " I
make them come late and leave soon. I fill them with
disgusts and distractions, so that they do ill whatsoever
they have to do." " And here ? " asked Dominic, leading
him to the refectory. " Who does not eat too much or too
little ? " was the reply; " and so they either offend God or
injure their health." Then the saint took him to the parlour,
where the brethren were allowed to speak with seculars, and
to take their recreation. And the devil began maliciously
to laugh, and to leap and jump about, as if with enjoyment,
and he said, " This place is all my own; here they laugh
and joke, and hear a thousand vain stories; here they utter
idle words, and grumble often at their Rule and their
Superiors; and whatsoever they gain elsewhere they lose
here." And lastly they came to the door of the chapter-room,
but there the devil would not enter. He attempted to fly,
saying, " This place is a hell to me: here the friars accuse
themselves of their faults, and receive reproof, correction,
and absolution. What they have lost in every other place
they regain here." And so saying, he disappeared, and
Dominic was left greatly wondering at the snares and nets
of the tempter; whereof he afterwards made a long discourse
to his brethren, declaring the same unto them, that they
should be on their guard.

Another night as the holy Father entered the church he
saw the evil one seated, as it were, with a paper in his hand,
which he appeared to be reading by the light of the lamp,
and his hand was hideous to behold and furnished with iron
claws. The saint approached him, and asked him what he
was reading. " I am reading the sins of thy brethren," was

the reply. Then the blessed Dominic laid hold of the paper, and commanded him in the name of God to give it up, which he was forced to do. And the saint found written therein several things wherein the brethren had transgressed, for which he duly corrected them.

But if, at the risk of wearying the reader, we have given these instances of the infernal malice related in the language of the ancient legends, it is time for us to present him with other and more lovely pictures, as they are left us in the narrative of Sister Cecilia. The first, as is fitting, shall be of the maternal love of the Blessed Virgin. Before reading it, we must remember that Dominic seldom or never had cell or bed of his own, and slept, when he slept at all, in the church or the dormitory. "One night, Dominic having remained in the church to pray, left it at the hour of midnight, and entered the corridor where were the cells of the brethren. When he had finished what he had come to do, he again began to pray at one end of the dormitory, and looking by chance towards the other end, he saw three ladies coming along, of whom the one in the middle appeared the most beautiful and venerable. One of her companions carried a magnificent vessel of water, and the other a sprinkler, which she presented to her mistress, and she sprinkled the brethren, and made over them the sign of the Cross. But when she had come to one of the friars, she passed him over without blessing him; and Dominic having observed who this one was, went before the lady, who was already in the middle of the dormitory, near to where the lamp was hanging. He fell at her feet, and though he had already recognized her yet he besought her to tell him who she was. At that time the beautiful and devout anthem of the *Salve Regina* was not *sung* in the convents of the friars or of the Sisters at Rome; it was only recited, kneeling, after Compline. The lady who had given the blessing said therefore to Dominic, 'I am she whom you invoke every evening, and when you say *Eia ergo advocata nostra* I prostrate before my Son for the preservation of this Order.' Then the blessed Dominic

inquired who were the two young maidens who accompanied
her, and she replied, 'One is Cecilia, and the other
Catherine.' And the blessed Dominic asked again why
she had passed over one of the brethren without blessing
him; and he was answered, 'Because he was not in a
fitting posture;' and so, having finished her round, and
sprinkled the rest of the brethren, she disappeared. Now
the blessed Dominic returned to pray in the place where
he was before, and scarcely had he begun to pray when he
was wrapt in spirit unto God. And he saw the Lord,
with the Blessed Virgin standing on His right hand; and
it seemed to him that our Lady was dressed in a robe of
sapphire blue. And looking about him, he saw religious
of every Order standing before God; but of his own he did
not see one. Then he began to weep bitterly, and he
dared not draw nigh to our Lord, or to His Mother; but
our Lady beckoned him with her hand to approach. Nevertheless, he did not dare to come until our Lord also in
His turn had made him a sign to do so. He came,
therefore, and fell prostrate before them, weeping bitterly.
And the Lord commanded him to rise; and when he was
risen, He said to him, 'Why weepest thou thus bitterly?'
And he answered, 'I weep because I see here religious of
all Orders except mine own.' And the Lord said to him,
'Wouldst thou see thine own?' And he, trembling, replied,
'Yes, Lord.' Then the Lord placed His hand on the
shoulder of the Blessed Virgin, and said to the blessed
Dominic, 'I have given thine Order to My Mother.' Then
He said again, 'And wouldst thou really see thine Order?'
And he replied 'Yea, Lord.' Then the Blessed Virgin opened
the mantle in which she seemed to be dressed, and extending
it before the eyes of Dominic, so that its immensity covered
all the space of the heavenly country, he saw under its
folds a vast multitude of his friars. The blessed Dominic
fell down to thank God and the Blessed Mary, His Mother,
and the vision disappeared, and he came to himself again,
and rang the bell for Matins; and when Matins were ended,
he called them all together, and made them a beautiful

discourse on the love and veneration they should bear
to the most Blessed Virgin, and related to them this vision.
It was on this occasion that he ordered his friars, wherever
they might sleep, always to wear a girdle and stockings."[8]

Theodoric of Apoldia relates the last incident almost in
the words of Sister Cecilia, and cannot suppress a word of
devout exultation. "Oh, with what love and veneration
ought we not to regard that incomparable Virgin, the holy
Mother of Jesus Christ, and our Mother also, to whose care
we have been entrusted by the Divine Majesty, under whose
wings we are protected, by whose loving hand we are
blessed, who bestows on us the dew of so many graces, and
who preserves us by her intercession from countless dangers!
Let us be on our guard lest by any fault of ours we cause
her to turn away from us those eyes of mercy which look
with clemency on those who carefully follow the right way!"

Another story of a more familiar character is thus related
by Sister Cecilia: "It was the constant habit of the venerable
Father to spend the entire day in gaining souls, either by continual preaching, or hearing confessions, or in other works of
charity. And in the evening he was accustomed to come
to the Sisters, and give them a discourse or a conference on
the duties of the Order, in presence of the brethren; for
they had no other master to instruct them. Now, one
evening, he was later than usual in coming, and the Sisters
did not think he would come at all, they having finished
their prayers and retired to their cells. But, lo! suddenly
they heard the little bell, which the friars were used to ring
to give the Sisters a signal of the approach of the blessed
Father. And they all hastened to the church, where, the
grating being opened, they found him already seated, with
the brethren, waiting for them. Then he said, 'My daughters,
I am come from fishing, and the Lord has this night sent me

[8] This vision of the children of the Order gathered under the mantle
of the Blessed Virgin is recorded as having been granted to various persons
on no fewer than four occasions; once (as above) to St. Dominic himself;
once to a certain recluse in Lombardy; once, as Thomas of Cantimpré
relates, to another German recluse, and once to Blessed Ceslaus (See
Danzas, ii. p. 19, and Nanni, p. 582).

Q

a great fish.' He spoke of Brother Gandion, whom he had
received into the Order; he was the only son of the Lord
Alexander, a Roman citizen, and a man of consequence.
Then he made them a long discourse, which gave them great
consolation. After which, he said, ' It will be well, my
children, if we drink a little.' And calling Brother Roger,
the cellarer, he bade him go and bring a cup and some wine.
And the friar having brought it, the blessed Dominic desired
him to fill the cup to the brim. Then he blessed it, and
drank first, and after him also the other friars who were
present. Now they were of the number of twenty-five, as
well clerks as laics; and they drank as much as they would,
yet was not the wine diminished. When they had all drunk,
the blessed Dominic said, ' I will that my daughters drink
also.' And calling Sister Nubia, he said to her, ' Come in
thy turn, and take the cup, and give all the Sisters to drink.'
She went therefore, with a companion, and took the cup, full
up to the brim, without a drop having been poured out. And
the prioress drank first, and then all the Sisters, as much as
they would, the blessed Father saying to them, ' Drink at
your ease, my daughters.' They were a hundred and four,
and all drank as much as they would; nevertheless the cup
remained full, as though the wine had just been poured into
it; and when it was brought back, it was still full. This
done, the blessed Dominic said, ' The Lord wills me now
to go to Santa Sabina.' But Brother Tancred, the prior of
the brethren, and Odo, the prior of the Sisters, and all the
friars, and the prioress, with the Sisters, tried to detain him,
saying, ' Holy Father, it is near midnight, and it is not
expedient for you to go.' Nevertheless he refused to do as
they wished, and said, ' The Lord wills me to depart, and
will send His angel with me.' Then he took for his companions, Tancred and Odo, and set out. And being arrived
at the church door, in order to depart, behold! according to
the words of the blessed Dominic, a young man of great
beauty presented himself, having a staff in his hand, as if
ready for a journey. Then the blessed Dominic made his
companions go on before him, the young man going first, and

he last, and so they came to the door of the church of Santa Sabina, which they found shut. The young man leaned against the door, and immediately it opened; he entered first, then the brethren, and then the blessed Dominic. Then the young man went out, and the door again shut; and Brother Tancred said, 'Holy Father, who was the young man who came with us?' And he replied, 'My son, it was an angel of God, whom He sent to guard us.' Matins then rang, and the friars descending into the choir, were surprised to see there the blessed Dominic and his companions, for they knew that the door had been left shut."

Such are some of the legends of these early times. Traces of them may yet be found on the spots they have enriched with their associations. Over the door of Santa Sabina, a half-defaced fresco commemorates this visit of the angel; within is still preserved the fragment of stone which was hurled at St. Dominic in prayer. And the spot on the pavement, where he was wont to take his scanty rest, is marked by a Latin inscription.

The room, too, where St. Hyacinth and the Blessed Ceslaus received the habit is still shown, and a picture in the choir recalls the history of their vocation. At St. Sixtus the ancient chapter-house still stands as the monument of St. Dominic's greatest miracles; and the Bull of Pope Clement VIII. before alluded to, which restored that ancient sanctuary to the Order of Preachers, sums up all the wonderful events connected with his history which happened within its walls and which entitle it to be numbered among the holy places of Rome.

According to the most trustworthy authorities, it was during this period of his residence at Santa Sabina that St. Dominic instituted his Third Order, known by the title of the *Militia of Jesus Christ*. The idea of such an Order, in which persons still living in the world should be enrolled, and whose special duty it should be to defend the Church and her members from the violence of the heretics, had first suggested itself to his mind during his labours in Languedoc. He witnessed the great disadvantage to which the Catholic

leaders were exposed by the constantly shifting character of
the forces at their command, the pilgrims, as they were
called, seldom remaining with the army after their forty
days of service were accomplished. There was also a
particular danger to which the Catholic population were
exposed in every country where the heretics had obtained
the upper hand. In many places these latter had seized the
goods of the Church, and reduced the bishops and clergy to
beggary. This was notoriously the case in the provinces
infested by the Albigenses, where, as we have seen, the
enemies of religion were powerfully supported by the temporal lords of the country. Things were not much better
in many parts of Italy, where the Emperor Frederic II. had
seized forcible possession of ecclesiastical property, con-
fiscating to his own use not merely church lands, but all
church treasures, even to the sacred vessels of the altar. It
is probable that the saint had taken some steps towards the
realization of his design before quitting Languedoc, but if
we may believe Père Réchac, who draws his authority from
certain documents found in the Vatican library by the
historian, Bzovius, the immediate occasion of his laying
his plan before the Pope was the desolating war then being
waged against the Christians of Poland by the Prussians
and other people of the north, who were still plunged in
the darkness of idolatry, and who from time to time laid
waste the surrounding countries with fire and sword. In
the February of the year 1218 an appeal for protection had
been sent to Pope Honorius from the bishops of Poland,
and it is probable that the visit to Rome of the Bishop of
Cracow was connected with the same subject. The Pope in
consequence addressed letters to the princes and bishops of
Germany and England, calling on them to come to the
succour of the Polish Christians. St. Dominic deemed
the time a suitable one for proposing to the Pope the
foundation of a military Order, whose members should
devote themselves exclusively to the protection of the
faithful against the enemies of religion, and the defence of
the goods of the Church. Honorius not only approved the

design, but recommended it in letters addressed to all the bishops and rulers of Italy, requiring them in no way to molest those who should enroll themselves in the new Order by requiring services of them that should interfere with the duties to which they had devoted themselves. Many accordingly took arms and joined the forces which were raised to oppose the Prussians, Tartars, and other heathens of the north, and it is probable that St. Dominic, who saw in these events an opening for the realization of his long cherished hopes, offered himself to depart and preach the faith to these idolatrous nations, but Honorius would not suffer it. Nevertheless he judged it a fitting opportunity for despatching brethren to found the Order in Poland, and other parts of the north, and thus the vocation of St. Hyacinth and his brother Ceslaus, came at a moment most opportune. In its origin, therefore, the Third Order of St. Dominic was essentially military. By their Rule its members were bound if called on to bear arms in defence of the Church. They wore white tunics and black mantles, on the latter of which was fastened the black and white cross of the Order. For their Office they recited a certain number of *Paters* and *Aves;* those only were received who were of exemplary life, and whose wives (if they were married) were willing to bind themselves not to prevent their husbands from discharging the duties imposed on them. During the lifetime of the holy Father the Order preserved its original name and its military character. After his canonization the brethren petitioned Pope Gregory IX. that their Institute might in future bear the title of *the Order of Penance of St. Dominic;* and as time went on, and the necessities of society changed, the military duties of the Order were laid aside, and women, both widows and virgins, were received into its ranks. The duties of military service were exchanged for those of penance and charity, and something of the sanctity of the cloister passed into family and secular life. So rapidly did the Third Order of St. Dominic and St. Francis spread in all countries where the friars established themselves that no later than the year 1255, we find the secular clergy of England addressing a petition to King Henry III., in which among other things they complain of the number both of men and women who have entered these new-fangled fraternities, "insomuch that it is difficult now to find any one who has not joined one or other of them."

Such was the origin of the Third Order of St. Dominic, which has continued to flourish down to our own times, and which has produced a progeny of saints, among whose names stand illustrious those of St. Catherine of Siena and St. Rose of Lima, with many others enrolled in the catalogue of the *Beati* of the Order of Preachers.

ST. DOMINIC LED BY THE ANGEL.

A BRIEF notice has been given in the foregoing chapter of
the manner in which the two Polish brothers, Hyacinth and
Ceslaus, were called to the Order, in the list of whose
apostolic men their names were to fill so illustrious a place.
We have reserved for a separate chapter the history of
another vocation as being yet more specially connected with
the early history of the Friars Preachers. Short as was his
religious career, few men exerted a more powerful influence
in the Order than the Blessed Reginald of Orleans. Regarded
with uninterrupted veneration from the date of his death
until our own time, it was only during the Pontificate of
Pius IX. that he was formally numbered among the *Beati*
of the Order, and the process of his beatification has thrown
much additional light upon his history. While still young
his rare gifts had acquired for him a brilliant reputation at
the university of Paris, where he graduated as doctor, and
taught for five years as professor of canon law. His fame
as a scholar no less than as a man of singular piety attracted
the notice of the canons of St. Aignan, whose college had
from very early times existed at Orleans, and enjoyed large
revenues granted them by successive monarchs. The kings
of France in fact assumed the title of abbots of St. Aignan,
and claimed as suzerains to give the investiture to the deans,
by delivering to them the sword, the belt, and the golden
spurs of knighthood. This investiture was bestowed on
Reginald by Philip Augustus in 1211, and the young dean
at once found himself in possession of all the advantages

which wealth and rank can bestow. Nevertheless his position
was a difficult one. The very privileges enjoyed by the
canons, which included exemption from the jurisdiction of
the ordinary, exposed them to attacks from various quarters,
and at the time of Reginald's promotion a lively conflict was
being waged between the chapter and the bishop, who claimed
certain episcopal rights which the canons would not admit.
This dispute had been both tedious and vexatious, but
Reginald had not long been installed in his office before he
succeeded in making peace between the contending parties.
The confidence with which he inspired his brethren, rendered
them well content to leave their interests in his hands, whilst
a good understanding was established between him and the
bishop, which soon ripened into a friendship so close and
intimate that, to use the words of one of his biographers,
"you might have thought the dean was bishop and that the
bishop was dean." Manasses de Seignelay, who then filled
the see of Orleans, was one of the most illustrious men of
his time, and the tie which bound him in such close relations
with Reginald was based on their mutual sympathy in the
things of God. He, and he alone perhaps, discerned that
in spite of possessing everything which the world holds most
precious, wealth, fame, dignity, and a position in which he
could amply gratify his taste as a scholar, Reginald, with all
his gifts of nature and of fortune, carried about with him
a heart as yet unsatisfied. His was one of those natures that
can be happy only in proportion as it is generous towards
God. And the lavishness with which he had hitherto spent
himself, his talents, and his means for the good of others,
did not yet come up to the level of that unlimited sacrifice,
the idea of which he had conceived in his heart. Day and
night he was consumed with two thoughts which gave him
no rest: a profound compassion for perishing souls, and the
thirst to devote himself without reserve to labour for their
salvation. His riches were a burden to him; freely as he
dispensed them for the relief of the poor and the enfranchise-
ment of the poor serfs dependent on him as their feudal lord,
a voice within seemed constantly demanding of him some-

thing more; and he dreamed in secret of embracing some way of life which to the apostolic work of preaching should unite the obligations of poverty and the holy folly of the Cross. In short, to use the words of Blessed Humbert, "he was secretly preparing himself for the ministry, though as yet he knew not in what way to carry it out; for he was ignorant that the Order of Friars Preachers had been founded." The way which at length opened to the fulfilment of his desires, came to him through the invitation of Manasses to accompany him on a double pilgrimage to Rome and Jerusalem, a proposal which he accepted the more willingly, in hopes that God would bless this act of piety by more clearly making known to him His holy will.

It was then in the May of 1218 that the two friends arrived in Rome, and were well received by many to whom they were known by reputation, among others by "a certain Cardinal," probably the Cardinal Ugolino, with whom Reginald soon came to be on terms of familiar intimacy. One day in a confidential discourse with the Cardinal, Reginald opened to him his whole heart, and confessed that he had long cherished the secret desire to abandon all things that he might devote himself to the work of preaching Jesus Christ in a state of voluntary poverty. The rest must be told in the words of Blessed Humbert: "Then the Cardinal said to him, 'Lo! there is an Order just risen up, whose end is to unite the practice of poverty with the office of preaching; and the Master of this new Order is even now present with us in the city, who also himself preaches the Word of God.' When Master Reginald heard this, he hastened to seek out the blessed Dominic, and to reveal to him the secret of his soul. The sight of the saint, and the graciousness of his words, captivated his heart, and he resolved to enter into the Order. But adversity, which proves so many holy projects, failed not in like manner to try his also. He fell sick, so that the physicians despaired even of saving his life. The blessed Dominic, grieving at the thought of losing a child ere as yet he had scarcely enjoyed him, turned himself to the Divine mercy, earnestly imploring God (as he himself

has related to the brethren) that He would not take from
him a son as yet but hardly born, but that He would at
least prolong his life, if it were but a little while.   And even
whilst he yet prayed, the Blessed Virgin Mary, Mother of
God, and Mistress of the World, accompanied by two young
maidens of surpassing beauty, appeared to Master Reginald
as he lay awake and parched with a burning fever ; and he
heard the Queen of Heaven speaking to him, and saying,
' Ask me what thou wilt, and I will give it to thee.'   As he
considered within himself, one of the maidens who accompanied the Blessed Virgin suggested to him that he should
ask nothing, but should leave it to the will and pleasure of
the Queen of Mercy ; to which he right willingly assented.
Then she, extending her virginal hand, anointed his eyes,
ears, nostrils, mouth, hands, reins, and feet, pronouncing
certain words meanwhile appropriate to each anointing.   I
have heard only those which she spake at the unction of his
reins and feet : the first were, ' Let thy reins be girt with the
girdle of chastity ; ' and the second, ' Let thy feet be shod
for the preaching of the Gospel of Peace.'   Then she showed
to him the habit of the Friars Preachers, saying to him,
' Behold the habit of thy Order,' and so disappeared from
his eyes.   At the same time Reginald perceived that he was
cured, having been anointed by the Mother of Him Who
has the secrets of salvation and of health.   The next
morning, when Dominic came to him, to ask him how he
fared, he answered that nothing ailed him, and so told him
the vision.   Then both together rendered thanks to God,
Who strikes and heals, Who wounds and Who maketh
whole."

Three days later Dominic again came to his room
bringing with him a religious of the Hospitallers of St. John ;
and, as they all three sat together the same scene was
repeated in the sight of all.   The above narrative is related
almost in the same words by a great number of writers,
among others by Blessed Jordan of Saxony, who says he
received it from the lips of St. Dominic himself.  Bartholomew
of Trent, who was himself clothed by St. Dominic, adds the

important explanation that the habit displayed by the Blessed
Virgin was that afterwards adopted by the brethren, not that
which they were wearing at the time of the vision, and that
Reginald, who was clothed a few days later, received the said
habit according to the form which had been shown him.
Bernard Guidonis, who is regarded as the most careful
among the early historians of the Order, is very clear and
precise on this point. "After the heavenly vision aforesaid,
and the showing of the habit," he says, "the blessed Dominic
and the other brethren laid aside the use of surplice, and
took in its place as a distinctive portion of the habit the
white scapular, retaining the black mantle which they wore
over their white tunics, as Canons Regular."[1]    Thenceforth
the white scapular became the distinctive garb of the Friars
Preachers: and the words which accompany the ceremony
of giving it, mark at once its origin and the reverence with
which it is regarded. "Receive the holy scapular of our
Order, the most distinguished part of the Dominican habit,
the maternal pledge from heaven of the love of the Blessed
Virgin Mary towards us."

Among all the traditions of the Order none perhaps is
more cherished than that which assures us, that the habit
which has clothed so many saints throughout the long lapse
of seven centuries, was first bestowed by the hands of our
Lady herself.    Hence Stephen de Salagnac calls her the
*Ordinis Vestiaria*. "Blessed are those," exclaims Theodoric
of Apoldia, "who are found worthy to wear this habit, the
symbol of grace unspeakable, woven by the hands of the
true *Mulier fortis* for the members of her household! Let us
ever cherish with veneration this royal and virginal garment,
and never soil its spotless whiteness."

Reginald had been brought back from the very gates of
death by the prayer of St. Dominic, who, in the moment
of anguish caused by the thought of so soon losing a son
whose extraordinary merits he had quickly discerned, had
besought of God, Who never refused the prayers of his
servant, that He would yet spare him for a little while.

[1] Bern. Guid. *Acta S. Dom.* ch. xxxiv.

He felt only too surely that the time would indeed be short.
There are certain souls who bear on them the stamp of
coming immortality; a something that reveals to us that
God has already marked them for Himself. As has been
beautifully said by a recent biographer of Blessed Reginald,
it is as though we beheld some magnificent forest tree, spreading abroad its boughs and covered with richest foliage, but
bearing on its bark the sign that it is marked for the wood-
man's axe, and in a brief space will be laid low amongst its
fellows. Short as it was, the time during which Reginald
was granted to the Order was to be rich in fruit, and
Dominic did not seek to prolong it by detaining him at
Rome. According to the custom of the times, the two
pilgrims had bound themselves by vow to pass the sea and
visit the holy places of Jerusalem, and this duty was regarded
as far too sacred to be set aside. Dominic therefore offered
no opposition to the departure of his newly-won disciple,
who before leaving him, made profession in his hands. And
a little trait of fatherly tenderness has singularly enough
been preserved in a tradition which survives in our own
day, and which represents the saint as bestowing on the
young pilgrim as his parting gift, a stick made of cypress
wood to carry during his journey. This stick was to have
its history. For it is said that Reginald, returning from the
Holy Land about the end of October in the same year,
touched at the port of Agosta, near Syracuse, in Sicily,
where, having won the hearts of the people by his preaching, he laid the foundations of a convent, planting on its
site this stick, which took root, and grew into a flourishing
tree.[2] To this day in the convent garden of Agosta may be
seen the trunk, now dried up and barren, but still sending
forth the odour of cypress. It is called the *wood of St.
Dominic*, and is held in great veneration, fragments being
distributed to the sick, especially to those suffering from

[2] The tradition affirming the foundation of the convent of Agosta by
Blessed Reginald, and the origin of the miraculous cypress-tree is attested
by the inhabitants of the city, and their attestation is inserted in the
process of beatification. See *Le Bienheureux Réginald d'Orléans*, by
Mdlle. Theresa Alphonse Karr, pp. 66, 67.

fever, whose confidence is often rewarded by miraculous cures.

Reginald arrived in Rome only in time to bid adieu to St. Dominic, who was on the point of setting out on a long journey, in the course of which he proposed to visit all the convents of the Order as yet founded. But before doing this he appointed Reginald to act as his Vicar, and desired that after remaining in Rome till the close of the year, he should remove to Bologna, and assume the government of the convent founded in that city. The fervent and loving heart of the new disciple had then at the very entrance on the life of obedience to bow to the law of separation, Manasses de Seignelay returned to his diocese to mourn the loss of its most brilliant ornament and his own dearest friend, and Dominic bidding farewell after only a few days' reunion to the son he so highly prized, set out for Bologna, on his way to Toulouse and Spain.

ST. DOMINIC MEDITATING ON THE GOSPELS.

# CHAPTER XIX.

### PORTRAIT OF ST. DOMINIC.

WE have now reached a period in the life of St. Dominic
when it may be well to pause for awhile and bestow a
more careful study on his character, one so little known
and so grievously misrepresented in our age and country.
Fortunately there is no need to appeal to the imagination
in order to place before us the true portrait of that dear
and venerable Father, every line and lineament of which
has been drawn by the hands of those who lived with him
and watched him day and night, who were trained by his
instructions, who were the companions of his apostolic
journeys, and who after his departure from this world,
gave their united testimony to the incomparable sanctity
of his life.

Of all faithful Christian souls, it is safe to say that they
must reproduce in one way or another the likeness of their

Divine Lord. If no feature of that likeness is to be found on a human soul, it can surely be none of His. But if this be in its measure true of the humblest disciple of Jesus Christ, much more may it be asserted of those great servants of God who stand as lights of the Church. In the meekness of St. Francis of Sales, in the charity of St. Vincent de Paul, in the wonderful conformity with the Sacred Passion exhibited by the Saint of Assisi, and in the thirst for the salvation of souls which formed the noble passion of St. Catherine of Siena, what do we see but reflections of that Divine Exemplar in one or other of the perfections of His adorable Humanity? ✝ Let it not, then, be thought irreverent, if we say of the holy Father St. Dominic that the special stamp which marks his character as a saint was his likeness to our Lord.✝ It was indicated in his name, it is said even to have been impressed on his very features. If there was less of human passion and personality about him than distinguishes many other great saints, it is because he stands amongst them pre-eminently as the minister of the Divine Word. Thus St. Catherine says in her Dialogue, "He took on him the office of the Word, the only-begotten Son of God, and appeared in the world as an apostle, scattering the darkness of error and giving light."[1] The ray of light indeed, which shines through thickest darkness, contracting thence nothing that can stain its transparent purity, is a fit emblem of him whose Order was to earn the glorious title of "The Order of Truth." "Like the light itself," says Père Danzas, "he represents the Word; he passes over the earth, but to the earth he seems not to belong; he passes everywhere like the Word of God, bringing men grace and truth; his existence is in some sort immaterial; if he speaks the language of men, it is only to reveal to them the things of heaven."[2] Nothing had power to disturb that matchless serenity which was his peculiar grace. The lives of some saints present us with a history of trials and temptations, of early struggles and

---

[1] *Dialogo*, c. 158.
[2] *Études sur les temps primitifs de l'Ordre*, tom. i. p. 272.

the final victory of grace. But in the life of St. Dominic, from the first moment when the star shone on his forehead as he was held at the baptismal font, down to the last sigh which he breathed in the presence of his brethren, we find no single moment when he did not belong to God. The evil one attacked him indeed, but had no power over him. Never during his life of fifty-one years was he once seen troubled or disturbed. Full of a tenderness which found its expression both in word and deed, he would yet seem to have been a stranger to passionate emotion of any kind; it was always the ray of light which kept its purity unstained. Theodoric of Apoldia says that "in his efforts to attain the perfection of sanctity it seemed as if the flesh were always in harmony with the spirit, for the latter was so constantly led by the Spirit of God, that the lower nature was completely under its dominion. Hence such peace reigned in his conscience that it was reflected on his very countenance, which always shone with a serenity that penetrated the hearts of those who beheld it." To the same effect are the words of Blessed Jordan, who says that "nothing ever disturbed his tranquillity but compassion for others, and that if the interior peace lost by Adam were to be found restored in any human soul, it was in that of the blessed Dominic."

Yet was there one sentiment within him to which may almost be given the name of a passion : it was his ceaseless, burning thirst for the salvation of souls. As his Divine Master had come into the world to save sinners, and loved them even unto death, so he too gave up all that was most dear to him in this life to win souls to Christ. He was always giving himself, it was the very keynote of his existence. He would have sold himself as a slave, he would have been cut to pieces by the heretics, he would spare himself neither by day nor by night if by any means he might save some. The source from which sprang this love of souls, is to be found in that other deeper love which reveals to us the secret of his heart. Before all things, and above all things, St. Dominic was the lover of Jesus

Christ. The Sacred Humanity of his Lord and Master, as made known in the Gospels, was the subject of his daily meditation and the theme of all his discourses. He preached nothing but Jesus Christ and Him crucified, delivering to men the mysteries of His Life and Passion; and after studying in the book of charity, all his care was to make known to the world the incomprehensible mystery of Divine Love. Hence the glorious title by which he was known amongst his own children was that of the "friend of Jesus Christ," a title to which Blessed Jordan touchingly alludes in the prayer which he composed to the holy Father.[3] If by friendship we understand an intimate knowledge and close union of hearts, it must be manifest that by prayer alone can such relations be acquired and maintained between the soul and God; and it is precisely as a man of prayer that St. Dominic stands pre-eminent. The habit of prayer knit his heart so closely to God, that nothing had power to move him from that centre, wherein, says Castiglio, "he reposed with marvellous and undisturbed tranquillity." We may say that his prayer was in a certain sense continual. There was neither place nor time in which he did not pray, but especially in those night-hours which he spent with God in the church. Very often his brethren watched him, unknown to himself, and saw how, when he believed himself entirely alone, he would pour out all the fervour of his soul without reserve. Blessed Humbert tells us that John of Bologna watched seven nights in order to observe him at these times. Perhaps of no saint have there been preserved more minute particulars of the methods of prayer which he practised himself and taught to his brethren. These form the subject of a distinct treatise, which is added by Theodoric as a kind of appendix to his Life of the saint, but which is supposed by the Bollandists to have been written by Father

---

[3] "I hope out of thy great familiarity with Jesus Christ thy Beloved, chosen out of thousands, that He Who, though thy Lord and God *was nevertheless thy Friend also*, will refuse thee nothing, but that thou wilt obtain from Him whatsoever thou mayest desire. For what will not the Beloved grant to His beloved one?"

R

Gerard, provincial of Lombardy, who gathered his information from the familiar companions of the holy Father, and
specially from Sister Cecilia.[4]

"There is a manner of praying," says the author of this
treatise, "in which the soul makes the body itself serve as an
instrument of devotion, and this method was often used by
the blessed Dominic.  By it the soul acts on the body, and
the body again upon the soul. . . . Besides that devout
exterior which he constantly exhibited, whether in the
celebration of Mass, or the chanting of the sacred psalmody,
at which times he was often seen wrapt in extasy, he had
various habits of prayer," nine of which the writer proceeds
to enumerate.

The first was to humble himself before the altar, as though
Jesus Christ were there, really and personally present, remembering the words, "The prayer of the humble shall pierce the
clouds."  Nothing was so dear to him as humility, for which
reason he would often repeat to the brethren those words of
Judith, "The prayer of the meek and humble is always
pleasing to Thee, O Lord."  "It was by her humility," he
would say, "that the woman of Canaan obtained her desire,
and so also was it with the prodigal son.  But as for me,
O Lord, I am not worthy that Thou shouldst come under my
roof—humble my spirit even to the very dust."  And as he
pronounced such words the saint would bow his head and
his whole body, inclining profoundly before his Lord and
Master, and so expressing the reverence that was His due.
He taught his brethren to do the same whenever they passed
the crucifix, that before that image of His greatest humiliation our Divine Lord might behold us also humble ourselves.
And in the same way he desired that they should do homage
to the Holy Trinity whenever they solemnly repeated the
*Gloria Patri*.  In training his disciples indeed, there was

---

[4] Not to overload our pages with references, it will suffice to say that
the contents of this chapter are almost entirely drawn from the Life of the
saint by Theodoric of Apoldia, and from the testimonies of the witnesses
for his canonization, commonly called the Process of Bologna, which are
given as far as possible in their own words.

nothing for which the saint cared more than to form them
to these habits of reverent devotion. He would often invite
them to this in the words of Holy Scripture, saying,
"Come and let us fall down before God and adore Him,
and let us weep before the Lord Who made us." "It
was thus," he would say, "that the Kings of the East
entered the house where they found the Holy Child with
Mary His Mother. And we, if we do the same, shall never
fail to find God made man, with the Blessed Mary, His
handmaiden."

He often loved to pray in imitation of our Lord in the
Garden, kneeling with his face bowed down upon the
ground; and he would remain in this posture for a long
space, repeating passages from the Psalms of the most
profound self-abnegation, and shedding such an abundance
of tears that the place where his face had leaned was often
wet. Or he would prostrate himself at full length upon the
ground, and at such times his heart would be torn by
compunction, and he would repeat aloud the words of the
Gospel, "O God, be merciful to me a sinner!" or weeping
and groaning bitterly he would exclaim, "I am not worthy
to behold the height of heaven by reason of my iniquities,
and because I have done evil in Thy sight;" or those other
words of the Psalm, "My soul is humbled to the dust:
quicken me, O Lord, according to Thy word." Then rising
from the ground he would take the discipline with the iron
chain which he always wore, or he would receive this terrible
chastisement from the hands of others. Another of his
favourite devotions was to stand before the crucifix either in
the church or the sacristy, looking at it fixedly, genuflecting
before it as many as a hundred times, praying aloud for
himself, for sinners, or for the brethren he had sent out to
preach, and repeating verses from the Psalms or other
portions of Holy Scripture. Sometimes, however, he would
pray silently, and then he might be seen to pause from time
to time as one surprised and overwhelmed by some great
revelation of Divine love, which drew copious tears from
his eyes; or he would kneel as if unconscious of aught save

the presence of God, and then it seemed as if he would
penetrate the distance that separated him from his Beloved,
his countenance now beaming with joy, now bathed in
devout tears.   Then with renewed ardour as one wholly out
of himself, he would recommence his genuflections which,
however rapid, were always performed with wonderful
reverence and dignity.   He was so accustomed thus to
bend his knees in prayer, that when he stopped at wayside
inns, after the fatigues of a long journey on foot, he always
performed this devotion when his companions were resting,
as though accomplishing a kind of office.

Another of his customs was to stand upright before the
altar, with his hands clasped before his breast, as though
holding a book, out of which he had the air of reading; then
he would press them over his eyes, or raise them above his
shoulders.   In these postures he had the appearance of a
prophet, now listening or speaking with God and the angels,
now thinking within himself on what he had heard.   He
would stand also with his arms stretched out in the form of
a cross, and would so pronounce steadily and at intervals
sentences like these : " O Lord God of my salvation, I have
cried before Thee day and night.   I have cried unto Thee,
O Lord; all the day long have I stretched out my hands to
Thee.   I have stretched out my hands unto Thee: my soul
gaspeth to Thee as a land where there is no water."   This
was when he prayed for any special grace or miracle, as on
the raising of Napoleon, when restoring to life the widow's
son, and also when he saved the English pilgrims.   At such
times his face breathed an air of indescribable majesty, so
that the bystanders remained astonished, without daring to
question him of that which they beheld with their own eyes.
Often, in rapture, he was seen raised above the ground;
his hands then moved to and fro as though receiving
something from God, and he was heard exclaiming, " Hear,
O Lord, the voice of my prayer, when I cry unto Thee, and
when I hold out my hands to Thy holy temple."   At such
times, says Theodoric, he seemed to obtain special favours
from the Holy Spirit, and to enter into the very Holy of

Holies.[5] But, above all, his devotion when celebrating the Holy Sacrifice is spoken of as something which kindled a like sentiment in all who beheld it. Bonviso of Placentia, who often served his Mass, says that he would sometimes look at the countenance of his beloved Father as he then prayed, and "that the tears flowed down his face so copiously, that one tear did not wait for another." His favourite prayer was the Our Father, which he loved above all others, as having been given to us by our Lord Himself. He never wearied of repeating it, not hurrying over it hastily, as is too often the custom, but dwelling upon every word and syllable, as though he would draw out all their hidden sweetness, and this was specially observable when he recited it in the Mass. Next to this devotion he prized the *Ave Maria*, "for indeed," says Castiglio, "there was no name after that of our Lord so welcome to his ears, or so constantly on his lips, as the sweet name of Mary. He never undertook anything of importance without invoking her aid, and left it as a charge to his brethren to do the same."

Nor was his devotion less apparent during the sacred psalmody in choir, at which he assisted with so much recollection that no noise or disturbance had power to distract his attention. As soon as the hours and the grace after dinner were ended, he would retire alone to some secret place, where, sitting down and making the sign of the Cross, he would meditate on those things which he had heard read. Then taking out that book of the Gospels which he always carried, he would kiss it reverently and press it to his breast, and those who observed him could mark how, as he read, he would seem to fall into arguments with another, smiling or weeping, beating his breast, or covering his face with his mantle, rising and again sitting and reading, as the passing emotions of his soul sought for expression.

Even on his journeys his habits of reading and medi-

[5] In the library at Carcassonne is preserved a very ancient MS. of Father Gerard's treatise, in which all the above methods of prayer used by the saint are illustrated by figures, showing the different positions he assumed at these times.

tating were never neglected, but, as his companions testified, he prayed as he walked along; and they would see him make the sign of the Cross, or use gestures as if brushing away flies, or driving from him all troublesome or distracting thoughts. These habits of prayer were accompanied by practices of penance that were never relaxed. Thrice every night he disciplined himself to blood, the first for his own sins, the second for the sins of others, and the third for the souls in Purgatory. John of Navarre describes his discipline as made of an iron chain having three branches, and says that it was well known among the brethren that besides taking this penance himself he often caused others to inflict it on him. He never laid aside his hair-shirt, or the iron chain he wore round his loins, even when he took his scanty repose, lying on the floor of the church or some other equally incommodious place. Rodolph of Faenza, in his deposition, declares that never had he known any one who gave his body so little sleep or food. "Though he willingly dispensed others when they needed it," says William of Montferrat, "yet he would never dispense himself." At table, having finished his repast before the others, he often fell asleep, being wearied out with his long vigils. In his journeys he slept on a heap of straw or on the bare ground, in his clothes and stockings, just as he had been walking; and if he happened, as was often the case, to be more than usually ill-provided, ill-lodged, or ill-received, he never complained, but seemed rather to rejoice at it.

In the above account of the prayer of St. Dominic, two things cannot fail to be noticed, the profound humility that penetrated his heart, and his deep compunction, whether for his own sins or those of others. Not one of those who gave their testimony concerning him, drawn from the most intimate daily intercourse, have failed to record that in the grace of humility he surpassed all men they had ever known. How could it be otherwise with one who placed his whole idea of sanctity in the imitation of his Divine Lord ? " Never did I know a man so humble," exclaims one witness. Others describe him as "patient, humble, merciful, and benign," and declare that he counted himself as nothing, and rejoiced most when receiving indignities or contempt. Preserving unstained his robe of baptismal innocence, he abased himself to the very dust before the majesty of God: whilst the thought of sin by which that majesty was offended caused him not merely horror but an unutterable sorrow. We speak often enough of zeal for souls, but it must be remembered that there are many kinds of zeal. That which moved the heart of St. Dominic was the zeal of an intense compassion. He hated sin because it offended God, but he loved and had compassion on the guilty ones, purchased by the Blood of Christ; and during his long night-watches, he was heard again and again repeating with bitter tears, the words, " O Lord! have mercy! What will become of sinners?" He often exhorted his younger brethren to cherish in their hearts similar dispositions. "If you have no sins of your own to weep for," he would say, " think of the multitude of unhappy souls who stand in need of mercy, over whom our Lord Jesus Christ Himself shed tears, and of whom the Prophet David said, ' I have beheld sinners and have withered away with sorrow.'" This loving compassion he manifested also in correction, imposing penances with such sweetness and benignity, that even when most severe the brethren patiently accepted them. It was the same fund of compassionate charity that made him, to use the words of Paul of Venice, "the sovereign consoler of his brethren." "If any one," says the same writer, "whether of his own or another Order, had a temptation or trouble, and went to ask his counsel, his words were so full of sweetness that none ever left him without being consoled." Others call him " most affable and compassionate," "not rendering evil for evil, or cursing for cursing, but blessing those who cursed him." Never did any one behold him angry or disturbed. Rodolph of Faenza, after saying that he was always joyous and cheerful, adds that if he saw a Brother doing anything amiss, he would pass it by at the time as though he saw it not, but afterwards, with a pleasant countenance and gentle words, he would say, " Brother, thou hast done wrong, confess thy fault," and

by his kindness he would lead all to confession. Nevertheless, he never failed to punish the faults of the brethren, and
that even severely, yet always with so much humility that
they departed from him consoled. To the same effect are
the words of John of Navarre, who says that when he
corrected an offence he compassionated the offender, and
grieved much when he had to punish. And not to multiply
these testimonies, we may conclude with the words of
Theodoric, that, "as he could show himself a father in
giving correction, so as a mother he could administer the
milk of consolation, for he watched over the souls of his
brethren as though they were his own." He had a mother's
tenderness for his children, which he showed even by his
care for their bodily comfort, trying by every means to
alleviate the hardships they endured, and to encourage them
to perseverance. In the midst of his long night-watches he
would sometimes leave the church and visit the dormitory to
see how it fared with the brethren, and if he found any who
were without a covering, he would cover them up with his
own hand.[6] Nor was his compassion manifested only to
his brethren, for "he showed himself loving and amiable
to all men," says John of Navarre, "to rich and poor, to
Jews and Gentiles, of whom there were many in Spain;"
and Ventura adds that "he was a true lover of souls,
extending his compassion not only to the faithful, but also
to heretics and unbelievers, and even to the lost souls in
hell, over whom he wept bitterly."

This tenderness of heart, however, he knew how to unite
with a singular firmness of purpose, for his humility was
allied to no touch of weakness. In times of doubt or

---

[6] The author of the *Recognitions* says that he received from St. Peter
certain particulars concerning our Lord's life with His disciples, which that
holy Apostle could never relate without tears. "He usually passed His
nights in prayer," he would say, "but He often thought of us even then.
That Divine Master Who had not where to lay His head watched to see
that we wanted for nothing. During the day He thought of our food, and
of our sleep by night. More than once I have seen Him come up to the
room where we were sleeping, and fearing lest we might suffer from the
cold, He would deign to strip off His own mantle and lay it across our
feet, and then He would go back to His prayer."

difficulty, before determining on any course, he always said Mass, and then having maturely taken his resolution he adhered to it without passion or anger, but with a constancy that nothing could move. Closely allied to this firmness was the courage which gave such a stamp of nobility to his character. He feared God too much to fear anything that man could do to him. Amid the plots of his enemies or the perils of his solitary journeys, he showed himself wholly indifferent to danger. It is too little to say that he did not fear death : to obtain the grace of martyrdom was the most ardent desire of his heart, a grace of which, in his humility, he counted himself unworthy. " Often have I heard him confess," says John of Navarre, " that he longed for nothing so much as to be scourged and cut to pieces for the faith of Christ." And this desire not being granted to him, he supplied for it by the severity of his penances, and by the constancy with which, in the midst of his immense labours, he never in any way spared or dispensed himself, but followed community life most exactly in the choir, the refectory, and all other things.

His life was almost equally divided between prayer and labour, and it was one of his maxims that we should give the day to our neighbour and the night to God. Blessed Jordan says that he taught this maxim both by word and work. "By day no one was more accessible and cheerful among his brethren, and by night no one was more watchful in prayer. In the evening weeping had place, and in the morning gladness. Thus he gave the day to his neighbour and the night to God, knowing that in the day-time the Lord hath commanded mercy, and a canticle in the night." In his active work for souls he had to discharge the duties both of a confessor and a preacher. As a confessor he possessed a singular grace for drawing souls to true penance, and devoted himself with unwearied patience to this office, for which he received plenary faculties from the Pope, enabling him to hear confessions in all places, and to absolve from all offences, whatever they might be. His extraordinary skill in the tribunal of penance, drew great numbers to seek his assistance, over whose sins he wept tears of compassion, moving them to weep for themselves. It is said that our Blessed Lady was known at various times to help her devout servant in this ministry, and to suggest to his penitents the sins they had forgotten. But his labours in the confessional never prevented him from daily breaking to the multitude the bread of Divine doctrine. God having called him to be the dispenser of the Word, he devoted himself to this duty with unremitting ardour. In this respect, as in so many others, we behold him treading closely in the footsteps of his Master. As we study the Life of our Lord in the holy Gospels, we seem to follow Him passing from town to town and from village to village, preaching the Word of God to all classes and to all listeners. On the mountain and on the plain, in the synagogue of Nazareth and by the sea-shore of Tiberias, regardless of fatigue, and allowing Himself no repose, it was His daily labour to teach the multitude. And Dominic, His faithful servant and disciple, followed closely in His track. "He preached," says Blessed Jordan, "by night and by day, in houses, in the fields, and by the roadside." Stephen of Bourbon tells us that his sermons "abounded with examples" drawn for the most part from Holy Scripture. "He was most assiduous in preaching," says Rodolph of Faenza, "and when he spoke his words were so touching that he often moved both himself and his hearers to tears, nor did I ever listen to any man who had such power to touch the heart with compunction." Unfortunately, no fragments of his discourses are preserved, but we know that he constantly explained the mysteries of the holy Rosary; in other words, that the favourite topics on which he dwelt were the Life and Passion of Jesus Christ, and it is said that he never preached without preparing by a previous meditation. Not content with this public ministry of the Word, he gave himself with unwearied diligence to the instruction of his own brethren, to whom, unless prevented by some great necessity, he every day gave a spiritual conference.

The courage of which we have spoken above, as so conspicuous in the character of St. Dominic, had its root in his unshaken confidence in God. Rodolph of Faenza, who for several years filled the office of procurator, said that whenever bread or wine or any other food was wanting, he used to go to the blessed Father, saying: "Father, we have nothing to set before the brethren," and he would reply, "Go and pray, my son, and God will provide." Then he would go to the church, and the blessed Dominic often went and prayed with him, and God always brought it about that they were supplied with all that they required. At other times the saint would bid him put upon the table such scraps as were in the house, and in one way or another they always had enough. He taught the same unwavering confidence in the goodness of God to those amongst the brethren who through ignorance or timidity feared to undertake the work of preaching. "Not only did he constantly preach himself," says John of Navarre, "but he used every means to induce his brethren to do the same; and he would send out even the unlearned to preach, saying: "Go securely, my children, for our Lord will put His words into your mouth. He will be with you, and nothing shall be wanting to you," and it always happened to them even as he had said. In like manner he encouraged those whom he sent out to new foundations, to endure with courage and patience the hardships of their first beginnings, assuring them that in due time God would abundantly provide; and it never failed to turn out as he had promised. This confidence was the more admirable from the conditions under which it was seen to be exercised. For he gradually established in his Order a poverty so absolute that the brethren depended on alms alone for their daily support. To many of his best friends and advisers the rules of human prudence seemed thus to be unwisely transgressed; but nothing moved the saint from his determination, nor did his sublime confidence ever fail of its reward. He knew in Whom he believed, and the trust of that perfect friendship was never disappointed.

In his own person he gave an example of the poverty which he taught to others. "Everything about him," says Gerard de Frachet, "breathed of poverty; his habit, shoes, girdle, knife, book, and all like things. You might see him with his scapular ever so short, yet did he not care to cover it with his mantle, even when in the presence of great personages. Summer and winter he wore the same tunic, which was very old and patched, and his mantle was of the worst." He not only required his brethren to live on alms, but himself very often went on the quest. Yet he knew how to unite the practice of poverty with that of liberality, and liked the brethren to be well provided. Poor as he was, moreover, he was a lover of hospitality, always ready to share what he had with others in greater need than himself. In the same spirit of large-hearted generosity he showed a great love and respect for other religious Orders, among whom perhaps the first place in his affections was held by the Franciscans and the Cistercians. With the latter he had been on intimate terms even in his boyhood, and after-wards in maturer years had shared with them the labours of the apostolate.[7] If such were the qualities of his heart, those of his intellect were not less admirable. In the con-troversies held with the Albigensian heretics he exhibited a profound knowledge of sacred science, as well as a singular skill in argument. "Most rich must have been the resources of that mind that could pour forth day after day such an abundant store of instruction, whether in his sermons, his lectures, or his spiritual conferences, without ever betraying the least token of exhaustion." It was as though there were an ever-flowing fountain within him, the waters of which were never dried up. Whilst he encouraged even the unlearned among his brethren to preach, trusting in the Divine assistance, he was careful to supply them with the means of instruction, and to guide them in their studies, insisting chiefly on their acquiring a thorough knowledge of Holy Scripture. Theodoric says that he constantly urged on them the study both of the Old and New Testaments, but

[7] In the *Menologium Cisterciense* many notices are given of the friend-ship existing between St. Dominic and various members of the Cistercian Order, and of the assistance given by them to the Order of Preachers, when it was newly instituted.

that as for the fables of philosophers and poets he made no great account of them. For himself, he always carried about with him the Gospel of St. Matthew and the Epistles of St. Paul, which he read so constantly that he knew them almost by heart. The very idea on which he founded his Order was that of supplying to the Church a body of religious men, qualified to defend the faith by their learning and eloquence. With the keen eye of a master-mind he fixed on the sites of the great European universities as suitable for his principal foundations; and so trained the brethren whom he placed there, that they drew to their ranks men of learning and ability in great numbers. When he himself appeared in any of these great seats of learning he was recognized as a master, and many of the wisest doctors of his time were proud to give him this title, and to reckon themselves his disciples.

This, then, is the outline of his character as we gather it from the testimony of those who knew him best, and who had held him company "going and returning, eating and sleeping, by day and by night, in sickness and in health." There is no sort of disagreement in the witness that they bear; one and all present us with the same portrait of a man "most perfect in humility," "zealous beyond all other men for the salvation of the human race," "who was never known to speak an idle word, or one that savoured of distraction," "wise, discreet, patient, and benign," so that as one witness says, "though he had known many holy persons in many parts of the world, yet he had never seen one so perfectly adorned with all virtues as the blessed Dominic."

And it pleased God that this richly gifted soul should inhabit an earthly tabernacle which by its beauty and majesty seemed a worthy temple of the Holy Ghost, "for truly," says Theodoric, "may we so call that holy body which was never stained by mortal sin or sullied by the least touch of concupiscence." It is the constant tradition of the Order, that even in his exterior he bore a certain resemblance to our Divine Lord. We have first the description left us by Sister Cecilia, who says, " He was about

the middle stature, but slightly made; his face was beautiful,
and rather sanguine in its colour, his hair and beard of
a fair and bright hue, and his eyes remarkably fine. From
his forehead and between his brows there seemed to shine
forth a radiant light, which drew respect and love from
those who saw it. He was always joyous and cheerful,
save when moved to compassion by the afflictions of his
neighbours. His hands were long and beautiful, and his
voice was clear, noble, and musical. He was never bald,
and he always preserved his religious crown or tonsure
entire, mingled here and there with a very few white hairs."
Père Réchac adds a few particulars gathered from other
authorities, who described his forehead as broad and majestic,
and his eyes as possessing a singular beauty of expression
which attracted the heart of those on whom he looked with
kindness, while they were capable of striking terror into
those of evil-doers. His head was generally a little inclined,
in an attitude of thoughtfulness and humility. "His voice,"
says Theodoric, "was very powerful and musical, like the
sound of a silver trumpet." His chestnut hair and sanguine
complexion were probably derived from his northern ancestry,
and correspond with the description given by Nicephorus[8]
of the appearance of our Lord; another trait of supposed
resemblance being the shape of the beard, which in St.
Dominic was cleft in twain, similar to that with which our

[8] The description given of our Lord's person by Nicephorus Callistus,
the Greek ecclesiastical historian, bears a striking similarity to that of
St. Dominic as drawn by Sister Cecilia. It is as follows: "The countenance of Jesus Christ was beautiful and full of life. He was somewhat
above the middle height. His hair was a light chestnut, not very thick,
and somewhat curled at the extremities, His eyebrows dark and slightly
arched. From His eyes there shone forth a marvellous grace of expression;
His nose was long, His beard brown, but moderate in size. His hair
was rather long, for no razor had ever passed over His head, nor had the
hand of any person touched it, save that of His Mother in His infancy.
His neck inclined slightly forward, so that there was nothing stiff or
haughty in His bearing, and His complexion was the colour of ripe wheat.
His face was neither round or sharp, but rather long like His Mother's,
and was slightly tinged with a ruddy hue. Gravity and prudence shone
therein, joined with great sweetness and serenity. To conclude, in all
respects He greatly resembled His Holy Mother" (Niceph. Callis. lib. i.
c. 40).

PORTRAIT OF ST. DOMINIC.

PRESERVED IN HIS CELL AT ST. SABINA.

Lord is commonly represented. Although several so-called portraits are preserved, yet none of them can be regarded as the *vera effigies* of the saint, though that preserved at Santa Sabina probably presents us with a kind of traditionary likeness. If we compare this with the engraved gem which professes to be the true portrait of Jesus Christ, a certain resemblance may be traced between them, specially in the straight line of the nose and forehead, which according to the rules of Greek art, was deemed to belong to the highest type of humanity. St. Antoninus has dwelt on the resemblance, as well interior as exterior, existing between the Master and His disciple, and has drawn out the parallel at some length, which Réchac sums up by saying that in the heart of St. Dominic as in that of our Lord, next to the sovereign love of God, three other loves reigned paramount : the love of the Blessed Virgin, the love of souls, and the love of the Cross. But the most remarkable passage which touches on this subject, is that which occurs in the Life of St. Catherine of Siena : " On the eve of the feast of St. Dominic, in the year 1370, she was praying in the church, and meditating on the glory of the saint. Seeing her confessor, Blessed Bartholomew Dominic, enter the church, she begged him to hear her, as she had something to communicate. Then she began to speak to him of the holy Father, St. Dominic. ' Do you not see him, our blessed Father ?' she said. ' I see him as distinctly as I see you. How like he is to our Lord ! his face is oval, grave, and sweet, and his hair and beard are the same colour.' Then she went on to declare how in a vision she had seen the Eternal Father producing from His mouth His Beloved Son, and as she contemplated Him, she beheld St. Dominic coming forth, as it were, from His breast. And a voice declared to her, saying, ' Behold, daughter, I have begotten these two sons, one by nature, the other by adoption. For as this My natural Son in His Human Nature was ever most perfectly obedient to Me even to death, so this My son by adoption was obedient to Me in all points from his childhood to his dying day, and directed all his works according to My commandments, and kept that purity both of body and soul, which he received of Me in Baptism, clean and unspotted to the end of his life. And as this My natural Son spoke openly to the world, and gave a most clear testimony to the truth that I put into His mouth, even so did this My son by adoption preach the truths of My Gospel, as well to heretics and schismatics, as among My faithful people. And as this My natural Son sent out His disciples to publish the Gospel to all creatures, so does this My son by adoption send out his children and brethren under the yoke of his obedience and discipline. And so for this cause it is granted to him and to his, by special privilege, that they shall have the true understanding of My Word, and shall never swerve from the same. And as this My natural Son ordained the state of His holy life in deeds and words to the salvation of souls, even so did My son by adoption employ himself wholly both in doctrine and example, to deliver souls from the snares of the devil. For it was his principal intent when he first founded his Order, to win souls out of the bondage of error and sin, and to bring them to the knowledge of truth and the exercise of a godly life, for which cause I liken him to My natural Son.' "[9]

With this quotation we may fitly conclude the present chapter, for none would care to add to the words with which a saint in extasy proclaims the glory of a saint.

[9] Process. 1330. *Life of St. Catherine* (Fen's translation), part 2, c. xxv.

# CHAPTER XX.

IN the autumn of the year 1218, St. Dominic prepared to leave Rome, in order to visit the various settlements which had been made by the brethren since their dispersion at St. Romain. In particular he desired to travel into Spain, that he might strengthen the young foundations in that country, which had hitherto met with very partial success. A feeling of humility is also said to have urged him at this time to absent himself from Rome, where the fame of his preaching and miracles was earning him a homage of popular applause, from which he shrank with horror. He accordingly appointed Reginald of Orleans to be his vicar in Italy during his absence, and chose Bologna as his place of residence, whence it appears probable that Reginald had returned from the East, before the holy Father's departure from Rome, which took place about the feast of All Saints.

Leaving the city therefore with his stick, his little bundle, and his copy of the Gospels, Dominic set out, together with a few of his religious, and took the road to Bologna. On the way they were joined by a Franciscan, named Brother Albert, who greatly rejoiced at finding himself in such good company. As they journeyed along, engaged in pious discourse, they encountered a fierce dog, who attacked the poor Franciscan, and tore his habit to rags. In sore distress he sat down by the wayside, not knowing what to do; but the saint compassionating his trouble, applied a little mud to the torn garment; and when the mud dried the rents were found to be perfectly joined together. Passing through Florence, he reached Faenza, where the following incident

s

occurred as related in the ancient memoirs preserved in the convent of that place. ♱Albert, the bishop of Faenza, was so charmed by his eloquence and the fascination of his discourse, that he would not allow him to lodge anywhere but in the episcopal palace. This did not, however, prevent Dominic from pursuing his ordinary course of life; every night he rose at the hour of Matins, as was his custom, and proceeded to the nearest church to assist at the Divine Office. The attendants of the bishop noticed this; and on watching him secretly to observe how he was able to leave the palace without rousing the inmates, they observed two beautiful youths who stood by the door of his chamber with lighted torches, and so led the way for him and his companions, every door opening for them as they went along; and in this way they were every night conducted in safety to the church of St. Andrew, whence, after the singing of Matins, they returned in like manner. When this was made known to Albert, he himself watched and became an eye-witness of the fact, and in consequence he procured the above church for a future foundation of the Order.♱ A memorial of this circumstance is preserved in the name given to the ground lying between the bishop's palace and St. Andrew's church, which is still called "the Angels' Field." St. Dominic often returned to Faenza and preached to the inhabitants, who so greatly valued his ministrations among them that they erected for his use on the public road going to Imola a pulpit, in which he preached several times, as did also St. Peter Martyr and St. Thomas Aquinas. Michael Pio describes this pulpit as still existing in his time, and says that out of reverence for the saints who had stood therein no other preacher had presumed to use it.[1]

Thus journeying, Dominic arrived at Bologna, where the brethren were still inhabiting their first convent of Santa Maria della Mascarella, and enduring much poverty and many hardships. The arrival of the saint among them was therefore doubly welcome. Some of those who had joined the community since their establishment in the city

[1] *Prog.* 91, 92.

had never seen the holy founder, and rejoiced greatly in the opportunity of doing so; and all gathered fresh courage from his presence and the burning words he addressed to them. In spite of their poverty, the prospects of the community had brightened in some respects since their first arrival. It happened that Cardinal Ugolino was at that time appointed Legate of Bologna, and moved by the great love he bore to St. Dominic, he desired to obtain for the friars a more suitable residence than the narrow and inconvenient quarters they then occupied.

The hospice attached to the church of Santa Maria was quite insufficient for their rapidly increasing numbers, and was incapable of enlargement, being surrounded on all sides by buildings. The Cardinal therefore decided on removing them to a different quarter of the city, and made choice of a church which at that time stood outside the walls, and occupied an open space in the midst of vineyards, whence it took its name of St. Nicholas delle Vigne. The rector of this church was a priest of holy life, named Rodolph of Faenza, to whom Ugolino proposed that he should resign the church and the plot of ground on which it stood, for the foundation of a convent of Friars Preachers. To this suggestion the good man acceded with generous promptness, but it was also necessary to obtain the consent of the patron of the church, a Bolognese nobleman named D'Andalo,[1] a matter of much greater difficulty. The proposals of the Cardinal, however, found an unexpected and powerful advocate in the person of Diana D'Andalo, a daughter of this noble house, who persuaded her father and grandfather, not only to make over to the friars their rights in the church, but also to bestow on them as a free gift, a small house adjoining it with ground attached to serve as a site for their convent.

Tradition had long pointed out this spot as destined to become a place of special prayer and pilgrimage. There was a certain devout woman of the city whose custom it

---

[1] Or more correctly Andalo Degli Andalotti, though the name is commonly given as above.

was to kneel and pray whenever she came that way, and when the passers-by used to laugh at her for her folly, "Yours is the folly," she would reply; "if you knew all that will one day happen on this spot you would kneel and worship with me, for those who are to live here in time to come will make our city illustrious throughout the whole world." Others spoke of a mysterious music which had been heard by the labourers among the vines, and which they believed to be the voices of angels. A citizen of Bologna passing there one day with his little son, whose name was Chiaro, told the child that the field through which they were walking was a spot favoured by heaven, and that the angels had been heard singing over it. "But, father," said the boy, "perhaps they were only men and women who were heard singing." "My child," replied his father, "know this, that the voices of men are one thing, and the voices of angels are another."

These traditions found their fulfilment when the white-robed children of St. Dominic were established on this spot, and the songs of the angels were exchanged for the chant of their midnight Office; a holy place indeed, for here were laid the foundations of that noble convent, the nursery of so many illustrious members of the Dominican Order in time to come. The buildings necessary for the accommodation of the brethren, which were planned at first on a very humble scale, had been begun before the arrival of the saint in Bologna, and pending their completion the community continued to occupy their first quarters at the Mascarella.

In spite of this welcome benefaction, however, the poverty of the friars continued to be extreme, and it was no rare thing for them to find themselves in want even of the small portion of bread which formed their only fare. One day the procurator came to the man of God, and complained that though the brethren were very numerous, he had nothing to set before them for dinner but two little loaves. Dominic desired him to cut them into a number of very small pieces, and himself assisted him in doing so; he then desired the server to go round and put two or three of these little pieces on each table. When he had made the round of the refectory, and had still some morsels left, he went round a second and a third time, adding a little each time to what he had at first laid on the table. And thus he went on until he had set before the brethren abundance and to spare, so that by the gift of God, much more bread was cleared away when they had finished their repast than what was originally set before them.[3]

As may be supposed at a time when the brethren were so often in want even of bread, they could not allow themselves the luxury of wine, even for the use of the infirmary, unless it chanced that some was given them as an alms. One day the infirmarian came to the holy Father, and pleaded the cause of the sick, for whom he much desired to procure a little wine, of which there was not a drop in the house. According to his custom the saint bowed his head in prayer, bidding the other pray with him. Then he bade him go and look at the empty vessel, in which the wine which they sometimes received was commonly kept, and make sure if perhaps a little had not been left in it. The Brother obeyed, and on opening the vessel discovered to his great joy that it was full of excellent wine.

On another occasion the same miracle was renewed that had formerly been witnessed in the refectory of St. Sixtus, and the community was fed by the hands of angels. The narrative is thus related by Father Ludovico of Palermo:

"After our sweet Father St. Dominic had finished the arduous business committed to him by the Holy Pontiff at Rome, he came to Bologna and lodged at the Mascarella, where the friars still abode, not being able to go to St. Nicholas by reason of the rooms being yet too fresh and damp. And it happened on a day that, on account of the great multitude of the brethren, there was no bread except a few very little pieces; and the blessing being given, the good Father raised his eyes and his heart to God, and lo! the doors being closed, there appeared two beautiful youths with two baskets of the whitest loaves, and giving one thereof

[3] *Vit. Frat.* part 2, c. xx.

to each friar, they so multiplied that there remained an
abundance, enough for three days. This great miracle
happened twice at Rome and twice at Bologna. And my
dear friend the rector of Santa Maria Mascarella, told me that
every year on the same day when the holy angels brought the
heavenly bread, most sweet odours which lasted forty hours
were perceived in the space then occupied by the refectory."

The table on which the miraculous loaves were placed
was left at Santa Maria, when the friars removed to
St. Nicholas, and was carefully preserved in a niche guarded
by iron bars, where Father Ludovico mentions having seen
it. It was constantly regarded as a precious relic, and was
supposed to have been adorned at a very early date with a
painting representing the miracle, but no steps were taken
for verifying the fact till 1881, when the parish priest of
Santa Maria, wishing to add to the decorations of the altar
over which it was then placed, caused the table to be
removed for a time to the house occupied by the Confraternity of the Blessed Sacrament, on which occasion it was
carefully examined by command of the Cardinal Archbishop
of Bologna. It was found that besides being much decayed
and worm-eaten, the wooden planks had suffered not a little
from the depredations of the devout, who had cut off small
portions to carry away as relics. Moreover, to fit it into the
space it had formerly occupied, the table had been sawn into
three parts, which were placed one above the other, and
fastened by iron cramps. But in spite of these injuries
there was plainly visible on the upper surface, a roughly
executed painting, belonging, as it seemed, to the early part
of the fifteenth century. It represents twelve persons seated
at an oblong table, in the midst of whom appears the holy
Patriarch with his hand raised in benediction. Standing
before the table are two angels, only their heads and wings
being now discernible. A yet more ancient painting of the
same subject, attributed to the thirteenth century, was
discovered on the other side of the table, with the remains
of an inscription, of which but a few words are now legible.
Santa Maria in Mascarella preserves other memorials of

this first visit of St. Dominic within its walls. The room once occupied by the saint has been turned into a chapel, over the altar of which is preserved a very ancient picture of our Lady, which is said once to have spoken to him. Between the chapel and the parish church is a large hall which, according to tradition, was formerly used as the refectory of the friars, and was the scene of the angels' visit.[4]

St. Dominic's stay at Bologna was of very brief duration, for he was anxious to reach Spain before Christmas, stopping at St. Romain on his way. He therefore set out, accompanied by Bertrand of Garrigua and the brethren who had come with him from Rome. The only incident recorded of the journey is amusingly related by Castiglio, who, however, does not inform us where it took place. The saint having one day stopped at an inn with his companions, the hostess was much disturbed at the small gains she saw herself likely to make by them, for they being many, and eating little, she was put to much trouble to little purpose. Wherefore, as the servants of God conversed together on spiritual things, according to their wont, she went about grumbling and blaspheming, saying all the evil words that came into her mind ; and the more the holy Father sought to appease her with fair speeches, the more violent she became, not being willing to hear reason. At length, being greatly disturbed by the noise of this virago, St. Dominic spoke to her and said, " Sister, since you will not leave us in peace for the love of God, I pray Him that He will Himself silence you," which words were no sooner uttered than she lost the power of speech, and became entirely dumb. She continued so until the saint's return from Spain, when, as he stopped at the same inn, she threw herself at his feet to implore his pardon, and

[4] *Cenni Storici sulla tavola di S. Domenico.* Bologna, 1883. In this little brochure is given a fac-simile of the paintings described above. By the greater number of writers the foundation of St. Nicholas is assigned to Blessed Reginald of Orleans. The actual removal thither of the friars undoubtedly took place under his government, but from Father Ludovico's narrative, given above, it is plain that the grant of the church had already been made, and the building of the convent begun before Reginald arrived at Bologna.

he restored to her the use of her tongue, with a warning that she should use it in future to the praise of God.

It was some time in the month of November when the travellers reached Toulouse, where the community of St. Romain had endured incredible hardships during the siege of that city, which had lasted nine months, and ended in the death of De Montfort and the temporary triumph of the heretics and their supporters. As the staunchest champions of the faith they had everything to fear from the enmity of Count Raymund VII., and the malice of the heretics of Toulouse, which had been so openly manifested against Peter Cellani, that Dominic judged it prudent to despatch him to Paris, at the same time summoning thence his brother Manes, whom he purposed taking with him into Spain. He remained a few days at St. Romain, during which time he did his best to encourage and advise the brethren; then leaving Bertrand to support them in their difficult position, he continued his journey, being anxious to complete it before the winter set in. The whole time occupied in his progress from Rome to Segovia, including that taken up by his visits to Bologna and St. Romain, did not exceed seven weeks, and when we remember that he had to cross both the Alps and the Pyrenees, and that the journey was made on foot, and in the season of winter, the energy and resolution that could have accomplished such an undertaking in so short a period, appear truly wonderful. We have again to remind ourselves that our story belongs to a date from which we are separated by nearly seven centuries, and that those wild mountain-passes now traversed by military roads, or pierced by railway tunnels, were then savage wildernesses, where every kind of peril had to be encountered by the traveller. But neither fatigue nor danger had power to daunt the heroic resolution of the saint; they did but raise his courage higher, as, singing aloud the *Veni Creator* or the *Ave Maris Stella*, he passed fearlessly over rocky steeps and foaming torrents till his feet once more pressed that native soil of Spain from which he had been absent for more than thirteen years.

THE ALCAZAR OF SEGOVIA.

# CHAPTER XXI.

### ST. DOMINIC IN SPAIN.

#### 1218, 1219.

ON a steep hill which rises in the midst of the plains
stretching north of the Guadarrama mountains, stands the
city of Segovia, ancient even at the period when it was
visited by St. Dominic, and still unchanged in many of its
features from the aspect which it must then have presented.
The stupendous Roman aqueduct, built of blocks of un-
cemented granite, the rocky hill, washed at its base by
the river Eresma, on the summit of which the Alcazar,
or Moorish castle, stands at the verge of a giddy precipice,
present much the same spectacle as that on which his eyes
must have rested as he entered the city towards the festival
of Christmas, in the year 1218, an unknown and wayworn

traveller, seeking hospitality in some house of entertainment frequented by the poor. As he travelled hither from the frontiers of France, he must necessarily have passed through that part of the country familiar to his youth: for Segovia is situated only a few miles to the south-west of Osma and Calaroga. Doubtless his return to this well-known neighbourhood brought back many memories of his friendship with Diego, and the long, quiet years of his early life, before at the call of God he exchanged his cloistral retirement for the labours of the apostolate. But on all this history is silent, nor does he seem to have stopped anywhere on his road before reaching Segovia. There he took up his abode in the house of a poor woman, who was not long before she recognized the sanctity of her guest. Dominic chanced to discover that she had in her possession a very rough hair-shirt, and desiring much to obtain this treasure for himself, he besought her to give it to him, offering an under-tunic that he wore in exchange. She willingly consented, and laid by the tunic in a box wherein she kept her little store of valuables. Some time afterwards a fire broke out in her house and everything was consumed excepting this box, which, as she believed by the merits of St. Dominic, was saved with all its contents. The larger part of the tunic she afterwards gave to the Fathers of Segovia, only reserving for herself the sleeves, which were long preserved in the monastery of Valladolid.

Dominic had not been many days in the city, before he began his usual work of preaching, and that with more than usual success. Possibly the freedom of speaking once more in his own mother-tongue, and the sight of those Spanish hills after long years of absence, gave fresh inspiration to his words. Priests and seculars, magistrates and citizens, all flocked to hear him, and conjured him to deal out liberally to his countrymen the bread of life. It pleased God to confirm the words of His servant by several special manifestations of Divine power.

A long drought had afflicted the country of Segovia, and reduced the inhabitants to the utmost distress. One day, as they gathered together outside the walls to hear the preaching, Dominic, after beginning his discourse, as if suddenly inspired by God, exclaimed, "Fear nothing, my brethren, but trust in the Divine mercy. I announce to you good news, for this very day God will send you a plentiful rain, and the drought shall be turned into plenty." His hearers looked about them with surprise, for the sun was at that moment shining brightly in the heavens, and there were no signs to indicate any change in the weather. Nevertheless, before the sermon was ended, dark clouds overspread the sky, and soon such torrents of rain fell, that the assembled crowds could scarcely make their way to their own homes. On another occasion, as he was preaching before the senate of the city, some letters from the king were delivered to the councillors present, who at once withdrew in order to open and read them. The preaching had to be suspended until their return, and when the man of God resumed his discourse he did not fail to make an application of what had just taken place. "You have listened to the words of an earthly king," he said, "now hear those of Him Who is eternal and Divine." One of the senators took offence at the freedom of his speech, and mounting his horse rode off, exclaiming contemptuously, "A fine thing, forsooth, for this fellow to keep us here all day with his fooleries! Truly it is time to go home to dinner." Then the blessed Dominic, looking at him with sorrow, and being filled with the spirit of prophecy, replied, saying, "You go away now, but before the year is over that horse of yours will want its rider, and you will not be able to reach the castle you have so carefully prepared as a place of refuge, for it will have fallen into the hands of your enemies." These words were fulfilled to the letter, for within the year this nobleman, together with his son and cousin, was slain on the very spot where he was then mounting his horse, and his strong castle, as the saint had foretold, was seized by the assassins.

Dominic soon endeared himself to the people of Segovia, who were proud of him as a fellow-countryman, and thronged

about him in crowds whenever he appeared in public.  There
is a green meadow outside the city through which rushes
the river Eresma, its beautiful banks thickly shaded by
alders and willows, where, according to tradition, the saint
often preached to the assembled multitudes, and where a
little chapel has since been erected in his honour.  He very
shortly gathered together a number of fervent disciples, with
whom he was able to lay the foundations of a convent
dedicated to the Holy Cross.  Very different is the present
convent which bears that title, and which is to be seen
nestling under the turfy slopes, displaying its rich flamboyant
entrance, adorned with statues of the saints of the Order,
and the royal badges of Castile and Aragon, from the austere
abode in which St. Dominic placed the first brethren of
Segovia.  The rocky hill on which the city stands is pierced
with a number of grottos, and adjoining one of these the
saint caused a few cells to be erected, so poor and narrow
in their proportions as to excite the wonder of all who
beheld them.  The site bore an aspect of rugged severity
well suited to the dwelling of those who embraced a life
of poverty and mortification.  The grotto itself was deeply
sunk in the rock, and had been chosen by the holy
Father as a place to which he could retire at night, in
order to fulfil those exercises of prayer and penance which
he never laid aside.  This kind of solitude had a singular
attraction for him, and local traditions point out more than
one such spot to which he was in the habit of withdrawing,
as at Castres, where a cave is still shown bearing the title
of the cave of St. Dominic.  At none of these, however,
has his presence been so well attested as at the grotto
of Segovia.  Its rocky walls (as those testified who secretly
watched him) were often wet with his tears and watered
with his blood.  The ruddy stains are still shown, which
bear witness to the heroic constancy with which this true
martyr of penance offered his scourged and bleeding body
as a sacrifice to God.  For when in process of time a stately
monastery was raised upon the site, this grotto was included
within its circuit, and converted into a chapel often visited

by pious pilgrims. Among these was one whose name is scarcely less illustrious in the history of her country than that of St. Dominic himself. In the year 1574, St. Theresa, before leaving Segovia to return to Avila, "desired," says Ribera, "to visit the Dominican monastery of the Holy Cross, in which is that celebrated chapel which the glorious St. Dominic so often watered with the blood of penance. She entered the chapel accompanied by the prior and by Father Diego de Yanguas, who at that time acted as her confessor. Having approached the altar, she prostrated on the ground in prayer, and being wrapt in extasy, beheld at her left side the glorious patriarch St. Dominic. After awhile Father Diego called her, and she at once arose, bathed in tears, which according to her custom she tried to conceal. The Father heard her confession, said Mass and gave her Communion, after which, returning to her prayers, she saw St. Dominic as before, standing on her left side. Then she asked him why he placed himself there, and he replied, ' Because the right side belongs to my Master.' At these words she turned, and beheld our Lord standing on her right hand side. He remained there for some minutes, and before withdrawing His sacred presence, He spake to her these words, ' REJOICE WITH MY FRIEND.'

"St. Theresa spent about two hours in the chapel, during which time the holy Father St. Dominic remained by her side relating to her what he had suffered in that grotto, and the great graces which our Lord had there bestowed upon him. Moreover, he promised to assist her powerfully in the affairs of her Order, and added many words of encouragement and consolation. She often afterwards declared that God at this time bestowed on her so many graces, and filled her soul with so much spiritual joy, that she could have desired never more to have left that holy sanctuary."[1]

In this most interesting narrative, our Lord is represented as conferring on His servant the very title by which he was known amongst his own followers. " Rejoice with MY FRIEND." How singular a happiness was his in being thus

[1] Ribera, *Vie de Ste. Térèse*, lib. iv. c. xiii.

named by the voice of Truth itself; and how justly is that
sanctuary to be held in honour wherein was granted a
revelation so touching, for ever linking the holy memories
of St. Dominic and St. Theresa! *Nimis honorati sunt amici
tui Deus.*

Dominic appointed to the government of this convent
a certain Brother commonly known as Blessed Corbolan the
Simple, who was beloved and venerated by the holy Father
for the purity and innocence of his life. As soon as the
foundation of the convent was complete, he set out for
Zamora, then one of the principal cities of Old Castile,
being an important mercantile centre, and having in consequence a large Jewish population. It offered, therefore,
a great field to the apostolic zeal of the saint, who desired
greatly to secure a foundation for his brethren within its
walls. The charm of his preaching won the good-will of
the citizens, and according to Polidori, his aunt, Donna
Sancia Guzman, purchased a piece of land called *las Sageras*,
used as a burial-place for the Jews outside the walls, and
gave it for the site of the future convent, which was actually
established a few months later. St. Antoninus, in his
Chronicles, speaks of this convent as one favoured by special
tokens of heavenly protection. Once as the brethren were
singing Office in choir they heard a voice bidding them fly
with haste. Obeying what they deemed a Divine warning, they
had hardly left the spot when the walls of the building fell
in, and so they escaped a cruel death. Here was preserved
a crucifix which had belonged to the blessed Dominic, and
was said on one occasion to have spoken to him, and a bell
which was often heard to toll untouched as a sign that one
of the brethren was about to pass out of this life. This was
so well understood that whenever the bell thus sounded each
member of the community was accustomed to prepare for
death.[2]

---

[2] Nanni, lib. 3, c. ii. The same is told of a bell belonging to the
convent of Salerno; and at Santa Catherina at Naples another signal,
resembling that given for the midnight Office, always sounded before a
death. P. Nanni declares having himself often heard it when living there
as a novice.

From Zamora, Dominic hastened on to Madrid, where a community had been already established by Peter of Medina, the same who was despatched into Spain at the time of the dispersion from Prouille. He and his brethren had met with a hospitable reception from the citizens, who furnished them with sufficient alms for their support, and assisted them in the erection of a little house outside the gate of Palnadù. It was poor and incommodious enough, but its poverty only recommended it the more to the heart of Dominic, who rejoiced greatly at the condition, both spiritual and temporal, in which he found the brethren. He carefully examined into their manner of life, their exercises of piety, and the labours they had undertaken for the good of their neighbour; and gave hearty thanks to God that He should have made choice of his children to be instruments of the salvation of souls, "the greatest and most honourable dignity," says P. Nanni, "that can be conferred on any creature." The people of Madrid earnestly desired to see the holy founder, whose reputation was already great amongst them; and the welcome they gave him, and the extraordinary fruit which attended his preaching, induced him to make a longer stay in the city than he had at first intended.

The change of manners indeed that was effected by the ministry of himself and his companions was so great and wonderful, "that," says Castiglio, "he could not satisfy himself with weeping, so great was the heavenly joy he felt at these manifest tokens of God's favour." Desiring in return to bestow some lasting benefit on the people who had so generously received him, he resolved on founding amongst them a convent of religious women to receive those pious souls who were desirous of flying from the vanities of the world and consecrating themselves to God, but for whom no suitable asylum then existed, for convents for women were still rare in Spain. Having once formed this design, he lost no time in carrying it into effect, and in order as soon as possible to provide his nuns with a dwelling, he and his brethren gave up the little house they had hitherto inhabited, and set about enlarging it and adapting it to the use of its proposed occupants. This undertaking was regarded with singular favour by the people of Madrid, who contributed liberally towards both the erection and endowment of the new monastery. So anxious was the saint to forward this work that, assisted by the brethren, he laboured at the building with his own hands. Though he was careful to provide his nuns with whatever was needful for religious observance, yet he desired that everything should be on a scale befitting holy poverty. " Their little chapel," says Castiglio, " resembled that of a hermitage, and the common dormitory had neither curtains nor partitions of any kind." All the necessary offices of the convent were provided with grates and turns according to the custom already adopted in France and Italy, in order the better to secure the observance of strict enclosure. As the building was not finished before his departure from Madrid, Dominic received the vows of the religious, but arranged for them to remain in their own homes until their new dwelling should be ready to receive them.[3] Meantime, he showed himself not less solicitous for their well-being, both spiritual and temporal, than he had been for that of his other religious daughters. He gave them the same rule and habit that had been adopted at Prouille and St. Sixtus, and appointed his own brother, Manes, to be their director and Superior. To provide for their support he renounced in their favour all the revenues that had been granted to the brethren since their coming to Madrid, leaving the latter in that state of absolute poverty which he desired to be the rule of the friars, though in the case of religious women he acknowledged it to be unsuitable.

The convent of Madrid was then, the third convent of nuns founded by St. Dominic. It was dedicated by him to St. Dominic of Silos, though after his canonization he himself was regarded as its titular patron. The singular interest with which he watched over this foundation is

[3] Danzas, *St. Raymond de Pennafort*, p. 158. It will be remembered that the year of novitiate before pronouncing the vows was not at this time required.

evident by the letter which after his departure he addressed
to the nuns on hearing of their final establishment in their
conventual home. This possesses a special value as being
almost the only authentic fragment of his writing which has
been preserved to posterity.

Brother Dominic, Master of the Friars Preachers, to the
Prioress and Sisters of the Convent of Madrid, health and
increase in all virtue.

We rejoice greatly at the report we have received of your
holy conversation, and give thanks to God that He has
delivered you from the mire of the world. Continue, then,
my daughters, to combat your ancient enemy with prayer
and watching, knowing that none shall be crowned save
those who have fought valiantly. Hitherto you have
had no house suitable for following your religious rule, but
now you will have no such excuse for negligence, seeing
that you are provided with a convent in which you can
perfectly carry out every detail of religious life. I desire
therefore that henceforth silence be better observed in the
places of silence, such as the choir, the refectory, and the
dormitory, and that you live in all other respects according
to the Constitutions that have been given to you. Let no
one go outside the enclosure, and let no one be admitted
within it, unless it be some bishop or prelate who shall
come to preach or to visit you. Do not neglect vigils
and disciplines, and let all be obedient to the prioress. Let
none waste time in idle conversation about unnecessary
things. And inasmuch as we cannot help you in your
temporal necessities, we desire not to be a burden to you,
nor will we permit that any Brother should have authority
to receive novices, but only the prioress with the council of
her convent. We command our dearest Brother, who has
laboured so much for you and has gathered you together in
this holy state, that he will dispose all things as seems best
to him, to the end that your life may be ordered in a holy
and religious manner. Therefore we give him full faculties
and authority to visit and correct you, and if need be, to

T

remove the prioress from her office, with the consent, however, of the majority of the community, and also to grant any dispensations that he may consider necessary.

Farewell in Christ.

The convent of St. Dominic the Royal, as it came to be called, went through many vicissitudes of fortune, both prosperous and adverse. The holy king St. Ferdinand III. regarded the community with special favour, and five years after the death of St. Dominic granted them a kind of charter written partly in Latin, and partly in Spanish, in which he took them under his protection. In spite of his good-will towards them, however, attempts were made to declare them incapable of inheriting or holding property, and the question was only set at rest in 1237 by a Bull from the Pope affirming the rights of the religious and charging the King to defend them. But another trouble arose about the same time from a quarter whence it was least expected. The Superiors of the Spanish province thought good to withdraw the Fathers of the Order whom St. Dominic had left at Madrid for the direction of the nuns, leaving them to be supplied in their spiritual necessities by secular priests. This was the more sensibly felt, as according to Castiglio, there were at that time in Spain very few ecclesiastics, and those but poorly educated, the incessant wars with the Moors and the troubles thence arising giving no facilities to the secular clergy for following their studies, so that few or none were then to be found among them qualified to act as guides in the spiritual life. In their distress, therefore, the nuns appealed to Pope Gregory IX., trusting that out of the great friendship he had borne towards the person of their holy founder, he would not suffer them to be thus abandoned. Nor were their hopes disappointed, for he at once despatched a Brief addressed to the General of the Order and the Provincial of Spain, in which he peremptorily required that the brethren should resume the spiritual direction of the nuns. One little incident related by Gerard de Frachet as happening at a time " when the Sisters were still living who

had received the habit from the hands of St. Dominic," may
be given here as a warning to the impatient.  Two brethren,
possibly of the number of those who had sought to escape
from the responsibility of directing the nuns, were sent to
Madrid, and one of them, who was charged with the duty of
delivering an instruction to the community, seems to have
found his task a difficult one and set about it unwillingly.
Lodged in a little house adjoining the convent, he tried to
prepare his discourse, but was greatly hindered and disturbed
whilst doing so by the incessant crowing of a cock belonging
to the religious.  At last he could stand it no longer, but
seizing his stick rushed out, and dealt the unfortunate bird a
blow which laid him dead at his feet.  Ashamed of his fit
of passion, he picked up the dead bird, and prayed it might
be restored to life, promising our Lord if the favour were
granted, that he would never again give way to his impatient
temper.  As he did so the cock fluttered out of his hands to
the ground, and began to crow gently, as if he desired not
again to exasperate the Brother.  Brother Giles, from whom
Gerard received this story, assured him that he had heard
it from the friar who was the chief actor in it.  Doubtless,
the history of their cock was not soon forgotten by the nuns
themselves.

As to the convent itself, the little building which
St. Dominic had laboured with his own hands to raise, did
not last many years.  Whether from its poor materials, or
from the hasty manner in which it had been constructed,
it soon fell into decay, and not long after the death of the
saint had to be replaced by another and much more stately
edifice, some portions of which are said still to remain.
Here the community continued to flourish for several
centuries, during which it produced many holy religious,
worthy descendants of those first planted here by their
holy founder.

It was with unbounded regret that the people of Madrid
at length took leave of the saint whose presence had brought
them so many precious graces.  " His teaching and conversation," says Castiglio, " had so captivated the souls of all,

that they felt themselves raised on high to great and heavenly things, whilst their affections were drawn to him with singular tenderness." Nor was he indifferent to the regard which they showed him and the generous response they had given to his words. On returning to Italy he failed not to make known to the Pope their fervent and devout dispositions, and in consequence Honorius despatched a Brief to the inhabitants of Madrid, in which he declared how acceptable to him had been the welcome they had given to his beloved sons the Friars Preachers, seeing that no good work can be more pleasing to God than thus to show charity to those who labour for the salvation of souls.

On leaving Madrid, Dominic directed his steps towards the city of Saragossa; but on his road thither a sorrowful trial was in store for him. Like his Divine Master, he was to taste the bitterness of being deserted by his own disciples. He was warned of the coming trouble by a vision in which he beheld a terrible dragon that seemed ready to attack and devour his companions. In fact, when they reached Guadalaxara many of them, discouraged by the hardships of the journey, broke out into murmurs, and even determined to cast off the habit and return to the world. It would seem that these religious were not those who came from Italy with the saint, but some young Castilian novices who had been attracted to him by the fame of his eloquence and miracles, but whose fervour cooled as soon as they made closer acquaintance with the austerity of his Rule. Their discontent was soon discovered by Dominic. He did his best to deter them from their purpose, but in vain: three only remained with him, a cleric named Adam, and two lay-brothers; the rest having put their hands to the plough, looked back and left him. Turning sadly to those who remained faithful, Dominic addressed them in the words of our Lord on a like occasion: "Will ye also go away?" "May God forbid, my Father," replied one of them, "that we should follow the feet, and abandon the head."

The saint, according to his custom, took refuge in

prayer, and that with so happy a result, that those who had yielded to the force of temptation soon repented of their cowardice, and, returning with tears, cast themselves at his feet and prayed to be received back into the company of his children. The tender heart of their loving Father did not reject them, nor from that time did they show any further signs of inconstancy in their holy vocation.

The memory of this incident has been preserved in a touching passage of the Constitutions of the Order, introduced at a later period, with an evident allusion to these circumstances. "Whenever novices," it is said, "wish to return to the world, we command all the religious freely to let them go, and to return them all that they have brought. Nor must they give them any vexation on this account, after the example of Him, Who, when some of His disciples went back, said to those that remained, 'Will ye go away?'"[4]

Arriving at Saragossa, Dominic and his companions took up their abode in the convent that had already been founded on the banks of the Ebro by some of the brethren sent from Prouille. Here Dominic gathered great fruit of souls, and according to Flaminius effected many striking conversions through the medium of the Rosary. On one occasion, as he expounded to a crowded audience those words of St. John, "He who commits sin is the servant of sin," it chanced that one of the chief men in the city, named Peter, who is said to have been a near relative of the saint, came to the church rather out of curiosity than devotion, for he was plunged in every kind of evil living; and conscious of his miserable condition, without having the will to amend it, had given himself up to despair. St. Dominic seeing him enter, by the Spirit of God discerned the state of his soul, which he beheld, as it were, possessed by evil spirits as many in number as

---

[4] Const. FF. Præd. d. 1. c. 14. Several writers relate the defection of St. Dominic's disciples as occurring on his first entrance into Spain. But in this case we should have to suppose that the deserters were of the number of his old and tried companions, including his brother Manes, a thing which is evidently incredible. Malvenda examines the question carefully, and places the incident after his departure from Madrid.

were the vices to which he had abandoned himself. He therefore adapted his words so as to touch the heart of this unhappy reprobate, and succeeded so far as to rouse within him not only a sense of salutary fear, but a feeling of love towards the preacher which he could not explain to himself. In fact, the charity which kindled the heart of the saint often thus communicated its flame to those who heard him, and attracted them to him, as it were, in spite of themselves. The next day, Peter came again, unable, as it seemed, to resist the secret influence that drew him to the feet of the preacher. St. Dominic perceived him amidst the crowd of listeners, and as he continued to speak, raised his heart to God, earnestly recommending to Him the salvation of this soul. Then it came to pass by Divine permission, that the same spectacle that he had himself beheld on the previous day, was made sensible to the eyes of the congregation. They saw the unhappy man (whose sins were indeed open and notorious) compassed about with evil spirits, who held him as their bond-slave fast bound with cruel chains. Filled with terror they all fled from the church, leaving him covered with confusion. But the saint did not abandon him. Giving him a rosary and teaching him how to use it, he won the poor reprobate to resume the long-forgotten exercise of prayer, and to seek for mercy through the intercession of our Lady: and before leaving the city, he had the happiness of reconciling this soul to God, and of seeing him embrace a life of sincere penance.[5]

It seems probable that many other places were visited at this time by St. Dominic, besides those above enumerated, but there is no period of his history the events of which have been less carefully recorded. We are justified, however, in supposing that his labours were really of a far more extensive

---

[5] We have omitted from the above narrative a number of prodigies which seem to possess no sufficient authority, though they do not necessarily invalidate the story of Peter's conversion. The fact that some member of St. Dominic's family was converted by him during his visit to Spain, is obscurely referred to by several writers. Père Réchac, on the authority of Alan de la Roche, supposes it to have been a certain noble lady, recalled by the preaching of the saint from a worldly and vicious life.

character than would appear from the scanty notices preserved by his biographers.[1] From the words used in his
deposition by Brother John of Navarre, it is clear, that
not Christians only, but Jews and Saracens, fell under the
benignant influence of the preacher.[4] "He showed himself
amiable to all men, rich and poor, Jews and Gentiles, who
were then very numerous in Spain ; and he was beloved by
all except the heretics, whom he refuted in his sermons and
disputations. Yet even these he exhorted with charity, and
sought to win them to penance and the true faith." These
words afford the only indication that St. Dominic addressed
himself to the conversion of the infidels, who at that time
mingled so largely with the Christian population of Spain.
Nor have we any certain information as to the route he
followed after leaving Saragossa. Castiglio contents himself
with saying that he preached and heard confessions in every
place through which he passed, and that neither weariness
nor the pressure of his immense labours, ever interrupted his
habits of devotion.

"Prayer had become so habitual with him," says this
writer, "that whether at home or abroad, in the church
or by the wayside, his heart was always united to God as
to a centre wherein he abode with marvellous tranquillity.
Like the three children who walked unharmed amid the
flames of the fiery furnace, so did St. Dominic maintain the
peace and quiet of his soul in the midst of every kind
of outward distraction. Never did he lose that interior
repose which is essential to the spirit of prayer, but in
all his cares and labours, amid hunger, thirst, fatigue, long
journeys, and continued interruptions, his heart was free
and ready to turn to God at all times, as though conscious
of none else but Him. Therefore many consolations were
granted to him that are not given to others ; and of this we
have evidence in his words and all his actions, wherein there
appeared a certain grace and sweetness of the Holy Ghost,
showing how dearly favoured was his soul."[6]

That in the course of these journeys he visited Palencia

* Castiglio, part i. lib. i. cap. 43.

seems certain from the important document quoted in a
former chapter, which firmly establishes the two facts that
confraternities of the Holy Rosary existed in the time of
St. Dominic, and that he himself actively propagated the
devotion.   We refer to the will of Anthony Sers, a citizen
of Palencia, who left a sum of money for supplying candles
for the use of the Confraternity of the Rosary, founded in that
city by the "good Dominic Guzman." Polidori speaks of
the warm welcome which he received from the bishop and
citizens of Palencia, among whom the memory of his charity
during the great famine still survived, and says that he
prepared the foundation of that celebrated convent of
St. Paul, which afterwards produced two of the *beati* of the
Order, Blessed Peter Gonzalez and Blessed Giles of
Portugal.   He adds that, passing on to Compostella, the
saint was present at the translation of the relics of St. James,
and preached on that occasion in the church dedicated to
the holy Apostle.

Another incidental proof of his having revisited the
scenes of his early life is to be found in the fact that the
nuns of St. Stephen of Gormas, near Osma, who had
hitherto lived under the Rule of St. Augustine, petitioned
to receive the Constitutions given to Prouille and the other
convents of women founded by St. Dominic, and to be
adopted into his Order.   These nuns afterwards removed
to the convent which was founded at Calaroga, a foundation suggested by the Blessed Manes after the death of
St. Dominic.   Preaching once in their native village, he
proposed to the people to raise a convent of the Order
on the very spot which had given birth to its great
founder.   "Only," he said, "let it be of modest proportions; if my brother sees fit, he will know how to enlarge
it."   Thirty years later, Alphonsus the Wise, King of
Castile, transformed the ancient abode of the family of
Guzman into a noble monastery, and the nuns of Gormas
were brought hither to occupy it.[7]

[7] Rod. de Cerrat, c. 50, in Append. t. i. *Ann. Præd.* This Brother
Rodriguez was confessor to King Alphonsus.

THE CONVENT OF CALAROGA.

[To face p. 296.

Unfortunately, no particulars of these visits have been preserved, and the last spot in Spain where we can with any certainty track the footsteps of the holy Father is at Barcelona, in Aragon. Here he was entertained in the house of a citizen named Peter Grunio, who lived in the parish of St. James, and in the street which now bears the name of St. Dominic. "There is a constant and most ancient tradition in Barcelona," says Malvenda, quoting from the historian Francis Diago, "that St. Dominic, returning into Italy out of Spain, passed some days in the house of Peter Grunio, now inhabited by the Friars Preachers." In this house was long preserved a portrait of the saint, having at his feet Berenger de Palon, bishop of Barcelona, and founder of the convent of Preachers in that city. For the statement of some writers to the effect that this foundation was made by St. Dominic himself, must be interpreted in the same sense as that in which so many other convents claim to have been founded by the saint, when, as a fact, he only prepared the way for their foundation by his presence and influence.

In reply to the pressing solicitations of the citizens, he promised shortly to despatch thither a colony of his brethren; and his host, Peter Grunio, generously offered his own house to be their residence.

Nothing is preserved that enables us to follow the course taken by St. Dominic after leaving Barcelona. It is believed, however, to have been during his homeward journey that an incident took place related by Gerard de Frachet without anything to indicate the date of its occurrence. "On a certain day," he says, "the saint was travelling with several companions, and when the time came for them to dine they found they had no more wine than would fill one small cup. The holy Father compassionated their needs, for some of his companions had been delicately nurtured in the world, and the want of wine was felt by them as a hardship, specially during the heat and fatigue of a long foot journey. He therefore desired the cup of wine to be poured into a large vessel, the bottom of which it scarcely covered, and then bade them fill it up with water. When this was done the vessel was found to be full of wine up to the very brim, and those who drank of it, who were to the number of eight, declared that in their whole lives they had never tasted any more excellent."[8]

So journeying, the saint once more crossed the Pyrenees and arrived at Toulouse by the end of April, in the year 1219, his visit to Spain having occupied altogether something less than five months.

[8] *Vit. Frat.* part 2, chap. v.

ROCAMADOUR.

## CHAPTER XXII.

### FROM SPAIN TO PARIS.

#### 1219.

The return of St. Dominic to Toulouse was warmly welcomed by the community of St. Romain, one which, together with that of Prouille, was always specially dear to the saint as first among the foundations of his Order. Castiglio observes that besides the support of which the friars stood greatly in need at a time when the prospects of the Catholics of Languedoc were so gloomy and threatening, they were desirous of receiving from his lips more complete instructions in the rule and ceremonies of the Order, in order that the brethren who went out from the mother-house to open fresh foundations might be able to establish therein a perfect uniformity of observance. For in spite of the difficulties

with which they had to contend, their ranks were daily
recruited by new members, who needed to be thoroughly
informed with the spirit of the founder. Some of these were
men of eminent sanctity, and among them was a certain
Brother Maurice, who going to preach in the town of Albi,
was given hospitality in the convent of the Friars Minors,
there being as yet no house of his own Order in that place.
The Franciscan community occupied a very poor residence,
and suffered much from the want of water. Maurice, therefore, had recourse to prayer, and pointed out with his stick a
spot in the enclosure where he bade them dig, and on their
doing so, there sprang up a fountain of water not only sweet
and delicious but possessing powerful medicinal virtue, so
that many who drank of it were healed of sundry diseases.[1]
Dominic, therefore, willingly consented to spend some little
time at St. Romain before continuing his journey to Paris.
Unconsciously to himself it was to be his last journey to
these familiar scenes, and before bidding them adieu, he had
it much at heart to rouse the courage of the Catholics of
Toulouse, and strengthen them in the faith. His was not a
spirit to quail in the face of danger; and the very depression
under which the Catholic cause then laboured made it the
more urgent that its champions should show a bold front to
the enemy. Once more, therefore, Toulouse listened for
awhile to the mighty eloquence of that voice which had
before carried the Gospel of peace over the hills and villages
of Languedoc. Such crowds flocked to hear him, that
St. Romain could not contain them: it was in the cathedral
church of St. Stephen, before the bishop and chapter, that he
was obliged to deliver his sermons, and their fruit was an
abundance of conversions. Here again he gave himself up
without reserve to all the labours of his apostolic calling.
All day long he was in the city, or in the surrounding
country, preaching and instructing the people, whilst the
night was devoted to prayer and sharp austerities. At the
same time his care and devotion were lavished on his
children, whom he strove to form to sanctity. Prouille and

[1] Castiglio, part i. lib. i. c. 44.

St. Romain were to him now what St. Sixtus and Santa Sabina had already been at Rome; and another miracle of the multiplication of the loaves is said to have taken place in the refectory of St. Romain. Some writers tell us that it was at this time, before leaving Toulouse, that the saint despatched the two brethren, Arnold and Romeo of Livia, to Lyons, though the precise time when the brethren established themselves in that city is involved in some obscurity. Arnold was distinguished no less for his courage than his eloquence. Some prudent friends warned him that his uncompromising defence of the Catholic faith was not acceptable to all his hearers, and suggested that possibly if he did not somewhat measure his words, the alms would flow into the convent but scantily, and he and his brethren might chance to find themselves without the necessaries of life. "That does not greatly concern us," was his reply, "we do not fear lest our granaries should become empty, for our Lord Himself is our procurator. Even if the alms of men should fail, why need we be troubled? Have you not read, 'Those who fear God shall want no manner of thing that is good'?" The Blessed Romeo, as he is commonly called, was a Catalan by birth, and distinguished even among the disciples of St. Dominic for his devotion to the Mother of God. Her name was ever on his lips; every day he recited kneeling a thousand Hail Marys, which he counted on a knotted cord. He had made it a law to himself never to preach without saying some word in reference to the mystery of the Incarnation, in speaking of which his whole soul seemed to melt with love, and which he made the great means of winning souls to God. In all his labours he was wont to console himself with a verse from the 126th Psalm: *Cum dederit dilectis suis somnum ecce hereditas Domini filii merces fructus ventris,* in which last words he saw an allusion to those of the Hail Mary, as though the reward of the servants of God was none other than the blessed "fruit of the womb, Jesus." He filled the office of Provincial of Provence for many years with great prudence and sanctity, and lived to a great age, ever increasing in the love of Jesus and Mary.

His closing days were spent in almost uninterrupted prayer. As he expired angelic voices were heard singing around his bed the words which in life he had loved so dearly, *Cum dederit dilectis suis somnum, ecce hereditas Domini.* Many miracles were worked at his grave, and twenty-four years after his death his incorrupt body was translated to a more splendid tomb before the altar of the Blessed Virgin, which bore this inscription :

Hac sunt in fossa, fratris venerabilis ossa
Dicti Romei, qui fuit Arca Dei,
Hic Jesum, atque piam dilexit valde Mariam.

The convent of Lyons became the nursery of many religious eminent both for learning and sanctity, such as William Perrault, author of the work entitled, *De Eruditione Religiosorum,* Stephen of Bourbon, and the Blessed Galibert, who evangelized every part of the Burgundian Alps, "a country," says a contemporary writer, "most barren and difficult of access."

It was in company with Bertrand of Garrigua that the saint at last bade farewell to Toulouse, and set out on the road to Paris. That road passed by Cahors, in the near vicinity of a celebrated place of pilgrimage, already more than once visited by the saint, and where the memory of his visit on this occasion has been religiously preserved down to our own time. The sanctuary of Our Lady of Rocamadour was ancient even in the thirteenth century, and to trace its history we must go back to the very origin of Christianity in Gaul, for to use the words of Pope Pius II. in a Bull published by him in 1463, "this sanctuary was founded at the same time that the Church herself was first planted in the land." It was in the year 70 of the Christian era that a certain devout solitary established himself on the lofty rocks which rise above the narrow ravine dug out by the waters of the Lauzon. So gloomy and desolate was this valley that it then bore the title of the Val Tenebreux, and together with the rocks with which it was overhung was inhabited only by wild beasts. Here, however, the holy hermit fixed his dwelling; he built himself a poor cell on the very summit of one of the rocky heights, together with a little oratory which he dedicated to the Mother of God, and in which he placed her image carved by his own hands.

Who was this solitary, and whence had he come? A constant and venerable tradition declares him to have been no other than Zaccheus, the disciple of our Lord, who landing on the coast of southern France, together with Lazarus, Martha, and Mary, travelled into this wilderness, and became the founder of a place of pilgrimage, which the author of *Notre Dame de France* hesitates not to call "the most curious and picturesque in the entire world."

The holy hermit had come hither seeking solitude, but it was not long before he became the apostle of the surrounding country. The inhabitants of the beautiful valleys of Figeac and St. Ceve sought him out, attracted by that sweet mysterious odour of sanctity which betrays itself even in the desert, and gave him the name of *Amator rupis* (the lover of the rock), which in their southern dialect was gradually changed into that of *Amadour*, under which title the saint has since been known.

Rocamadour grew in time to the proportions of a town, containing not one church alone, but a very assemblage of sanctuaries. Even in its present ruined condition it presents a spectacle of unparalleled grandeur. On a gigantic rock, crowned by an ancient castle, stand groups of chapels and hermitages surrounding one church which rises high above the rest, whilst at its feet clusters the town composed of a single street, whence from an immense height you look down into a green and narrow valley through which rushes a mountain torrent. The eye beholds with wonder the distance that separates that smiling valley from the lofty ramparts that tower above those rocks of strange fantastic forms and varied tints, whence on platforms that overlook giddy precipices there arise ancient buildings which seem to form a part of the very rocks to which they cling.

At the gates which lead into the town from the valley below begins the magnificent flight of steps which conducts to the chapel of our Lady perched at the very summit of the rock. These steps, formerly 278 in number, though now reduced to 216, are still, as in old times, ascended by devout pilgrims on their knees. At the 140th step a platform is reached on which stand the houses of the canons who serve the sanctuary; then at the top of a second flight of steps appears the church of St. Saviour, having at its right twelve other sanctuaries dug out of the rock and dedicated to the twelve Apostles, and on its left the chapel of our Lady in which is still preserved the ancient image brought hither by St. Amadour. The chapel is not that raised by his hands, which was unfortunately destroyed in the fifteenth century by the fall of an immense rock by which it was overhung. It was replaced in 1479 by another building raised on the same spot, which again was almost entirely destroyed in 1562 by the fury of the Huguenot heretics. Certain portions of it however remain, and within the restored sanctuary are still preserved three precious relics, the image of our Lady, the altar said to have been consecrated by St. Martial, and the miraculous bell. The image is rudely carved in wood, and represents our Lady enthroned and wearing a crown, whilst seated on her knee, but resting there unsupported by her hands, appears the figure of the Holy Child. Blackened and decayed with age, this image was at a very remote period covered with a thin coating of silver in order the better to preserve it, but this also is now discoloured and falling into fragments. The altar consecrated by St. Martial consists of a rude and simple block of stone, and there is every reason for believing as authentic the tradition that attaches it to his name. From the roof of the chapel is suspended the ancient bell, believed to be the same which once hung in the hermitage of St. Amadour, and to have summoned the faithful to prayer in those remote ages whence the sanctuary dates its origin.

Its form and material certainly betoken an extraordinary antiquity, and the records of many successive centuries bear witness to the fact whence it derives its title of *miraculous*. Hanging from a rope, but without any apparatus necessary for tolling it, it has been repeatedly known to sound without being touched or moved by mortal hand; and the occasions when this has taken place have been when persons at sea in danger of shipwreck have invoked the aid of Our Lady of Rocamadour.[2]

BELL AT ROCAMADOUR.

The church of St. Saviour, spoken of above, is exclusively reserved for the use of the canons. Beneath it is a sub-terranean crypt, which serves as the parish church, and is dedicated to St. Amadour. Here all that remain of the relics of the saint are preserved. In 1166, more than a thousand years after his decease, his holy body was found perfectly incorrupt in the tomb where it had first been laid, and was solemnly removed thither. In the thickness of the wall an arched vault was constructed wherein it reposed for another three centuries, its state of preservation being so well attested as to pass into a proverb. "Such a thing,' men would say, "is as whole and entire as the body of St. Amadour." But in the year 1562, the Huguenot heretics, after ravaging many another holy sanctuary, arrived at Rocamadour, and after plundering it of all its treasures, they laid their sacrilegious hands on the holy

[2] *History of Rocamadour.* By P. Odo de Gissey, S.J., 1631. In this work the author, quoting from older writers, enumerates fifteen well attested instances of this prodigy.

U

body, which they first endeavoured to burn; but failing in this attempt, they tore it from its niche, and tried to cut it to pieces with their halberds. Seizing a smith's hammer, the captain of this band of brigands dealt it blow after blow, exclaiming as he did so: "Since thou wilt not burn, thou shalt break." An eye-witness of this horrible scene, declared to Père Odo de Gissey that the body was at that time perfectly incorrupt, the venerable face being adorned with a long white beard; and Père Odo himself having inspected the remains, which were carefully collected by the canons on the departure of the heretics, found one arm and hand quite perfect, with marks of vermilion blood which had flowed from the broken fingers.

Besides the sanctuaries already named, a great number of other chapels have been erected in different parts of the mountain, of which we will only notice that of St. Michael, which is formed out of a kind of cavern, and is by far the most ancient edifice now remaining. It is reached by steps cut out of the solid rock, and contains within it a little cell, said to be that inhabited by St. Amadour during his lifetime, and forming afterwards his first place of sepulture. Outside the chapel, suspended by a chain to the wall, hangs an enormous mass of iron, called the *Sword of Roland*. The words recall one of the most poetic legends which belong to the history of the sanctuary. When the great Paladin was crossing France in order to join his uncle, Charlemagne, then fighting against the infidels in Spain, he visited Rocamadour, and offered at our Lady's altar the most precious of all his possessions, his renowned sword, *Durendal*, but as he could not go into battle without his trusty weapon, he ransomed it, paying its weight in silver. The tragic end of the story is well known to all lovers of the tales of chivalry. In the fatal defile of Roncesvalles, Roland is betrayed and surrounded by the enemy; he and his knights perform prodigies of valour, but they are overwhelmed by numbers, and Roland is left almost alone, with his friends and comrades lying dead around him. Then he takes in his hand his good sword Durendal, that bright and shining weapon, sparkling with gems, and so sharp and strong that no blow dealt by human hands is powerful enough to break it: "Oh, fair and shining sword!" he exclaims, "how often have I borne thee into battle, and wielded thee against the enemies of Christ! Who now will carry thee when I am gone? Certes no caitiff Saracen or misbelieving Jew shall be thy master; rather will I break thee in pieces with my own hand." Raising the sword he strikes three mighty blows with it on a block of marble which lies before him, but though the marble is cleft in twain, Durendal remains uninjured. Then perceiving a deep chasm hard by, he flings the weapon down into the abyss, and standing with his back against a tree and with his face turned towards Spain, he joins his hands in prayer and yields his gallant soul to God.

> Jointes ses mains, l'a la mort entrepris.
> Saynt Gabriel et bien des autres dis [anges]
> L'âme de lui portent en paradis.

Durendal was recovered by Roland's brothers-in-arms and solemnly deposited at Rocamadour. There it remained till 1183, when that unhappy prince, Henry Court-Mantel, coming to Rocamadour, carried off the sword as well as all the treasures of the sanctuary, with which he paid the army of ruffians he had hired in order to make war on his father, King Henry II. of England; the mass of iron named above being afterwards placed there to represent the ancient weapon.

This was but one among many of the occasions when Rocamadour became a prey to the spoiler. It arose from the ruins to which the Huguenots had reduced it, only again to be laid desolate in 1793 by the hands of the revolutionary hordes; but though in our own day it is despoiled of the riches with which its many sanctuaries were once adorned, and though their walls are crumbling into dust, the holy rock remains a place of pilgrimage resorted to by thousands of the faithful who still, as in old time, invoke the aid of Our Lady of Rocamadour.

It was, then, at the gates of this venerable sanctuary that

one midsummer's day in 1219, two wayworn pilgrims presented themselves, staff in hand, and asked for hospitality.
They had travelled on foot along the *Cami Roumion*, the
pilgrim's road, which led from Cahors, along which rude
pyramids, surmounted at night by lighted lamps, served to
guide the way. They were received no doubt into one of
the hospitals founded for the reception of pilgrims, and paid
their devotions at those shrines and altars which have been
above described. On those rocky heights, adorned with
their battlemented ramparts and their many sanctuaries,
rested the eyes of St. Dominic and the Blessed Bertrand;
up those very steps they ascended on their knees, and in
the subterranean church of St. Amadour they kept watch
during the entire night. What passed during that vigil of
silent prayer? Did Our Lady of the Rosary bestow on her
servant any fresh tokens of favour, any vision of maternal
sweetness to strengthen him during the time that yet
remained of his glorious warfare? So it is currently
believed, and fragments of a tradition exist which hint at
yet more ineffable graces as at this time bestowed on the
servant of God.[3] However that may be, the passing visit
of the two saints has left behind it indelible traces, and the
memory of it is cherished among the glories of Rocamadour.
The walls of that subterranean church are adorned with
paintings of the most famous personages who have visited
this spot. There may be seen the brave knight Roland
offering to our Lady his good sword Durendal and redeeming
it by its weight in silver. There are his valiant comrades
bringing back the wondrous weapon. There are the great
apostles, St. Martial of Limoges and St. Sernin of Toulouse,
and there, too, are the figures of St. Dominic and Bertrand
of Garrigua, who have left behind them in this time-
honoured sanctuary an odour of sanctity, the memory of

---

[3] Some writers represent the saint as having received the stigmata
during his vigil at Rocamadour. There seems no sufficient ground for
such an assertion, which may, however, be taken as expressing the general
belief that spiritual favours of a very special kind were at that time
granted to him.

which seven centuries has not sufficed to banish. The two saints are represented standing, with the pilgrim's staff in their hands, and their eyes raised towards heaven. In the hall of the canons is another picture of St. Dominic kneeling before our Lady, who is giving him a rosary. The first of these pictures is the more ancient of the two, and at the time when petitions were being presented for the beatification of Blessed Bertrand, its existence was appealed to, as affording evidence of a cultus which had existed from time immemorial. Nor is this all; so dearly is the memory of St. Dominic cherished at Rocamadour, that in the year 1876, at the petition of the Rev. Père Rouard du Card, then provincial of Belgium, an altar dedicated to the saint was erected in St. Saviour's church by the Bishop of Cahors.[4]

The morning dawned, and the two pilgrims, consoled and invigorated by their night of prayer, once more set forth, staff in hand, on their road towards Paris. An incident which befell them on the road must be told in the words of Gerard de Frachet. " The holy Father Dominic, going from Toulouse to Paris by way of Rocamadour, spent the night devoutly in our Lady's church, having as the companion of his journey, as he was also of his holiness, Brother Bertrand, afterwards first prior of Provence. The next day as they travelled along they overtook some German pilgrims, who, hearing them singing and reciting litanies, devoutly joined, and when they came to a town invited them to eat with them, and as the manner of this nation is, regaled them sumptuously; and thus they did for four successive days. One day, therefore, the blessed Dominic said to his companion: ' Brother Bertrand, I have a conscience to be thus reaping temporal benefits from these pilgrims without sowing any spiritual seed for them in return. If you think good, let us kneel down and pray to God that He will give us

---

[4] The Rev. Père Rouard du Card considered that there were grounds for believing in a vision of Our Lady of the Rosary having been granted to St. Dominic during his vigil at Rocamadour. He purposed to have published the result of his researches on the subject, but was prevented from doing so by his much regretted death.

to understand and speak their language, that so we may speak to them of our Lord Jesus Christ.' When they had prayed they were able, to the astonishment of the other pilgrims, to speak German quite easily; and for four days more they travelled with them and talked to them of our Lord. At last they reached Orleans, and as the Germans were going on to Chartres, they there parted company with them, humbly recommending themselves to their prayers. The next day the holy Father said to Blessed Bertrand: 'Brother, we are about to enter Paris; and if the brethren hear of the miracle which our Lord has wrought for us, they will take us to be saints, whereas we are only poor sinners, and if it come to the ears of seculars we shall be exposed to much vanity. Therefore, in virtue of holy obedience, I forbid you to reveal this to any one until after my death.' And so it was kept secret at the time; but after the death of the saint, Brother Bertrand made it known to his brethren." [5]

Thus we are able to follow the course taken by the travellers: from Toulouse to Rocamadour, from Rocamadour to Orleans, and from Orleans to Paris. They entered by that gate which was afterwards called the Gate of St. James, close to which stood the little hospital bestowed on the friars by the dean of St. Quentin, which bore the same title, and where Dominic found a loving welcome awaiting him from Matthew of France and the thirty religious whom he had gathered together since his establishment in the capital.

[5] *Vit. Frat.* part 2, ch. x.

# CHAPTER XXIII.

IT was with feelings of singular joy that Dominic greeted his tried and faithful follower the abbot Matthew, and beheld the group of young disciples who stood around him. Among them were some, the very *élite* of the university, men who had before them a noble career, and who bore on their brows the impress of their future greatness. Vincent of Beauvais,[1] Andrew de Longjumeau, Guerric of Metz, the Englishmen, Robert Kilwarby, Clement and Simon Taylor, Stephen of Bourbon, and the German, Henry of Marburg, these are the names of men, each one of whom has a place in the history of the Order. They had been gathered from the ranks of a society unequalled in Christendom for its brilliant renown. It is difficult for us in the present day to form any adequate idea of the position occupied by Paris university at the opening of the thirteenth century. To understand it aright, we must realize the passionate enthusiasm which had seized men's hearts as they emerged from the semi-barbarous ages during which the sword alone had held sway, and began to recognize the new dominion of the intellect. Those young and ardent spirits who in previous centuries would have dreamt of no other distinction than such as was to be gained

---

[1] Vincent of Beauvais, afterwards chaplain and librarian to St. Louis IX., Andrew de Longjumeau, who accompanied him to the Crusade and was his ambassador to the Mussulman chiefs of Egypt and Palestine; Guerric, founder of the convent of Metz; Kilwarby, afterwards Archbishop of Canterbury, and Cardinal of St. Ruffina; Clement and Simon Taylor, first founders of the Order in Scotland; Stephen of Bourbon, author of the *Tractatus de septem donis Spiritus Sancti*, in which occur many valuable historical anecdotes; and Henry of Marburgh, one of the greatest preachers of his time, whose sermons are said to have stirred the whole city of Paris.

on the battlefield or in the tournament, were now crowding into the lists of learning and seeking for the novel honours of the schools. ⟨ No matter what career he intended to follow, it was the first object of every young man's ambition to have studied at Paris. She was the capital as of pleasure, so also of science, the *Cariath-sepher*, the home of letters, and amid her thirty thousand students she numbered the *jeunesse dorée* of every civilized nation. "All the sons of nobles nowadays," says an English chronicler, "are sent to Paris to be made doctors." That among a throng so large and varied there should have been found many grave disorders, cannot be subject of surprise. The scholars of Paris were subject to no collegiate discipline: they lodged in the houses of the citizens and lived as their own masters; and thus they were exposed to a thousand dangers, the existence of which was fully recognized by all wise and good men. If writers abound who extol in florid language the charms of their favourite city, which they declare to possess whatever is most precious on earth, "lessons of wisdom, the glory of letters, refinement of manners, and nobility of thought,' others are to be found who discerned another aspect of the brilliant picture and failed not to raise the warning voice. "Oh, Paris," exclaims Peter of the Cells, writing to one of his monks who had gone thither to study, "resort of every vice, source of every disorder; thou dart of hell! how dost thou pierce the heart of the unwary!" But without attempting to dissimulate evils so great and notorious, or to represent the world as at all less worldly and corrupt in the age of St. Dominic than it is in our own, there was one great difference in the principles which then ruled society as contrasted with those which govern it in the present day. We have said all when we speak of these times as belonging to the *ages of faith*. Scandals were as numerous then as now, perhaps even of a more shocking character than those which meet the eye in the midst of our own more polished civilization. But there had not yet come about that divorce between society and faith which we now have to deplore. Whatever license men allowed themselves, they never ceased to believe. They might violate the commands of God, but they did not ignore His right to impose them. The eternal truths were never banished from their memory. The belief in God, the sense of sin, the hope of heaven, and the fear of hell—these things abode ever, as it were, on the threshold of their hearts; and together with them, as is evident by a thousand examples, a true and keen estimate of time and eternity. Hence it needed but a word to awaken in the most profligate soul thoughts which faith had clothed with so intense a reality that when once aroused they could neither be forgotten nor disobeyed. Moreover, human respect, the tyrant of modern society, had not yet assumed the upper hand, and the comparative simplicity of manners then existing left men free to act on any impulse that moved within them without greatly caring what the world might say. Thus we find the records of the time, crowded though they may be with examples of violence and lawlessness, rich also with tales of conversions as sincere as they were sudden, and exhibiting to us those who were one day, as it seemed, votaries of the world, and the next cut to the heart by some passing word, and flying to the cloister.

Thus we come on a history, like that of Guerric of Metz, one of Matthew's disciples, who had already gained a great name in the university, and who was sitting in his chamber at a late hour preparing for a scholastic disputation on the morrow. At last, weary and exhausted, he rose and, opening his casement, looked out into the night. From the street below there came the voice of some midnight reveller who, as he made his way homewards, was carelessly singing the refrain of a popular song :

> Le temps s'en vait
> Et rien n'ai fait ;
> Le temps s'en vient
> Et ne fais rien.[2]

---

[2] The time flies day by day
And I fling my life away ;
The hours, how fast they run !
And still I've nothing done.

The story of Guerric is related by Stephen de Bourbon.

As he listened to the words they seemed to place before him a picture of his own state. "Alas," he said to himself, "it is even so: life is passing and judgment approaching, time is flying fast and I am flinging it away in vanities; but I will free myself from their bondage, and that at once," and the next morning hastening to the convent of St. James he asked and received the holy habit.

Another scholar of the same name, Guerric of St. Quentin, was called into the Order in a manner somewhat similar. He had applied himself chiefly to natural science, and taught mathematics at Paris with great success. One day he entered a church almost by accident at the moment when a Lesson was being read aloud from the book of Genesis, and these words fell on his ears: "Adam lived nine hundred and thirty years and he died," and so of the other patriarchs, the Sacred Text always concluding with the same expression, "he died"—*mortuus fuit.* "Ah, Lord!" exclaimed Guerric, "all the world then dies; no matter how many years he lives, a man must die at last. What then is there worth living for, except to prepare for death?" and with this thought in his heart he repaired to the convent of the friars and asked admission amongst them.

A few years passed away, and Guerric found himself established at Bologna, where he filled the chair of theology. A young Frenchman was then studying in the university whom Guerric loved, and whom he tried by various means to win from a life of worldliness. The youth felt the attraction of grace, but was reluctant to yield to it. When Good Friday came, therefore, desiring to assist at the Divine Office, he was, nevertheless, careful not to go to the church of the Friars Preachers, lest on that day of tears and compunction they might exhort him to embrace their way of life, and he might not have the strength to resist. But as he opened the psalter which he held in his hand, his eyes fell on the following verse, "Except you be converted, the Lord will brandish His sword; He hath bent His bow, and made it ready."[3] The words pierced his heart, and he understood them as a warning to himself. He closed the

[3] Psalm vii. 13.

psalter, and at once ran to seek Brother Guerric, crying out to him without any sort of preamble, " Brother Guerric, why do you delay?" and as the other stood astonished, not understanding his meaning, he continued, " Ring at once for Chapter." Then Guerric, perceiving with joy what was passing in his soul, gave the signal, and the community being assembled the young man received the habit, whilst the brethren praised God for so admirable a conversion, for he who now entered their ranks had delayed neither a day nor an hour, and had not even given himself time to return to his lodgings. Another anecdote shall be given, though it belongs to a later date, and the scene is also placed not at Paris, but Bologna. A certain Brother received in prayer a Divine intimation regarding one of the masters of the university, named Recaldo, whom he understood to be called by God to better things, though he habitually turned a deaf ear to the call. As the subprior of the convent happened to be a fellow-countryman of Recaldo, the Brother entreated him to call on him, and see what he could do with him. Recaldo consented to receive the subprior's visit, stipulating only that he would not speak to him about God. They met accordingly, and conversed on indifferent subjects. When the subprior rose to depart, he glanced around him and took notice of the rich profusion that was everywhere apparent. The clothes of the young master were of the finest texture, and the couches in his chamber were soft and luxurious. "I bid you farewell for to-day," said the subprior, "but I should like to say two words before I go." "Very well, say them," said the other, "only take care you say no more." "Well then," said the subprior, "have you ever thought on what sort of bed those will lie through all eternity, who refuse to do penance during this life?" "I know nothing about it," replied Recaldo, carelessly. "Listen then," said the subprior, "and the Prophet Isaias shall tell you, 'Rottenness shall be thy bed, and worms thy covering,'"[4] and so saying, he left him. But

---

[4] Isaias xiv. 11. The Douay version runs thus, " Under thee shall the moth be strewed, and worms shall be thy covering."

his words remained in the memory of Recaldo, and left him no ease by day or by night. In vain he sought to drive away the terrible image by laughter and revelry; it remained ever before him, and would not be banished. A few days later he came to the convent, and begged to be received among the friars, choosing rather to endure a hard life in this world, and then to be carried by the angels into heaven, than to enjoy the delights of the flesh for a few short years, and then to be buried in hell.

Other narratives breathe the sweetness of those liturgical associations, so characteristic of a time when the Office of the Church was by no means restricted to the use of priests and religious, but when its sacred language was familiar to all the faithful. It is thus that Humbert de Romans relates the story of his own vocation to religion. He had already attained the degree of Master of Arts, and by the grace of God had preserved his innocence unstained, practised many works of penance, and daily assisted at the Divine Office in the church of Notre Dame. One day he had gone, in company with some others, to hear Vespers in St. Pierre des Bœufs, and when his companions had departed he stayed behind to assist at the Office of the Dead. They had reached the second Nocturn, and whilst the Lessons were being read the chaplain of the church came up to him and said, "Dear friend, you are one of my parishioners are you not? Suffer me then to ask you some questions that concern your soul. Do you remember what you promised at your baptism?" "Assuredly I do," replied Humbert; "but why do you ask?" "You promised," continued the chaplain, "to renounce Satan and all his pomps, but alas, how many scholars of Paris spend their days in follies and vanities, which are nothing else but his pomps. They say to themselves, 'When you have mastered such a branch of learning, and have taken such a degree, you will become a great clerk, and will obtain a rich benefice;' and what is all that but the pomps of Satan? Ah, dear sir, beware of such things. They do better who quit the world, and enter among the friars of St. James; for all that the world can give is only part of the pomps of the devil." As he finished speaking, the Lesson that was being read ended, and the voice of a young cleric entoned the response, *Heu mihi Domine, quia peccavi nimis in vita mea; quid faciam miser, ubi fugiam nisi ad te, Deus meus?*[5]—"Alas, O Lord, I have sinned greatly in my life past, what shall I do, miserable man that I am, and where shall I fly for refuge save to Thee, O Lord?" The words so plaintively chanted sank into his heart; and when he left the church they came back to him again and again. "What shall I do? Whither shall I fly?" And a voice seemed to answer within him: "There is no other refuge for thee save the convent of St. James." Before yielding to the interior voice, however, he sought his friend and the master of his studies, Hugh de St. Cher (afterwards the first Cardinal of the Order), and opened to him his whole heart. "Fear nothing," said Hugh; "go at once and accomplish what you propose. So soon as I have settled certain worldly affairs, it is my intention to do the same thing;" and in fact, both of them shortly after entered the Order, which they adorned by their learning and virtue.

The pages of Gerard de Frachet abound with similar examples of the persuasive power which in the ages of faith often made itself felt in the language of the Divine Office. Two students of Paris were accustomed to recite together the Office of the Blessed Virgin. One of them cherished the desire of entering among the friars, and often urged his companion to do the same. As they were one day saying Vespers together, the latter felt all his hesitation give way. "I can resist no longer," he said. "Where you go I will go; and as a beginning let us both go to the convent to-night and hear Matins." It was the second Sunday in Advent, and when the Office was over, at which they had assisted with great devotion, they asked one another what portion of it had most touched them. One said it was St. Gregory's exposition of the Gospel, "There shall be signs in the sun and moon." "As for me," said the other, "what went to my heart was that eighth

[5] Offic. Defunc. Resp. v.

Responsory, *Docebit nos Dominus vias suas*—'The Lord will teach us His ways;' and then those other words, *Venite, ascendamus ad montem Domini, et ad domum Dei Jacob*—'Come and let us go up to the mount of the Lord, and the house of the God of Jacob.'[6] It seemed to me as if our Lord were Himself inviting us to enter into the convent of St. James, the true house of God, standing on the mountain."

So too we read of another scholar, who had long debated within himself whether or no to obey the call of God. As he recited Compline of our Lady he came on this verse, " How long, O Lord, wilt Thou forget me, and how long shall I take counsels in my soul and sorrow in my heart all the day."[7] Seized with sudden emotion, he melted into tears, exclaiming again and again, " How long indeed, O Lord, how long—how long shall I halt between two opinions—how long shall my enemy triumph over me? O Lord, enlighten my eyes that I sleep not in death !" Unable to finish Compline, he spent the night in tears and prayers, and no long time passed ere he put an end to his mental struggle and yielded to the impulse of grace.

We will add the story of one more vocation which, though differing in character from those given above, is equally redolent of the spirit of faith. It is that of Henry of Marburgh, who has been already named as one of the disciples of abbot Matthew whom Dominic found awaiting him in Paris. He had been sent to study at the university by an uncle who stood to him in the place of a father, and passing through his course of studies with blameless reputation, he returned to his own country to teach what he had thus acquired. While thus engaged, his uncle died, and appearing to him in a vision of the night, besought him to do somewhat for the expiation of his sins and the relief of his soul then suffering in purgatory.

---

[6] The full force of the application of the text will be seen if we remember that the convent of St. James (*Jacobus*) was situated on *Mount St. Genevieve*.

[7] Psalm xii. 1, 2.

" What would you have me do?" inquired Henry. " Take the Cross and pass over the sea," was the reply, " and after you have borne arms for awhile against the enemies of Christ, return to Paris, where you will find the brethren of a new Order serving God by the ministry of preaching. Enter among them, and you will deliver my soul and find for yourself the way of salvation." Awaking from sleep, Henry delayed not a day in obeying what he deemed an intimation of the Divine will. Abandoning all things, he took the Cross and joined the holy war, and returned to Paris just at the time when the first followers of St. Dominic were establishing themselves in the city. He at once entered the community, and became in due time one of the most renowned preachers in Paris.

Further illustrations of this subject will present themselves in the course of our narrative, but enough has been said to explain how it was that an Order which bore the stamp of a poverty and austerity so severe and appalling, was able to recruit itself from the most brilliant society in Europe. To hearts powerfully touched by the grace of compunction, its severity was its attraction. A novice entered among the friars who had been used to every kind of luxury and delicate living. " How can you expect to persevere in such a life?" said one of his friends, who sought to recall him to the world; " you who have lived a life of ease and indulgence, amid good fare, and soft couches, and rich clothing, and all the delights of the flesh— how will you be able to endure the life of these friars?" " The thoughts you put before me are just those which move me to persevere," replied the other, " for I ask myself if I cannot endure the hardships of religion, how shall I bear the fire of hell?"

Possibly, however, the severity of the Rule would not alone have attracted disciples had not the friars from the very first taken a foremost place among the scholars of the university. This had entered into the mind of St. Dominic as one of the primary ideas of his Order. They were to study and to preach. In their cells only three occupations were allowed them: they were to study, to write, and to pray—*legere, scribere, et orare.* The character of the Order was perfectly seized by the Cardinal James de Vitry when he described it as " a congregation of the scholars of Christ "— *Sancta et honesta Christi scholarium congregatio.*[8]  " Every day," he says, " they listen to a lecture on the Holy Scriptures, delivered by one of their own number, and as soon as they have made any progress in these studies they are sent abroad to teach to others what they have learnt."

Scarcely had they established themselves at Paris when their reputation as scholars seems to have been fully recognized. At first they had no schools of their own, but as at Toulouse, attended those of the Cathedral Chapter. Within their own convent, however, they pursued their studies, and to excellent purpose. When William de Montferrat arrived from Rome, he came furnished with letters of recommendation from the Pope, who, addressing the prior and brethren of St. James, prays them to receive the bearer of these despatches with all charity. " We took great pleasure in his society," writes Honorius, " but he preferred to join you at Paris. Wherefore we earnestly recommend him to you, and beg of you to give him every facility of study which is permitted by your Constitutions." The holy Pontiff need have had no misgivings on this point. The facilities for study (*opportunitatem studendi*) of which he here speaks, were freely afforded to all who joined the Friars Preachers. They did not abandon the pursuit of learning when they assumed the religious habit, they only added to it the work of preaching, thus uniting these two means of extending the Kingdom of Him among Whose titles is that of " the Lord of knowledge."[9]  Their studies were of course chiefly, but not exclusively, theological. We may gather some idea of their breadth and extent from the words of Vincent de Beauvais, who, in his *Triple Mirror*, proposed nothing less than to present an epitome

---

[8] Echard, t. i. p. 24.

[9] "Deus scientiarum Dominus est " (1 Kings ii. 3). *Les Dominicains dans l'université de Paris,* p. 127.

of all human knowledge, whether in the domains of art, science, history, or philosophy. And he did this not as though these branches of secular learning were to be cultivated apart from sacred science, but rather in connection with it. "All the arts," he says, "stand grouped around theology, as servants round their queen, and those which we call liberal can be used to good purpose for the demonstration of Catholic truth." Humbert de Romans, afterwards fifth General of the Order, has much to say, in his *Commentary on the Rule of St. Augustine*, on the subject of study, and evidently does but expound the views generally received in the Order. He takes it for granted that study forms a necessary part of the life of the brethren, and quotes the words of St. Jerome, that "Reading should succeed to prayer, and prayer to reading." "If," he says, "religious perfection is one good, and the study of sacred letters is another, the union of both will result in a yet greater good. The Cherubim, whose name signifies the plenitude of science, are not only enlightened by the splendour of the Divine Majesty, but communicate it by an act proper to them. And so those religious Orders which unite to sanctity the light of science, are preferable to those which offer sanctity only; and are so to be esteemed." This is entirely in accordance with those words of St. Thomas, that it is greater to give light than merely to have light: to communicate to others the fruit of contemplation than only ourselves to contemplate. And after enumerating all the advantages that are to be found in sacred study, Humbert names, as the last and principal one, that it helps to the increase of charity. "For the knowledge of God, which is increased by sacred studies, helps us to advance in love; for the more we know God, the more we love Him." This doctrine has been introduced into the very Constitutions of the Order, wherein it is declared that "the pursuit of sacred learning is most congruous to the design of the Order," both because the brethren profess the contemplative life, and the study of sacred things is useful to that end, and also because it is designed for teaching to others that

v

Divine knowledge which its members have acquired by learning.[10]

The Friars Preachers, then, were students not by indulgence or permission, but by the very necessity of their state. The pursuit of sacred learning was the main object for which they were founded. But the charm, the beauty of their lives, consisted in this, that they were not *only* students and preachers. St. Dominic did not fear to cast his children into the very midst of a society steeped through and through with every element that could seduce the heart, because he had provided them with two safeguards, to the strength of which he trusted—they were prayer and poverty. If during the day they studied and preached, by night they watched, and prayed, and sang God's praises. One night a certain rich citizen, who lived in a house in the near neighbourhood of St. James's, heard as he lay awake the voices of the friars as they were singing Matins. "Ah, wretch that I am!" he thought to himself, "who spend my days in ease and pleasure, and at night rest here on a bed of feathers, when the servants of God, after toiling all day in His service, spend the night in singing His praises!" And obeying the grace which stirred in his heart, he next day entered among them.

St. Dominic, who was now observing with a master's eye this newly-developed phase of the Order, as it shaped itself to the requirements of a life of study in the midst of a busy capital, relaxed nothing at all of the rigour with which he required that his children should hold fast to the duties of the choir and the obligations of poverty. The men who drew crowds to the pulpits of the university were to live on alms, and from day to day to beg their bread. Often suffering actual want, they were as often relieved in ways that revealed the watchfulness of a tender Providence. An incident given by Gerard de Frachet, as related to him by Henry of Marburg, evidently belongs to this time, for he speaks of it as happening " about the beginning of the Order." Two brethren who were journeying towards Paris,

[10] Const. FF. Præd. dist. 2. n. 2.

found themselves still fasting when the hour of None arrived, and knew not where or how to procure a meal. As they debated between themselves what to do, a tall man in the garb of a pilgrim suddenly stood before them. "Oh, ye of little faith!" he said; "of what do you discourse together? Seek first the Kingdom of Heaven, and all things shall be added to you. You have left all things for God; do you now fear that He will leave you unfed? But this shall be a sign to you. When you have crossed the field, you will reach a little village in the next valley, and going to the church, the priest will come and invite you to dine with him, and even while he is speaking a soldier will pass by, and try to take you from him by violence to make you his guests. Whilst they are disputing the lord of the district will arrive, and will provide amply for all of you. Always, therefore, trust in the Lord, and bid your brethren confide in Him also." Having said this the pilgrim disappeared, and everything happened as he had said. And the brethren returning to Paris, related these things to Brother Henry and the other brethren, who were at that time living there in great poverty.[11]

St. Dominic spent an entire month in Paris, during which time he busied himself in adapting the hospice occupied by the brethren to the necessities of conventual life. Nothing could exceed the poverty of their first dwelling. They had no cloisters; for the chapter-house they used a kind of wooden shed, and the chapel itself was small and incommodious. Though well content that his brethren should practise poverty in its severe reality, the saint, nevertheless, was well aware that the maintenance of regular observance often depends on exterior conditions, and what was needed for this purpose he carefully provided. He also made himself thoroughly acquainted with the inconveniences to which they were exposed owing to the jealousy of the royal, ecclesiastical, and university authorities. The friars were indeed surrounded by a very network of opposing interests. The king, the municipality, the university, the bishop, the

[11] *Vit. Frat.* part 1, c. v.

cathedral chapter, and the parish of St. Benedict, all possessed their several rights and privileges, which they showed no disposition to abandon. In consequence, the brethren of St. James found themselves unable to say Mass or celebrate the Divine Office in their own chapel. For these purposes they had to frequent the parish church of St. Benedict, or sometimes the neighbouring Benedictine monastery of Notre Dame des Vignes. The abbot Matthew, familiar from his youth with the ways of the university, perfectly understood the tenaciousness of these various bodies, which he endeavoured to conquer by patience and conciliation. Nevertheless, he strongly represented to Dominic the necessity of obtaining from the Holy See permission for them to celebrate their own Offices within their own precincts, and on his return to Rome the saint did not fail to plead the cause of his children. Honorius promptly despatched a Brief addressed to Father Matthew, granting him and his brethren the desired privilege, but both the parish and the chapter opposed its execution, unless on the condition of the payment of certain dues to the dean, which dues they took care to fix at a sum utterly beyond the means of the friars. On hearing this, Honorius appointed a Commission to inquire into and arrange the affair, expressing his astonishment that, instead of opposing the execution of his orders, the chapter should not rather have hastened to forward the just petition of the servants of God; and at the same time addressing a letter of warm encouragement to the friars. By the January of the following year they succeeded in getting leave to use the Pontifical privilege, but the vexatious conflict with the chapter continued for some time longer. In the end, however, the prudence and patience of Father Matthew were amply rewarded. Not only did the university espouse the side of the friars, but they found a powerful protectress in Queen Blanche of Castile, and by the August of the year 1220 the community were left free to worship God in peace within their own walls, and to live in harmony with their neighbours. It seems certain that the support which the friars received on this occasion from

Queen Blanche was in no small degree owing to the personal interest she felt in their founder, and the intimate relations which had long existed between them. It is a very general tradition in the Order that the birth of her son, afterwards St. Louis IX., was a grace obtained by her through the devotion of the Holy Rosary, which had been taught to her by St. Dominic himself. As the birth of the holy king took place in the year 1215, this will carry us back to a period before which we find no notice of any meeting between the saint and the illustrious princess, who was his countrywoman. But bearing in mind the very meagre records of his earlier history, and their most imperfect chronology, this need not be regarded as any reason for rejecting the tradition. Certain it is that Blanche always showed a special favour to the Order of Preachers. Out of their ranks she chose the tutors of her son; and, as we have seen, it was owing to her firm and resolute government that measures were at last taken for the extinction of that malignant heresy to which they opposed themselves as invincible champions.

Important to the community as was the settlement of the dispute above mentioned, it by no means engaged the whole of Dominic's attention. True to his principle, that the grain must be scattered and not hoarded up, he saw in the brethren gathered around him at Paris fit instruments for extending God's work by the formation of fresh foundations. No fewer than six such undertakings were decided on, though all were not begun at once. Limoges was chosen to receive the first colony, and the religious whom Dominic selected to be the leader of the little community was Peter Cellani, his first disciple at Toulouse. Peter hesitated, not from any want of obedience, but from an honest diffidence in his own powers, for he possessed little or no learning, and had entered the Order too late in life to supply for his deficiencies. He therefore exposed his fears and weakness to the saint, and begged him to choose some one more suitable for Superior. But Dominic knew the character with whom he had to deal, and was well convinced that Peter possessed other qualities which would amply compensate for his want of letters. "Go, my son," he replied, " and fear nothing; twice a day I will think of you before God. He will be with you, and will make you to increase and multiply. You will gain many souls, and your labours will be abundantly fruitful." Peter bowed his head in obedience, and the result proved that the holy Father had indeed been led by the Spirit of God.

At Limoges they received an affectionate and hospitable welcome from the bishop and clergy, and a site was given to them near the bridge of St. Martial. When the building of the convent was begun, one of the citizens named John Botis declared that, having no children, he should adopt the friars in their place; and taking on himself the direction of the works, at his own expense brought into the cloister the waters of a fountain, still called at the beginning of this century by the name of "the fountain of Preachers." Few convents produced more illustrious members than Limoges, and among those who received the habit from the hands of Prior Peter were Stephen de Salanhac, Bernard Guidonis, and Gerard de Frachet, all of whom became eminent in the Order, and to whom we are indebted for much valuable history regarding the early period of its existence. Gerard de Frachet, the author of those charming *Lives of the Brethren* which have furnished so many of the anecdotes given in the foregoing pages, succeeded Peter in the government of the convent at a time when the rapid increase of the community, and the inconvenient distance from the city of the site they at first occupied, rendered it necessary for them to move to a more suitable position. He chose a house situated in one of the faubourgs, on ground where it was said a procession of religious clad in white had twice been seen in a dream or vision, and agreed with the owner to purchase it for the sum of six thousand *sols tournois*.[12] The bargain was concluded, and the friars took possession of their new abode; but when it came to producing the purchase-money, difficulties made themselves felt. The brethren were sent out to gather alms, but without success; day after day those who had gone on the quest returned home with empty hands to report their

[12] A sum equal to about three hundred livres.

disappointment to the prior. At last his patience and confidence began to fail him, and he fell into despondency. One day one of the Fathers came to visit him in his chamber, and found him very sad and pensive. The community were just then singing the *Salve Regina*, and as they came to the words, *Et Jesum benedictum fructum ventris tui, nobis post hoc exilium ostende*, prior Gerard heaved a deep sigh. "Ah, Lord!" he exclaimed; "whatever are we to do!" "Dear Father," said the other, "do not afflict yourself thus. Listen to the brethren, who are invoking the Blessed Virgin and asking her, not for temporal things, but that she would show them her Divine Son." "True enough," replied the prior. "I am in the wrong, I know. Whilst my brethren are asking our Lady to show them her Son, I am breaking my head to know where to find six thousand *sols tournois*."

From that moment he renewed his confidence in God and our Lady, and the next morning being Saturday, as the brethren were singing our Lady's Mass, a certain Sieur Aymeric, canon of the church of Daurat, called at the convent, and hearing of their trouble begged the prior to summon them all to chapter, as he had a word to say to them. The brethren being assembled, the canon addressed them as follows: "I know, dear Fathers, that you have bought this place, and can find no one to advance you the purchase-money. But the Blessed Virgin, whom you love so dearly, and who is the special Mother of your Order, will certainly not fail to provide, and I think it must have been she who moved me to come here to-day; for last night, after singing Matins with the other canons, I felt such an inspiration to do so without knowing why, that I could not rest till I had saddled my horse and set out: and now I promise to send you the money without delay." He was as good as his word, and next morning very early the six thousand *sols tournois* were brought to the prior. Not only so, but the brother of Sieur Aymeric, also a canon, gave sufficient alms to build part of the convent, as well as the church, in which both of them were afterwards buried as signal benefactors.

Limoges became in time the fruitful mother of other convents, among them that of Brives, which was begun in great poverty, the brethren for a time having no other shelter than tents. Better days came at last, and they were able to lay the first stone of a humble convent. Bernard Guidonis has described the ceremony, and the joyful gathering of clergy and people who awaited the coming of the friars at the site chosen for the new building. They came walking in procession and carrying the cross, whilst the air was filled with their chants of joy, when a singular circumstance occurred which all the bystanders interpreted as a token of Divine favour. It was the month of April, before the time when bees commonly swarm; but as the brethren advanced a swarm of these little creatures appeared and settled on all those who stood around. They neither stung or annoyed any one, but showed themselves friendly and sociable, selecting as their chief resting-place the processional cross, whence they removed to the foundation-stone, on which they settled in the form of a crown. What are we to understand by such a sign, asks the old writer, given at this moment, unless it were to show that these spiritual bees of Jesus Christ were about to build their cells, and thence to distil the honey of the Divine Word?

We cannot take leave of Limoges without noticing the closing career of its founder, Peter Cellani. What kind of spirit he infused into his community may be gathered from the fact that within the first century of its existence it produced more than two hundred religious who died in the odour of sanctity. Throughout the length and breadth of the diocese, says Stephen of Salanhac, he was regarded as a kind of prophet. But he was not allowed to end his days therein. By desire of Pope Gregory IX., he was recalled to Toulouse to labour once more, in concert with the Blessed William Arnald in conflict with the Albigensian heretics, who under the protection of Raymund VII. were as busy and as formidable as ever. For Blessed William was reserved the crown of martyrdom, which he received at Avignonet in 1242. In nowise intimidated by his cruel fate, Peter only showed the greater zeal in preaching the faith.   Constantly exposed to every kind of danger, he continued his apostolic labours until the year 1257, when he died full of years and of merits, in the city where forty years before he had received into his house the blessed Dominic and his first six companions.

Among the foundations of 1219 must be named that of Dinan, in Brittany, which owed its origin to the piety of Alan Lanvalay, a Breton knight who had fought in the wars of the Albigenses, and had at that time formed an intimate friendship with St. Dominic, from whom he learnt the devotion of the Holy Rosary, which he afterwards preached in many parts of France.   Being admitted into the Order by the saint himself (as the ancient register of Dinan declares), he gave his own lands for the foundation of a convent, which claimed to be reckoned among the most ancient of the Order, though it did not actually receive a colony till the year 1219. After Alan's death a rose-tree is said to have sprung up out of his grave, bearing a profusion of flowers which bore on their petals the *Ave Maria*, the words of which had been so constantly on his lips.   In this convent, moreover, is said to have been preserved until the seventeenth century an autograph letter from St. Dominic, which having been borrowed by a certain Augustin du Pas, who was drawing up a history of Brittany, was lost by him among his papers and never recovered.[13]

The other foundations which St. Dominic decided on making besides that of Limoges, were Metz, Rheims, Poitiers, Orleans, and Scotland.   It was in response to the earnest entreaties of the Scottish King, Alexander II., that the saint promised to send brethren to establish the Order in his dominions.   Alexander was present in Paris at the time of St. Dominic's visit to the capital, having come for the purpose of renewing the ancient alliance of his crown with the royal house of France. At his request eight religious

[13] Réchac, 138, 338.  This Alan is not to be confused with Alan de la Roche, the restorer of the Rosary, also a Breton, and commonly, though incorrectly, given the title of *Blessed*, for he has never been beatified.

were named for this distant mission, and among them were Simon Taylor and Clement, who is described as a man of great learning and singularly skilled in languages. In 1233 he became bishop of Dunblane,[14] but always regretted the retirement of his religious cell, and at the Chapter held at London in 1250 obtained a promise that he should still share in all the suffrages of the Order.

While thus engaged, Dominic did not neglect the work of preaching. On the feast of St. John Baptist he was invited to preach in the cathedral of Notre Dame, and according to his invariable custom, prepared himself previously by an hour of mental prayer. Whilst he was uncertain what subject to choose for his discourse, our Lady is said to have appeared to him and shown him a book wherein was written the text on which she desired him to speak. The saint raised his eyes and read the words, *Ave, gratia plena*.[15] Entering the pulpit, he explained them with a devout simplicity which disappointed some of his hearers, who had gathered together expecting to hear something very profound from the lips of so renowned a preacher, and who were a little disconcerted on having to listen to nothing more than an exposition of the Hail Mary. The preacher, they complained, was giving them a child's lesson. The murmurers were chiefly four learned doctors, who did not enjoy a very spotless reputation; but so great was the power and sweetness which our Lady infused into the words of her faithful servant, that the rest of the immense audience who had gathered to hear him were moved as one man with sentiments of admiration and devotion, and during the rest of his stay in Paris the churches in which he preached could not contain the crowds who flocked to hear him.

Père Croiset tells us that it was with him the custom first arose among preachers of introducing the *Ave Maria* at the opening of their sermons, and that before beginning a discourse he always knelt and repeated the versicle, *Dignare*

[14] Not Dublin, as erroneously stated by several writers (See Dempst. l. 3, *Hist. Scot.* n. 308).
[15] Millin, *Antiq. Nat.* t. iv. c. 39.

*me, laudare te, Virgo sacrata.* The historians of the Rosary represent him as doing much to propagate that devotion at Paris, where he is said to have admitted great numbers into the Confraternity.

Before he left he had the happiness of giving the habit to his old and dear friend, William de Montferrat. The circumstances of their first acquaintance at Rome two years previously will not have been forgotten by the reader. William had at that time engaged to enter the Order as soon as he should have completed his course of theology at the university of Paris. He now joyfully redeemed his pledge, and thenceforth became the constant companion of the saint, and was one of those who gave their evidence at his canonization. He lived to carry into execution the design over which they had conferred together in the first days of their friendship, and departing to the East about the year 1235, consecrated the rest of his life to labours for the conversion of the Saracens and the Eastern schismatics.

But there was yet another of the scholars of Paris with whom Dominic at this time became acquainted, and who was destined to do a greater work in the Order than any of those who have yet been named. No more winning character greets us from the pages of Dominican history than that of Jordan of Saxony, destined to become the successor of him whom he called the master of his soul, and to give to the Order a greater extension than it obtained even in the days of its founder. Noble in birth, for he was a member of the family of the counts of Eberstein, he had from his earliest years shown a disposition to virtue and a love of letters. Coming to Paris as a youth of twenty, he had passed ten years in the schools, applying himself with success to the study of philosophy, mathematics, and rhetoric. He even composed two little treatises on geometry, and a volume of his notes on Priscian, the standard grammarian of the middle ages, was long preserved. But whilst thus cultivating his rich intellectual gifts, the innocence and simplicity of his heart remained unchanged. He had bound himself by vow to give an alms every day to the first poor person whom he might happen to meet, and his fidelity in accomplishing this obligation deserved to receive a token of the Divine approval. It was the custom at that time for seculars, and among them the more pious of the university scholars, to be present at Matins, then commonly recited at midnight not merely in religious choirs, but even in most parish churches. One night Jordan rose, intending to assist at the Office at Notre Dame, and believing himself to be late, he hastily threw on his mantle, girding himself with a belt richly ornamented with silver clasps. As he left the house a poor beggar accosted him and asked an alms, and Jordan, not having his purse with him, stripped off his belt, as the only valuable article he had about him, and gave it to the beggar. When he reached the church he found to his surprise that it was still early and that the doors were closed; he therefore waited patiently outside until they were opened, and as he entered went, according to his wont, to say a prayer at the foot of the great crucifix. What was not his astonishment as he looked at the sacred figure to see it girt with the very same girdle which he had parted with but an hour before for the love of Christ, recalling to his mind those words of his Master, "What you did to one of the least of these My brethren, you did it to Me."

Jordan had taken his degree as bachelor, and had received the subdiaconate when St. Dominic came to Paris. He was present at some of the saint's sermons, and felt his very soul captivated by the power of that inspired word. Seeking his presence, he placed the direction of his conscience in the hands of one who from the first moment of their acquaintance had gained his entire confidence. " I went frequently to confession to him," he says, " and by his desire received the diaconate." But intimate as was the friendship established between them, the saint, guided by the Spirit of God, did not press what he clearly discerned to be the vocation of his penitent. He was content to cast the seed, leaving it to another hand to bring it to maturity.

The month of Dominic's stay in Paris passed swiftly away, and he prepared to set out on his return journey to

Italy. We are told that both at Toulouse and also in the capital he was strongly urged to remain in France and there fix the centre of government for the whole Order. To the arguments brought in support of this proposal, however, he turned a deaf ear. The decisions of those to whom God commits the foundation of great works are guided by other considerations than those of human prudence; and having fully weighed the question in the balance of the sanctuary, the saint adhered to his resolution with that invincible constancy which was a part of his character. Despatching Bertrand of Garrigua, therefore, to Toulouse to resume the government of St. Romain, Dominic took as his companions William de Montferrat and a lay-brother named John, whom he had brought from Spain, and left the capital about the middle of July, this time passing through Burgundy, and bending his steps southwards by the way of Avignon.

# CHAPTER XXIV.

August, 1219.

THE first place where we come on the track of the travellers is the town of Châtillon-sur-Seine, where they were charitably received by a worthy ecclesiastic whose generous hospitality Dominic had an opportunity of abundantly rewarding. For while they were still being entertained within his house it chanced that a young man, his nephew, fell from the roof, and was picked up, having received mortal injuries. While the relations of the youth were mourning over him as dead or dying, the saint prostrated in prayer, and with tears, besought God to restore the sufferer; then, taking him by the hand, he gave him back safe and sound to his weeping mother and the rest of the afflicted family, who knew not in what words to pour forth their joy and gratitude. The kind old priest himself could not be satisfied without inviting his friends and neighbours to a modest banquet in honour of his guest, and among those present was his sister, mother to the youth in whose favour the miracle had been wrought. There was set on the table, among other things, a dish of eels, of which, being invited to partake, the good woman excused herself, giving as her reason that she was then suffering from a quartan fever. When the saint heard this, he took a small portion of one of the eels, and making over it the sign of the Cross, bade her eat it without fear, which she did, and from that moment was completely cured of her fever.[1]

[1] The house where he lodged at Châtillon, and the room in which he slept, are still shown.

Escaping from the demonstrations of respect which these miracles drew on him, Dominic pursued his way to Avignon, where many of the inhabitants had long desired to see him. The position of the city was at that time altogether exceptional. It was a little republic, governed by seven consuls and two judges. Deeply infected with the Manichean heresy, the citizens were for the most part adherents of Count Raymund, who in acknowledgment of their services had granted them a considerable territory. Dominic, however, during the few days he spent in the city, fearlessly preached the faith; and his eloquence so charmed his hearers that many were found who entreated him to send thither a colony of his brethren, that they might support the Catholic cause by their preaching. The saint undertook to do so at some future time, if they on their part would find him a suitable site for a convent. They invited him at once to choose one for himself, and all going forth together they left the city by the gate of the Rhone, and came to a spot by the riverside, where was a green and pleasant island, planted with willows and poplars. As they were looking about them, a man called out from the midst of the crowd, saying, "This is the very spot where St. Martha is said to have preached, and where she restored to life a young man who had been drowned, as he was swimming across the river in order to come and hear her." St. Dominic hearing him speak thus, inquired of the bystanders, and was assured by them of the truth of the story.[2] "This, then, is the place for me," he said; "if you will grant it to me, it is here that our convent shall be erected." One of those who stood near him pointed out that there were pools of stagnant water in the place, which would render it unhealthy; but the saint making the sign of the Cross over these pools, one portion of them dried up, and the rest gathered together and formed a kind of well or fountain. These marshy waters had until then been quite unfit for drinking, but from this time they became sweet and salubrious. The magistrates, therefore, did not hesitate to

[2] For the story referred to see Bollandists (July, vol. vii.), who accept it as authentic.

grant him the site of ground, of which Dominic at once took possession by planting a cross; but the convent does not seem to have been actually founded until five years later, when Bertrand of Garrigua, then provincial of Provence, succeeded in establishing a community there in spite of immense difficulties. But the faction of the Albigenses was so strong within the city, that the brethren had for a time to retire. In 1226, however, Louis VIII. entered Comtat at the head of one hundred and fifty thousand men, and laid siege to Avignon, which at the end of three months was forced to surrender to his arms. The Catholic cause had triumphed at last. The city, long left without a bishop, now opened its gates to king and clergy, and on the 14th of September, the feast of the Holy Cross, the King and the Cardinal Legate walked behind the Blessed Sacrament in a solemn procession of expiation, wherein the Friars Preachers, headed by the Blessed Bertrand, also bore a part. After this the brethren resumed the peaceable possession of their convent, in the sacristy of which was long shown the famous well, which down to very late times continued to bear the title of "the well of St. Dominic."[3]

Returning to our travellers, we must now follow them in their course over the Lombard Alps, the passage of which was difficult and laborious. Not all the companions of the saint shared either his physical strength or his heroic courage, and at length Brother John, the Spanish lay-brother, became utterly spent and exhausted. Overcome with hunger and fatigue he sat down, unable to proceed further. "What is the matter, my son?" asked the saint. "It is, Father," he replied, "that I am simply dying of hunger." "Take courage," said the saint, "yet a little further, and we shall find some place in which we may rest." But as Brother John replied again that he was utterly unable to proceed any further, Dominic had recourse to his usual expedient of prayer. Then he desired him to go to a spot he pointed out,

---

[3] For the above account compare Jean Mahuet, *Prædicatorium Avm-ionese*, c. ii. pp. 7, 8, *Semaine Religieuse d'Avignon*, wherein are quoted the ancient Archives of the Convent, and Réchac, p. 760.

and take up what he should find there. The poor Brother dragged himself to the place indicated, and found a loaf of exquisite whiteness, which, by the saint's orders, he ate, and felt his strength restored. Having asked him if he were revived, Dominic bade him take the remains of the loaf back to the place where he found it; and this done, they continued their journey. As they went on, the marvel of the thing seemed to strike the Brother for the first time. "Who put the loaf there?" he said; "I was surely beside myself to take it so quietly! Holy Father, tell me whence did that loaf come?" "Then," says the old writer, Gerard de Frachet, who has related this story, "this true lover of humility replied: 'My son, did you not eat as much as you needed?' And he said, 'Yes.' 'Since, then,' replied the saint, 'you have eaten enough, give thanks to God, and trouble not yourself about the rest.'"

This story was related to the brethren by Brother John himself after he returned into Spain, at a later period. In spite of his seeming delicacy, he had a brave heart, and accompanied some of the friars into Morocco, where they went to preach the faith and where, we are assured, he made a holy end.

And now Dominic was once more on that soil of Italy which thenceforth he was never again to quit. Since he had set out from Rome in the November of 1218 he had spread his Order throughout Spain and France; the cities of Italy were now one after another to receive as their apostles colonies of his white-robed children. The first place which he visited was Bergamo, where he accepted the site for a convent, and gave the habit to several religious, among whom was the Blessed Guala dei Romononi, afterwards bishop of Brescia. At Asti he was also warmly received, whence proceeding to Milan he was again given hospitality by the canons of St. Nazzario, with whom he had formerly lodged when travelling to Rome in 1217. Here he preached with much success, and received into the Order three very eminent doctors of law, Guidotti di Sexto, Roger di Merati, and Amizo, or Arditio, di Solar. The latter held the office

w

of Apostolic Notary, and is described by Taegius as "a
man endowed with every virtue, possessed of rare prudence,
zealous for the faith, and perfect in the observance of regular
discipline."

In the course of a familiar conversation held among some
of the brethren, one of them is reported to have said that
were it possible to exchange his soul for that of another,
the one he would choose would be the soul of Brother
Amizo.[4] Dominic esteemed him highly, and kept him near
his own person. Becoming thus very intimately acquainted
with the holy founder, he was chosen as one of the witnesses
who gave their testimony to his sanctity. Though he does
not add any important particulars to those given by the
other witnesses, yet his words are worthy of notice as bearing
evidence with how close and loving an eye he had studied
the character which he thus portrays. "Master Dominic,"
he says, "was a most humble, mild, good, patient, and
pacific man; sober and modest, full of wisdom in all his
acts and all his words; he delighted in consoling his neighbours and specially his brethren, and he was most zealous
for regular discipline. As an ardent lover of poverty, he
desired that it should be observed by the brethren in their
food and clothing, their convents and churches, and even in
the vestments used in the Divine worship. During his life
he was specially solicitous that they should not make use
of silk either at the altar or elsewhere, and that neither gold
nor silver should be used except for the chalices." Amizo
eventually became prior of the great convent of St. Eustorgio,
founded in his native city, and in that capacity had the
happiness of witnessing the heroic virtues and intrepid death
of St. Peter Martyr. It was he who collected the evidence
and drew up the *procès-verbal* regarding the saint's martyrdom, presented to the commissioners appointed by Pope
Innocent IV., to inquire into the circumstances of that
event, a document used in the process of canonization, and
still preserved.

Some writers represent that so far back as the year 1217

---

[4] Father Michel Pio, *Prog. in Italia*, 86.

there had been given to the saint a little house in Milan
near the Roman Gate, afterwards called St. Domenichino,
and that a small community had been sent to reside here
the year following. If such had been the case, it is most
improbable that he should have taken up his residence with
the canons rather than with his own brethren. But it may
here be observed once for all that the chronology of these
Italian foundations is most confused, owing to the contra-
dictory statements to be found in the records of the different
convents. The most that can be aimed at is to give the
more probable conjectures, and those which involve the least
amount of contradiction, and appear supported by the best
authorities. In most cases, as has been observed before,
the confusion has arisen from convents claiming as the
date of their foundation that of some early visit of the saint
to the city where a foundation was afterwards made. And
this confusion often extends to the history of the brethren
themselves, concerning whom it is sometimes hopeless to
ascertain with any certainty either the place or precise date
of their reception into the Order. This remark applies to
the history of one who may nevertheless be safely numbered
among St. Dominic's Milanese novices, Brother Giacomo
Xuron, who was without doubt one of the religious who took
part in the foundation of the first convent in this city. He
was a man of great learning and sanctity, and his life was
illustrated by miracles.

As he was some years later discharging the duties
of lector in the convent of Genoa, he heard a voice as
from heaven which said to him, "Arise, and pass the
sea, and go into the East. There you will do great
things for My glory, and gain many souls." Asking permission from his Superiors to obey this Divine command,
Xuron took with him one companion, and set out for
Greece. In the first town which he entered in that country
he saw lying in the street a poor cripple, both of whose
legs were deformed and contracted. In his compassion,
Xuron stooped down to speak to the poor sufferer, seeking to
console him with kind words; and chancing to touch one

of his legs the man at once arose, with the limb straight and vigorous. Full of surprise, Xuron fled from the spot, not daring to touch the other leg, says Taegius, and desirous only of escaping from the occasion of vainglory and human praise. He finally passed over into the island of Candia, where he effected many conversions by his preaching and miracles, and died universally honoured by the people as a saint.

Attended by these and other disciples whom he had gathered on his way, St. Dominic set out for Bologna, and reached that city towards the end of August, nine months only having elapsed since his departure from Rome in the previous year.

CLOISTERS OF SAN DOMENICO, BOLOGNA.

## CHAPTER XXV.

### REGINALD AT BOLOGNA.

#### 1219.

It will be remembered that St. Dominic, before setting out on his journey into Spain, had appointed Reginald of Orleans to be his vicar in Italy, and had assigned him the convent of Bologna as his residence. The appointment to a post of such responsibility of one who was as yet wholly untrained in the religious life would, in any ordinary case, and on the part of any ordinary man, have seemed to violate the laws of prudence. But of St. Dominic, if of any man, might be said that, like his great patron St. Paul, he had the Spirit of God. He possessed in an extraordinary degree that gift of the discernment of spirits, so essential to those who hold rule over other souls, which enabled him to choose the instruments who were fittest to build up the work of God. From the day when they had first met, the heart of the

disciple lay open to the eye of the master like the pages
of a book, and he recognized therein a power and a force of
attraction which qualified him to be a leader amongst his
brethren. After passing a few weeks in Rome, therefore, and
bidding farewell to his old friend the Bishop Manasses,
Reginald set out for Bologna, where he arrived on the 21st
of December, 1218. He found the community still occupying
their first quarters in Santa Maria in Mascarella, and in spite
of the recent visit of their Father suffering extreme poverty
and depression.   To appreciate the spirit that Reginald
brought with him, and which he found means to infuse into
those over whom he was now placed, we must remember
what had been his previous position and life in the world.
Almost every social advantage had been at his command :
wealth, dignity, a learned reputation, and a wide sphere of
credit and influence.   Of all these he had stripped himself
to satisfy the two desires of his heart, poverty and freedom
to teach the Word of God.   The true vocation of a Friar
Preacher had revealed itself to him with an irresistible
attraction before he had even heard of the existence of the
Order.   When therefore he came into the presence of that
life, its austere reality had no terrors for him.   He embraced
it as the answer from God to the prayer of a lifetime; and
whilst to the eyes of the world he was making a sacrifice
of stupendous heroism, he himself was only conscious of
those floods of sweet consolation which inundated his soul
amid the burning throbs of sensible fervour.   No doubt
among those who were acquainted with the particulars of
his former life, there were plenty to whom it seemed a kind
of miracle, that a man who used to have at his command a
splendid dwelling, numerous servants, and all the appliances
of good living and luxury, should be willing to wear the poor
dress of a friar, and sit at a table rarely furnished with
anything better than broken morsels of bread, which had
been begged in alms.   They did not guess, and probably
would not have believed, that the subject of their compassion found in each circumstance of his new life, only
matter for secret joy.   He could not rest until he had begun

the work to which he longed to consecrate the span of life
which had been given back to him at the intercession of
our Lady. "No sooner had he established himself in the
convent," says Blessed Jordan, "than he began at once to
devote himself to preaching, and his words were so fervid
and vehement that they kindled the hearts of his hearers
like a burning torch. All Bologna seemed on fire, as though
a new Elias had appeared amongst them." In eight days
Reginald was master of the city. Men of law, as well as
ecclesiastics, professors no less than students, yielded to the
magical charm of his eloquence. Soon the church was too
small to contain his audience, and he was obliged to preach
in the streets and public piazzas. The people came from all
the surrounding towns and villages to hear him, and the age
of the Apostles seemed to have returned. The first-fruits of
the harvest of souls that Reginald was afterwards to reap in
such abundance, was one of the professors named Moneta,
a man famous for his learning throughout Lombardy. The
kind of rage that had set in for attending Reginald's sermons
filled him with uneasiness, and he did his best to keep his
own pupils from exposing themselves to the dangerous
attraction. The attempt, however, was vain, and on the
feast of St. Stephen, within a week after Reginald's arrival,
they not only expressed their intention of going to hear the
preacher, but insisted on his accompanying them. Unable
to give any good reason for refusing, yet unwilling to
comply, Moneta proposed that they should first hear Mass
at St. Proclus. They went, and stayed during three Masses,
till, unable to delay longer, Moneta was obliged to accompany the others to Santa Maria, where Reginald was then
delivering his sermon. The doors were so crowded that
they could not enter, and Moneta remained standing on the
threshold. But as he stood there he could command a
view of the whole scene, and every word reached his ear.
A dense mass of people filled the church, yet not a sound
broke the words of the preacher. He was speaking on the
words of St. Stephen, the saint of the day: "Behold, I see
heaven open, and Jesus standing at the right hand of God."

"Heaven is open to-day also," he exclaimed; "the door is ever open to him who is willing to enter. Why do you delay? Why do you linger on the threshold? What blindness, what negligence is this! The heavens are still open!" As he listened, Moneta's heart was changed and conquered. When Reginald came down from the pulpit, he was met by his new penitent, who abandoned himself to his direction, and even made a vow of obedience in his hands. But as his engagements did not admit of his at once entering religion, he remained in the world for a year, during which time he laboured incessantly to bring in other disciples, and at each new conquest his joy was so great that it seemed, says the chronicler, as if he were taking the habit himself each time another received it. After his entrance into the Order, Moneta became the founder of several convents. His *Summa against the Cathari* is still preserved, and attests his learning, which was equalled, or rather surpassed, by the sanctity of his life. He died full of years and of merit, and blind, it is said, from his constant weeping. It was in his cell that the great patriarch breathed his last, as we shall hereafter relate.

But whilst this enthusiasm reigned outside the convent, the brethren within were passing through one of those seasons of trial permitted by God in the history whether of communities or individuals, a time of purgation preparing the way for one of spiritual fecundity, as the frosts of winter make the earth ready for seed-time and harvest. Possibly the very fervour which was burning in the heart of Reginald led him to demand of his brethren a degree of sacrifice to which, at the moment, they were unequal; he had yet to learn by experience that lesson of discretion, that souls must not be forced beyond their present grace. Some weeks had passed since Reginald's arrival, and the brethren had removed to their new convent of St. Nicholas; few disciples had yet actually joined them, and the heavy cloud of depression still hung over the community. This had attained such a point that many debated the question of leaving the Order altogether, and two had even obtained letters from the

Apostolic Legate empowering them to do so. These letters they brought to Reginald, and made known to him their intention of abandoning the new Institute, the failure of which, it was plain to them, could only be a question of time. It was Ash Wednesday, and Reginald assembling the chapter, addressed the brethren in words of bitter sorrow, whilst they on their part could only answer by their sobs. Then Brother Clare (or Chiaro) arose (the same whose father had spoken to him when a child of the singing of the angels). He had grown to be a man of great repute and learning, and before entering the Order had taught arts and canon law in the University. With manly earnestness he now exhorted his brethren to have courage, trusting in the Providence of God, Whose hour of mercy was perhaps even then close at hand. Reginald raised his eyes to heaven, and listened in silence; possibly that moment of sorrow and humiliation was bringing to his generous soul, together with lessons of Divine wisdom, a precious interior grace. In fact, the words of the speaker were about to receive a remarkable fulfilment. There was at that time in the university of Bologna a famous doctor named Roland of Cremona, renowned throughout the whole of Italy as a professor of philosophy. His success in the schools, however, did not prevent him from taking his full share of worldly amusement, and the day before he had entered with a number of young companions into all the mad revelry of the last day of the Carnival. Dressed in a new suit of clothes, which included a splendid scarlet doublet, he spent the entire day in games and dances, and other customary diversions, and went home in the evening tired and worn out. But as he lay on his bed he could not rest. What satisfaction had he got out of his day's pleasure? Nothing but weariness and satiety. The dances and the wild mirth in which he had taken part, he could only think of them with disgust. "Truly," he said to himself, "did the Wise Man say that the end of laughter is sadness. I know well enough that these things can never give me real happiness; that is to be found only in the service of God. As to the service of the world, at best

it is but a slavery, and a very foolish one. To-morrow I
will seek out that holy man, Brother Reginald, and will
place the decision of my future life in his hands." So when
morning dawned, he repaired to St. Nicholas, and abruptly
entered the chapter-room just as Brother Clare was finishing
his discourse. Moved by the Spirit of God, he at once
asked for the holy habit, and Reginald, like one transported
out of himself, took off his own scapular, and flung it over
his neck. A sudden impulse of joy seized the whole community, the sacristan tolled the bell, whilst the brethren
entoned the *Veni Creator*, and as they sang it, their voices
stifled with tears of thanksgiving, the people came together,
and the church was invaded by a crowd of men, women,
and students, among whom the rumour had run like wildfire
that Master Roland had joined the friars. The dark cloud
of temptation rolled away, and the two brethren who had
resolved to quit the Order threw themselves at the feet of
Reginald, and declared their resolution of persevering even
until death.

One of the community, however, and he not the least
worthy of its members, still retained in his heart some
shadows of doubt and misgiving. It was Rodolph of
Faenza, the procurator of the convent, whose office brought
daily before his eyes in a very practical shape the difficulties with which they were beset. Profoundly afflicted
as he had been at the discouragement of his brethren, he
could not at once dismiss the impression it had left on his
heart. But our Lord Who never abandons a soul of good-
will and upright intentions, deigned that night to appear
to him, having at His right hand the Blessed Virgin, and
on His left St. Nicholas, the patron of the convent. The
latter, placing his hand on Rodolph's head, addressed him,
saying, "Brother, fear nothing, all will go well with thee
and thy Order, for the Blessed Virgin will have care of it."
At the same moment Rodolph seemed to see upon the river
which runs through Bologna a vessel filled with a multitude
of friars. "Seest thou all these?" continued the saint;
"fear nothing, I say, fear nothing, for these are all brethren

who shall go forth from this house, and spread themselves through the entire world." Roland's entrance into the Order was, in fact, the beginning of a new era for the convent of St. Nicholas. His example was followed by many, both of the professors and students, till at length it passed into a common proverb that no man should go and hear Master Reginald who did not mean to put on the habit of a friar. An historian quoted by Malvenda declares that it would be impossible to enumerate all the illustrious men who at this time joined the community. "Archdeacons and deans," he says, "several abbots and priors, together with doctors in every learned faculty, abandoned their benefices in order to profess an apostolic life in the Order of Preachers."[1]

Moreover, among the brethren themselves the season of discouragement and temptation was followed by a renewal of fervour as lasting as it was wonderful. Reginald's own example, far more even than the power of his words, communicated to others the flame of devotion. The auguries drawn of old from the voices of the angels began to be fulfilled, and the life led within the walls of St. Nicholas gradually came to exhibit the strictest and most fervent realization of the Rule of St. Dominic which has perhaps ever been seen. Many of the brethren closely imitated him in their nightly watchings and disciplines, and in the devotions which were dear and peculiar to himself. At no hour of day or night could you enter the church without seeing some of the friars engaged in fervent prayer. After Compline they all visited the altars, after the manner of their holy founder; and the sight of their devotion, as they bathed the ground with their tears, filled the bystanders with wonder. After singing Matins very few returned to bed; most of them spent the greater part of the night in prayer or study, and all confessed before celebrating the Holy Sacrifice. Their devotion to the Mother of God was of the tenderest kind. Twice every day they visited her altar, after Matins and again at Compline, walking round it three times, as they sang canticles in her honour, and recommended themselves

[1] Suset. in Chron. ap. Malv. an. 1219.

and their Order to her love and protection. They held it a matter of conscience never to eat till they had first announced the Word of God to some soul. They also served in the hospitals of the city, adding the corporal to the spiritual works of mercy; and in spite of the excessive austerity of their lives, it is said such was the joy of their hearts, shining out in their countenances, that they seemed none other than angels in the habit of men. The strict observance of the rule of silence practised among them is illustrated by the following anecdote. One night a friar, being in prayer in the choir, was seized by some invisible hand, and dragged violently about the church, so that he cried aloud for help. These disturbances, arising from diabolic malice, were very frequent in the beginning of the Order; and at the sound of the cry more than thirty brethren, guessing the cause, ran into the church and endeavoured to assist the sufferer, but in vain; they, too, were roughly handled, and like him, dragged and thrown about without pity. At length Reginald himself appeared, and, taking the unfortunate friar to the altar of St. Nicholas, he delivered him from his tormentor. And all this while, in spite of the alarm and horror of the circumstances, not one of those present, who amounted in all to a considerable number, ventured to speak a single word, or so much as to utter a sound. The first cry of the vexed Brother was the only one uttered during the whole of that night.

This admirable discipline was certainly attained and preserved by the practice of a somewhat rigid severity; yet its very sharpness attests the perfection which must have been reached by those who could have inflicted or accepted it. In the following anecdote, as given by Gerard de Frachet, the supernatural and passionless self-command exhibited by the chief actor, robs the story of that austere character which might make an ordinary reader shrink, and clothes it with a wonderful dignity and sublimity. A lay-brother had committed an infringement of the law of poverty, and on conviction of his offence, refused to accept the penalty imposed. He had accepted and concealed a piece of cloth given to him by a secular. Reginald perceived the rising spirit of insubordination, and at once prepared to extinguish it. He burnt the cloth in the cloister, then calling the culprit before the chapter he denounced the fault committed, and required the Brother to accept the penance he had deserved. Causing him to bare his shoulders, he raised his eyes to heaven, bathed in tears, and calmly and gently, as though presiding in choir, pronounced the following prayer: "O Lord Jesus Christ, Who gavest to thy servant Benedict the power to expel the devil from the bodies of his monks through the rod of discipline, grant me the grace to overcome the temptation of this poor Brother through the same means. Who livest and reignest, with the Father and the Holy Spirit, for ever and ever. Amen." Then he struck him so sharply that the brethren were moved to tears, but the penitent was reclaimed, nor did he ever again relapse into a similar fault.

This sort of chastisement was a very ordinary means which he used to deliver his subjects from the assaults of the enemy. A Brother tempted to quit the Order was taken in the act of escaping from the convent, and brought into the chapter over which Reginald was presiding. Recognizing the presence of the great enemy of souls, he resolved to deliver the Brother from his snares by the severity of penance. As the culprit confessed his fault and declared himself ready to accept the prescribed penalty, Reginald bade him prepare himself for the discipline. Then he administered the chastisement with no sparing hand, saying as he did so, "Go forth, thou evil one, from this servant of God!" while from time to time he turned to the others, saying, "Pray, my brethren, pray!" for he understood that the malignant spirit was of the number of those that come not forth, save by prayer and fasting. When this had gone on for some time, the penitent asked leave to speak. "What would you say, my son?" said Reginald. "I think, Father," he replied, "that the devil has left me now and will trouble me no more." At these words all present gave thanks to God, and the Brother himself remained faithful ever after.

Such then was the kind of discipline that reigned in the convent of St. Nicholas. It could not have been established save by one who ruled over the hearts of his subjects. They all knew that if the hand of their Father was firm and strong, his heart was tender as that of a mother. It is the very expression of Blessed Jordan, who knew him well, and bore testimony to the love with which he inspired those whom he governed. Under such a rule the community grew in numbers and in perfection, and such was its reputation for sanctity that men spoke of it as a kind of harbour of salvation; as may be illustrated by the following beautiful story given us by Taegius and others. There was a certain cleric in Bologna of great learning, but devoted to worldly vanities, and to other than a holy life. One night he seemed suddenly to be in the midst of a vast field, the sky above him was covered with clouds, rain fell in great abundance, and there was a terrible tempest. He, therefore, desiring to escape from the hail and lightning, looked all around him, to see if by any means he might find a place of shelter, but he found none. Then at the last he perceived a small house, and going to it he knocked, for the door was fast shut. A voice spoke to him from within, saying, "What wantest thou?" And he said, "A night's lodging, because of the great storm that is raging." But the keeper of the house answered him, saying, "I am Justice, and this is my house; but thou canst not enter here, for thou art not just." Then he went away sad, and presently he came to a second house, and he knocked there likewise; and the keeper answered and said, "I am Peace, but there is no peace for the wicked, but only to them of good-will. Nevertheless, because my thoughts are thoughts of peace, and not of affliction, therefore I will counsel thee what thou shalt do. A little way from hence dwelleth my sister, Mercy, who ever helpeth the afflicted; go, therefore, to her, and do even as she shall command thee." So he, continuing on his way, came to the door of Mercy, and she said to him, "If thou wouldst save thyself from this tempest, go to the convent of St. Nicholas, where dwell the Friars Preachers. There thou shalt find the food of doctrine, the ass of simplicity, the ox of discretion; Mary who will illuminate, Joseph who will make perfect, and Jesus Who will save thee." And he, coming to himself, and thinking well on the words of Mercy, went quickly to the friars, and asking for their mercy,[2] with great devotion received the holy habit.[3]

While Reginald was thus engaged in building up the spiritual edifice, he was not wholly unmindful of temporals. It will be remembered that the patronage of the church of St. Nicholas was vested in the family of D'Andalo, and that some difficulty had been offered by them to the acquisition of the property by the friars. Though the opposition of her relatives had been overcome by the influence of Diana, the whole affair does not seem to have been satisfactorily concluded until the 14th of March, 1219, at which date we find Peter de Lovello, and his son Andalo, making over to Master Reginald, in the name of the friars, the patronage of the church and the territory adjoining.[4] In the course of these negotiations, Diana necessarily became acquainted with Brother Reginald, and conquered by the ascendancy of his sanctity and genius, placed the direction of her conscience in his hands. "Attracted by the Holy Spirit," says a contemporary chronicler, "she had begun to despise the pomps and vanities of the world, and to seek more and more the spiritual direction of the Friars Preachers.[5] And she rejoiced as she watched the progress of the convent as it advanced day by day to completion in the close neighbourhood of her father's palace.

[2] This is an allusion to the words used in receiving the habit of the Order, at which ceremony the prior says to the postulant, "What do you ask?" And he replies, "*The mercy of God and yours.*"

[3] This story, says Gerard de Frachet, was related by Master Alexander in the schools, when commenting on that verse in the Psalm, "Mercy and Truth have met together," and he noted it in his marginal comments. He was a most truthful and honourable man, and an Englishman by birth, becoming afterwards a bishop in his native country.

[4] See document, printed by Mamachi, Append. n. clvi. col. 369.

[5] *Origines du Monastère de Sainte-Agnès.* By a contemporary writer. Published by Melloni in his *Memoirs of Men illustrious for Sanctity,* vol. i. p. 194.

Such was the position of the community of Bologna when St. Dominic once more appeared among them. "He found at the convent of St. Nicholas," says Blessed Jordan, "a large community of brethren who were being carefully trained under the discipline of Reginald. They all received him with joy, and showed him reverence as to their Father, and he abiding with them formed the yet young and tender family by his teaching and example." Great indeed must have been the consolation of the holy founder at finding himself surrounded by so many fervent religious, for in the short space of eight months, Reginald had received more than a hundred novices. Here, then, as at Paris, Dominic rejoiced in beholding a rich promise for the future, and gave thanks to God, Who thus poured out on his Order the blessing of fertility. On their part, his new children could not satisfy themselves with contemplating that noble presence in the full vigour of his glorious manhood, so gracious in speech, so admirable in every act, ever joyful in the presence of men, yet freely pouring out his tears in the hours of secret communing with God.[6]

The first practical lesson they learnt from him was one of poverty. "When the blessed Dominic came to Bologna," says Rodolph of Faenza in his deposition, "the Lord Oderic Galiciani wanted to give the brethren some lands worth more than five hundred Bolognese pounds. The deed had already been executed in presence of the bishop, but Brother Dominic caused it to be annulled, and would not allow them to have those or any other possessions, desiring that they should live only on alms, and that but sparingly." In fact, we read that the saint tore Oderic's contract in pieces with his own hands, declaring his resolve that his children should never depart from the law of poverty.

There was another law that he was no less inflexible in enforcing; it was that which invariably required the dispersion of the brethren to new centres. During his late progress through Lombardy, where the Manicheans were

[6] "Omnibus hilarem se præbebat; in orationibus crebro lachrymabatur" (Deposition of John of Navarre).

rapidly spreading their pestilential errors, the saint had seen how urgent was the necessity for planting communities of Preachers in all the cities of Northern Italy, that they might oppose themselves as a phalanx against the attacks of heresy. In many of the places which he had visited in the course of his various journeys between France and Italy, he had prepared the way for foundations to be made as soon as the number of the brethren would allow. The large accession of new subjects gained since the coming of Reginald to Bologna now permitted him to undertake some of these, and several bands of religious were sent out in the course of this and the ensuing year. Echard enumerates among the foundations made or decided on at this time, those of Milan, Bergamo, Asti, Verona, Florence, Brescia, Faenza, and Placentia. Those chosen for these important missions accepted their assignations not only with obedience, but joy, well knowing that, as Jordan writes, the holy Father followed the disciples whom he sent forth with his prayers, and that the power of God was with them to bless their work. And such was the fervour which at that time was found among the brethren, that when there was question of choosing subjects for undertakings which involved any special hard- ships or suffering, the number of those who voluntarily offered themselves exceeded what was required. For those who remained at Bologna a far harder sacrifice was reserved. Perceiving how great a work had been accomplished by Reginald among the students of the university, Dominic resolved to send him to Paris, then the very heart and centre of the scholastic life of Christendom. As he himself purposed to make Bologna his own place of residence, they would thus occupy the most important posts in the Order, and command the two great universities of Continental Europe. Blessed Jordan does not conceal the fact that the separation was a sorrowful one, and that in the judgment of some the saint seemed to be destroying the work so prosperously begun. "Having come to Bologna," he says, "the blessed Dominic sent Master Reginald thence to Paris, to the great grief of those children whom the latter had but recently

x

begotten by the Word of the Gospel, and who wept to see themselves so soon torn from their mother's breast. But all these things happened by the Divine will. It was something wonderful to see how the servant of God, in sending his brethren hither and thither in the world, acted as boldly and unhesitatingly as if he had been already certain of the future, or had received a revelation from the Holy Spirit. And who shall dare to say that it was not so? He had with him at first but few brethren, and those for the most part simple and unlettered men, and he separated them, scattering them through the Church, so that to the children of this world, who judged according to their own prudence, he seemed to be pulling down what had been begun, rather than to be building up."

But the supernatural wisdom of the holy founder was justified by the result. Reginald departed to Paris to communicate to the population of that great capital the same burning flame he had kindled at Bologna; and Dominic himself remained at St. Nicholas, as the centre whence he could direct and govern the foundations of Italy. If this demanded a sacrifice, by none could it have been more sensibly felt than by himself, for he was parting from his child of predilection, and in this life the Father and his beloved disciple were never to meet again.

But before Reginald took his departure he had committed one of his penitents to the direction of St. Dominic. Diana D'Andalo had already made the acquaintance of the saint on the occasion of his first visit to Bologna; she now became his spiritual daughter, "and loved him with her whole heart, committing to him the care of her salvation." He recognized in her one of those rare souls that are sometimes to be found, as richly adorned with the gifts of nature as with those of grace. She confided to him her desire of consecrating herself to God, and approving of her resolution, he consented to receive her vows, permitting her for a time to remain in her father's house and make no change in her exterior life. It was, therefore, in the convent church and before the altar of St. Nicholas that Diana took her irrevocable engagement, in the presence of all the community, including Reginald, and a number of noble ladies of Bologna, who in their turn became benefactresses and disciples of the friars.

This ceremony was the last in which Reginald bore a part, and the following day he set out for his new destination.

THEY were no new scenes which met the eye of Reginald of Orleans when, at the end of his long foot journey, he found himself at the gate of St. James's convent, in the September of the year 1219. There had been a time when every street in the great capital had been like a home to him, who first won honour and renown among the schools on Mont St. Geneviève. And though eight years at least had passed since he closed his university career, he soon found that he was not forgotten in Paris. Many days had not elapsed before it was rumoured abroad that the white-robed friar who now appeared in the pulpit of Notre Dame was the same Master Reginald whose reputation as a professor of canon law was still held in honourable memory; and at once masters and scholars gathered together to hear him. "With unwearied fervour," says Blessed Jordan, "he preached Jesus Christ, and Him crucified," and never had his eloquence been felt more captivating or more irresistible. Not a few of those who crowded round his pulpit sought him out in his convent and placed the direction of their consciences in his hands, and among these was Jordan of Saxony. The work in his soul which had been begun by Dominic was completed by Reginald, and he at length resolved to enter the Order, believing (as he says) that he should find therein that way of salvation concerning which he had so often deliberated. But before taking the final step he desired to win over to a similar resolution one bound to him in ties of holy and tender friendship, who was then studying theology at the university of Paris. This was Henry, then canon of the church of Utrecht, afterwards better known under the title of Henry of Cologne. " I loved him in Christ above all other mortals," says Jordan, "as being truly a vessel of honour and grace, than whom I do not remember ever in this life to have seen a more gracious creature. . . . He lodged in the same house with me, and dwelling together we were joined in a sweet and close union of hearts. . . . The purpose of my own mind being fixed, I began to labour that I might draw along with me this chosen friend of my soul, feeling sure that he would be most useful for the office of preaching. He however refused, but I ceased not to solicit him. I therefore managed that he should go to confession to Brother Reginald, and when he returned he opened the book of Isaias, as if seeking direction in the pages of Holy Writ. The first words on which his eyes rested were these: ' The Lord hath opened my ear and I do not resist, I have not gone back.' [1] Whilst I was interpreting to him these words as fitly answering his intention, and was exhorting him to place his youth under the yoke of obedi-ence, we noticed a verse that came a little further on, ' Let us keep together '—*Stemus simul*, as though we were admonished not to desert one another. Recalling this word afterwards, when I was at Bologna and he at Cologne, he wrote to me, saying, ' Where is now the *stemus simul* ? You are at Bologna, and I at Cologne.' . . . . That night, there-fore, he went to Matins at the church of Notre Dame, and remained there till daybreak praying and entreating the Mother of God that she would bend his will; but it seemed to him as if his prayer profited him nothing, and that his heart still remained hard within him. Then, as if pitying himself, he turned to her, and said, ' Now then, O Blessed Virgin, I feel that you regard me as unworthy, and that there is no portion for me among the poor of Christ.' For, indeed, God had long before made known to him how great a safeguard to the soul was holy poverty when we stand before the tribunal of the Judge. For once in a vision he had found

[1] Isaias 1. 5.

himself there standing amid a great multitude, and being
conscious to himself of no crime, he thought to escape
without condemnation, when one seated by the Judge's side
arose and said to him, 'Thou who standest there, what hast
*thou* ever forsaken for the sake of Jesus Christ?'   Thus
admonished, he had indeed conceived a desire to embrace
perfection in the state of poverty, if the sluggishness of his
will could be overcome.   As he was about to leave the
church, sad and disconsolate, the foundations of his soul
were suddenly shaken, and bursting into tears, all the hard-
ness of his heart seemed broken up, and the sweet yoke of
Christ, which awhile before he had thought so heavy, now
appeared to him lovely and delightful.   In the impulse of his
fervour, therefore, he went to Brother Reginald, and having
made a vow in his hands,[2] he returned to me.   Perceiving
the traces of tears on his angelic countenance, I asked him
whence he came, and he replied, 'I have vowed a vow to the
Lord, and I will perform it.'   We agreed, however, to put
off our novitiate till the season of Lent, and meanwhile we
gained another of our companions, named Brother Leo.

" When Ash Wednesday approached (which fell that
year on the 12th of February), we prepared to fulfil our
vow, our companions who dwelt in the same house with us
knowing nothing of the matter.   When, therefore, Henry left
the house, one of them asked him whither he was going, and
he answered, 'I go to Bethany,' which word indeed signifies
'the house of obedience.'   We three then met at St. James's,
whilst the brethren were singing the antiphon, *Immutemur
habitu;* and laying aside the old man, we were clothed with
the new, so that what they were singing with their voices
was fulfilled by us in very deed."

Such was one of the spiritual conquests achieved by
Reginald during his short but splendid career in Paris.   It
seems to have lasted little more than five months, during
which time his fervent soul spared itself neither in labour nor

---

[2] It will be observed from this, and from other examples, that the
custom of receiving the habit, and making a certain period of novitiate
therein, before taking the vows of religion, was not then established.

austerity. The abbot Matthew, who continued to preside over the community as Superior, perceived with mingled fear and admiration how rapidly the powers of nature were being consumed by the ardour of the spirit. He had known Reginald intimately in early years, and recalling the delicacy and luxury of his former life, he could not refrain from asking him once how he found it possible to endure the hardships and sacrifices to which he was now exposed. Reginald cast down his eyes, and a blush suffused his countenance as he replied : " Truly I count myself to have merited nothing by what you call sacrifices ; for indeed, so long as I have been in the Order, I am conscious only of having been too happy."

To this soul then, so rich in grace, the crowning happiness was given of a speedy summons to his reward. He was utterly consumed in the fire of that great love which had been enkindled in his heart, and in a short space he had accomplished a long time in the service of the Master Who now called him. Early in the month of February, 1220, and before the day on which Jordan and Henry received the habit, he fell sick, and in a very short time it became evident that his end was at hand. Matthew, who loved him dearly, proposed to administer Extreme Unction. " I do not fear death," said Reginald, " but rather wait for it with joy. At Rome the Mother of God anointed me with her own merciful hands ; nevertheless, lest I should seem to despise the unction of Holy Church, I humbly ask for it." When this ceremony had been accomplished they laid him on ashes at his own request, and thus, in the presence of the brethren praying around him, he gave up his soul to God. He was buried in the church of Notre Dame des Champs, for at that time the friars had no cemetery of their own. His brethren mourned over his loss as that of an angel of God, and it is said that Matthew could never speak of him without tears. " The very night that his spirit took its flight towards God," says Blessed Jordan, " it seemed to me, who did not as yet wear the habit of a friar, though I had made profession in his hands, that the brethren were being carried over the water in a vessel, which sank, but those who were in it escaped in safety. I think this ship represented Brother Reginald, whom indeed the brethren at that time regarded as their chief support. Another person also beheld a clear fountain which suddenly dried up, and in place of which two other fountains presently sprang forth." He adds with touching humility, "Conscious of my own unworthiness, I dare not interpret this vision; I only know that he received to profession only two persons whilst at Paris, of whom I was the first and the other was Brother Henry of Cologne."

Jordan's subsequent career in the Order, which he governed after the death of St. Dominic, and to which he gave so wonderful an extension, leaves us in no difficulty how to accept the interpretation he so modestly suggests. As a fact, he filled the exact place which in the judgment of the brethren had been assigned to Reginald; for by most the latter had come to be regarded as the probable successor of the holy founder. It must have been but a few days after he was laid in the grave that Jordan and Henry received the holy habit in the manner above described, nor was it long before the community of St. James's understood how fully their great loss had been replaced.

Having related the tale of Jordan's vocation in his own words, we cannot close this chapter without saying something more concerning the friend whose story was so closely bound up with his own. The sweetness of friendship is not forbidden to those who love God, as a thousand beautiful examples in the lives of the saints will amply prove. Yet this is certain, that the heart which loves must consent to suffer loss. After the entrance into the Order of Brother Henry, he for awhile gained a reputation in Paris as a preacher which surpassed even that of Reginald himself. "Never in the memory of man," says Jordan, "had there before been seen a man so young, so eloquent, or so attractive as a preacher. Every sign of grace seemed gathered together in him, for he was prompt in obedience, placid in meekness, pleasant in cheerfulness, and open-hearted in charity. . . . After a time he was sent to Cologne as prior; and Cologne still bears witness how diligently he kindled in all hearts there the fire which our Lord came to cast upon the earth. He used to admonish his hearers that the Name of Jesus, which is above every name, is most worthy of love and worship, so that to this day whenever that sacred Name is mentioned in the church, the hearts of all are moved to manifest their reverence."

But the earthly career of this highly-gifted soul was as brief as it was brilliant. He was attacked by an illness brought on by overfatigue in the October of 1225, and by what seemed a fortunate accident, Jordan, then Master General of the Order, was present at his happy death. He describes it in a letter to a German Benedictine[3] nun with whom he corresponded, and who was also linked in bonds of holy friendship with Brother Henry. "Alas!" he writes, "the voice of the turtle-dove will no more be heard in our land. Let us weep over the flower that is faded, over the turtle-dove who will never sing any more. I speak of Brother Henry, your friend and mine, or I should rather say everybody's friend, for indeed he strove to gain all souls to Jesus Christ. Let us mourn together over him who is mourned for by Cologne and by all Germany. . . . On the night of the 23rd of October, just as they were ringing for Matins, I went to see him before going to choir, and finding him already in his agony, I asked him if he would receive Extreme Unction. He replied that he earnestly wished it, and we decided on satisfying his desire before beginning the Office. During the ceremony it seemed as though he were giving himself the Holy Unction rather than receiving it from another, so fervent were his prayers. . . . Then we went down to Matins, . . . during which my eyes shed torrents of tears, which were yet mingled with unspeakable sweetness. Returning to him when the Office was over, I found him quite transported in God, singing, and exciting in himself and others the desire of paradise. Sometimes

---

[3] She was a religious in the Benedictine monastery of Horreen, and the letters addressed to her by Blessed Jordan are printed in the *Thesaurus Nov. Anec.* of Martene, pars 1, 920.

he would address the brethren who surrounded him, saying,
' Dear brethren, my soul is wholly poured out over you ! '
At others he would sing with joy, often repeating the
invocation, ' Oh, Blessed Virgin Mary, make us worthy
to partake of this heavenly bread ! ' . . . And with these
and similar words he prepared for his departure. . . . After
a time he said, ' The prince of this world has come, but he
is powerless against me.' Then he fell into his agony, and
we began the recommendation of his soul, but our voices
were choked with our tears. I could not lose him without
anguish ; but no, I have not lost him, I have but sent him
before me ; and young as he was, I well know that he had
accomplished a long life." In another letter he writes :
"God, Who will one day wipe all tears from our eyes, in
this life separates friends and brethren as seems good to
His wisdom. But I cannot yet console myself. Since the
day that Brother Henry was taken from us I have not ceased
to weep over a friend so faithful and so beloved, and so
perfectly worthy of love. . . . Oh, my brother Jonathan,
you were given to me by the glorious Virgin herself, for
when I resolved to enter the Order I asked her to give
you to me as my companion, and she granted my request.
She it was then who bestowed on the Order the precious gift
of this dove. Faithful labourer in the vineyard of our Lord,
he was called to receive his reward not at the close of the
day, but at the sixth hour. O good and faithful servant,
enter into the joy of thy Lord ! "

Such were the tender accents in which the loving heart
of Jordan dwelt on the memory of his friend. That memory
always remained fresh and verdant. It was the custom of
the friars in these early times before ascending the pulpit to
preach, to kneel and ask a blessing from one of their companions, who recited a prayer prescribed for the purpose.
After the death of Henry it was observed that Jordan
discontinued this practice, and Gerard de Frachet has
explained the reason. Each time he prepared himself to
preach he saw standing before him, in the midst of a
company of angels, the form of his departed friend, as

though ever present to inspire and encourage him. From him, then, and from no other lips, he asked the customary blessing. Of him, too, it doubtless was that he spoke, when relating to his brethren the story of two students who had entered the Order together, but whose names, through modesty, he did not reveal, he said that being tenderly attached to one another, the one who died first appeared to his friend resplendent with light, and said, " My brother, that which we have heard, that of which we so often spoke together, I now behold in the city of our God ! " [4]

What Jordan says in the above notice concerning the devotion of Henry to the Holy Name of Jesus is not without a particular interest. This devotion, it is well known, has always been much cherished in the Order of St. Dominic, and there seems reason for thinking that the preachers of the Order had some share in bringing about the introduction of the Holy Name into the Hail Mary. Thomas of Cantim-pré tells a story of a German religious named Walter de Meysenberg, who had been received into the Order by Blessed Jordan, and who was heard crying out in his sleep, and repeating the words, " Blessed be Jesus, blessed be the fruit of thy womb." " Next morning," says the writer," I questioned him on the subject, and he replied : " For many years past I have been in the habit of adding the Holy Name of Jesus to the Angelic Salutation, and of saying, *Blessed be the fruit of thy womb, Jesus*. Last night the devil tried to strangle me, and in my terror I invoked the Blessed Virgin, using those same words, and at once the enemy left me." St. Peter Martyr, Blessed John of Vicenza, and Blessed Ambrose of Siena are among those named as propagators of this devotion, and somewhat later was established that Confraternity of the Holy Name which still exists and is attached to the Order of Preachers.

[4] " Sicut audivimus, sic vidimus in civitate Domini virtutum, in civitate Dei nostri " (Psalm xlvii. 9).

# CHAPTER XXVII.

THE loss which had been sustained by the community of St. Nicholas in the departure of Reginald was abundantly supplied by the presence of the holy founder himself, who henceforth established himself at Bologna and made it his head-quarters. He desired indeed at no great distance of time to revisit Rome, and to present to the Pope a report of his late visitation of the Order, but before doing so he remained for some time at Bologna, in order to consolidate the position of the convent in that city, and to fill up the gaps that had been made in the ranks of the community by the dispersion of so many brethren.

Like most other cities of Italy, Bologna was at this time a prey to rival factions, whose quarrels often enough ended in bloodshed, giving rise to lasting feuds, which troubled the peace of families and occasioned shocking scandals. The factions of Bologna were perhaps not greater or more bloody than those which reigned in other cities, but they had one element of danger in them which did not exist to the same degree elsewhere, and which arose from the large number of young students, belonging to every European nation, who flocked to the university, and made a point of taking part in all the civic disturbances. To establish peace in such a society was a work worthy of a saint, and one which truly needed a saint to accomplish it. The influence of the friars, and of Reginald in particular, had already been beneficially exerted in this direction, but to the mediation of St. Dominic himself was reserved the glory of ultimate success. It is impossible to say with what unremitting fervour he sought to establish the reign of Jesus Christ among the citizens, to heal their feuds, and to unite their hearts in mutual charity. Advice, exhortations, reproofs—he spared none of them, while to the grace and power of his words in public he added in private the secret and more efficacious means of unceasing prayers and penances. Those who know the unhappy force and persistency of a spirit of discord can alone appreciate the success which crowned the saint's labours. In the course of them he entirely won the hearts of the people of Bologna, and the mutual love that sprang up between him and his fellow-citizens subsisted until his death. For with Dominic, he could not work in any other spirit save that of love, and it sufficed that he was called on to labour for any souls to make him speedily carry them in his heart. Henceforth Bologna and its people became very dear to him; he never left them but with regret, and how-ever frequently he was called away on those apostolic journeys through Italy in which the last two years of his life were consumed, it was here that he always returned as to the home of his rest.

Meanwhile, the tide of novices flowed in without abate-ment. Among those received was Bonviso of Placentia, who enjoyed much of the confidence of Dominic, and was often chosen as his travelling companion. He was one of those who afterwards gave his evidence at the saint's canoni-zation, and his deposition is of particular value and interest. During the time which he spent at Bologna in company with the holy Father, he temporarily exercised the office of pro-curator, and had to provide food for the brethren. On a certain fasting-day, all being seated in the refectory, the blessed Dominic gave the signal for bread to be set on the table. Bonviso approaching him, made known to him the fact that there was no bread in the house. "Then," he says, "the holy Father, with a cheerful countenance, lifted up his hands and blessed God; and presently two young men entered the refectory carrying two baskets, one of bread and the other of dried figs, so that the brethren all had abundance." This was that *second* repetition of the miracle at Bologna to which Father Louis of Palermo alludes in his narrative. " The *second* time," he says, " after the loaves they gave a handful of good figs. And a Brother who made oath of the same to Pope Gregory IX. added ' that never had he tasted better figs.' Then replied the Pontiff, ' Grammercy to Master Dominic, for they were not gathered in your garden,' as though he had said, ' God did at that time produce them.' And the brethren who were thus fed, were more than a hundred in number."

Bonviso was afterwards sent to preach in his own country, and he tells us that being still a novice and quite unaccustomed to preaching, he tried to excuse himself on the ground of want of learning, for he had come to the university to study law, and had not as yet applied himself greatly to theology. But the saint encouraged him sweetly, saying, " Go with confidence, my son, for the Lord will be with you, and will put the word of preaching into your mouth." He obeyed therefore, and went to Placentia, where he preached with so much success that he gained three men of considerable note to the Order.

The vocation of Stephen of Spain, another of the witnesses of Bologna, is related by himself in his deposition. He was a student in the university, and as a countryman of the holy founder appears to have been acquainted with some of the particulars of his early life in Spain, for he says, " Before knowing him personally I had heard much good of him from men worthy of credit," and he goes on to relate the story[1] of his selling his books at Palencia at the time of the famine. " After he came to Bologna," continues Stephen, " I went to confession to him, and I thought he loved me. One evening, as I was at supper in my lodgings with some of my companions, Brother Dominic sent two of the brethren to me, who said, ' Brother Dominic desires you to come to him at once.' I replied that I would come presently,

---

[1] As Echard points out, not quite correctly, for he makes out St. Dominic to have been at the time subprior of Osma. It is just such a mistake as a man might make who was not relating facts that had come to his own knowledge, but was relating them from hearsay.

when I had finished supper, but they said that I must come at once. Rising therefore, and leaving everything, I went to St. Nicholas, and found him there surrounded by several brethren. As I entered, Brother Dominic said to the others, 'Teach him how to make the *venia*.' Having made the *venia*, I placed myself in his hands, and he clothed me in the habit of the Friars Preachers, saying, 'I will give you arms wherewith you may fight against the devil all the days of your life.' I have often wondered much both then and later what moved him thus to call and clothe me in the habit, for he had never before spoken to me of entering religion; but I fully believe that he did so by Divine inspiration."

Stephen has preserved several little traits of the holy Father which show him to have been much in his company, and a close observer. He dwells much both on his great love of poverty and the severe austerity he himself practised. If the brethren had two kinds of cooked dishes (he says), Brother Dominic contented himself with one, though, as another witness adds, he would taste of the second dish, to encourage the brethren to eat sufficiently. He nearly always slept at table, being tired out by his long watches, and because he ate and drank so little that he had finished before the others, and was thus overpowered by sleep. Stephen often served his Mass, and was witness of the copious tears he shed, and of the singular devotion with which he repeated the *Pater noster*. He also testifies to the extraordinary influence exercised both by the saint and his disciples in the extinction of feuds and the pacification of the cities and provinces into which they were sent. That which had passed at Bologna had taken place under his own observation, and the same followed on the settlement of the friars in the cities of Lombardy and the Marches. "Many of these cities," he says, "deliver their statutes into the hands of the friars to be changed and amended as they think good. They do the same in what regards the putting an end to wars and the making peace among themselves, as well as the restitution of ill-gotten goods, and other things it would be too long to enumerate."

In Paul of Hungary, another of his novices, St. Dominic had the consolation of receiving and forming in his own spirit, a disciple whose happiness it afterwards was to realize the two great desires of his own heart, and to win the grace of an apostolate to the Cumans, and the palm of martyrdom. Paul, a Hungarian by birth, had come to Bologna to study in the university, where he received the doctor's cap. But the charm of Dominic's preaching, and yet more the example of his life, determined him on abandoning all his prospects of worldly advancement and embracing an apostolic life. During the short space of time which he spent under the spiritual direction of the holy Father, he was filled with so ardent an admiration of his virtues that he made it his one aim to imitate them. The saint on his part discerned in his new disciple the true spirit of an apostle, and hesitated not to send him while still young in religion to plant the Order in his native country.

To these names we must add those of two afterwards numbered among the *beati* of the Order, namely, John of Salerno and Nicholas Palea. Of the first of these, who was a native of the south of Italy and of Norman extraction, we shall have to speak more particularly in connection with the foundation of the Order at Florence. Powerfully tempted by his family to abandon his vocation, he owed his perseverance to the prayers of St. Dominic, who early discerned the rare gifts with which he was endowed, and fully understood the purpose with which the great enemy of souls sought to draw back to the world one so fitted to make war against the powers of evil. Singularly small in person, he was powerful in mind, and attaching himself to Dominic as to his true spiritual Father, he sought to imitate him in all things, but specially in his practices of prayer and mortification. He would spend entire days and nights in prayer, often rapt in extasy, and seeming hardly to belong to earth, but rather to heaven, so wholly was he detached from all thought or care of the body.

Nicholas Palea was likewise from southern Italy, being a native of Giovenazzo, a town near Bari, in the kingdom of Naples. Even from his cradle he had shown signs of singular sanctity, and seemed to have received intimations of his future vocation. When but eight years old he began to practise entire abstinence from meat, and being reproved for this singularity by the priest who directed his education, the child crossed his arms on his breast, and kneeling down with great humility, replied, "Master, one day when I was alone in my father's house a young man of wonderful beauty stood before me and said, 'Son of obedience, from this day eat no meat, for the time will come when you will enter an Order which will observe perpetual abstinence.'" Being a youth of great promise, his parents sent him to study at Bologna, and there the preaching of the blessed Dominic made a speedy conquest of his heart. His angelic purity endeared him greatly to the saint, who often chose him as his companion in some of the expeditions which he made into the surrounding country for the purpose of preaching. The gift of miracles which he possessed manifested itself when he was still a young novice, for passing through a village with some of his companions, they met a poor woman with a withered arm, the sight of whom touched Nicholas with compassion. "Poor woman!" he exclaimed, "what have you done to your arm?" His companions sharply reproved him, saying he had broken the Rule by speaking to a secular. "I only did it out of compassion," he said. Then turning to the woman he added, "Have confidence in God, and He will certainly heal you." "Are you sure of that?" asked the woman. "Yes," he replied, with great simplicity, "your faith will save you if you will but believe;" and repeating the words, *In nomine Patris, et Filii, et Spiritus Sancti*, he had scarcely ended when the poor sufferer found she had recovered the use of her arm. At Giovenazzo, where he was sent shortly after his profession, many other miracles attested his sanctity, one of which was the raising to life of a child who had fallen into a well and been drowned. He became founder of a very famous convent at Trani, near his native place. Having preached the Lent in the cathedral of this city, the citizens with one accord entreated him to found a

Y

convent among them. He willingly consented to do so, but there was great difference of opinion as to the choice of a site. Nicholas recommended the people to cease disputing over the question and make it a matter of prayer, and next day in the sight of the archbishop, and many of the clergy and faithful, a cross of fire appeared in the air over the spot afterwards chosen for the convent.

The Blessed Nicholas is also famous as the undoubted founder of the great convent of the Order in Perugia. St. Dominic more than once visited this city and preached in it, and on one occasion, according to a constant tradition, he and St. Francis met here at the Gate of St. Angelo, and embraced one another tenderly. It was not, however, until 1233 that Nicholas, coming to Perugia to announce the Word of God, was entreated by the citizens to make a foundation in the city. The *podestà*, or chief magistrate, supported their petition, and taking the standard on which were represented the arms of the city (a griffin *argent* on a field, *gules*), he placed it in the hands of Nicholas and declared to him that wherever he might plant it the convent should be built. Nicholas took the standard and planted it by St. Peter's Gate, on a spot which overlooks the beautiful valley of Valliano, with Assisi in the distance. There rose a convent, with a magnificent church dedicated to St. Dominic, in which took place the canonization of St. Elizabeth of Hungary and St. Peter Martyr, which was consecrated by Pope Clement IV., and in which Blessed Benedict XI. lies buried.

It would take us too long to relate one half the beautiful legends which are attached to the life of the Blessed Nicholas. He united the perfection of simplicity to that of learning. Preaching once at Brescia to a crowded audience, the unseemly conduct of two young men who were present drew from him a grave rebuke. But as they paid no heed to his exhortation, the saint, filled with a sudden inspiration, exclaimed aloud, "O God, Thou seest that men will not listen to Thy Word, but do evil even in Thy sacred presence!" and going forth out of the church He ascended a little hill hard by and continued, "Birds of heaven, since men reject the Word of God, come and listen to it in the name of Jesus Christ!" Immediately a vast number of birds gathered about him, and remained as though listening to him until he had concluded his sermon, when having received his blessing, they flew away.

Such were some of St. Dominic's Bolognese novices. We need not wonder that among them were not a few who in later times have been raised to the altars of the Church, when we bear in mind by whom and in what manner they received their religious training. All the rich treasures of his mind and of his heart were poured out on the task of rearing to maturity these precious souls on whom all the hopes of the future rested. He instructed them daily, and often shed tears as he did so, those who listened to him being moved to weep also. He cared for their health no less than for their spiritual training, and indeed it was necessary to set limits to the fervour which some would have pushed beyond the bounds of prudence. When the hour came for them to retire to rest it was necessary to look for them in the different corners whither they retreated that they might devote themselves to prayer. Their silence was unbroken, and their devotions were accompanied with many mortifications. Frugal as were their meals, many added other practices of penance, such as passing eight days without drinking, or pouring cold water over their portions. These external practices, however, would have been of little worth had they not been united to a charity which embalmed their daily life. There was a holy emulation among them who could be most serviceable to his brethren. Constantly on the watch against temptation, they avoided everything that could tarnish the spotless purity of their consciences. When they considered the beauty and innocence of the life to which they were called, all their regret was not sooner to have embraced it. Neither the business nor the pleasures of the world were even so much as named among them, and the virtue which was thus so jealously guarded they were careful to place under the special protection of the Queen of Virgins.

Whilst carefully cultivating these religious virtues in the souls of his children, Dominic knew how to blend with them an ardent love of souls, without which indeed they would have been no worthy disciples of his. Though more than one instance has been given of his sending out some to preach who were possessed of no learning and felt themselves unfitted for the task, this is not to be understood to imply that as a rule he neglected to train his novices for the work of preaching. On the contrary, we are assured that he attached very great importance to their pursuing those studies which best fitted them for the office, and if any showed a particular aptitude for it, he withdrew them from other occupations and employed them exclusively in what he regarded as the primary duty of the Order. The character of their preaching resembled his own; it was simple in form, and based upon the Holy Scriptures. Following the example of their holy Father, when they went forth to announce the Word of God, they took with them no book save that of the Gospels.[2] This marked love of the Holy Scriptures on the part of St. Dominic and his religious was well understood by their hearers, as is illustrated by a story related by Nanni. There was, he says, a certain priest who, attending at the sermons preached by the saint and his brethren, was deeply impressed by their teaching and conceived a great desire to embrace so holy a rule of life. But he was not so fortunate as to possess a copy of the New Testament, which he imagined to be a necessary condition to his becoming a friar. "Ah! how happy should I be," he said to himself, "could I but be received among them, but that cannot be till I can provide myself with a New Testament." As he considered within himself how he should set about providing himself with this treasure, an unknown youth accosted him with a Testament in his hands, and asked him if he would buy it. Eagerly accepting the offer, the priest took the book, but then a new trouble beset him. How could he be sure it was God's will that he should join the friars? At length he

---

[2] Theodoric, c. 22, n. 255; Boll. p. 605.

determined to seek a solution to this question in the pages
of the book itself, and opening it at hazard he read these
words in the Acts of the Apostles: " Arise and go with this
man, nothing doubting, for I have sent him," and taking it
as a word from heaven, he presented himself to St. Dominic,
and was received among the brethren.[8]

A similar means for solving his doubts was resorted to by
Conrad of Zähringen, bishop of Porto, a Cistercian monk,
who at one time entertained grievous and perplexing
suspicions as to the character of the Order.   He opened
his Missal, and read in the Preface to the Mass of our Lady
the words, *Laudare, benedicere, prædicare;* and embracing the
saint the next time he met him, he exclaimed: " I am all
yours.   My habit is Cistercian, but in heart I am a Friar
Preacher."   The above words have since been adopted by
the friars as in some sort their motto or device, as briefly
expressing the two-fold character of the Order, at once
monastic and apostolic.   They are to be found sculptured
over an ancient doorway belonging to the ruined convent of
Grenoble.

The writers who have given us so beautiful an account
of the fervour which in these early times filled the cloisters
of St. Nicholas with the odour of sanctity, do not, however,
pretend to represent that the perfection which was there
followed was without a flaw, or that faults more or less
grave did not from time to time call for correction.   On
the contrary, they notice some of these transgressions with
singular frankness and simplicity.   Thus we read of a lay-
brother who was tormented by the enemy in punishment
for having eaten in secret the remains of some better food
served to the sick in the infirmary.   Gerard de Frachet in a
remarkable passage takes notice of the various devices to
which the enemy of souls has recourse in order to disturb
those newly-entered into religion, which show plainly that
even in these ages of primitive fervour human nature was
not always proof against temptation.   " Who," he says,
" can number up the snares which the enemy employs to

[8] Nanni, lib. 4. cap. 20.

tempt novices? He makes use sometimes of indiscreet fervour, at other times of relaxation and the omission of small practices enjoined by the Rule. Sometimes he takes occasion of too great an attachment to friends and relatives, or again, of disputes among the novices themselves. He attacks them by the remembrance of worldly pleasures; he stirs up antipathy towards their companions; he excites an over-attachment to books, or even to more contemptible objects. I knew one youth who was greatly troubled at having to part with a little dog that he had brought up from puppyhood; in short, the devil is a skilful artisan and can ply many trades, and he is a wise man who holds himself on guard against his devices."

One anecdote related by Malvenda, shows how keenly Dominic watched over the words and actions of his brethren, and how promptly he repressed the first approaches of evil. As he was one day engaged in giving them a spiritual con- ference the sacristan entered, and calling out one of the priests, told him that a woman was in the church who desired to go to confession, adding in a whisper a jocular remark on the good looks of the penitent. The words were not so privately spoken as to escape the saint's ear, and levity of this kind was the last fault to which he ever showed indulgence. Sternly reproving him for a remark so unseemly, he bade him kneel down, and in the presence of all adminis- tered a severe chastisement.

But if the hand of the saint was prompt to correct, his heart was equally ready to console and to encourage; and in enforcing the Rule he continually led the way by his own example. Doubtless to men who had filled positions of importance and consideration among their fellow-citizens, it can have been no light humiliation to be sent out into the streets day by day to beg their bread, and to meet with scoffs and ridicule far harder for human nature to bear than even blows. If so, the humiliation was lightened and made easy when they beheld it shared by their venerable Father. He himself often went on the quest, accepting such scraps and broken morsels as the charity of the faithful saw fit to bestow on him. Once, indeed, he was so fortunate as to receive a whole loaf by way of alms, and in gratitude for so unusual a benefaction, knelt down in the street to thank the generous giver.

It can be no great wonder that, in presence of facts like these, the influx into the Order of so many men of note, and specially of so many scholars of the university, was regarded with great disfavour by friends and relatives. They sent their sons to Bologna to study canon law and fit themselves for worldly dignities, not to put on a coarse habit and beg alms in the public streets. Whatever might be the sanctity of Brother Dominic, fathers and mothers were to be found in abundance who keenly resented his attracting into a life so obscure and penitential those whom they desired should make a figure in the world. On one occasion special indignation was felt at the entrance into the convent of a young lawyer whose friends had conceived great hopes of his advancement. Not content with angry words, they were determined to drag him out of the convent by violence. The brethren became alarmed, and entreated the saint to apply to the magistrates for an armed force to protect the house. But he replied with his usual equanimity, "We have no need of soldiers to defend us; I see standing round the church more than two hundred angels who are sent to guard us." And indeed, when the friends of the youth came, intending to attack the convent, they were suddenly seized with a kind of panic, and withdrew in confusion, and the novice was left undisturbed in his vocation, wherein he happily persevered.

Whilst St. Dominic was still at Bologna, there arrived in the city a certain merchant of Florence named Diodato, brought thither in a somewhat singular manner. Having confessed certain sins of injustice which called for restitution, he had been required by his confessor to build a chapel, and to place some religious therein. He had in consequence made choice of one of the faubourgs of Florence, called Ripoli, and having there built his chapel with a house attached, he was considering to whom he should offer it,

when he heard such great things reported of the sanctity
of St. Dominic and the rare example of his brethren, that
he resolved to come to Bologna and judge for himself,
intending, if he found the reports true, to make over the
chapel to the new Order. Thoroughly satisfied with the
result of his observations, he proposed to Dominic to accept
the buildings at Ripoli for a foundation of the brethren.
The saint joyfully accepted the offer, desiring greatly to
establish the Order in the city of Florence. He therefore
chose twelve brethren, at the head of whom he placed John
of Salerno, in whom, though the youngest of the company,
he discerned qualities that fitted him to undertake the
direction of an important work. They accordingly set
forth, and arrived at the little hermitage—for so it might
more justly be called—which was situated about three miles
out of the city on the road leading to Arezzo.

With great joy, singing hymns and psalms of thanksgiving, the brethren had taken possession of their new
home, which, narrow as it was, sufficed for their accommodation, while their generous patron, Diodato, supplied them
with all that they required in the way of food and other
necessaries. The retired position of the convent, however,
seemed to fit it rather for contemplatives than for those
whose calling was to labour for the salvation of souls, and
remembering what manner of life Brother John had hitherto
led at Bologna, it is possible that his brethren prepared
themselves to enter on a course of prayer and penance
rather than one of apostolic labour. They were, therefore,
a little astonished when, a few days after their arrival,
their young prior called them together and set before them
in eloquent terms the true character of their vocation and
the duties to which it bound them. They were come there
not for themselves alone, but for the people; and in order
to reap that fruit of souls which the Lord of the harvest
designed to give them, they must be prepared to devote themselves without sparing to the work of preaching and teaching,
and to the drawing of sinners to true penance. This work
they would begin on the very morrow, going into the city

and preaching the Word of God, if need were, in the very streets.

The brethren heartily entered into the spirit of their prior, and their apostolic labours were at once begun, and followed by most happy results, to which the sanctity far more even than the eloquence of Blessed John so greatly conduced as to earn for him the title of the Apostle of Florence. They continued to inhabit the same spot during the lifetime of Diodato, but after his death removed into the city, giving up their little hermitage to the use of some Franciscan friars.

One other visitor to Bologna must be named whose connection with a foundation of the Order has already been alluded to. Beranger de Palou, bishop of Barcelona, was returning from Rome into Spain, and, passing through Bologna, made some stay in that city. One object which he had in doing so was the hope of carrying back with him to his own country an illustrious ecclesiastic who had for nine years past fixed his abode in the university, where he had gained great renown as a doctor of canon law. Raymund of Pennafort was as distinguished by birth as by learning. His fame as a canonist extended far beyond the limits of the university, and attracted a crowd of scholars whom with characteristic disinterestedness he taught gratuitously; but the magistrates of Bologna, conscious of his value, had assigned him a yearly *honorarium*, in the hopes of thus keeping among them a man of such rare merit. Bishop Beranger was no less desirous of regaining possession of one who had been among the chief ornaments of his diocese, and succeeded in persuading him that he belonged of right to Barcelona, and could not lawfully prolong his absence. Meanwhile, he rejoiced in the opportunity of making a personal acquaintance with the founder of the Friars Preachers, of whose fame he had heard at Rome, and whom he greatly desired to speak with. What if he could persuade the saint to give him a colony of his brethren, and should so be able to return to his cathedral city with ample spiritual treasures! He was fortunate enough to succeed in this attempt also, for as it will be remembered, Dominic in his recent visit to Barcelona, had already engaged to send thither a foundation, and could not hope to do so under more favourable auspices.

It can hardly be doubted that in the course of these negotiations, Dominic and Raymund must have become mutually acquainted, but on this point history is entirely silent. If the two saints met, as we may reasonably suppose that they did, there was nothing at the time to indicate the tie which was hereafter to connect St. Raymund of Pennafort with the Order of Preachers. It was not until two years later that he entered that Order of which, in the year 1238, nineteen years after his departure from Bologna, he became the third Master General, and to whose Constitutions he was to give the form which, in the main, they preserve to the present day.

ENTRANCE TO SANTA SABINA.

## CHAPTER XXVIII.

### ST. DOMINIC'S FIFTH VISIT TO ROME.

#### 1219, 1220.

It was in the month of November, 1219, that St. Dominic set out for Rome, taking with him as his companions the two brethren, William de Montferrat and Bonviso of Placentia. The first place to which he directed his steps was Florence, where he found the community under John of Salerno in a good state of discipline, and making fair progress in their apostolic labours. In these labours he took an active part, preaching daily in the city and effecting many conversions. Among these was the notable case of a woman named Benedicta, who had attained an unhappy notoriety not only from her irregular life, but from certain

extraordinary visitations to which she was subject, and
which were commonly attributed to possession. St. Dominic
addressed himself to the task of recalling this soul into the
way of salvation, and having brought her to true penance
and the desire to repair her past scandals, he also, by means
of his earnest prayers, delivered her from the vexations of the
enemy. He exhorted her to continue faithful to grace, and
to persevere in the recitation of the Holy Rosary, and many
wonderful things are related of the assistance she received
from our Blessed Lady, who is said to have appeared to
her and shown her five lilies, on the leaves of which were
inscribed those holy truths the meditation on which should
preserve her in the path of virtue. This conversion became
widely known, and was much talked of in the city; and
while some recognized in it the power of God, others were
not wanting who remained in doubt as to the sincerity
of the penitent. Among these last was a priest, who in
his misdirected zeal not only caused much annoyance and
suffering to the poor woman, but freely expressed his contempt for the friars who supported her. Benedicta poured
out her trouble to the holy Father, who, as usual, showed
no disturbance at what was said against him and his
brethren. "Have patience, my daughter," he said, "the
time will come when he who now speaks evil of you and
of our Order, will see things in another light, and will
himself wear the friar's habit," and this prophecy was
verified a few years later, when the priest in question
entered into the Order of Preachers.[1]

As one of the saint's chief objects in undertaking his
present journey was to see and confer with Pope Honorius
on many important affairs, he travelled by way of Viterbo,
at which city the Pope was then residing. Not only had he
to make a report on the general condition of the Order of
which he had recently made the visitation, but he desired

---

[1] The story of the conversion of Benedicta is related by Constantine of
Orvieto and other ancient authors, and is considered as perfectly authentic.
But a great number of marvels have been introduced into it by later
writers, to whom less credit is due; and these, therefore, we have omitted.

to obtain the sanction of the Pontiff to an important step which he was now contemplating, with a view to its more perfect consolidation. This was the convoking of a General Chapter, in which should be drawn up such laws as seemed necessary for preserving uniformity of observance and unity of government in an Institute now fast spreading over the length and breadth of Christendom. Needless to say, he was well received by the holy Pontiff, who fully entered into all his plans, and granted him several Briefs, one of which, addressed to the prelates of Spain, recommending all the religious of the Order to their favour and protection, is dated as given at Viterbo, on the 15th of November, 1219. Three weeks later, that is to say, on the 8th of December, the Pope published a second Brief, addressed to the prelates of the Catholic world, in like manner affectionately recommending to them "the prior of the Order of Preachers and his religious, . . . whose ministry for souls, as we are well aware, becomes every day more necessary." In the absence of more precise dates (a luxury with which the historians of St. Dominic rarely indulge us), we may take those attached to the above Briefs as fixing the time of the saint's visit to Viterbo, though it seems certain that he returned here on more than one occasion.

His stay was unfortunately prolonged by an attack of illness, of which he had felt the first symptoms at Bergamo, and which returned in a severe form before he reached Rome. William of Montferrat speaks of this illness as being a grievous one, "yet he did not on that account break the fast, nor eat meat, nor take any extra pittance, unless it were sometimes a few apples or radishes." Neither did it induce him in any way to change his ordinary manner of travelling, which is graphically described by his other companion, Bonviso of Placentia. "When I travelled with him to Rome," he says, "whenever he left any town, or village, he used to walk barefoot, he himself carrying his shoes slung on his shoulders, for he would not suffer me to carry them, though I much wished to do so. Thus he would travel on until we came to the neighbourhood of another town, when he would put his shoes on again before entering. Once in the same journey there came on great floods of rain, so that the rivers and streams were much swollen, but he, praising God, sang with a loud voice the *Ave Maris Stella* and the *Veni Creator*, being always joyful amid tribulations of this sort. And as he came to a certain river that was much swollen on account of the floods, the blessed Dominic made over it the sign of the Cross, and bade me, who was much afraid of water, to enter in without fear, which I did, trusting in the name of the Lord, and we passed over without danger."

So travelling, they reached Rome, and took up their quarters at Santa Sabina, which the saint had quitted rather more than a year previously. Here he rejoiced to find his two communities increased in the number of their subjects, and flourishing in all good discipline. To the nuns of St. Sixtus he brought a welcome gift—doubly welcome as a pledge of his fatherly affection and remembrance of them. "When the blessed Dominic returned from Spain," writes Sister Cecilia, "he brought the Sisters as a loving little gift, some spoons of cypress wood, for every Sister one. And one day, having finished his preaching and other works of charity, he came in the evening to the Sisters, that he might deliver to them these spoons from Spain." Amid all his fatigues and journeys, and with his mind preoccupied with weighty cares, he still had room enough in his heart to think of the pleasure and comfort of his beloved daughters, and these spoons, carried in his little bundle over the hills of Spain and Italy, were doubtless treasured by them as precious relics.

During his stay in Rome, Dominic resumed the discharge of his duties as Master of the Sacred Palace, as well as his customary work of preaching. A great number of signal conversions are said to have been effected by him at this time, which by the historians of the Rosary are attributed to the spread of that devotion. One of these shall be given as reported by Flaminius, though its authenticity is not undisputed. There was in Rome a woman named Catherine,

whose house was the resort of the most dissipated society
in the city, and who lived in the habitual neglect of all
religious duties. Hearing much, however, of the preaching
of St. Dominic, she one day went to hear him out of curiosity,
and even received one of the rosaries he was accustomed to
distribute among his audience. This she kept about her,
and began to recite the prayers, though for long years
previously she had abandoned every practice of piety. One
evening, as she was returning homewards, she was accosted
by a man of majestic appearance, who bade her hasten home
to prepare supper, as he meant to be her guest. Catherine
did as she was bid, and they sat down to table; but she was
surprised to see that everything the stranger touched was
*tinged with blood.* Thinking he had perhaps cut himself, she
offered to bind up his wound, but he said, "I am not
wounded, but do you not know that a Christian should
eat no food that has not first been steeped in the Blood
of Christ?" "For God's sake," exclaimed Catherine, "tell
me who you are, and what you require of me." Then she
beheld his aspect change into that of a Child of wonderful
beauty, whose head was crowned with thorns, while bleeding
wounds were to be seen in his hands and feet. Presently,
as she looked at him, the figure changed again to that of
a Man fastened to a Cross. The vision lasted but a minute,
and in its place appeared the same form, but glorious and
beautiful, and shedding forth rays of light. "Oh, wandering
sheep!" he said, "return to the fold, for in what has been
shown thee, thou hast seen the way of salvation." Catherine
understood that in what she had beheld, there had been
represented to her the Joyful, Sorrowful, and Glorious
Mysteries of the Rosary, the contemplation of which should
indeed lead her into the way of salvation. She sought out
St. Dominic, and making to him a general confession of her
whole life, entered under his direction on a course of penance,
distributing all her goods to the poor, and living for the rest
of her life in prayer and poverty. She is said to lie buried
in the church of St. John Lateran. Another story is told in
connection with the Rosary, though without anything to

indicate the precise date to which it belongs. When the holy Father was preaching the devotion in Italy, a certain knight came to confession to him. To whom, when he had finished, the blessed Dominic said, "My son, you have confessed your lesser sins, but have omitted those that are graver," and he told him what they were, for the Lord often thus revealed to him the secrets of hearts. Then the knight, full of wonder, said, "Those to whom we commonly confess do not thus instruct us; who will guide me, Father, when you depart?" "I will leave you a teacher who will instruct you," replied the saint; "it shall be this rosary, on which you see five large beads, on each of which you shall say an Our Father, and fifty smaller ones for the *Ave Marias.* Now these five larger beads are of different colours. The first, which is variegated, shall represent to you the various ways in which a man can sin against God, himself, or his neighbour, in thought, word, and deed; and the ten smaller beads that follow shall stand for the particular sins of which you yourself have been guilty. The second large bead by its pale colour represents the pallor of death, and the ten smaller ones that follow shall remind you that all men must die. The third bead, which is the colour of fire, is the figure of the wrath of the Eternal Judge against sinners, Who yet in His mercy delays to pronounce against them the sentence which they deserve; and the ten smaller ones shall warn you of the peril which they incur who delay their repentance. The red colour of the fourth bead represents the torments of hell, on which meditate as you recite the ten beads that follow. And the fifth bead, which is the colour of gold, shall speak to you of the joys of heaven, on which dwell one by one in your heart whilst reciting the ten smaller beads. This is the guide that I leave you—it will teach you how to live well, and how to escape from the wrath of God, if you diligently consider these things." The knight took the rosary, and carefully complied with the saint's directions. He continued for the rest of his life to recite it daily, and before he died, was permitted in a vision to see an angel, who for each angelic salutation that he pronounced placed a stone in the hands of our Blessed Lady; and out of the hundred and fifty stones so collected there was raised an edifice of surpassing beauty, which represented to him the heavenly palace into which by his sincere repentance he should be admitted. This story, which is given by Malvenda, bears a certain resemblance to that before related of Benedicta, the penitent of Florence, to whom our Lady gave the five lilies whose leaves were inscribed with salutary instructions; but the authenticity of both may be considered as somewhat uncertain.

Castiglio and other writers assign to this fifth visit of the saint to Rome the narrative of several miracles wrought by him, as well as others in which the malice of the enemy appears, as manifested in various vexatious ways, having chiefly for their object the disturbance and discouragement of the nuns of St. Sixtus. There was also one of the brethren of Santa Sabina against whom his attacks were specially directed, he being distinguished both for his rare virtue and his indefatigable labours for the salvation of souls. This was Brother Rao, or Raoul, who had received the habit of religion from the hands of St. Dominic, together with Giacomo di Melle and Audio of Rome. Portraits of the two latter brethren may be seen represented over a door which leads into the garden, near to the spot where stands the famous orange-tree of St. Dominic. Many wonderful things are told both of the sanctity of Brother Raoul and the torments he endured from the malice of the infernal enemy, insomuch that there was not a part of his body that was not bruised and torn by the blows of the demons, who feared him as their mortal foe. They also sought to terrify him by frightful apparitions and terrible howlings. Raoul had a most tender devotion to the dead, and was accustomed to say that he feared nothing so much as dying before he had accomplished the suffrages for them to which he was bound. He was most dear to the blessed Dominic, whom he regarded with unbounded love and veneration, and he was one of those to whom was granted a revelation of his glory after death.

z

Not content with exterior annoyances such as those inflicted on Raoul, the evil spirit sought to injure the holy Father in another way, by dragging back to the world the children who were dearer to him than his own life. " There was in the convent of Santa Sabina," says Theodoric, " a young Roman citizen named James, who, overcome by a powerful temptation, had one night resolved to leave as soon as the church doors should be opened in the morning. The venerable Father knowing this by the Spirit of God, sought him out and warned him gently not to abandon the holy company to which he was joined, but the youth, turning a deaf ear to his words, stripped off his habit and declared himself determined to go. Then Dominic, touched with compassion, and understanding that he was under the influence of a violent temptation, spoke to him, saying, " My son, wait a little, and afterwards you will not act as you now purpose to do." Then, prostrating in prayer, he prayed to our Lord for the son whom he saw was about to perish. Before he had ended his prayer, the young man came and cast himself at his feet with tears, entreating him to restore him the habit which he had cast off, and promising to remain faithful to God in the holy Order into which he had entered. The next day some of the brethren, going to St. Sixtus, related to the Sisters what had passed, and the holy Father was forced to admit the truth. " My daughters," he said, " the enemy of God sought to tear from me a little sheep, but the Lord delivered him out of his hands."

It was at this time, according to the most probable conjecture of historians, that the interview took place between Dominic and Francis, in the palace of Cardinal Ugolino, which the Franciscan writers give as occurring at Perugia, in the year 1219, but which is placed by St. Antoninus and Malvenda as occurring in this year, at Rome. After a spiritual conference of some duration, the Cardinal asked them whether they would agree to their disciples accepting ecclesiastical dignities. Dominic was the first to reply. He said that it was honour sufficient for his brethren to be called to defend the faith against heretics. The words of St. Francis were equally

characteristic. " My children," he said, " would no longer
be Friars Minors if they became great ; if you would have
them bring forth fruit, leave them as they are." Edified by
their replies, Ugolino did not, however, abandon his own
views : when he was elevated to the Papacy, he promoted
a great number of both Orders to the Episcopate, as many
as forty-two of whom were of the Order of Friars Preachers.

The marked preference shown to St. Dominic and his
children by Cardinal Ugolino was fully shared by Pope
Honorius, as is proved by the renewed favours which he
liberally poured out at this period in the shape of Briefs and
privileges, one of which constituted Dominic the Superior or
Master General of the entire Order, an office he had hitherto
only held by tacit consent, and which was doubtless formally
given him at this time with a view to the assembling of the
brethren in the General Chapter which was now in contemplation.  In another decree, dated the 17th of December,
His Holiness ratified in perpetuity the gift of the convent of
St. Sixtus to the Order of St. Dominic, for hitherto, owing to
the circumstances explained in a previous chapter, it had
only been granted to the saint conditionally, pending the
conclusion of the negotiations with the Gilbertines and the
final resignation of their claims.  Moreover, in various letters
addressed to bishops and other prelates, the Pope made
known his high esteem for the friars and his sense of the
immense good they were effecting wherever they were
founded.  " In these latter days," he says, writing to the
Archbishop of Tarragona, " when the charity of many has
grown cold, we verily believe that God has in His goodness
raised up the Order of Friars Preachers not only for the
extirpation of heresy, but to combat in general whatever is
opposed to His glory and the salvation of souls."

Cardinal James de Vitry, who lived and wrote in the time
of St. Dominic, thus describes the Order, and his words are
interesting and valuable as giving us the impression of a
contemporary.  " There is in the city of Bologna," he says,
" a new Congregation of Canons Regular, very agreeable to
God and man, who serve God under one Superior whom they

obey with fervour, promptness, and humility.   Delivered
from all temporal cares and living solely on alms, and that
only to such an amount as suffices each day for the necessities of a most frugal life, they imitate the poverty of Jesus
Christ and despise all superfluities for His love.   They sing
the Canonical Office according to the Rule of St. Augustine.
They follow the studies of the university, and one of their
number each day delivers to his brethren a lecture on the
Holy Scriptures.   What they have learnt and meditated
they then preach to others, for according to the will of the
Pope, and by his authority, they join to the life of Canons
the duty of preachers."[2]

Another very singular testimony to the esteem in which
the founder of the Friars Preachers was held, is to be found
in a Brief addressed by Honorius to various religious of the
Order of Vallombrosa, those of St.Victor, and others, giving
them leave to quit their solitude and employ themselves in
active labours for the salvation of souls, provided always
that without laying aside the habit of their respective Orders,
they place themselves under the direction of Brother Dominic
and obey him in all things connected with the ministration of
God's Word.[3]

The exact time spent by St. Dominic at Rome is uncertain, but it is probable that it was from thence that he
despatched letters convoking the assembly of the first
Chapter General of the Order, which was appointed to
meet at Bologna on the feast of Pentecost, 1220, not four
years from the date of the confirmation of the Order. Having
therefore taken every measure in his power for the good
government of the Roman communities, the saint set out
some time early in the new year on his return to Bologna,
that he might prepare all things for the reception of the
brethren who were coming to take part in this important
assembly.

Flaminius tells us that on his road he stopped at a
certain place in the diocese of Orvieto, called St. Christina,

<hr>

[2] Jac. Vit. *Hist. Occid.* c. 17, ap. Echard, t. i. p. 24.
[3] Bull. Ord. FF. Præd. t. i. p. 10.

where there lived a gentleman whose custom it was to give hospitality to any of the friars who passed that way. He accordingly entertained St. Dominic with much joy, and showed him every kindness, and his charity met with its reward. For a terrible tempest visiting that part of the country soon afterwards, the fields and vineyards all around were completely laid waste by the hail, and their fruits entirely destroyed, the lands of this gentleman alone escaping: a favour he did not hesitate to ascribe to the blessing of heaven which had been bestowed on him in return for the hospitality shown to the servant of God.

Thus passing on he arrived at Bologna, where it is probable that the first news which greeted him on his arrival was that of the death of Reginald of Orleans, which took place in the February of 1220; but the sorrow of this bereavement, deep as it must have been, has left no traces on the page of history.

PIAZZA OF SAN DOMENICO, BOLOGNA.

## CHAPTER XXIX.

### THE FIRST GENERAL CHAPTER.

#### 1220.

It was on the 17th of May, 1220, that the Fathers of the
Order met in the convent of St. Nicholas at Bologna. Jordan
of Saxony, who was one of the four brethren sent from Paris
to represent that house,[1] has left us a brief and most unsatisfactory account of the proceedings. "In the year of our
Lord, 1220," he says, "the first General Chapter of this
Order was held at Bologna, at which I was present, having
been sent from Paris with three other brethren; for the
blessed Dominic had ordered by his letters that four brethren
should be sent to Bologna from the house at Paris. When I
was sent I had not yet spent two months in the Order. In

---

[1] Abbot Matthew could not himself attend the Chapter, being detained
in Paris in consequence of the troublesome negotiations which were still
being carried on with the cathedral authorities. Easter having that year
fallen on the 29th of March Whit Sunday (on which day the Chapter
opened) must have fallen on the 17th, not the 27th of May, as is sometimes incorrectly stated.

that Chapter it was decreed by common consent that a General Chapter should be held every year, at Bologna and Paris alternately, in such sort, however, as that the Chapter of the ensuing year should be held at Bologna. It was also ordained that henceforth our brethren should hold no possessions or revenues, and that they should renounce those which they held in the neighbourhood of Toulouse. Many other things were also there ordained which are observed to this day."

This extremely meagre account is supplemented by the narrative of Theodoric of Apoldia, who writes as follows: "In this Chapter, presided over by the venerable Father, Master Dominic, by the inspiration of the Holy Ghost and with the consent of the illustrious men whom he had gathered together, were laid the foundations of the laws of the Order. The chief foundation-stone thereof was the obligation of Evangelical poverty. In fact, by a perpetual statute, they agreed to give up all possessions and temporal revenues, renouncing even those granted to them at Toulouse, and preferring the poverty of Christ to the riches of the Egyptians. After this the humble servant of Christ, who presided over the Chapter, said to the assembled brethren: 'I deserve only to be dismissed from my office, for I have grown cold and remiss, and am no longer of any use.' Thus he who was above them all, both by his sanctity and his authority, humbled himself before all.

"But as the brethren absolutely refused to accept his resignation, he decided with their consent, that definitors should be appointed, who should have power both over him and over the whole Chapter, to define, decree, and ordain all things so long as the Chapter should last, the authority of the Master General continuing unchanged after its conclusion. Moreover, in order to extirpate those abuses which might spring up as weeds, and to plant the germs of all virtue, it was further decreed that the Chapter General should be held every year."

It would have been of interest to have known more particularly what were the "other things" of which Jordan speaks as regulated in this first Chapter. Of one ordinance we are certain, that, namely, which provides that in each cell there should be a crucifix and an image or picture of the Blessed Virgin.[2] "For the crucifix," says Gerard de Frachet, "is a book ever open which teaches us the art of loving God; and this decree was made to the end that, in all they did, in their studies no less than in their prayer, nay, even in their very sleep, the brethren might accomplish every act under the merciful eyes of the Virgin Mother and her Divine Son."[3]

We also know that in this Chapter the alteration in the form of the habit, which had been introduced after the vision granted to Reginald of Orleans, was fixed by law. During the lifetime of Reginald, Dominic had been unable to explain to the brethren his reasons for making the change, but now that Reginald had departed to God, they were made known to all.

These are all the details which we possess regarding the proceedings of this venerable assembly. The number of friars present at the first Chapter of his Order held by Francis has been carefully preserved; but no similar reckoning was made of the Friars Preachers. We know only that France, Spain, Italy, Poland, and as some say, Scotland, had their representatives in that assembly. Dominic was then fifty years of age, having lost nothing of that manly vigour of mind and body which ever distinguished him. If we seek amid the scanty materials which history has left us, to find some token which may reveal to us the secret feelings of his heart at a moment of such deep interest, we shall find that power, and success, and a government over other men which gave him a personal empire of souls extending over half Christendom, had produced no change in the simplicity and humility of his heart. It tended Godward as it had ever done; and his first act, as we have seen, was to implore permission to renounce a superiority of which he accounted himself unworthy. Some, perhaps, may be

---

[2] Const. FF. Præd. dist. i. c. ix. 175.

[3] "Utpote liber expansus, et liber de arte amoris Dei (*Vit. Frat.* part iv. c. i.).

tempted to look on this as an easily assumed modesty, and to doubt how far he hoped or expected his resignation would be accepted. But the evidence of Brother Paul of Venice shows that even at this time the darling hope of his soul had never been abandoned; he still cherished the thought, so soon as the Order was firmly established, of carrying the light of the Gospel among the heathen. "When we shall have fully instructed our brethren," he was wont to say, "we will go to the Cumans, and preach the faith of Christ;" and this deeply-rooted intention was no doubt in his mind when he made the effort to rid himself of the government of his Order.

By far the most important regulations of the Chapter were those which bore reference to the law of absolute poverty, henceforth to be embraced as an obligation by the brethren. That they were not made without opposition on the part of some is abundantly evident. The expressions used by John of Navarre seem to indicate that it cost the holy Father some labour to bring all to accept these decrees, especially the brethren of Toulouse, where the Order held considerable possessions. "When the brethren had many lands in the neighbourhood of Toulouse and Alby," he says, "and carried money with them on their journeys, and went on horseback, and wore surplices, Brother Dominic laboured much, and brought it to pass that they should renounce all temporal goods, and should not go on horseback, and should live on alms, and should carry nothing with them on their journeys. And so the possessions in France were given to the nuns. And that the brethren might devote themselves more entirely to study and preaching, he desired that the unlettered lay-brethren of the Order should have the management and administration of temporal things; but the brethren who were clerics would not allow the lay-brethren to take precedence of them in this, lest the same thing should befall them that had befallen the brethren of Grammont with regard to their lay-brethren."

St. Dominic, with characteristic humility, deferred to the very reasonable objection raised by the other brethren to this last-named proposal. Nevertheless, as we learn from the deposition of Rodolph of Faenza, he succeeded in obtaining such regulations as should limit the care of temporal things to certain officers. Speaking of his great love of poverty, and his dislike of all show and superfluity in the convents and churches of the Order, Rodolph goes on to say: "He would not have the brethren mix themselves up with temporal things, or with the management of the house, nor with consultations about temporal matters, excepting those to whom the care of the house was entrusted. The others he wished to be always intent on study, prayer, and preaching, and if he knew any Brother who was specially useful for preaching he would not allow any other office to be imposed on him."

These words partly explain to us the motive which the saint had in establishing in his Order the absolute poverty he so highly prized. What he aimed at was the deliverance of the brethren from the cares of this world and the deceitfulness of riches. He lived in an age when monasteries were in possession of extensive lands, over which they often exercised the rights of feudal lords. Such institutions were productive of enormous benefits to the society amid which they were planted, but it was a condition of things which could not fail to weaken the apostolic spirit of those who were engaged in it. But the mind of the blessed Dominic was formed entirely on the apostolic standard, and this was the character he desired to preserve among his children. In the lands and revenues so liberally granted to the convent of Toulouse by Bishop Fulk and the Count de Montfort, he saw the germ of institutions which would in time place the brethren so endowed with worldly possessions on the same footing as the monks of Cluny, whose riches had been a stumbling-block even in the eyes of St. Bernard. There was but one means for averting this result, and that was the enforcement of the Evangelical law of poverty, and hence the saint rested not till he had obtained the consent of the Chapter to its acceptance.

That in the course of six centuries a change should have been effected in the legislation of the Order, whose brethren are now no longer bound to the same rigorous form of poverty, need cause neither surprise nor scandal. Experience, the altered circumstances of the times, and the decision of the Holy See, afford the necessary explanation. It must be remembered that highly as St. Dominic prized this absolute form of poverty he never put it forward as an end, but only as a means, and as he deemed it, the most efficient means for delivering his brethren from the distracting solicitudes incident on the possession of lands and revenues. Had it ever come before him as likely to prove an obstacle rather than a help to the spiritual well-being of his brethren, we can have no manner of doubt that he would have rejected it. And it is not difficult to understand in what way it actually became so. The anxieties and solicitudes attendant on a state of want and indebtedness are certainly no less hostile to the religious spirit than those which accompany the possession of property. The picture which has been presented in a former chapter of prior Gerard de Frachet "breaking his head" to know where he could find six thousand *sols tournois* with which to pay for the site of his convent, does not strike one as particularly conducive to the habit of serene contemplation. He probably sang his *Salve Regina* on the following day with much greater devotion, when his debts had been paid by the good-natured canon Aymeric.

Yet such examples can have been by no means exceptional, when the friars had to build convents and churches, and supply large communities with the necessaries of life with no available resources, for it would hardly have been safe for all Superiors to reckon on the timely relief afforded to Gerard. The whole principle on which the present legislation of the Order is framed, is expressed in the Constitutions in words at once luminous and conclusive. "The possession of revenues in common (it is said) is not contrary to the Rule of St. Augustine which we profess, neither does it necessarily diminish religious perfection, for poverty is not perfection, but a means to perfection. As, therefore, an instrument is not used for its own sake, but because of the end to which it serves, it is not to be considered better in proportion as it is great, but rather in proportion as it meets its end; just as medicine is not said to be better, because of its quantity, but because of its fitness for expelling disease. A religious Order, therefore, is not more perfect simply on account of its greater poverty, but rather in so far as the poverty it professes adapts itself either to the general end of all religious life, which is the service of God, or to some special end, such as contemplation, or the instruction of our neighbour. And this seems best secured by that kind of poverty which provides frugally for the necessities of life, procured without incurring great solicitude, and used in common; and such is the poverty embraced by our Order."[4]

St. Antoninus explains the reasons of the change in a very simple way. "In earlier times," he says, "there were no other mendicant Orders, and hence alms were then given in abundance. But now these Orders are greatly multiplied. Moreover, wars, and the greater habits of luxury prevailing among lay persons, have diminished their resources, and restricted their alms; and they are now more disposed to spend their means on the fabrics or ornaments of churches, than to provide for the needs of the poor." In other words, what was a possibility in the thirteenth century became under altered conditions of society impracticable.

It is evident that the rule of absolute or mendicant poverty was not established without a certain amount of opposition on the part of some present at the Chapter. Neither did the decrees passed on this head find universal favour among the brethren at a distance. Flaminius tells us that the community of Toulouse in particular were by no means willing, in obedience to these decrees, to renounce the possessions which had been granted to them, neither did they relish exchanging the habit of the Canons Regular

---

[4] Const. FF. Præd. dist. ii. c. 1, dec. vii, 486.

which up to this time they had continued to wear, for the rough and poor garb substituted for it. They therefore resolved to appeal to the Pope, and despatched a deputation, who made the journey mounted on horseback and well provided with money. But St. Dominic was warned of their intention, and, furnishing himself with aid from the magistrates of Bologna, he took measures for arresting the malcontents as they passed through the city, so that when they dismounted at their inn they found themselves prisoners: their horses and money being taken from them, and they themselves delivered over into the hands of their holy Father. Having dealt with them as the occasion demanded, he sent them back to their convent, on foot, and clad in the friars' habit; and thus was promptly extinguished the spirit of insubordination.

This is the story as told by Flaminius, and repeated from him by Malvenda, Castiglio, and others. Touron rejects its authenticity on the ground that it is to be found in no writer earlier than Flaminius, and Père Réchac devotes a chapter to the refutation of this statement, drawing up his argument under eight distinct heads. Without presuming to decide between the disputants, it may be observed that there is a certain similarity between the points enumerated by Flaminius, as those on which the brethren offered resistance, and the words of John of Navarre (quoted above), which suggest the possibility of some facts having come to the knowledge of the latter not altogether unlike what Flaminius has reported.

Another particular in which the practice of the Order has gradually changed regards both the place and time for the celebration of the General Chapter. The inconvenience of limiting the place for their assembly to the two university cities of Paris and Bologna quickly became apparent, and other cities, such as Rome, London, Cologne, and Bordeaux were soon included. In the year 1370, the yearly Chapter was exchanged for a triennial one. In 1625, by authority of Urban VIII., the interval was prolonged to six years, which remains the present term, though in our own day a yet longer interval has been allowed. The article which directs that every cell should contain a crucifix and an image of our Lady, remains in force, a venerable relic of ancient legislation. It was very befitting to the children of him to whom from early years the crucifix had indeed been "the book of charity," and to religious whose tender devotion to the Mother of God had already earned for them the title of "the Friars of Mary."[5]

The beautiful words we have quoted from Gerard de Frachet had indeed a deep significance. They might truly be said to remain even in their sleep under the eyes of the Queen of Virgins, whose dormitories were visited by her, and blessed by her gracious hand. And in their turn they expressed their loyal devotion to her, by letting the first words which fell from their lips on waking be those of the *Ave Maria*, with which they began the Office of the Blessed Virgin, which they recited before quitting the dormitory. This practice was most acceptable to her in whose honour it was performed, but she desired that it should be accomplished devoutly. And we read how on one occasion, when perhaps the Office was being recited a little sleepily, she appeared in the dormitory accompanied by other virgins, and animated the brethren to greater fervour with the words, *Fortiter, fortiter, viri fortes.*

Before breaking up, the Chapter named certain religious to fill various offices, whilst others were set apart for distant missions and foundations. Jordan of Saxony was appointed lector for the convent of Paris, and on returning thither delighted his audience by his Commentaries on the Gospel of St. Luke. John of Waldeshusen, commonly called John the Teutonic, was despatched to Germany, where he effected great things for the extension of the Order. Of this holy Father, one of the most distinguished religious of his time, it is said that whilst only a child of ten years old, it was revealed to him that he should one day enter into a new Institute having for its title the name of Preachers, of which

---

[5] " In principio Fratres Ordinis dicebantur Fratres Virginis Mariæ " (St. Anton. *Chron.* part iii. lib. 23, c. 3, § 1).

he should in due time become the head. When in obedience
to the commands of the Chapter he left Bologna, and set
out for his native country, he passed by a certain Cistercian
convent near Constance, where he and his companions asked
for hospitality. It chanced that the night previously the
abbot, whose name was Eberhard, and who was a man of
great sanctity, had seen our Lord in a dream, Who said
to him, " To-morrow I will send you some of My horses;
do not fail to shoe them well." On awaking, he was perplexed what meaning to attach to such a dream, and he was
still considering the matter when he was told that some
religious were at the gate praying for admission. Bidding
them enter, they presented themselves before him, clad in
their white habits and black mantles, and carrying only a
stick, a breviary, and a copy of the Gospels. Never having
before seen any brethren of the Order, the abbot questioned
them as to who they were, and what was the meaning of
their habit, and the things which they bore. " We are,"
replied John, " Friars Preachers; we carry a stick to show
that our preaching rests on the Cross of Jesus Christ, which
is indeed that staff of which David speaks when he says,
*Virga tua et baculus tuus, ipsa me consolata sunt.* We also carry
the Book of the Gospels, in which the preachers of God's
Word should be fully instructed. And as to our habit of two
colours, your Reverence will remember how the prophet
Zacharias beheld four chariots, to the last of which were
harnessed " grisled horses and strong ones,"[0] which represented apostolic men who should be sent forth to preach the
Gospel among many people. We, then, are those grisled
horses, and the two colours of our habit signify by the white,
the purity of our doctrine, and by the black the austerity
of our life."

When Eberhard heard this explanation, he cast himself
at the feet of the speaker, saying, " You, then, are those
horses, of whose coming our Lord warned me last night
in a dream, bidding me take good care of you."

Then he washed their feet, and gave them new shoes

Zach. vi. 3, 6, 7.

(for theirs were worn out in the course of their long journey), and furnished them abundantly with every necessary, remaining ever after a great friend and protector of the Order. John became a great preacher, and was instrumental in spreading the Order throughout Germany and Switzerland, and the revelation made to him in his childhood received its full accomplishment when in 1241 he was elected its fourth Master General.

This seems the proper place in which to resume the history of Diana d'Andalo, who, it will be remembered, made her vows in the hands of St. Dominic before the departure of Reginald from Bologna. She did not at once, however, leave her father's house, but by the saint's advice, remained for a time there, leading a life of penance and devotion. Under her rich garments she wore a hair-shirt and an iron chain. She never left her private apartments before the hour of Tierce, spending her time until then in prayer and silence, and the rest of the day in good works and pious reading. Dominic, under whose direction she lived, thought it good thus to test her spirit before he consented to let her take any further steps; but on his return from Rome, before the opening of the Chapter, Diana implored his permission for her to abandon the world altogether, and enter the religious state. St. Dominic, who had marked her rapid progress in virtue, understood that God's time had come. He took counsel with the Cardinal Ugolino, who fully approved of Diana's spirit and vocation, and both of them frequently visited her at her father's house, and encouraged her in her holy purpose.

It was Diana's earnest desire that Dominic would found at Bologna a house of nuns of his Order, similar to those already established at Prouille, Rome, and Madrid, for she desired to wear no other habit than that which she had come to associate with all her ideas of the spiritual life. This plan the saint himself had also long and earnestly cherished, and calling the brethren together in Chapter, he placed the project before them, and desired to know their opinion. " Father," they replied, " we willingly agree to whatever you think good." "Well, then," said the saint, "before deciding aught, let us present it to God in prayer." The next morning, having, according to his wont, spent the night in prayer, he made known to them what he believed to be the will of God in the matter. "My brethren," he said, "our Lord demands of us this foundation, and I believe that we ought to begin it without delay, without waiting for the completion of our own convent." Then as the Chapter was at hand, after which he knew that he should have to leave Bologna for some little time, he placed the superintendence of the whole matter in the hands of four Fathers, Paul of Hungary, Guala of Brescia, Ventura of Verona, and Rodolph of Faenza.

Diana's wishes seemed now on the eve of their accomplishment, but her vocation was to be subjected to a yet severer test. Not only did her parents offer the most strenuous opposition to her entrance into religion, but the Bishop of Bologna objected to the site proposed for the new convent, and raised difficulties in the way of the whole plan. Diana therefore resolved on a decisive step. On the feast of St. Mary Magdalen, 1220, she left her father's house, and took refuge in the monastery of Ronzano, situated on a hill near Bologna. When this was known, it created a great commotion in her family; friends and relations all united in the determination to force her from her retreat, and coming to Ronzano they carried out their purpose, and that with such violence on their part, and such resistance on her own, that they actually broke one of her ribs. Brought home as a prisoner, she fell ill, and remained in a very suffering condition for nearly a year, during which time St. Dominic was unable to visit her, and could only encourage her by his letters. It was not until after his death that Blessed Jordan, his successor, inheriting all the interest which the great patriarch had manifested in the vocation of the young heroine, succeeded in carrying out his plan, and with the approval of the bishop founded the convent of St. Agnes in a spot not far from that of St. Nicholas; in which he placed four religious from the convent of St. Sixtus at Rome, among

AA

whom were the two sisters Cecilia and Amy. Sister Cecilia
became the first prioress of St. Agnes, dying in the odour of
sanctity at a very advanced age; and these two Sisters,
together with Diana, lie buried in the same grave, where
their remains have been twice discovered and honourably
translated.

The Chapter having terminated, the assembled Fathers
dispersed to their several convents, and Dominic resumed
his ordinary life, dividing his time between the training of
his novices and the public ministration of the Word of God.
His confirmation in the office of Master General, and the
decision of the Chapter not to allow of his retirement from
the government of the Order, seemed in his eyes as a call
for him to renew his fervour, and to exhibit in his own person
a model of those virtues he desired to form in others.
"Placed over the brethren as their Master and governor,"
says Theodoric, "he was distinguished only by a more
profound humility and a more rigorous austerity. His
watchings became longer, his fasts more continual, his mortification more universal. He excused himself from no one
point of regular observance; day and night he assisted at
the Office in choir, and in the refectory he never absented
himself from the common table, where his only singularity
was in the greater abstinence that he practised."

Yet the austerity of the saint was as far as possible
removed from harshness or severity. An anonymous writer
quoted by Theodoric, who knew him personally and greatly
loved him, has drawn a beautiful picture of him in his community life, which he gives in the form of a Divine revelation. "Never, so long as he lived in the flesh," he says,
"did the blessed Dominic raise bitterness in the heart of any
of his brethren; he never irritated them by word or deed;
for in truth, nothing bitter could flow from such a well-spring
of charity. His heart was so large towards others that he
provided for their bodily wants with the utmost tenderness;
not contenting himself with giving them only the frugal diet
that was customary, but often procuring other and better
provisions, for fear lest the young should be discouraged, or

lest the elder brethren, weakened by their long fasts, should
yield to infirmity. Thus condescending to the wants of all,
even when he had to administer correction his severity was
always mingled with compassion. When he laughed, as he
sometimes did, his laughter proceeded from the same spirit
of sweetness and simplicity. For he was, above all things,
true and simple, and to such a character laughter is not
unsuitable. In his prayers indeed he shed abundant tears,
pouring out before God the needs of His Church. But if
any of his brethren were troubled or tempted, he carried
them in the secret of his heart, and with a fatherly compassion, he comforted them with his words, and supported them
by his prayers. On the weak and infirm he lavished the
tenderest affection, providing for their wants with the utmost
solicitude. All therefore rejoiced at his prolonged presence
among them, and his delightful conversation rendered all the
privations of poverty supportable, and sweetened every
hardship which they had to endure."[7]

The writer who has preserved the account of the saint's
*nine methods of prayer*, tells us that he sometimes withdrew
to the garden of the convent, and there spent long hours in
contemplation, praising God amid the trees and flowers. He
loved this kind of solitude, and among the rare recreations
that he allowed himself was that of planting trees in his
convent gardens. Besides the orange-tree at Santa Sabina,
there was long shown a cypress-tree in the garden at
Bologna planted by his hands. In the present century it has
been cut down, and out of its wood have been carved two
images, one of Our Lady of the Rosary, and the other of
St. Dominic, which stand at the entrance of the sacristy.[8]

---

[7] Theodoric, lib. 5, c. vii. The above passage has been rather freely
translated, with strict adherence to the sense.

[8] Under the image of our Lady, which stands at the right hand, we
read—

> Virginis effigiem cernis; fuit ante cypressus
> Præscia Gusmani dextera fixit humi.

Underneath that of St. Dominic—

> Cypressus fit grata sui cultoris imago,
> Fili, gratus eris factus imago Patris.

It was at this time that a remarkable addition was made to the ranks of the Order, in the person of Conrad the German. He was a professor of the university, whom the brethren had long ardently desired to have among them. One evening St. Dominic received a visit from a certain Cisterian prior, who afterwards became bishop of Alatri. He was a man of great sanctity, whom the Pope had despatched into Germany on an important mission, and passing through Bologna he took the opportunity of becoming acquainted with the Saint of whom he had heard much, and with whom he desired greatly to confer on spiritual things. In their very first interview the hearts of the two servants of God opened one to the other. The instinct of true sympathy does not always need time to make itself felt; by a magic touch it sometimes reveals itself at first sight, and so it was in the present instance. They spoke together of their most secret thoughts and of the special favours granted them by our Lord. " Prior," said St. Dominic," I will tell you a thing which you must keep secret till my death. Never have I asked anything from God, but He has granted it to me." " Then, Father," said the prior, " I marvel that you do not ask the vocation of Master Conrad, whom the brethren desire so greatly to have among them." " The thing is difficult," answered Dominic; " nevertheless, if you will pray with me this night, I doubt not God will incline to our request." It was the 14th of August, the vigil of the feast of the Assumption. The brethren retired to their cells after Matins, but that night the prior kept watch in the church by his friend's side; and at the hour of Prime, as they intoned the hymn, *Jam lucis orto sidere*, Conrad entered the choir, and demanded the habit from the hands of the saint.[9]

Brother Conrad became known as a great preacher, and did much to extend the Order in his native country.[4] He died at Magdeburgh in the year 1239, singing out of the very joy of his heart. As the brethren recited the Gradual psalms

---

[9] Constantine of Orvieto, who received the narrative from the lips of the prior; also Theodoric, n. 206.

around his bed, he joined his voice to theirs, and at the words, *Hæc requies mea in sæculum sæculi*, he raised his finger and pointed to heaven as if he beheld a sight of surpassing glory, and expired with a smile of extasy on his lips.

St. Dominic's spiritual conquests were not all made or retained without difficulty. Among his novices was a youth whose singular gentleness and sweetness of disposition greatly endeared him to the holy Father. His name was Thomas of Paglio; and shortly after his reception his relatives forcibly carried him off by night, and dragging him to a neighbouring vineyard, stripped off his habit, and clothed him in his former worldly garb. St. Dominic, hearing what had happened, immediately betook himself to his only arms of prayer; and as he prayed, Thomas was seized with a strange and unendurable heat. " I burn, I burn," he cried; " take these clothes from me, and give me back my habit ; " and having once more gained possession of his woollen tunic, he made his way back to the convent in spite of all opposition, and at the touch of that white robe of innocence the fiery anguish was felt no more.

The engagements of his conventual life however, important as they were, were never suffered to interfere with the discharge of that public office of preaching to which St. Dominic held himself so solemnly bound. " The people of Bologna," says Flaminius, " were so eager to hear him that in order to satisfy their devotion he had to preach, not once only, but several times every day, choosing the largest church, and sometimes the public piazzas. At an early hour in the morning his hearers came to secure places, and when he left the church many wanted to accompany him back to the convent, and draw from him some word of edification." On one such occasion two young students presented themselves, one of whom addressed him, saying, " I beg of you, Father, to obtain for me from God the pardon of my sins, for I have just been to confession." " Have confidence, my son," replied the saint, " for God has indeed pardoned you." The other made the same request, but did not receive a similar reply; God had made known to His servant that the young man had concealed some of his sins. Of another who was living in open violation of the laws of God, we read that after resisting the power of the preacher's eloquence, he was conquered at last in another way. For happening one day to serve the holy Father's Mass, at the moment when he kissed his venerable hand, he was sensible of an odour of sweetness which took possession of his very soul, so that as it were in spite of himself he felt moved with the resolution to abandon his criminal habits. Nor was this the only occasion when a sensible grace was communicated by the person of the saint, for a certain usurer, whom he communicated, felt the Sacred Host burning against his mouth like hot coals, whereupon he was moved to penitence, and making restitution of all his ill-gotten gains, became sincerely converted to God.

Sometimes his discourses were followed by scenes which bore striking witness to the power which his words exerted over the hearts of his hearers. As he one day preached in a public piazza, there happened to be present the governor of St. Severino, a town in the Marches of Ancona, who was so moved by what he heard, that presenting himself to the saint as he ended his sermon, he knelt in presence of the vast audience, and asking his blessing, conjured him to give him some of his brethren; promising if he would do so, to give them a church, a convent, and everything necessary for their support.

The memory of these things is still cherished in the city which witnessed their occurrence. On the spot where six centuries ago devout crowds listened to the words of the great preacher, there now stands two columns, one of which is surmounted by a figure of the Blessed Virgin, the other by that of St. Dominic. It is the *piazza di San Domenico*,[10] and reminds us that amid a thousand political revolutions, Bologna still counts it among the glories of her past history that her streets and churches have resounded to the voice of one of God's greatest saints.

[10] The convent of St. Nicholas after the death of the saint was dedicated to St. Dominic, and gives its name to the piazza.

CHURCH OF SAN DOMENICO, SIENA.

# CHAPTER XXX.

### FOUNDATIONS IN ITALY.

#### 1220.

Soon after the conclusion of the Chapter, St. Dominic began a series of journeys through the provinces of northern Italy, visiting the communities of brethren who had been sent forth from Bologna in the previous year, and laying the foundation of convents in a great number of other places. It is impossible to follow his course with absolute certainty, though the careful researches of Father Michel Pio enable us to establish the regular succession of these foundations with tolerable accuracy. But it appears evident that they were not all made in the course of one excursion. From time to time the saint would seem to have returned to Bologna, spending some time at the novitiate house, so that the remainder of the year 1220 must be understood as occupied in these journeys, with interruptions of longer or shorter duration, during which he resumed his residence at Bologna. A mere cursory examination of the places he thus visited would give a very inadequate idea of the vastness of the work accomplished by St. Dominic in this closing portion of his life, or of the character of those disciples whom he gathered to the Order in every town and village through which he passed. We shall therefore follow him on his road as best we may, gathering up such fragmentary notices of his progress as have been preserved by local historians.

Before starting on his journey northwards, however, he paid a short visit to Viterbo, in order to render an account to His Holiness of the proceedings at the late Chapter. On his road thither, he passed through Siena, in which city he was no stranger, as besides his visit there in company with Bishop Fulk in 1215, when returning to France from the Council of the Lateran, there is evidence of his presence in the "city of the Virgin" on more than one subsequent occasion. He had early despatched thither a colony of his religious, whom the citizens received with open arms, assigning them for their residence the little hospital of St. Mary Magdalen, near the city gates. Here St. Dominic came, together with two brethren of Siennese origin, Tugerio and Bene, the latter of whom had formerly been parish priest of St. Quirico. His presence was warmly welcomed by the citizens; and Ranieri Piccolomini, to whom the hospital belonged, made it over by a deed of gift to him and to his Order, the contract still existing in which he is styled *Domnus Dominicus*. The friars continued to occupy it for seven years, but in the meantime a much better site was given to them by Fortebraccio Malevolti, on the hill known as the Campo Reggio, where arose that famous church of San Domenico inhabited at various times by the Blessed Ambrose of Siena, and by St. Thomas Aquinas, which had St. Antoninus for its prior, and which is so closely linked with the history of the glorious St. Catherine. Gigli calls it the most venerable sanctuary in Tuscany, and says it was the third convent built by St. Dominic in Italy. He, moreover, represents the saint as choosing the twelve brethren who formed its first

community, all of them Siennese by nation, and naming as
their prior, Brother Walter of Siena, all which implies the
foundation of St. Domenico to have been made during his
lifetime.

Leaving the question of chronology, however, we may
with more certainty gather up some of the records which are
preserved regarding the residence of St. Dominic at Siena,
and the many illustrious subjects whom he there drew into
the Order. Preaching constantly as was his wont in one or
other of the city churches, on a certain day he appeared in
the pulpit of the Duomo, or cathedral, where great numbers
assembled to hear him. Among those present was Tancred
Tancredi, a member of that noble family which has filled the
annals of Siena with the names of its illustrious members.
As he stood amid the crowd, listening and gazing at the
preacher, Tancred beheld another figure standing beside
him in the pulpit, and whispering in his ear: it was the
Blessed Virgin, who was inspiring the words of her faithful
servant. The sight filled him with admiration, but as the
saint descended the pulpit-stairs, that same glorious vision of
Mary floated nearer and nearer to the spot where he stood.
It pointed with its hand to the figure of the preacher, and a
low sweet voice uttered in his ear, "Tancred, follow that
man, and do not depart from him." Obedient to the call
thus given, he abandoned all things, and going to St. Mary
Magdalen's hospital asked and received the holy habit.
But they who are the elect of God are those against whom
Satan directs his deadliest temptations. That same night
the enemy appeared to him under the form of the Blessed
Virgin, and declaring to him that Brother Dominic was an
impostor and a deceiver, urged him to quit the convent.
Tancred seized a crucifix, and boldly presenting it to the
tempter, "If," he said, "thou art indeed the Mother of God,
adore Him Whom this crucifix represents; if not, depart
in the name of God," and with that the vision of evil
disappeared.

Many very beautiful records are left us of his life. He
had a singular familiarity with the angels, who stood by him

as he prayed. Once, as he was earnestly interceding in prayer for an obstinate sinner, the angelic friend beside him seemed to whisper, " Tancred, your prayer for that soul will be in vain." But the zeal and charity of this true Friar Preacher was not to be checked even by such a word as this: he only prayed the harder, as though he would be heard; and, lo! three days after, he saw the soul for whom he interceded flying up safe to heaven. After the death of St. Dominic he was appointed Vicar General of the Order in the Holy Land, where he spent eighteen years, his perfect knowledge of the Eastern languages enabling him to labour with great fruit among the infidels. Tenderly devout during his whole life to the Blessed Virgin, to whom he owed his vocation, she is said to have appeared to him as he lay on his bed of death, and to have sweetly summoned him to depart, with the words, *Veni, dilecte mi, veni in hortum meum; veni coronaberis a Filio meo ;* and he, smiling joyfully, exclaimed to the brethren who stood around, *Gaudete viscera mea, quia lætatus sum in his quæ dicta sunt mihi, in domum Domini ibimus.*

Another of the Siennese novices who received the habit from the hands of St. Dominic was Chiaro Landucci, also of noble blood, who had given promise of the extraordinary learning for which he was afterwards distinguished even in his cradle. For being yet an infant, if he saw a book, he never ceased crying till he got possession of it, so that his nurses had to provide themselves with volumes of some sort in order to keep him quiet. Going to Paris, he became doctor in every one of the learned faculties, and was at last elected rector of the university, which office he held for fifteen years. But his splendid acquirements gained him the jealous enmity of a certain canon, who had planned to take his life, a design he would certainly have put into execution had not Chiaro been warned by an angel to save himself by flight ; and returning to his native city, he there forsook all worldly honours, and devoted all his vast learning to the service of God, in the habit of religion.

From Siena, Dominic once more took the road to Viterbo. This city, which was the ordinary residence of the Popes during the thirteenth century, had been more than once visited by St. Dominic in the course of his many journeys between Lombardy and Rome; and the ancient palace of the Popes, which still stands in a half ruinous condition adjoining the cathedral of St. Lorenzo, must many times have received him within its walls. On the present occasion he met here Cardinal Ranieri Capocci, whom Ciacconi, in his *Lives of the Popes,* speaks of as "united to St. Dominic in bonds of familiar friendship, and a firm defender both of him and his Order." Himself a native of Viterbo, he had, when Legate of Tuscany, succeeded in delivering the city out of the hands of the Emperor Frederick I. and restoring it to the Holy See. He now made it his place of residence, and spent large sums in the adornment of a city so dear to him. Warned by our Lady in a vision by night, he had begun the building of a church outside the gates, which bore the name of Santa Maria in Gradi, and this church, with the monastery attached, he now bestowed on St. Dominic, a memorial of whose residence within its walls is still shown in a chapel, once his cell; the original cloister, with its pointed arches of severely monastic aspect and groined roof being also preserved. Accepting the gift, the saint planted a colony of his brethren at Viterbo, but before the building of the church was completed, the Cardinal, their benefactor, was taken away by death. In consequence, possibly, of this, the community in its early days had to struggle with much poverty, and one story is related by Gerard de Frachet, which may be given here as illustrative of the way in which the brethren lived by alms, and of the tokens of Divine favour which were often granted them when on the quest.

Two lay-brothers, Ranuzio of Orvieto, and Dominic of Viterbo, came once to a certain countess who had large estates near the city, and asked for alms according to their custom. With her own hands she measured out to them a quantity of flour, which they gratefully accepted and carried home with them. When the countess came next morning she found her sack full of flour, and imagined that the Brothers had been too proud to accept

such an alms, and had poured the flour back into the sack.
Next time that one of them presented himself at her house
therefore, she reproved him sharply, asking him why he
and his companion would not take what she had given them.
The Brother listened in astonishment, and assured her
they had carried it away. " How can you say that,"
said the countess, "when I found my sack here as full
as it was before ?" So they continued to dispute, till at
last she was forced to believe him, and supposed that
some one had come in her absence and had filled up the
sack. But when her servants assured her that no one
had gone near the place, she came at length to understand
that the thing had been wrought by the power of God,
Who liberally rewards those who are liberal to His servants.

His business at Viterbo concluded, Dominic returned
to Bologna, where, however, he made no long stay, but
accompanied by Bonviso of Placentia, set out on his journey
northwards, taking the road to Milan. It must be borne
in mind that, though the visitation of convents already
founded and the establishment of new ones were among
the principal objects which he had in view, this did not
prevent his continually devoting himself to the ministry
of the Word of God. As he travelled from place to place,
he preached in every town and village through which he
passed, converting heretics and sinners by his exhortations
and miracles. Thus at Modena he touched the heart of
a certain French canon, who, under the influence of grievous
temptation, had been driven almost to despair, but who,
opening his conscience to the saint, was by his prayers
and good counsels restored to peace. Here, too, he received
several excellent subjects into the Order, among whom was
Albert de Boschettis, who afterwards became bishop of
Modena.

The foundation of Milan, of which we next have to
speak, was one of very special importance, on account of
that city being the head-quarters of the Manichean heretics,
who at that time were almost as numerous in Lombardy as
they were in Languedoc. In consequence, St. Dominic had

very early seen the necessity of establishing there a community of brethren who should be well qualified to defend the faith by their preaching and disputations. He therefore chose two religious in whom he had great confidence, Brother Robaldo Albigania, a Milanese by birth, to whom he had himself given the habit, and Brother James of Monza, who coming to the city in the previous year had at once entered on their apostolic duties with great zeal and diligence. Robaldo was one of those ardent and courageous souls to whom fear is altogether unknown, and he plunged into a hand to hand conflict with vice and error of every kind. Milan, like most other cities of Italy, was torn by feuds and factions, and the servants of God in their apostolic labours had not only to contend with heretical doctrines, but with those deadly hatreds which were handed as a heritage from father to son, and were the fruitful sources of innumerable crimes. Against this particular kind of scandal, Robaldo opposed himself with determined vigour. " He was all fire and spirit, as well as charity," says his biographer, "and bent on healing these impious feuds, he spoke to his compatriots with power and authority, and turned souls about at his pleasure."

There was among the nobles of Milan a youth who absolutely refused to forgive the slayer of his brother, though the latter had sought his pardon and sued for peace. Robaldo urged him to yield by every argument in his power, but without success; wherefore moved by a sudden inspiration he seized his hand, saying, " I command you in the Name of Jesus Christ, Who forgave His murderers, that you do not stir from this spot until you have pardoned your enemy and promised peace." He spoke with such energy as struck terror into the hearts of his hearers, and the young man found himself powerless to move a step. As he stood thus, another of his brothers hastened to the spot, furious with desire of vengeance. But Robaldo mastered him also, and so brought things about, that that same day both brothers consented to dine in a friendly way with their enemy, and in Robaldo's presence signed a document by which they engaged themselves ever after to keep the peace.

As to the heretics, who began by insulting and ridiculing the new preachers, they soon found reason to fear their power with God. As Robaldo was one day in prayer before the high altar of the cathedral, a band of these miscreants determined to divert themselves at his expense, and sent one of their number to practise a joke upon him. "Father," said the heretic, "I well know you are a man of God, and able to obtain whatsoever you wish by prayer; I pray you, there-fore, to make over me the sign of the Cross, for I suffer from a cruel fever, and I would fain receive my cure from your hands." Robaldo knew well the malice of his enemy, and replied, "My son, if you have this fever, I pray God to deliver you; if you have it not, but are speaking lies, I pray Him to send it to you as a chastisement." The man instantly felt the approach of the malady he had feigned, and cried, impatiently, "Sign me with the Cross, I say, sign me; it is not your custom to send curses upon men, but cures." But Robaldo replied again, "What I have said, I have said; if you have it, may He deliver you; if not, you will certainly have it." Meanwhile, the others stood at the door, laughing to see the saint, as they thought, made a fool of; but their merriment was soon silenced, when they saw their companion return to them with every symptom of the fever he had before pretended. The result was his own conversion, and that of his entire family; and Robaldo, on his sincere peni-tence, restored him to health, and received him and all his children into the communion of the Church.

Under the direction of a Superior so energetic, the friars rapidly gained the respect both of friends and enemies, but they did not obtain any permanent settlement in the city until the arrival of Cardinal Ugolino, who came thither in 1220 to establish peace between Milan and Cremona, which cities had long been at war with one another. Trusting in his great love of the Order, Robaldo and his brethren besought him to grant them some place of residence, suitable for the duties which they had to discharge. Just outside the gates of the city, there was a church dedicated to St. Eustorgio, at that time served by canons. According to popular belief, this church, not then a place of great resort, was yet reserved for some glorious destiny in the future. A venerable hermit had foretold it would be one day the home of a company of preachers, and declared that he every night beheld a great light shining over its roof, which betokened the light of doctrine which, shining thence, would one day illuminate the city. The canons, too, from time to time heard in their choir the singing as of angels. When, therefore, in the May of 1220, Ugolino succeeded in placing it in the possession of the friars, it was held by many that these various auguries received fulfilment. Here it was then that St. Dominic found his children established, and here for a time he took up his abode among them. He had hardly done so, however, before he was attacked by a severe illness, of which some account is given us in the deposition of Bonviso of Placentia. " I was with him at Milan," says that witness, " and took care of him when he had a severe attack of fever. He never complained of what he suffered, and it seemed to me that he spent the whole time in prayer and contemplation. I thought so because of certain signs on his countenance which he used to have in time of health when he was absorbed in prayer. As soon as the fever left him, he spoke to the brethren of God, or he held a book, or made some one read to him ; or he praised God and rejoiced in his infirmity, as was his invariable custom." From another authority we learn what the books were that he desired to be read to him ; they were his life-long favourites, the Dialogues of Cassian and the Epistles of St. Paul.[1]

As soon as he had recovered from his sickness, Dominic resumed his journey northwards. In the course of it he found himself one night before the gates of St. Colomba, a

---

[1] Echard, on the authority of Taegius, represents St. Dominic as being present in Milan on the 11th of June. As we know him to have spent the feast of the Assumption this year at Bologna, it is evident that his progress through Lombardy cannot have been continuous. But it is impossible to say at what precise period of it, it was interrupted.

Cistercian house in the district of Piacenza, but the hour
was late, and he would not disturb the inmates. "Let us
lie down here," he said to his companion, "and pray to God,
Who will surely care for us." They did so, and both immediately found themselves transported to the interior of the
convent. Thus we see it was ever with the same simplicity
that Dominic journeyed; it was the poor mendicant friar,
with his wallet on his back, and nothing save the light that
gleamed on his noble forehead to distinguish him from other
men, who went barefoot up and down the hills and valleys of
Italy, preaching as he went.

Como was his next resting-place. A few brethren having
come hither from Milan on a preaching mission, had been
pressed to stay by the Catholic inhabitants, who promised, if
they would yield to their request, to give them the site for a
convent. The spot chosen was fit indeed to be the home of
those whose life was one of prayer and contemplation. On
the shore of the lake, rising amid the chesnut-woods which
clothe its banks, on soil carpeted with greenest turf, and
gemmed with flowers of every hue, stands the church of
St. Martino delle Selve, and here the friars at first fixed their
habitation. But these scenes, over which Nature has poured
forth all her charms, were darkened at that time by the
black cloud of heresy. Nowhere had the pernicious doctrines
and detestable practices of the Manicheans struck deeper
root than among these beautiful mountain regions of Lombardy; and as in Languedoc, they found their most zealous
supporters among the noble ladies of the country. Nevertheless, it was precisely among this class that the labours of
the new preachers proved most successful, and Humbert de
Romans relates the story of more than one great dame won
over from the sect by the example of their sanctity.

How welcome St. Dominic's presence must have been to
those engaged in carrying on the very struggle in which he
had spent his heroic ten years of apostolate may easily be
supposed. Beautiful as was the situation of St. Martin of
the Woods, he judged it too retired for the active duties of
the brethren, and accepted the offer made to him by the

abbot of St. Abondio of the church of St. John Baptist, which stood at the foot of one of the surrounding hills. The future sanctity of the spot had been revealed to a citizen of Como in a vision, wherein he saw a fountain of clear refreshing water burst forth in the church, and flowing thence through the town in sparkling streams, at which young and old of all classes came to quench their thirst; whilst one lady, who was at the time a heretic, saw, as she thought, two vessels standing in the same church, one of which was filled with honey and the other with wine, which being mixed together was distributed by the friars to the people; and she was given to understand that by this was signified that matchless form of prayer (wherein the honey of devotion to our Lady is mingled with the strong wine of the love of Jesus Christ) which was to be taught and preached within the walls of St. John the Baptist. We next find the saint at Bergamo, where he was no stranger, having passed through the city in the course of more than one journey between France and Italy. It will be remembered that he had made some stay here on his return from Paris in 1219, on which occasion he had given the habit to Brother Guala and some others. If we are to credit the account given by Borselli, Guala remained at Bergamo after receiving the habit, and became the actual founder of the convent. "After the first General Chapter," says this writer, "the blessed Dominic, taking with him Bonviso of Placentia as his companion, made the circuit of nearly the whole of Lombardy, preaching as he went. After leaving Milan he came to Bergamo, where the brethren lived on a certain hill in a place called the *Capella*, whence in those parts they were then called *Capellite*. Brother Guala, who had founded this convent, was confirmed in the office of prior by the blessed Dominic."

The convent here spoken of adjoined a very ancient oratory dedicated to St. Mary Magdalen, which occupied a hill to the west of the city. Here, then, St. Dominic remained for some days, preaching in the city and its neighbourhood, and receiving into the Order many notable subjects. Among these were Pagano of Lecco, who enter-

BB

ing religion as a mere youth, spent his life in incredible
labours for the faith, and finally, in the year 1256, received
the crown of martyrdom at the hands of the heretics;
Pinamonte Bembrate, a great canonist, won to the Order
by the preaching of St. Dominic, whose life he closely
imitated, who was the founder in Bergamo of the famous
charitable institution of the *Misericordia*, and who became
in later years a great friend of St. Thomas Aquinas; Peter
Scaliger, whom his biographers call "a prodigy of learning,
as well skilled in human as in sacred letters;" and Isnard
of Vicenza, wl.ose life was illustrated by many miracles,
and consumed in every kind of good work. His power
over souls was manifested in the conversion of the most
abandoned sinners, and also of a vast number of heretics.
One of these latter had publicly declared that he would
abjure his errors, provided that Brother Isnard would cure
a citizen named Martin, who was believed to be possessed
by the devil, and whose violence made him the terror of
his neighbours. When Isnard heard this, he set out in
quest of the unhappy sufferer, and, meeting him in the
street, kissed him tenderly. Overcome by this act of
charity, the evil spirit quitted his victim, and Martin, out
of gratitude, spent the rest of his days in the service of the
convent. The challenge given by another of the heretics
had a different kind of result. Isnard was of a heavy and
corpulent figure, which often exposed him to the ridicule
of his enemies. "For my part," said one of them, "I will
become a Catholic too, when that barrel there (which is
mightily like Brother Isnard in shape) comes and rolls to
me on the spot where I am standing." The words were
hardly out of his mouth when, to his surprise and terror,
the cask to which he pointed set itself in motion, and, rolling
against him, broke one of his legs.

It would be impossible to narrate one half of the wonders
attributed to Isnard, "the fame of which," says Michael
Pio, "resounded through all Lombardy." He died at the
convent of Pavia in 1244, under somewhat singular circumstances. A lay-brother saw in a vision all the clergy and

people of the city coming to the convent, and praying
the friars to give them one of their community to be their
patron before God.  Relating what he had seen, the brethren
treated it as an idle dream; but two days later Isnard died,
and the people of Pavia, weeping over the loss of one whom
they had regarded as their father and protector, chose him
indeed to be their patron and advocate in heaven.

The admirable example of these holy religious, and
the great fruit which followed on their preaching, led the
magistrates of Bergamo to desire their removal nearer to
the city.  They therefore laid the matter before St. Dominic,
and offered him the church of St. Stephen, with ground
adjoining it, for the erection of a convent.  This he accepted,
and here arose the celebrated convent of St. Stephen, which
was for more than three hundred years the nursery of
men illustrious in the history of the Order, but which was
finally destroyed by Sforza Pallavicino, in 1561, in order
to strengthen the fortifications of the city.

It was with the utmost regret that the people of Bergamo
bade adieu to the holy Father, who passed on from thence
to Cremona, where he once more met his friend and fellow-
labourer St. Francis, who was there, together with his
spiritual daughter St. Clare.  They lodged in the same
house, and an anecdote of their meeting has been preserved.
The water of a well belonging to the house had become unfit
for use, and the people of the place, bringing some of it
in a vase, begged one of the two saints to bless it that it
might recover its sweetness.  A graceful contest arose,
each wishing the other to perform what was asked of them;
but the humility of Francis conquered.  Dominic blessed
the water, which was immediately restored to its clearness
and sweet savour.[2]

This incident was painted in the choir of the Dominican
church at Cremona, but the painting was destroyed at a later
period when the choir was rebuilt.

---

[2] The above narrative is given as related by Flaminius, but in the
Franciscan Chronicles it is related somewhat differently, and the two
saints are represented as blessing the water together.

The last city in Lombardy visited by St. Dominic was
Brescia, and though the historians of the Order have not
given any particulars of this visit, it is noticed by the local
chroniclers, Giacomo Malvezzi, Capriolo, and others, whose
narratives are quoted by Father Michael Pio. "In those
days," says Malvezzi, writing in 1432, "the blessed Dominic,
father and founder of the Order of Preachers, going through
Lombardy, entered this city, and received hospitality near
the church of SS. Faustinus and Jovita *ad sanguinem*. Here
he established some religious under his holy Rule, and
commanded that our Lord should be served in this place
with all devotion and religious worship. And after spending
some days there he planted a juniper-tree near the church
on the north side, from the roots of which came forth several
little shoots; one of which in my time grew to be a large
and strong plant. It is believed he did this not so much
for his own recreation and that of his brethren, as to leave
there a memorial of himself." Caprioli gives us to understand that the people of Brescia had at that time been
enduring many troubles and afflictions, but, he says, "Our
Lord Jesus Christ permitted this to bring them back to
better things, and doubtless chose for this purpose the
blessed Dominic, a man endowed with learning, power, and
holiness, whom He sent to Brescia, and in His mercy
permitted to establish his religious in the Basilica of
SS. Faustinus and Jovita, under the rule of the Blessed
Guala." The church, or as it is here called, the Basilica
of St. Faustinus and St. Jovita, commonly bore the additional title of *ad sanguinem* in memory of its being erected
on the spot where thousands of Christians were put to
death under the Emperors Hadian and Trajan. Many
reasons concurred to make the foundation one of unusual
importance; and desirous to commit it to the charge of
one in whose powers he could fully confide, St. Dominic
appointed as its first prior Brother Guala, whom he had
left but awhile before at Bergamo. Here, then, began
the great career of this celebrated religious, who eight years
later was appointed by Gregory IX. Legate Apostolic in

Lombardy, of whom we will briefly say that in that capacity he made peace between Padua and Treviso, and between Bologna and Modena; that when prior of Brescia he fed the inhabitants in the time of a grievous famine; that he afterwards became bishop of the city, which he governed for fourteen years, at the end of which time he resigned the dignity to end his days in solitude, and whose character is summed up by his biographer, who calls him "the father of the poor, the protector of widows, the physician of the sick, and the entertainer of pilgrims." It was in a chapel of the church of St. Faustinus, that he had that vision which made known to him the death of St. Dominic, which will hereafter be spoken of, and by which, perhaps, the name of the Blessed Guala is most commonly remembered in the Order.

It seems probable that after thus making the circuit of Lombardy, St. Dominic returned for a brief space to Bologna, where, as we have seen in the last chapter, he spent the feast of the Assumption, and received Conrad of Germany into the Order. Soon after this, however, he again set out northwards, entering this time the Marches of Treviso, and directing his course towards Venice.

We infer that Verona was first visited by him from the certainty we possess that the convent at Verona was founded at this very time by one of the Mal avotti family There the founder began (for he did not live to complete it) the exquisite church of St. Anastasia, which still stands, one of the most perfectly beautiful Gothic buildings in Italy. Its lofty doorway, rich in many tinted marbles, "makes you feel," says a modern writer, "as if Fra Angelico might have painted such a door as opening into Paradise."[3]

No particulars, however, have been preserved regarding the saint's passage through this city, though it is included

---

[3] Street's *Brick and Marble in the Middle Ages*. The date of the foundation of this convent is fixed by an inscription on marble in the cloister, to the effect that it was begun by Rodolph Malvotti for the good of his soul in 1220, being the fourth year of the pontificate of Pope Honorius III., Brother Dominic of Spain being then Master General of the Friars Preachers.

among those named by Flaminius or visited by him. " In 1220," he says, " St. Dominic visited Mantua, Verona, Padua, Venice, and many other cities, in which he founded convents, and by his preaching drew many to enter the Order of Preachers."

Borselli, in his Chronicle of the Master Generals of the Order, also speaks of his visit to Padua, as having been made chiefly on account of the university there existing; and numbers up several religious to whom he at that time gave the habit. Among these was John of Vicenza, one of the *beati* of the Order. He had been sent to Padua by his father, Martin Schio, to study law. There, however, a more sublime vocation awaited him. St. Dominic being then in the city, no church in the place was large enough to hold the crowds who flocked to hear him, and he therefore preached in the great piazza known as the Piazza della Valle. John was there, and that day's preaching put all thoughts of law out of his head. As soon as the sermon was ended, he went to find the preacher, and begged to be instantly admitted among his followers, and to receive the habit of the Order. He made his novitiate at Bologna, but afterwards returned to the convent of Padua, where he became one of the most famous preachers of his time.

He was called the apostle of Lombardy, and indeed Lombardy needed an apostle in those unhappy days, torn as it was by the wars and desolated by the cruelties of Frederic II. and the tyrant Ezzelino. John was a preacher of peace amid all the terrible calamities of those times. He left one memorial of himself in the salutation, " God save you," which he introduced among the citizens of Bologna during a time of public commotion, to excite them to gentler and more courteous treatment of their opponents, and which soon spread through Europe, and has lasted to our own day. The angels were seen whispering in his ear as he preached, and his words had ever the same burden, purity and peace. He was a fervent lover of the Rosary, and sometimes, as he preached this devotion, a bright rose would appear on his forehead, or a golden sunny crown would glitter over his head. He had a marvellous power over the fiercest animals; eagles were obedient to him, and a wild, untamable horse became tractable at his bidding. His devotion to the memory of St. Dominic was very remarkable, and Father Stephen of Spain assures us that 100,000 heretics were converted by only hearing the account of his life and miracles as narrated by his devoted follower. The Pope at length appointed him on a mission of pacification to the north of Italy; and such was the success of his labours, especially after a discourse addressed to the populace on that very Piazza della Valle where he had first heard the eloquence of his holy Father, that all the contending parties agreed to abandon their differences and accept of peace. Ezzelino alone held out; and concerning him John had an awful vision. He saw the Almighty seated on His throne, and seeking for a scourge for the chastisement of Lombardy. Ezzelino was chosen as the instrument of His wrath, and surely a more terrible one was never found. At that time John had never seen him, and when first they met, and he cast his eyes on him, he wept, recognizing him as the man he had seen in his vision, and cried aloud, "It is he whom I saw—the scourge of Lombardy. Woe! woe to thee, unhappy country! for he shall execute judgment on thee to the uttermost." Nevertheless, even this monster was in some degree touched and softened by the preaching of Blessed John, and at his exhortation consented, for a time at least, to put a stop to the terrible wars which were laying waste the whole of Lombardy. He was present at that great assembly on the Campagna of Verona, when 300,000 people met, together with the princes and prelates of half Italy, to swear a universal peace. John harangued the immense multitude, and in the midst of a profound silence he addressed them from the words of our Lord, "Peace I give you, My peace I give unto you;" and such was the power of his eloquence that even Ezzelino hid his face and wept. Then was heard a cry that rose from that great multitude as from one man. "Peace, peace," they cried, "peace and mercy!" It was granted them for a brief space, and when Blessed John died there was engraven at the foot of the image raised to his honour in the church of Vicenza, the words which had formed the text of his sermon at " the festival of peace."

After a brief stay at Venice,[4] where the brethren were still occupying their narrow and incommodious quarters in the oratory of St. Daniel, 'St. Dominic again returned to Bologna, but we have no means of tracing his homeward course or of fixing the date of his return. All that can be affirmed as certain is that every portion of the above progress, however it may have been divided or interrupted, took place within the last seven months of the year 1220, as the Christmas of that same year was spent by him in his sixth and last visit to Rome.

---

[4] According to local tradition, two other convents owe their foundation to St. Dominic, namely, those of Cividale, in Austria, and Giustinopoli, in Capo d'Istria, but no certain records have been preserved concerning his presence at either place.

ST. PETER MARTYR.

# CHAPTER XXXI.

LAST VISIT TO ROME, AND THE SECOND GENERAL CHAPTER.

1220—1221.

IF St. Dominic's return to Bologna after an absence of several months caused joy to the hearts of his children, it brought him matter for sorrow, and even displeasure. Rodolph of Faenza, who as procurator superintended the completion of the convent, had made some additions to the building which the saint judged inconsistent with the profession of holy poverty. Before his departure he had himself left directions for the proposed alterations, and even a kind of plan or model to ensure the preservation of that rigorous observance of poverty which was so dear to him, and which he regarded as the indispensable condition of religious life. He gazed at the new building with tears flowing down his cheeks. "Will you so soon forsake poverty," he said, "and build palaces while I am yet alive?" "Wherefore," says Stephen of Spain, who relates this incident, "he commanded them to abandon this work, and so it remained unfinished as long as he lived." Yet the excess committed was nothing

more than raising some of the cells by one cubit. How
rigid, indeed, was the poverty and humility of the structure,
we may judge from another circumstance which occurred
about this time. St. Francis also came to Bologna on a visit
to the religious of his Order recently established in the city,
but when he found them living in a large and spacious house,
he was so indignant, that he ordered them to quit it, and he
himself took up his dwelling for the time in the convent
of the Friars Preachers, "which," says Father Candidus
Chalippus, in his Life of the saint, "he found more to his taste,
and where he passed some days with his friend, St.Dominic."

This was not the only occasion on which Rodolph's
notions on the subject of poverty did not entirely harmonize
with those of the holy patriarch. Like a good procurator,
he united liberality to frugality, and occasionally made
small additions to the scanty fare provided for the brethren,
serving them with some extra portions, known as pittances.
On such occasions he says, "Brother Dominic would whisper
to me, 'Why do you kill the brethren with these pittances?'"
Nevertheless, as Touron observes, it does not appear that
the good Father corrected himself of this fault. He
probably understood that the saint did not require from his
brethren what was beyond their strength, and that severe
as were his ideas on the subject both of poverty and penance,
he never refused his children a certain measure of indulgence;
for with regard to this very matter of pittances, John of
Navarre states that though he never dispensed himself concerning them, yet he willingly dispensed others.

The December of 1220 saw St. Dominic for the sixth and
last time at Rome. This was the occasion of a meeting that
must have been full of the tenderest interest to his heart.
Fulk of Toulouse was then in the holy city. Little more than
three years had elapsed since that dispersion of the sixteen
brethren of St. Romain, which had taken place in his own
presence, but this short period had sufficed to convert the
prior of Prouille, the leader of that devoted little band,
the destinies of which to every eye but his, seemed then so
hopeless and obscure, into the Master General of a great

Order, whose convents were spread through the length and breadth of Christendom. All things in their respective positions were changed, save Dominic himself; but Fulk could have detected no difference between the apostle of Languedoc and the master of the Friars Preachers, save in the adoption of a yet poorer habit and those few silver hairs which, we are told, his long labours, and not his years, had begun to sprinkle over his tonsured head. But the heroic heart, the patient, gentle spirit, the simple hearty joyousness of his friend, were still the same; and so, too, was the disinterestedness of his soul, of which Fulk had proof in a transaction whose acts are still preserved. This was the renunciation, on the part of the saint, of that grant, formerly made by the bishop, of the sixth part of the tenths of his revenues for the support of the Order when it was yet young and friendless. The principle of poverty had since then been more strictly developed in the Institute, and Dominic believed he could no longer in conscience accept these revenues, even though given, in the very terms of the grant, as an alms to the poor of Christ. Fulk, on his part, confirmed the donation of the church of Notre Dame de Fanjeaux to the religious of Prouille; for it will be observed that the rigid law of poverty which the saint enforced on the rest of his Order, he relaxed in favour of the communities of women, for whose state he judged a moderate revenue was requisite to be secured.

The deed expressing the above agreement is given by Mamachi, together with engravings of the three seals appended, namely, those of the bishop, of the cathedral church of St. Stephen, and of St. Dominic, of which latter we here give the *facsimile*. He is represented, as may be seen, dressed in the habit of the Order and bearing a stick. The inscription surrounding the figure is to be read thus, *Sigillum Dominici ministri pricationum*—" The seal of Dominic, minister of preaching."

It were to be wished that more particulars had been preserved of the great patriarch's last appearance in the Roman capital. Rome had witnessed the first development of his Order; henceforward St. Sixtus and Santa Sabina were to become classic names among his children; and if, as there is reason to believe, a prophetic knowledge had been granted him that the period of his death was not far off, there must have been a peculiar charm in his parting visit to these familiar scenes. We know only that he preached daily either at Santa Sabina or at one of the churches in the city, and that every day saw him at the grating of St. Sixtus, renewing his exhortations to the Sisters to keep fast to the holy rule which under his guidance they had embraced. The affection which he so faithfully preserved for these spiritual chileren is illustrated by one of the miracles related to us by Sister Cecilia as happening at this time. Upon a certain day he stopped at the gate, and, without entering, asked of the portress how Sister Theodora, Sister Tedrano, and Sister Ninfa were. She replied they were all three ill of fever. "Tell them," said Dominic, "from me, that I command them all to be cured;" and at the delivery of the message they all three arose in perfect health.

St. Dominic returned to Bologna in time to prepare for the second General Chapter, which was summoned to meet on the 30th of May. In this Chapter a great and important work was to be laid before the assembled Fathers, both in what regarded the completion of the form of government to be established in the Order, and its further extension throughout the world. Great interest was therefore felt in the coming proceedings, an interest shared by enemies as well as friends, as appears from the following story. Two of the brethren who were travelling towards Bologna, were met on the road by a man who joined himself to their company and fell into conversation with them. He inquired the object of their journey, and being informed of the approaching Chapter, "What," he asked, "is the business which is likely to be discussed?" "The establishment of our brethren in new countries," replied one of the friars; "England and Hungary

are among those proposed." "And Greece also," said the
stranger, "and Germany, is it not so?" "You say truly,"
returned the friar; "it is said that we shall shortly be dis
persed into all these provinces." Then the stranger uttered
a loud cry as of great anguish, and exclaiming, "Your Order
is my confusion," he leapt into the air, and so disappeared;
and the friars knew that it was the voice of the great enemy
of man, who was thus compelled to bear witness to the
power which the servants of God exercised against him.

✝ With regard to the government of the Order, it will be
borne in mind that in the older forms of monasticism each
abbey was complete in itself, the abbot exercising a paternal
jurisdiction within his own domain independent of any
central authority; but according to the plan devised by
St. Dominic, the Order was now to be divided into provinces,
the houses in each province, with their priors, being placed
under the government of priors provincial, who again were
subject to the authority of the Master General. In this way
unity and discipline, together with uniformity of observance,
were carefully secured; and the form of government thus
introduced has been adhered to until our own day. ✝

At the opening of the Chapter the saint addressed the
brethren at considerable length, laying before them the state
of the Order in the countries wherein it was already
established, and proposing its still further extension. It
appeared that sixty convents were already founded, and a
yet greater number in course of erection. The eight provinces
into which the Order was now divided were those of Spain,
France, Provence, Lombardy, Rome, Germany, Hungary,
and England. Among these newly-created provinces the
first place in order of rank was given to that of Spain, which
was committed to the government of Father Suero Gomez.
Father Peter of Rheims became provincial of France, Father
Bertrand of Garrigua of Provence,[1] Father Jordan of Saxony
of Lombardy, Father Clare de Sextio of Rome, and Father

---

[1] "Our holy founder [say the Acts of the Provincial Chapter of Aix]
appointed as first provincial of Provence, Bertrand of Garrigua, the
dearest companion in his labours and apostolic journeys."

Conrad of Germany; whilst the two provinces of England and Hungary, which yet had to be colonized, were placed respectively under Father Gilbert de Fresnoy and Father Paul of Hungary.[2]

The names of most of these illustrious men have been already mentioned. Peter of Rheims had very early joined the community of St. James, and attracted the notice of St. Dominic, who discerned in him special gifts for government as well as great power as a preacher. He twice filled the office of provincial of France, and was present on the occasion when, some years later, Jordan, then Master General of the Order, addressed the brethren of St. James in Chapter, and invited those who desired to be chosen for the missions in the Holy Land to notify their wishes. At once the whole assembly made the *venia*, and Peter beholding this expression of their devoted zeal, also did the same. Then, rising and addressing Jordan, "My Father," he said, "either leave me with these children, or let me go with them, for with them I would live or die." He was not, however, of the number chosen, but remaining in France, was in the year 1242 raised to the episcopal see of Agen.

In his address to the assembled Fathers, Dominic gave them an earnest exhortation to the pursuit of sacred learning, that they might be the better fitted for the charge laid on them by their vocation as preachers. He reminded them that the briefs granted so liberally by the Vicar of Christ, recommended them to the favour of the Universal Church, inasmuch as they were therein declared to be labourers for God's honour and the salvation of souls, and that this end could never be attained without a diligent application to the Divine Scriptures; he therefore enjoined all who should be engaged in the sacred office of preaching to apply without ceasing to the study of theology, and to carry always with them a copy of the Gospels and the seven canonical Epistles.

The foundation of the English province will be treated

[2] The names of the first provincials are given rather differently by different writers; the above is from Malvenda, 1221, cap. v. p. 332.

of in a separate chapter. Immediately on the conclusion of the Chapter, Father Paul of Hungary was despatched to his new destination, accompanied by four other brethren, one of whom was Blessed Sadoc of Poland, the tale of whose martyrdom, with his forty-eight companions, is among the most interesting incidents recorded in the annals of the Order. The crown of martyrdom was reserved for Paul also. He received it the following year, together with ninety of his brethren, from the hands of the Cuman Tartars, who infested the borders of Hungary, and whose conversion to the Christian faith had so long formed the cherished day-dream of St. Dominic. It would seem, indeed, as though this nation, whose barbarity exceeded that of any of the savage hordes that still hung round the boundaries of Christian Europe, was destined, if not to be converted by his Order, at least to fill its ranks with an army of martyrs. Another of Paul's earliest companions, Berengarius of Poland, the archbishop of Cracow, was slain by them a few years afterwards; and in 1260 seventy more were sent to join their company; all of whom, it is said, were children and disciples of the glorious St. Hyacinth.

On the conclusion of this Chapter the magistrates of Bologna, wishing to mark their veneration for the holy founder and their gratitude for the benefits he had procured to the city by the extinction of their internal feuds, bestowed the honours of citizenship both on him and on all who should hereafter succeed him in his office of Master General. The public act in which this proceeding is recorded declares the motives for making this grant to be the eminent learning of the saint, his great actions, his position as founder of the Order of Preachers, and the splendour of his birth, as a member of the illustrious family of Guzman.[9]

Jordan of Saxony was not present at the Chapter, having been detained in Paris by his duties as lector. On receiving the news of his appointment to the province of Lombardy, he set out, accompanied by a Brother whom he had recently

---

[9] This act is still preserved in the city records, and its text is quoted by Touron, p. 354.

gained to the Order, and who was a man of singular merit. This was Everard, archdeacon of Langres, who had refused several bishoprics and was renowned as a preacher throughout France and Burgundy. The great desire of Everard's heart was that he might see and become acquainted with the holy Father Dominic, and he rejoiced greatly in the hope that his assignation to Lombardy would give him a better chance of obtaining the fulfilment of this wish. The two friends travelled through Burgundy, Champagne, and Franche-Comté, preaching as they went. Entering Switzerland, they stopped at Lausanne, where Everard was taken ill, and in a few days his state was declared by the physicians to be hopeless. Jordan communicated the intelligence to him in deep grief, but he received it with calmness and even with joy. "It is those to whom the thought of death is bitter," he said, "who need that it should be concealed from them; for me I do not fear to be stripped of this mortal body, in the hope I have to be admitted to heaven. I had one desire, and it was that I might have lived to have seen the face of our Father Dominic, but I go where father and son will ere long meet in God's presence." He died a day or two later, "and I think," says Jordan, "that his death must indeed have been happy, for instead of the sorrow and trouble I thought to experience, my soul was filled with holy joy." He did not guess that in the providence of God, Everard would behold the face of Dominic before that happiness was granted to himself.

It was just before the assembly of this important Chapter that St. Dominic received into the Order a young student from Verona who was destined to become one of its brightest ornaments. Peter of Verona was the son of heretic parents, but, even as a child of seven, had ardently embraced the Catholic faith, the doctrines of which he had learnt at the school where his parents sent him to study grammar. One day his uncle, who was a great authority among the Manichees, questioned him as to what he learnt at school. "I learn the Creed," replied the child, and he began to repeat the words, "I believe in God the Father Almighty,

Creator of heaven and earth." "That is false," said the
Manichee, "heaven and earth were not created by God,
but by the devil." Peter repeated the words of the Creed
a second time, adding, "That is what I have been taught,
and what I believe, and what I shall always repeat." His
uncle, struck by the firmness of the boy, went to find
his father and said to him, "That little Peter of yours,
if you do not see to it, will pass over to the great harlot
(it was so the heretics commonly spoke of the Catholic
Church), and one of these days he will do us much harm."

At the age of fifteen he was sent to study at Bologna,
and, happening to hear one of the sermons delivered by
St. Dominic in a public piazza of the city, he was from
that moment filled with but one thought and desire, namely,
to place himself under the direction of the preacher and
receive the habit of the Order. The saint, with his usual
discernment, recognized in his young disciple the treasure
sent him by heaven, one destined in a special manner
to carry on his work as the champion of the faith against
the assaults of heresy.[4]

He did not live to see the glory of Peter's future career,
yet even now there were sufficient indications of it to make
him peculiarly dear to the heart of St. Dominic, who felt
himself drawn by a powerful attraction to the youth whose
angelic innocence of life had been united, even from infancy,
to an extraordinary courage in the profession of the Catholic
faith. "The hammer of the heretics," as he was commonly
termed, he died by their hands, writing on the ground in
his blood the word *Credo*, and so renewing even at the
very moment of death the same glorious profession of faith
which he had pronounced in childhood. His holy body
lies buried in the church of St. Eustorgio at Milan, but
the finger which wrote that memorable *Credo*, is preserved
with other priceless relics in the convent of SS. Domenico
e Sisto at Rome.

[4] "Post B. Dominicum, non immerito princeps appellari debet sacro-
sancti officii inquisitionis" (Sixtus V. Bull of Canonization of St. Peter
Martyr).

The eulogy of this great saint cannot be entered on in this place, but there is one fact connected with his death which deserves a brief notice. Carino de Balsamo, the assassin of St. Peter, was taken on the very scene of the crime and carried prisoner to Milan, whence, through the guilty connivance of the *podestà* bought over by the heretics, he succeeded in making his escape. Falling sick at Forli, he was taken to a hospital adjoining the convent of the Friars Preachers, and believing himself dying, made his confession with every token of real penitence to one of the Fathers. He did not however die, and on his restoration to health craved admission among the brethren of the saint whom he had slain. With extraordinary charity they received him among them, and he continued for forty years to lead a life of such true penance as earned for him the title of *il beato*. Four centuries later his body was laid in the sepulchre of the Blessed Marcolino of Forli; while in the church of St. Eustorgio he was painted among other saints of the Order, his head being surrounded by an aureole. St. Peter died praying for his murderers; and in the wonderful grace granted to Carino we may see what power is given to the intercession of a martyr.

We should form an imperfect idea of the life led by St. Dominic and his children, or the good which they achieved, if besides an enumeration of the provinces and convents founded by them, we did not also take into account the work which they undertook simply as preachers. From the different centres in which they were planted, the brethren were continually sent out into the surrounding districts to preach the Word of God in towns and villages after a fashion somewhat resembling modern "missions." "The first brethren of the Order," writes Stephen de Salanhac, "journeyed along the roads, scattering the seed of the Divine Word far and wide as they went. Every member seemed changed into a tongue, for everything about them preached penance and holiness of life."

Following the example of their holy Father, of whom Blessed Jordan says that he preached in the streets, in the houses, in the fields, or by the wayside, so did his children carry the Word of God into all parts, and announce it to men of all states and conditions. They raised their voice boldly and fearlessly at fairs and markets, in the lists of the tournament, or in the castle hall. At one time we see them holding disputations with the heretics, at another they are carrying the good tidings of salvation among the wild shepherds of the Alps. They went forth two and two without scrip or purse, as our Lord sent out His disciples— mere youths sometimes, as Thomas of Cantimpré describes them, "who had only just left the world, without experience, simple as doves, yet in all that regarded their conduct as prudent as serpents." Gerard de Frachet tells us of a devout woman in Lombardy who had heard of the new Order of Friars, and desired much to see some of them. It chanced that two of the brethren who were travelling in those parts, called at her house, and as their manner was, addressed her some words of edification. But she seeing them so young, and with such fair smiling countenances, despised them in her heart. She had prepared herself to see grave, bearded men of rigid and austere aspect, as if they had just come forth out of the desert, and could not persuade herself that these youths could preserve themselves from the contamination of the world, or be fit to speak of Divine things. So she shut her window in their faces and would not converse with them. That night our Lady appeared to her and said with a severe countenance, "Yesterday thou didst despise my servants and think evil of them in thy heart. Dost thou not believe that I am able to preserve those who go about the world preaching the doctrine of my Son?" And with that she opened her mantle and showed a great number of friars securely sheltered beneath its folds, and amongst the rest were the two young brethren whom the woman had seen the day before. It is manifest that the apostolic labours of the brethren could not have been accomplished under the conditions then imposed on them without exposing them to hardships and difficulties of every kind. Gerard de Frachet relates how one of the brethren who was sent to Hungary, was overcome by fear lest these difficulties would have to be encountered without obtaining any corresponding fruit of souls. Consulting a holy Cistercian monk in his trouble, his friend beheld in prayer a vision, wherein he seemed to see a vast river, spanned by a bridge, across which many religious were passing in ease and safety; while struggling in the waters appeared some Friars Preachers, swimming against the tide, and dragging after them a boat, laden with a crowd of people. The friars seemed exhausted with fatigue, when our Lady appeared and, extending her hand towards them, helped them to reach the river's bank in safety. This vision he understood to signify that if those who embraced the apostolic life had more to suffer than such as attended only to their own salvation, yet their labours would produce abundant fruits to other souls, and be the source to themselves of unspeakable happiness, which would be secured to them by the loving patronage of our Lady.

Some of the most charming anecdotes which are to be found in the *Vitæ Fratrum* and in the ancient chronicles of the Order, refer to what we may call the adventures of the brethren on their preaching expeditions, and the marks of God's loving providence over them. Theodoric relates a story of two young friars who arrived at a village in Hungary just at the time when the people were assembling in the church to hear Mass. When Mass was over, and the congregation were dispersing, the sacristan closed the church door, and left the two friars standing in the porch, no one having offered them hospitality. A poor fisherman saw them thus standing, and was touched with compassion, but having nothing to offer, he did not venture to invite them to his house. Going home to his wife, however, he spoke of what he had seen. "My heart aches for those poor young brethren," he said, "whom no one seems ready to receive into their house." "What can we do?" replied his wife. "I have nothing to give you for your supper but a handful of millet." "Well, then, let us give it to them," was his reply, "and look in your purse and see if possibly there may not be a coin or two with which we can buy them some bread." To his great joy two little coins were found, with which the good man desired his wife to purchase a loaf and a little wine, and to cook the millet and some fish he had caught, while he went in search of their guests and brought them home to his humble dwelling. The two friars ate the poor fare set before them with thankfulness, and next morn- ing, taking leave of their hosts, they prayed that God would bless them for their charity, and never suffer their purse that had furnished the much needed alms to be empty; a prayer that was answered to the letter, for from that day the two little coins were never found wanting.

↖ Another time we read of two brethren travelling through a wild mountain region in Germany, where they have lost their way. After wandering about in vain, they sit down and take counsel together what to do. One of them looks up, and sees a kite flying over their heads. " Kite," he cries, " I command thee in the Name of Jesus Christ to show us the way we must follow." Immediately the bird descends, and going before the brethren, leads them into the right road, which they had not seen, and then flies away.↖

Two others, Sigfried and Conrad by name, going out to preach, come to a river, on the other side of which they see a village church, into which the country people are flocking, and where they desire to go also that they may announce the Word of God. But how to cross the river, which is broad and deep? Suddenly they descry a little boat on the further side. " Cross over here, little boat," cries Sigfried, " in the Name of Christ, Whom we desire to preach." The boat obeys his word and comes across the river guided by no mortal hand, but getting into it, they find no oars with which to row it. Presently a little maiden comes running down the hill carrying an oar. " Do you want to cross, brethren?" she says, and joining them in the boat she pushes them across the stream and then disappears.

Again we come on narratives which make us understand the labours which these preaching missions entailed on those engaged in them, and the severity with which they neverthe- less observed their Rule. Two brethren had spent a whole

Lent preaching in a district in Germany, where the people came together in such numbers that from early morning until None they were incessantly engaged in hearing confessions, and then after breaking their fast, from None again until night, this labour being only interrupted by that of preaching. As Lent drew to a close they both fell ill, and feared they should not have strength enough to journey back to their convent. When the vigil of Easter came, one of the two brethren fell into such a state of prostration that his voice was scarcely audible. " Alas, Brother Ulrich," he said to his companion, " what are we to do? If only to-morrow we could get a *partridge*, I think that might restore our strength." " A partridge!" said Ulrich, " and where are you to get such a thing at this time of year!" " I know not indeed," said the other, " yet I believe our Lord could show us this favour if He thought fit." Ulrich, who saw that his comrade was really in extremity, despatched a messenger to a nobleman who lived at no great distance, begging him to send something that would restore the sick man. As the messenger journeyed along, he heard as he passed through a valley watered by the Molda, a whirring of wings. It was a covey of partridges, and one of the birds got caught in a bush and could not extricate itself. The man captured it easily, not knowing what kind of bird it was, and brought it to Brother Ulrich, saying : " See what a beautiful bird I have caught as I came along!" Ulrich took it to the invalid, who received it gratefully. " Did I not tell you," he said, " that our Lord could send me a partridge if He saw fit?" And fortified with this timely succour he found strength enough to get back to his convent.

The brethren on these journeys begged their bread, and for the most part took their scanty mid-day repast by the side of some stream or wayside fountain. It was thus as the little party of travellers were seated near a spring of water, having with them the young novice, Thomas Aquinas, that they were surprised by the armed company who carried off the novice as a prisoner. So common was this way of life, that we find in the acts of a very early provincial chapter an ordinance permitting the brethren to speak together at such times. "We do not regard it as a *breach of the silence at table*," are the words of this ordinance, "when the brethren on these journeys speak together as they take their refection by some spring of water on the roadside." So we read in the Life of Blessed Jordan that coming near a village at the time of dinner, he sent two of his companions to beg a little bread, bidding them bring what they could collect to a little fountain by the wayside, when they could all eat it together. The brethren returned with such a scanty supply as furnished only a handful of bread to each one. Jordan gave thanks to God for permitting them thus to practise real poverty, and bade the others rejoice with him. A woman passing by was scandalized at seeing a company of religious men giving way as she supposed to unseemly mirth, and at so early an hour; but when she inquired and found they were but rejoicing at their poverty, it so touched her heart, that she ran off to her cottage and brought thence bread, wine, and cheese in abundance, begging them to accept it, and remember her in their prayers. Sometimes hospitality of this kind shown to the brethren drew on their benefactors a special benediction. Thus we read of two Spanish brethren who were returning into their own country and passed through Poitou, preaching as they went. One day, having travelled far without taking any refreshment, they became weary and exhausted. The only village near was a wretched hamlet, where it seemed hopeless to apply for hospitality. "Never fear," said one of them to his younger companion, who was ready to sink with fatigue, "let us pray to God, and even in this poor hamlet He will know how to supply our needs." As he spoke, they saw approaching them a company of men and horses, in attendance on the châtelaine of Saint Maixent, who was travelling along the road in company with her young son. When she saw the two wayworn friars, she bade her son dismount and supply them with provisions out of those which her followers carried with them. With charming grace the boy accomplished his mother's orders, bringing them an excellent meal of wine,

fresh bread, eggs, and a good fish pasty, pressing them to
eat, and waiting on them as though he were their servant.
When the friars had finished their dinner, the elder of the
two said to his companion, " Let us kneel down and pray
to God for this good youth that God will reward him and his
mother for their charity towards us." So they knelt down
and said the *Veni Creator* and a *Pater* for their benefactors,
after which they continued their journey. Some time afterwards one of these friars going to the General Chapter at
Paris, stopped on his way at a convent in Poitou, where he
saw a young novice recently clothed whose face he seemed to
recognize. " Who is that young Brother ? " he asked of the
Prior, and hearing that he was son to the châtelaine of Saint
Maixent, he called him and said, " Dear Brother, do you
remember, at your mother's desire, giving a dinner once to
two travelling friars, when they were in great need ? " " I
do, indeed," replied the novice, "and I have often thanked God
for giving me the grace of vocation in answer to their pious
prayers." Then replied the Brother, " I was one of those
friars, and I have often prayed to God to give you a good
life and a happy end. The good life you have found the way
to, persevere in it, and it will lead you to a blessed end."

But we must not multiply quotations from these old
chronicles, which would readily furnish a collection of
anecdotes in no degree inferior in their picturesque beauty
to the Fioretti of St. Francis. Those given above are only
cited as illustrations of the work which was going on in
every country into which the friars penetrated. The plains
of Lombardy, the mountains of the Alps, the forests of
Germany, were everywhere made beautiful by the feet of
those who carried the good tidings of salvation to many
a remote district, where the rude inhabitants were left as
sheep without a shepherd; whilst at the same time they
feared not to declare their message also in the courts of
princes or to the learned audience of the schools. Thus
realizing the design of their great patriarch, they became the
true apostles of their time, carrying into practice the motto
which was adopted as their device, *Laudare, benedicere, prædicare!*

PREACHING YARD OF THE BLACK FRIARS, HEREFORD.

## CHAPTER XXXII.

### THE DOMINICANS IN ENGLAND.

THE religious chosen by St. Dominic to undertake the foundation of the English province was Father Gilbert de Fresnoy, of whom, before his appointment as provincial, we know no more than that he had been received into the Order at Bologna by Reginald of Orleans. Immediately after the close of the Chapter, he set out for his new destination, together with twelve companions, travelling in the suite of Peter de la Roche, bishop of Winchester, whose presence at Bologna, on his return from the Holy Land, may probably have hastened the despatch of the English mission. They arrived at Canterbury some time in the month of June, where the archbishop, Stephen Langton, was then residing. He received the new-comers with extraordinary kindness, and insisted on Gilbert's addressing a sermon to the people on that very day. It must have been a somewhat hard tax on

the preacher's powers, the more so as he probably felt the
future success of his enterprise, in so far as it depended on
the favour of the archbishop, was in no small degree likely
to hang on the good or bad opinion he might form of his
sermon.   Happily it was received with universal applause.
It was declared to be grave, elegant, and full of wisdom;
and Stephen promised both him and his companions that
they should never fail to find in him a friend and a protector.
They proceeded on their journey to London, and thence to
Oxford, where they arrived on the feast of the Assumption.
Here they erected a little oratory dedicated to our Lady, and
opened schools, which, from the name of the parish,[1] were
called St. Edward's schools.   The situation proving inconvenient, owing to its distance from the city, they betook
themselves to prayer that they might find favour with
the university authorities, and were able soon after to
establish themselves in the Jewish quarter, which was
assigned to them, to the intent, says Wood, "that they
might induce the Jews to embrace the Christian faith,
as well by the sanctity of their lives as by preaching
the Word, in which they excelled."   The canons of St.
Frideswide let them some lands at a low rate; and, aided
by further benefactions from Isabel de Bulbec, widow of
Robert, Earl of Oxford, and Walter Malclerk, bishop of
Carlisle, they built themselves a house, to which the
countess added an oratory and a burial-ground.   Here they
received a considerable number of new members, among
whom were Father John of St. Giles, Father Robert Bacon,
Father Richard Fishacre, and Father Robert de Kilwardby.
John of St. Giles was the first professor who taught in the
schools of St. Edward, and is called by Matthew of Paris
"a man skilful in the art of medicine, a great professor of
divinity, and excellently learned."   He was an intimate
friend of Robert Grosteste, bishop of Lincoln.   Robert Bacon
was brother, or as some say uncle, to the yet more celebrated
Franciscan friar, Roger Bacon.   He joined the Order when

---

[1] St. Edward's parish no longer exists, having been divided between the
two more modern parishes of All Saints and St. Aldate's.

an old man, out of the great love he bore St. Dominic. Richard Fishacre was his dear and bosom friend, whom Ireland calls "the most learned among the learned." He was a great admirer of Aristotle, whose works he ever carried in his bosom. "He was," says Wood, "renowned both as a philosopher and as a divine, for which reason he was so dear to Bacon that he became his inseparable companion; and as they were most constant associates in life, so neither could they be separated in death. For as the turtle-dove, bewailing its lost mate, dies, so, Bacon being dead, Fishacre neither could nor would survive." He was the first English preacher who commented on the "Book of Sentences."

Robert Kilwardby has been already named as having joined the Order at Paris, whence he was transferred to Oxford after the establishment of the friars in England. He afterwards became provincial; in 1272 was raised to the see of Canterbury, and six years later was created Cardinal of Santa Ruffina, by Nicholas III. In all these dignities he displayed the utmost humility, never laying aside the habit of his Order, and making all his journeys on foot, attended only by two friars. He died at Viterbo in 1280, leaving behind him many learned works of philosophy and theology.

The convent of Oxford soon became too small to contain the number of illustrious scholars who presented themselves for admission; and in 1259, King Henry III. made the friars  the grant of an island, formed by different branches of the river Isis on the south side of the city, where with the aid of abundant alms they built themselves what Wood calls a "beautiful habitation," together with a church dedicated to St. Nicholas. In their former quarters they had been much cramped for room, but here they had larger space; and the acts of divinity were given in the church and chapter-house, whilst the lectures on philosophy were delivered in the cloister. Of these buildings not a stone now remains, the whole having been pulled down at the dissolution of religious houses, and the materials sold piecemeal at a very cheap

rate, "unless [says Wood] we allow for the sacrilege." The
site is now entirely built over, with the exception of a small
piece of ground which formed part of the convent garden,
and which retains the name of " Paradise Garden," which it
bore so far back as 1221. The chief entrance to the convent
was over a bridge called the "Preachers' Bridge," built by
the friars in the reign of Edward I., and a portion of the
stream surrounding the island still bears the title of
"Preachers' Pool," whilst other memorials of the past are
preserved in the names of some of the surrounding localities,
such as Friars Street and Blackfriars Road. Many illustrious
persons were buried within the church of the friars, and to
this day tombs are disinterred together with human skeletons,
some with chalices on their breasts, as well as hearts cased
in lead. One of these latter remains was taken to King
Charles I. when he resided at Oxford, and on being opened
in his presence the heart was found fresh, and almost
unchanged.

The Dominicans of Oxford became in time some of
the greatest ornaments of the university, eminent in all the
learning of the age. It would be impossible to recount the
names of the great men whom they gave to England, or who
joined their ranks, but among these latter Walter Malclerk,
their first benefactor, must not be passed over. His history
is a remarkable one. His noble birth, attractive manners,
and extraordinary genius, raised him to the highest favour
at the court of Henry III., who, besides elevating him to the
bishopric of Carlisle, made him Lord High Treasurer of the
kingdom. In this position many years were spent in a life
of brilliant state services; but, as it would seem, the taint
of worldly ambition for a time obscured his better qualities
and his religious character. After a brief period of disgrace
at court, we find him again at the head of affairs in 1234;
and when, eleven years later, the king marched from London
against his revolted subjects, he left Walter Malclerk to
govern the kingdom during the period of his absence in
the field. But God had destined the conclusion of his life
to present us with another of those singular conversions the

stories of which crowd the annals of the Dominican Order. We are not told what was the immediate cause which wrought the change in his views and desires, and disgusted him with the very career which he had hitherto so ardently pursued; but as soon as grace had effectually touched his heart, he resolved on a generous and entire sacrifice; and, resigning his bishopric and distributing all he possessed to the poor, he took the habit of the Friars Preachers at Oxford, where he gave himself wholly to a life of penance, and "growing old in religious conversation," says Wood, "performed many memorable deeds in building and other things." This act of heroic renunciation filled all England with surprise, whilst the friars themselves were forced to admire the marvel which had transformed a courtier and a minister of state into the humble novice of a mendicant community. He died two years afterwards, and left behind him several learned works. From the words of Wood it would seem that the example set by Walter Malclerk was followed by other English prelates. Speaking of .the destruction of the convent at Oxford, he says, " The memory of the friars who dwelt there has a right, nevertheless, to be eternally preserved, for they lived with us to the immense benefit of the university, whilst the very prelates of the Church, attracted by their learning and their unspotted life, often laid down their honours and preferments, and repaired to Oxford to take that Rule upon them."

In 1229 took place that singular emigration of students from the university of Paris to that of Oxford, which was intended as a protest against the violation of their privileges, of which Du Bonlay gives the history. The Dominicans of the *Studium Generale* of St. James' convent were among the number, and it was on this occasion that Blessed Jordan, then Master General of the Order, visited Oxford, whence he wrote to his spiritual daughters, the nuns of the convent of St. Agnes at Bologna, a letter which is still preserved. " I write to you from England," he says; " pray that our Lord may direct me to do something for the honour of His Name, the glory of the Church, and the good of our Order.

He gives me hopes of making a good capture in the university of Oxford, where I now am." In the convent of Oxford was held one General Chapter, that of 1280, and the Great Council commonly known as "the Mad Parliament," which in 1258 made over all the real powers of government to Simon de Montfort, Earl of Leicester, son to the hero of Muret.

، From Oxford the brethren rapidly spread into other parts of the kingdom؛ Their first house in London was founded in the very year of their arrival in England, and was situated in Holborn, where two General Chapters were held, those namely of 1250 and 1263. In the first of these Chapters, according to Echard,[3] the letter to the religious of the Province of Poland, commonly but erroneously attributed to St. Dominic, was drawn up and despatched to its destination by John the Teutonic, fourth General of the Order. In the second, St. Thomas Aquinas assisted as definitor of the Roman Province, and took an active part in the deliberations.[4] It was in this Chapter that Humbert de Romans, the fifth General of the Order, resigned his office, and Peter of Tarantasia, afterwards Pope Innocent V., was chosen to govern the Order in his place as Vicar-General, until the next General Chapter.

In 1275, Robert de Kilwardby, being then archbishop of Canterbury, removed the community to a better position and, assisted by the King, built for them a church and convent on the site of Baynard Castle, which stood between Ludgate and the river, on ground now occupied by Printing House Square. The buildings covered a large space of ground, shut in by walls and gates, within which artisans of all kinds plied their trades. The convent enjoyed great privileges, and was the scene of many important events. Parliaments were more than once held within its walls, as well as the General Chapters of 1314 and 1335.

\ It would be tedious to enumerate all the English foundations of the Order, which was no less warmly favoured by Henry III. than by the popular leader, De Montfort.

---

[3] Echard, t. i. p. 113.     [4] Touron, *Vie de S. Thom.* ch. xxi.

Whilst "Sir Simon the righteous," as he was commonly
called, established the friars in his own town of Leicester,
the monarch whose government he opposed with so mighty
a hand, planted them at Gloucester, Ipswich, Canterbury,
and many other places. "This Order," says an Augustinian
chronicler, "flowing as a most rapid river from our Father
Austin, was truly a lucid fountain of paradise, which we
may fitly compare to the river Tigris, which was accounted
the swiftest and most impetuous of all rivers; and so this
Order is always deemed the most impetuous and boldest
against heretics." The waters of this swift river soon spread
into every part of the kingdom, so that within fifty years
of their arrival in England more than forty convents are
said to have been founded. They were established not only
in great cities such as Exeter and Bristol, but even in the
more remote valleys of Wales. At Gloucester, and again
at Norwich, their convents and churches still remain almost
perfect, the buildings being applied to secular purposes.

The seal of the Norwich Priory
is preserved, and represents St.
Dominic standing at a church
door with a friar behind him.
Opposite to him appear two men,
one wearing a high conical hat,
and between the two groups is a
fire, above which a book seems
as if tossed out of the flames.
The whole is of course a representation of the miracle of Fanjeaux. At Hereford, where in
1270, says Leland, "they made
a solempne pece of work," the
"preaching yard" is still shown,
with the hexagonal cross or pulpit, whence the friars were
wont to address the multitudes when the number of their
hearers was too large to admit of their assembling in the
church. In fact, we are told that their sermons were
generally delivered in the open air, and we find frequent

mention of the "portable pulpits" which they used, convenient to be put up wherever occasion might require.

A few years after their establishment in the country, they were employed by Pope Urban IV. to preach the Crusade throughout England and Scotland. Henry III., who chose his confessors from the friars and always had some of them with him, obtained leave from the Pope that they should ride on horseback, with a view to their accompanying him to the Holy Land when he took the Cross with the intention of proceeding thither. True to the traditions of their Order, the English Dominicans were ever active as missionaries among the infidels. Hardly were they planted in the island, before we find them sending forth apostles to preach the Gospel in Finland, Livonia, and Greenland. At Wisby, in the isle of Gothland, may still be seen the beautiful ruins of the Dominican church of St. Nicholas, built in 1240, and seeming, by the style of its architecture, to have been reared by some of these English missionaries. In the East also they were active at a very early period, and we find English friars filling the offices of provincials and bishops in the Holy Land in the reigns of Henry III. and Edward I. A memorial of one of these prelates has been almost accidentally preserved. In Flintshire, not far from Rhuddlan Castle, whose massive ivied towers stand on a commanding height overlooking the peaceful vale of Clwyd, may be seen the scanty remains of a convent of Black Friars. They consist of two ancient tombstones built into the walls of a barn. On one of these appears the figure of a bishop, round which may be traced the imperfect inscription :

✠ · · PVR LALME FRERE WILLAM FRENEY ERCHEVESKE
DE RAGES.

The prelate whose name is thus preserved was no other than William de Fresney, or Fresnoy, possibly a member of the same family as Gilbert de Fresnoy, the first provincial of England, who by Urban VI. was created archbishop of Rages, and who, after labouring for many years in the East, returned to England and ended his days in the remote convent of Rhuddlan, some time in the reign of Edward I.

But besides its distinctly apostolic and missionary character, the Order of Preachers in England, as elsewhere, devoted itself to the culture of letters and sacred science.' It thus kept true to the double design of its holy founder. The friars spread themselves over the land, taking part in every popular movement, and becoming the apostles of the English villages. They appeared at fairs and markets, and preached to the people from their portable pulpits or from the market cross; they spread the devotion of the Holy Rosary, which nowhere struck deeper root than in the kindly English soil, where it flourished like the wild rose, its sweet emblem, which clothes our summer hedgerows with its luxuriant blossoms. The Rosary quickly established itself in England as the devotion of all ranks; it continued in vigorous practice in this country at a time when elsewhere it fell into partial oblivion, and it even survived for a time the calamitous destruction of religion in the sixteenth century, and had to be sternly suppressed by law.[4]

'Thus the children of St. Dominic everywhere appeared as the friends and instructors of the common people. Yet at the same time their learned men were busy in the schools, where, as Leland says of one of their number, "they shone as the evening star among lesser luminaries."' Not to speak of other literary works, we must not pass without notice the share they had in the labours set on foot by Hugh de St. Cher to promote the study of the Holy Scriptures. That great man provided the convent of St. James with a beautiful corrected copy of the entire Bible, to the end that friars coming from all parts to the *Studium Generale* at Paris might compare their own Bibles with this authorized copy, and on their return to their own provinces might propagate the

---

[4] So late as 1590 we find it stated by the royal judges that "in Wales the people do carry their beades openly, and make such a clapping with them in church that a man can scarce hear the minister for the noise thereof; alledging that they can read on their beades as others on their bokes."

corrections. After this, about the year 1236, he began the first Biblical Concordance ever drawn up, and this work was completed and much enlarged by three English Dominicans, John of Derlington, Richard Stavensbury, and Hugh of Croydon, the first of whom became confessor to Henry III., and died archbishop of Dublin. The labours of these three learned religious were so considerable that the work when finished was very commonly known by the name of "the English Concordance."

It has been said that one object to which the friars in England from the first devoted themselves was the conversion of the Jews, and one fact in connection with this subject is deserving of record. The zeal which they elsewhere displayed as the champions of the faith against heresy, had, happily, nothing whereon to exercise itself in England up to the time of Wickliffe; for in old Catholic England of the thirteenth century heretical pravity was an unknown crime. But if heretics did not exist, Jews did, and in considerable numbers, and they often had much to suffer. They were generally the first victims to be plundered by any rapacious monarch in want of money; and from time to time it needed but a word or an idle rumour to raise against them the passions of some wild mob, who proceeded at once to pillage and massacre. Mr. John Kirkpatrick, in his valuable *History of the Religious Orders established at Norwich*, using the phraseology which obtained currency in most writings of the last century, speaks of the Dominicans as "a bloody kind of monks," to whom, we are led to suppose, persecution and bloodshed were a sort of second nature. Yet, strange to say, they appear in one period at least of English history not as persecutors, but as protectors of the persecuted. When, in 1255, the child-martyr, Hugh of Lincoln, was crucified by the Jews of that city in hatred of Christianity, a terrible storm arose over the whole country against the co-religionists of those who had committed the frightful crime, and many unhappy Jews were put to death, both in London and elsewhere, by the hands of infuriated mobs. But the Dominicans opposed themselves as a rock to the storm of popular indignation, and pleaded for the lives of those who were innocent of any participation in the guilt of their brethren. For this just and courageous conduct they had much to suffer, for the Londoners were so displeased with the friars for taking the part of the Jews, that they stopped the alms on which they depended, and for several days the community at Holborn was left without so much as a morsel of bread to eat.

The only convent of Dominican nuns existing in England was that of Dartford in Kent. Queen Eleanor of Castile, the beloved consort of Edward I., was much attached to the Order, and had purposed founding a house of Dominican nuns, but was prevented doing so by death. Her son, Edward II., took a vow to carry out his mother's intentions, but the troubles of his reign rendered it impossible for him to fulfil his purpose. Edward III., however, took on him the same vow, and not only founded the convent, but granted it a liberal revenue from the royal exchequer. Richard II., whose devotion to the Order is well known, and who is supposed to have enrolled himself in it as a tertiary, continued his grandfather's benefactions. It became a famous house of education, and among the noble personages who joined the community was a princess of the house of Plantagenet, Bridget, daughter of King Edward IV. The embattled gateway of this convent still remains. It was dedicated to our Lady and St. Margaret, and its seal represents the latter saint standing on a dragon and holding a cross, while below appears the figure of King Edward III., kneeling, and holding the convent in his hands. Dugdale, in his account of this convent, made the mistake of supposing that the nuns were sometimes Augustinians and sometimes Dominicans, not being aware that the nuns, as Dominicans, of course professed the Rule of St. Austin.

Father Michael Pio, in his *Uomini Illustri*, has collected a few fragments regarding the brethren in England, which refer chiefly to the happy deaths of some among their number. He tells us of one religious of the convent of Derby, who was visited on his death-bed by our Lady and

St. Edmund.   There are also notices of singularly happy
deaths in the convents of York and Cambridge, and mention
is made of one Brother from whose tomb there distilled a
miraculous oil.   Of two Brothers named Richard we read
that it was made known to them how greatly the souls in
purgatory complained of those who recited the Office of the
Dead negligently.   To another friar, Ivo (or John), a departed
Brother appeared with whom he had been on very intimate
terms, and who being in purgatory earnestly implored his
prayers.   The next morning, when he said Mass, Brother
John, holding in his hands the consecrated Host, addressed
our Lord with holy and loving boldness.   "O Lord Jesus
Christ," he said, "if the Sultan of Babylon held a person in
slavery, and his chamberlain, who had served him faithfully
for twenty years, asked for his deliverance, his master would
certainly grant it.   But Thou, O Lord, art surely not less
merciful than he, and I have served Thee faithfully these
many years; wherefore I confidently ask for the release of
my Brother's soul."   He said these words with many tears
and sighs, and the next night the Brother appeared to him,
and gave him the welcome assurance that his sufferings were
ended.

From England the Order was carried into Ireland by
Brother Reginald, or Ronald, the same who was present in
the refectory at Bologna when one of the visits of the angels
took place as before recounted.   After some years of labour
in that country he returned to Italy, when Pope Gregory IX.
appointed him his Penitentiary, and afterwards named him
archbishop of Armagh and primate of Ireland.   In Scotland,
as we have seen, the Order is thought to have been already
introduced before the arrival of the friars in England.

It is to be regretted that such very scanty records have
been preserved of the history of the Order in our own land.
Foreign writers, when they come to treat of the subject,
speak of the inhabitants of these remote islands as we should
describe some tribe of the interior of Africa; and perhaps
our own notions of the real condition of the country at a
time separated from our own by six centuries, and now so

utterly revolutionized, both socially and religiously, is hardly less vague. It seems like a dream to think of days when St. Thomas was sitting in council with his brethren in the convent of Holborn, and Blessed Jordan of Saxony was capturing souls in the schools of Oxford; when Blessed Bartholomew of Braganza was negotiating treaties at the English court, and St. Vincent Ferrer was preaching to the multitudes from those rocks on Clifton Downs which still bear his name; when the white habit of the Friars Preachers was worn by some of our greatest prelates, and was a familiar object in the thoroughfares of our great cities, or among the lanes and by-ways of our country villages. But it is a profitless thing to linger among dreams. Rather will we remind ourselves that the Lord's hand is not shortened nor does His grace ever fail. The orange-tree of St. Dominic still flourishes at Sta. Sabina and sends forth new shoots even in the midst of her desecrated cloisters, as though to remind us, when we are disposed to think of the ages of faith as something that have passed away for ever, that even in an unbelieving age God keeps a protecting hand over the ancient faith, the ancient devotions, and the ancient Orders of His Church.

SCALA CŒLI, FROM THE ARK OF ST. DOMINIC.

# CHAPTER XXXIII.

### VENI DILECTE.

#### 1221.

As soon as the Chapter had concluded its deliberations, St. Dominic prepared for what proved to be the last of those apostolic journeys in the course of which he established his Order in all the chief cities of Italy.[1] His immediate object was to visit Cardinal Ugolino, who then exercised the office of Legate of the Holy See in Lombardy, and whose residence in that capacity was fixed at Venice. According to some he had not yet laid aside his purpose of passing to the countries of the infidels, and the journey to Venice is thought to have been made in the hope that

an opportunity might present itself for realizing this desire.
Yet there can be little doubt that even before he left Bologna
he had received an intimation of his approaching release.
"Having attained the perfection of sanctity," says Theodoric,
"our holy Father St. Dominic received the gift of prophecy
from our Lord, Who deigned to make known to him the
precise time when He would call him out of this life, . . .
One night as he prayed, being consumed with his desire
to appear before the presence of God, he beheld a youth
of great beauty, who stood before him and said to him,
'Come, my beloved, come and enter into true joy.' Oh,
glorious call! oh, most delicious words, full of the sweetness
of Divine love! inviting this holy and happy soul not to
the vain and passing joys of this world, but to those that
are real and eternal! Happy soul indeed, who sought not
to delay out of fear of the Judge, but girding his loins and
holding in his hand a burning light, opened quickly to Him
Who knocked, and went joyously to meet his Lord!"

It was after receiving this precious assurance of his
approaching glory, that the saint before leaving Bologna
visited certain clerics of that city with whom he was on
terms of holy intimacy. After speaking to them for awhile
of the nothingness of this life, he said, before taking leave
of them, "You see me now, dear friends, in good health;
but be sure of this that before next feast of the Assumption,
I shall have quitted this world, and departed to God."

Early in the month of June, then, he left Bologna;
and after a short visit to Faenza, continued his route towards
Venice, for the purpose of taking counsel with the Cardinal
on the affairs of the Order, and it would seem that the
actual foundation of the convent of SS. John and Paul must
be referred to this date. Michael Pio says that he certainly
stopped on his way at Mantua and Ferrara, and preached
in both those cities. He also assigns to this date the
foundation of the convent of Trevigi, though it is doubtful
whether St. Dominic visited that city in person. He appears
to have made an excursion from Venice to Milan, possibly
with a view to meeting Jordan of Saxony, who had by

this time entered on his office as provincial of Lombardy; but if so, the latter has omitted to notice the fact in his Life of the saint.

When St. Dominic returned to Bologna after a few weeks' absence a marked change was visible in his appearance. His hair was thinning on his temples, the excessive heat of the summer appeared to render him languid and exhausted; and yet, in spite of what he was evidently suffering, he never relaxed in any of his usual labours. It was the first week of August. He had travelled from Venice to Bologna on foot as usual, preaching as he went; nay, there was even a more than ordinary zeal observable in his conduct, as if he felt the time was shortening, and desired that the last hour should find him watching and at work. As he approached Bologna, the extraordinary heat affected him painfully. It was evening when he reached the convent of St. Nicholas, yet in spite of his fatigue, and the severe headache to which he acknowledged, he remained until past midnight conversing with Father Ventura, the prior, and Father Rodolph, the procurator, and then proceeded to the church, where he continued in prayer until the hour of Matins, notwithstanding their earnest entreaty that for once he would consent to rest during the Office. As soon as it was finished, he was obliged to give way to the violence of the fever accompanied with dysentery, the advances of which he had hitherto disregarded. They begged him to allow himself a little repose on a bed, but he gently refused, and desired to be laid on a sacking which was stretched upon the ground. His head was swimming with the pain and heaviness of his malady; but even then he would not spare himself, but desired the novices to be called round him that he might speak to them, for what he felt would be the last time. " He comforted and exhorted them," says Ventura, in his deposition, " with sweet words and a smiling countenance; and indeed through his whole sickness he was so patient that he neither complained nor uttered a single groan, but always seemed cheerful and full of joy."

Well knowing that human skill would not avail for his

recovery, he desired that twelve of the most discreet brethren should be summoned, and in their presence made a general confession of his whole life to Father Ventura, who was his ordinary confessor. Having done this he addressed the brethren, saying, "By the mercy of God I have preserved my virginity unstained until this day. If you desire the same grace, avoid the company of women, which is always dangerous. If you would keep chastity, guard yourselves from dangerous occasions and watch over your hearts." But the moment afterwards a kind of scruple seemed to seize him: and turning to Ventura, he said with touching humility, "Father, I fear lest I may have sinned in speaking of this grace before the brethren."[1]

The whole community were now recalled, and as they stood around their dying Father, he gave them his last will and testament in the following words: "Persevere in serving our Lord with fervour, and apply yourselves to extend the Order, which is now only in its beginning. You know that to serve God is to reign, but we must serve Him with our whole hearts. Be firm then in a holy life, keep faithful to your Rule, and increase in all virtue. Behold, my children, what I leave to you as a heritage: HAVE CHARITY, GUARD HUMILITY, AND MAKE YOUR TREASURE OUT OF VOLUNTARY POVERTY."

The brethren were overwhelmed with affliction, and in the hopes that some relief might be afforded by removing him to a more healthy air, they conveyed him to a house situated on a hill outside the city, where was a little chapel dedicated to our Lady, called Santa Maria dei Monti. But though he suffered them to do this, he himself was in no doubt as to the issue of his malady; and as the prior and brethren stood around his couch he began to exhort them, moving them to compunction. "Never did I hear from his lips," says Ventura, "a better sermon." He had received

---

[1] Stephen of Spain, in his deposition, says that he firmly believed the holy Father to have preserved his baptismal innocence unstained, for that having often heard his confession he could never understand him to have committed mortal sin.

the Holy Viaticum before his removal from St. Nicholas; they now administered Extreme Unction, and after the performance of this holy rite some of those present observed one to another that in case of his death at Santa Maria, the rector of that church did not intend that his body should be carried away, but meant to have him buried there. When the prior repeated this to the saint he replied quickly, "God forbid that I should be buried anywhere save under the feet of my brethren. Rather take me out and let me die in that vineyard, that you may be able to bury me in our own church." They could not refuse to satisfy his desire; and though they feared lest he might die on the way, they carried him back to the city, weeping as they went. Having reached the convent, as he had no cell of his own, they took him to that of Brother Moneta, who also gave him a change of garments, for so absolute was the poverty which he practised that he had no habit assigned to his own use save that which he wore. But when he perceived that he was lying on some kind of bed, he earnestly begged that they would lay him on the floor in ashes, and they were obliged to comply with his request. Then he remained quiet for about an hour, during which time some of the brethren who had heard of his illness arrived from a distance, and among these was John of Salerno, who had the sad consolation of once more seeing his beloved Father, and receiving his blessing. Presently he called the prior to him, saying, "Prepare," (meaning for the recommendation of a departing soul); but as they were about to begin, he added, "You can wait a little;" and it was perhaps during these moments that, according to the revelation made to St. Bridget, the Mother of God, to whom he had ever shown himself so loyal and loving a servant, visibly appeared to him, and promised that she would never withdraw her patronage and protection from his Order.

He was now sinking so rapidly, that they saw a very short time would rob them of the Father to whom their hearts cleaved with so overflowing a tenderness. All were bathed in tears; Rodolph held his head, and gently wiped the death-sweat from his forehead; Ventura bent over him, saying, "Dear Father, you leave us desolate and afflicted; remember us, and pray for us to God." Then the dying saint summoned his fast-failing strength, and, raising his hands and eyes to heaven, he said in a clear and distinct voice: "Holy Father, since by Thy mercy I have ever fulfilled Thy will, and have kept and preserved those whom Thou hast given me, now I recommend them to Thee. Do Thou keep them; do Thou preserve them." Then, turning to his children, he added tenderly, "Do not weep, my children; I shall be more helpful to you where I am now going, than I have ever been in this life." One of them again asking him to tell them exactly where he would be buried, he replied in his former words, "Under the feet of my brethren." "For," says Theodoric, "though he knew himself to be invited to the heavenly nuptials, he chose the lowest place; but the Father of the family made him pass to the highest, and raised him in honour and glory above other guests." A little later, feeling that his last moment approached, he said to the prior and brethren, "Now begin." They therefore began the solemn recommendation of the soul. "And I believe," says Ventura, "that the blessed Father repeated the prayers with us, for his lips continued to move whilst we recited the Office; at the end of which, and whilst we were pronouncing the words, *Subvenite Sancti Dei; occurrite, Angeli Domini, suscipientes animam ejus, offerentes eam in conspectu Altissimi*, he stretched his arms to heaven and expired. It was about noon on the 6th of August, which fell on a Friday, in the year 1221, when the saint thus departed to God, being in the fifty-first year of his age." [2]

His weeping children stood for awhile around the body, without venturing to touch the sacred remains. "Good reason indeed had they to sorrow," says Castiglio, "at the loss of one whom God had given them as their father, their

[2] The above account is drawn from the depositions of the two brethren, Ventura and Rodolph of Faenza, who were both present at the death of the saint, and from his Life by Theodoric of Apoldia, liv. v. ch. i. ii.

pastor, and their best friend. He had been their refuge in every trouble, their resource in every need, always ready to console with his words of counsel or compassion those who had left all things for the love of God. What greater calamity could befall them than to be deprived of such a saint and such a father, and what wonder that over such a loss they should weep bitter tears?" When at length it became necessary to prepare for the interment, they began to strip off the tunic in which he died, and having done so, their tears of tenderness flowed afresh, for they discovered an iron chain tightly bound round his waist, and from the scars and marks it had produced, it was evident that it had been worn for many years. Rodolph removed it with the utmost reverence, and it was afterwards delivered to Blessed Jordan, his successor in the government of the Order, who kept it as a precious relic.

To Rodolph also belonged the duty of providing all things for his burial. He caused a wooden coffin to be made, in which the body was enclosed with iron nails, shutting up and nailing the coffin with his own hands, and attesting that no spices or aromatical perfumes of any kind were placed therein, and he himself kept careful watch over the precious remains until the interment. "It was," says Theodoric, "by the special disposition of Providence that the venerable Cardinal Ugolino, bishop of Ostia, came to Bologna, and in his own person rendered to the saint the honours of a devout burial." The people of Bologna, who had shown extraordinary sympathy with the friars during the last days of the saint's illness, and had made unceasing prayers for his recovery, followed the procession in a dense body. Patriarchs, bishops, and abbots from all the neighbouring country swelled the train. Among them was one who had been a dear and familiar friend of the departed saint, Albert, prior of the convent of St. Catherine in Bologna, a man of great piety and warm affections. As he followed, sorrowful, and bathed in tears, he observed that the friars chanted the psalms with a certain joyfulness and calm of spirit; and this had such an effect on him, that he too stayed his tears and began to sing with them. And then he began to reflect on the misery of this present state, and the folly of mourning it as an evil when a holy soul was released from bondage and sent to the presence of his God. With this thought in his heart, he went up, in an impulse of devout affection, to the sacred body, and, bending over it and conquering his grief, he embraced his dead friend, and congratulated him on his blessedness. When he rose, an emotion of wonderful happiness was observable on his countenance. He went up to the prior of St. Nicholas, and taking him by the hand, "Dear Father, rejoice with me," he said; "Master Dominic has even now spoken to me, and assured me that before the year is ended we shall both be reunited in Christ." And the event proved his words, for before the close of the year Albert was with his friend. Brother Rodolph had caused a tomb to be prepared, surrounded by large stones solidly cemented together, for he feared lest any impious person should lay hands on the sacred remains. This tomb was closed in by another great stone, also carefully cemented, "and thus was laid to rest this treasure, more precious than gold, purer than silver, and nobler than all imaginable jewels." Cardinal Ugolino himself wrote the epitaph which was placed over the tomb, and which ran as follows:

"Here lies the body of the venerable servant of God, Dominic de Guzman, born at Calaroga in Spain, in the diocese of Osma; founder of the Order of Friars Preachers, of which he was made first Master General by Honorius III. and confirmed in that dignity by the suffrages of his brethren, in the Chapters held here in Bologna in 1220 and 1221. On the 30th of May of the latter year he was declared a citizen of Bologna, together with all others who should succeed him as Master General of the Order. He slept in our Lord at noon on Friday, August 6, 1221, under the pontificate of Honorius III., and I, Ugolino, Cardinal Bishop of Ostia, and Apostolic Legate, after having celebrated his obsequies, have herewith by our hands placed his venerable body. May the Name of the Lord be praised for ever!"

Theodoric adds that many revelations were granted of the glory of the saint, among others to a cleric of Bologna of holy life, who, not having been able to assist at the obsequies, next night saw in a dream the blessed Dominic seated in the church of St. Nicholas on a kind of throne and crowned with a glorious diadem. "Are not you Brother Dominic," he asked, " who are recently dead ? " " My son," replied the saint, " I am not dead, because I have a good Master with Whom I live." The next morning the cleric went to the church of St. Nicholas and found that the holy body had been buried precisely in the spot where in his vision he had beheld the saint enthroned. We also read that on the day of the saint's death, being the 6th of August, Brother Raoul had gone from Rome to Tivoli in company with Tancred, the prior of Santa Sabina, and at the hour of Sext he celebrated Mass, and made an earnest *memento* for the Father, whom he knew to be then lying in the extremity of sickness at Bologna. As he did so, he seemed to see the great road reaching out of that city, and walking along it was the figure of St. Dominic between two men of venerable aspect, crowned with a golden coronet, and dazzling with light. But the most celebrated of these revelations was that received by Blessed Guala of Brescia, who as he fell asleep leaning against the bell-tower of his church, seemed to see two ladders let down from an opening in the sky above him. At the top of one stood our Lord, and His Blessed Mother was at the summit of the other. Angels were going up and down them, and at their foot was seated one in the habit of the Order, but his face was covered with his hood, after the fashion in which the friars are wont to cover the face of the dead when they are carried out for burial. The ladders were drawn up into heaven, and he saw the unknown friar received into the company of the angels, surrounded by a dazzling glory. Guala awoke, not knowing what the vision could signify; and hastening to Bologna, he found that the great patriarch had breathed his last at the very moment in which it had appeared to him, and he judged it as a certain token that the soul of Dominic had been taken up to heaven.

Not long after the holy body had been deposited in its tomb, a sweet and penetrating perfume became sensible, as if issuing forth from it, and spreading thence through the whole church. This odour was perceived both by Brother Ventura and many other persons. Moreover, the miracles wrought and graces received at the tomb were so abundant that crowds came thither day and night in pilgrimage, and the citizens, seeing how wonderfully Almighty God was manifesting His power on this spot, brought rich stuffs and hangings, with which they desired to enclose the place of sepulture. But the brethren would not allow this to be done. They feared the appearance of vainglory and ostentation, and the solemn injunctions of their departed Father to hold fast to evangelical poverty were still fresh in their minds. In spite, therefore, of the daily increasing number of prodigies and Divine favours, they allowed the body to remain under the plain flagstone placed over it by Rodolph, without any token of exterior honour, and took no steps for obtaining his canonization. By some this conduct has been censured as neglect, but it was probably rather the result of that simplicity and poverty of spirit which St. Dominic had bequeathed to his children as their inheritance. The answer of one of the friars, when questioned on the subject, may be taken as a sample of the feeling under which they acted. "What need for canonization?" he said. "The holiness of Master Dominic is known to God; it matters little to declare it before men." Nevertheless, the devotion of the faithful continued to be manifested with ever-increasing fervour. Some remained at the tomb day and night, invoking the intercession of the saint, or thanking him for favours received. Others brought testimonies of their cures, hanging up waxen figures of eyes, hands, and feet, according to the different infirmities from which they had been delivered. One English scholar, by name Nicholas Wood, of the diocese of Worcester, is specially mentioned by Jordan as instantly cured of a hopeless paralysis, after making a vow to the Blessed Dominic. But none of these things moved the friars to depart from the line of conduct on which they had decided, and dreading lest, under the appearance of piety, they should be thought to be seeking for their own emolument, they broke and threw away the images and other votive offerings brought by the people, and would not permit any of these exterior marks of devotion to be exhibited.

Necessity at last obliged the religious of St. Nicholas to undertake the first translation of the sacred relics. The convent had to be enlarged on account of the ever-increasing size of the community, and the church stood in need of repair and alteration. The tomb of St. Dominic had, therefore, to be disturbed, and to do so, the Pope's permission was first required. Honorius III. was dead, and his successor in the Papal chair was none other than Cardinal Ugolino Conti, who had been consecrated Pope under the name of Gregory IX. He acceded to the request with joy, at the same time sharply reproving the friars for their long negligence. The solemn translation accordingly took place during the Whitsuntide Chapter which assembled at Bologna in 1233, under Blessed Jordan of Saxony, who had succeeded to the government of the Order. The Pope wished to have attended in person at this ceremony, but, being prevented doing so, he deputed the archbishop of Ravenna to represent him, in company with a crowd of other distinguished prelates. Three hundred Friars Preachers, from all countries, assembled to assist at this function, not without a secret fear on the part of some as to the state in which the sacred remains should be found; and this doubt agitated many of them during the day and night preceding that on which the translation was appointed to take place, with a painful emotion. Among those who shared this uneasiness was Brother Nicholas of Giovenazzo, but it pleased God to reassure him by a special revelation. For, as he prayed, there appeared to him a man of majestic appearance, who spoke these words in a clear and joyous tone: *Hic accipiet benedictionem a Domino, et misericordiam a Deo salutari suo.* And he understood them to signify the blessedness enjoyed by St. Dominic, and to be a pledge of the honour which God would cause to be shown to his relics.

On the 24th of May the ceremony of translation took place, the person who showed himself most active in directing the proceedings being Stephen of Spain, then acting as provincial of Lombardy, who had been far from sharing the indifference of his brethren, and greatly desired to see the holy Father inscribed in the catalogue of saints. Blessed Jordan, then Master General of the Order, and all the Fathers of the General Chapter, together with the bishops, prelates, and magistrates who had come to be present on the occasion, stood round in silence whilst the grave was opened. Rodolph of Faenza, who still held the office of procurator, and who had been so dear a son to the great patriarch, was the first to raise the stone. Hardly had he begun to remove the mortar and earth that lay beneath, when an extraordinary odour was perceptible, which increased in power and sweetness as they dug deeper, until at length, when the coffin appeared, and was raised to the surface of the grave, the whole church was filled with the perfume, as though from the burning of some precious and costly gums. The bystanders knelt on the pavement, shedding tears of emotion as the lid was raised, and the sacred remains, now reduced to bones, were exposed to their eyes. Thomas of Cantimpré, in his second book *De Apibus*, relates a singular circumstance, which has been repeated by Malvenda. He says that among the Fathers present at the ceremony was John of Vicenza, whose singular zeal and sanctity had always greatly endeared him to St. Dominic. As he stood by the coffin, he stepped aside to give place to William, bishop of Modena; but immediately the holy body was seen to turn in the direction where he stood. His humility moved him again to change his place, when the same thing was observed; as though on this first day, when public honours were being paid to the holy patriarch, he desired to show by evident token that he counted his chief glory to consist, less in such honours, than in the sanctity of his children.

It was Blessed Jordan who raised the body of his beloved Father, and reverently laid it in a new coffin. Eight days later, this also was opened, to satisfy the devotion of some

EE

noble personages who had not been present on the previous occasion. Then it was that Jordan, taking the sacred head between his hands, kissed it, while tears of tenderness flowed from his eyes; and, so holding it, he desired all the Fathers of the Chapter to approach and gaze at it for the last time. One after another they came and kissed the venerable relics. All were conscious of the same extraordinary odour; it remained on the hands and clothes of all who touched, or came near the body; nor was this the case merely when the grave was first opened. The tomb remained unclosed for fifteen days, during which time it was watched and guarded by officers appointed by the city magistrates, and during all this time the same exquisite odour was sensible to all who visited it. Flaminius, who lived three hundred years afterwards, thus writes in 1527: "This divine odour of which we have spoken, adheres to the relics even to this present day."

The body was removed to a marble tomb prepared for it, and, as Jordan says, "was buried amid its own perfumes. . . . It was Whit Tuesday, and as the choir intoned the Introit for the day, ' Receive the joy of your glory, giving thanks to God, Who has called you to the heavenly kingdom,' the brethren in their gladness of heart took the words as if spoken from heaven. The trumpets blew, the people displayed a countless multitude of tapers; and as the procession moved along there everywhere resounded the words, ' Blessed be Jesus Christ.'" It is thus that Jordan writes in the circular letter which he addressed to the brethren of the Order, in which he also speaks of the vast number of miraculous graces which were poured forth both before and after the ceremony. "Sight," he says, "was granted to the blind, power of walking to the lame, soundness to the paralyzed, speech to the dumb. . . . I myself saw Nicholas the Englishman, who had long been paralyzed, leaping at this solemnity."

Stephen of Spain declares in his deposition that from the time that John of Vicenza began to preach to the people the life and miracles of the saint, a wonderful increase of grace manifestly shone forth, both among the friars and their audience, specially in the cities of Lombardy, where more than a hundred thousand people, who had hitherto doubted whether to adhere to Holy Church or join themselves to the heretics, were converted to the Catholic faith.

The miracles duly attested as having been wrought by the saint's intercession since his death, are of all kinds, and belong to all countries. Their simple enumeration would fill a volume, and however glorious to the memory of our saint, might prove but tedious to the reader. Many also, as we are assured, were performed during his lifetime, besides those which have been noticed in the foregoing pages. Examples of both kinds are given in the history of Theodoric of Apoldia. " But what was far more resplendent and magnificent than his miracles," says Blessed Jordan, " was that purity of life and force of Divine fervour which proved him indeed to be a vessel of honour, adorned with every precious stone. . . . Who will ever be able to imitate his virtue? We may admire it, and judge from his example of our own sluggishness. But to be able to do what he did belongs not to the ordinary strength of man, but only to a singular and special grace. . . . Let us nevertheless imitate as far as we can the example of our Father, and render thanks to our Lord, Who has given us such a leader, beseeching Him that walking in a straight course along the paths which our fathers have marked out, we too may deserve to win the goal of eternal bliss into which that happy soul has entered."

# CHAPTER XXXIV.

In the same year which witnessed the translation of St. Dominic, Pope Gregory IX. appointed an Apostolic Commission to begin the necessary inquiries for proceeding to the canonization of the servant of God. The members of this Commission therefore required of Father Ventura, who still filled the office of prior of Bologna, that he should collect the depositions of those who had been eye-witnesses of the life of the saint. The depositions thus given constitute what are known as the Acts of Bologna, being the testimonies of those brethren who had been on the most intimate and familiar terms with the holy Father during his life. They were nine in number, viz., Fathers Ventura of Verona, William de Montferrat, Amizio of Milan, Bonviso of Placentia, John of Navarre, Rodolph of Faenza, Stephen of Spain, Paul of Venice, and Fugerio of Penna. Besides these depositions, which were sworn to before the Commissaries with all accustomed forms, twenty-nine other witnesses were heard; inquiries were set on foot throughout France, Spain, and Italy, and a vast number of miracles were examined and proved. The Process being submitted to the Holy Father, he determined without delay to proceed to the canonization of one to whose sanctity he himself bore witness in the memorable words spoken by him to the assembled Cardinals, " I have no more doubt of the sanctity of this man, than I have of that of St. Peter and St. Paul."

Strange to say, the statements of historians vary both as to the place and time of St. Dominic's canonization.

Malvenda supposes it to have taken place in 1233, the same
year as the translation; but this involves the impossible
supposition that all the necessary forms and inquiries were
gone through between the 24th of May and the 13th of July,
that is, in less than two months. We are, however, safe in
following the authority of Bernard Guidonis, who affirms it
to have taken place at Rieti, on the 13th of July, in the year
1234, thirteen years after the death of the saint, a year and
two months after his translation, and eighteen after the
Confirmation of his Order.

In the Bull of Canonization, which is of very considerable
length, Pope Gregory, after enumerating the great actions
of the holy patriarch, and declaring that his Order and that
of the Friars Minors had "renewed Christian piety throughout the world," goes on to draw his character in the language
of one to whom it was intimately known by personal observation, and in words which describe with singular felicity
that blending of the contemplative with the active life which
was the salient feature of his sanctity. "He hungered and
thirsted," says the holy Pontiff, "after the practice of the
strictest virtue, and seemed always to watch with his
spiritual weapons in his hand. As far as he could, he dwelt
before the tabernacle of our Lord, making it his special object
to subject the flesh to the spirit, and to unite himself entirely
to God. It was in no half way that he exerted himself to
obtain the happy transformation of his spirit into that of
God, but he devoted himself to this work with all his
strength, and seemed as though wholly liquefied in the
ardour of Divine love. At the same time, his heart being
ever full of compassion towards others, he did not allow
himself to be entirely taken up with these spiritual exercises,
but employed himself for the good of his neighbour, yet
moderately, so as not to hinder his own perfection. But
when he exercised the functions of an apostolic preacher, it
was as though the thunder of heaven broke the hearts of the
wicked; he seemed like a bow discharging a thousand sharp
arrows against the delights of the flesh; and whilst the sects
of the heretics trembled at his words, the hearts of the

faithful were filled with joy unspeakable. . . These things,''
he adds, "were well known to us from the familiar conversation which we formerly had together, when we ourselves
were engaged in employments and offices inferior to that
which we now exercise."

The 6th of August, on which day St. Dominic departed
this life, being already occupied by the festival of the Trans-
figuration, his feast was appointed to be kept on the 5th,
but at a later period, when the 5th was set apart by Pope
Paul IV. for the feast of Our Lady ad Nives, St. Dominic's
feast was fixed for the 4th of August, on which day it is still
celebrated.

The Office of the saint is attributed by some to Blessed
Jordan, but Altamura, in his *Biblioteca Domenicana*, tells us
that two Fathers, John of Castile and Constantine of Orvieto,
were each appointed to draw one up, when that of Constantine was finally chosen, being preferred for its greater
elegance.   When this Office was celebrated for the first time
at Bologna, Guala of Brescia was present, and assisted at
the ceremony.   By common consent he was appointed to
sing the antiphon, *Scala Cœli*, which is now the third antiphon of Lauds, and in which a reference is made to the
vision of Guala above related.   On this occasion he again
related the circumstances of this vision to Bartholomew of
Trent, who was also present, and who was united with
Guala on terms of intimate friendship.[1]

Most touching, indeed, must have been the first celebration of this Office in the convents of the brethren.   Stephen
of Salanhac was present on this occasion at St. Romain of
Toulouse, and relates the following singular narrative: "In
the year 1234," he says, "the day before the feast of the
blessed Father, I met in the city of Toulouse Brother
Aymeric of Solemniaco, a monk of the Cistercian Order,
and I begged him to come the next day to assist at the feast,
as he had been an old friend and companion of the saint in
the house of Bishop Fulk.   He rejoiced much at receiving
this invitation, and said, 'O Lord, I give Thee thanks that

[1] Bart. Trid.

THE ARK OF ST. ...

(To face p. 491.)

Thou hast glorified Thy servant Dominic! All last night I spent with him in vision, and after many holy colloquies, he begged and even commanded me that the next day I should go to the convent of his sons and assist at the first celebration of his feast. I shall do so, therefore, with all my heart,' which indeed he did, praising God in His saint."

A second translation of St. Dominic's relics took place in 1267, when the holy body was removed to a more richly ornamented tomb. This translation, like the first, was made at the time of the General Chapter, and the head of the saint, after being devoutly kissed by the brethren and several bishops who were then present, was exposed to the veneration of the people from a lofty stage erected outside the church of St. Nicholas. The tomb was again opened in 1383, when a portion of the head was placed in a silver shrine, in order the more easily to satisfy the devotion of the faithful. This shrine is a work of extraordinary magnificence, formed somewhat like a monstrance, the urn containing the sacred relic resting on a pedestal surrounded by angels, the whole being surmounted by a bust of the saint. Finally, in 1469, the remains of the saint were deposited in the magnificent shrine in which they still rest, and which is regarded as the greatest work of Nicholas Pisano. The ark of St. Dominic, as it is commonly called, occupies a chapel dedicated to the saint, and is adorned with six large bas-reliefs and several smaller ones, together with a great number of statues. The six large bas-reliefs are arranged two in front, two at the back, and one at either extremity. They represent the following subjects: (1) the Confirmation of the Rule, (2) the Vision of the Holy Apostles, (3) the Raising to Life of Napoleon Orsini, (4) The Miracle at Fanjeaux, (5) the Visit of the Angels to the Refectory of St. Sixtus, (6) the Recovery and Profession of Blessed Reginald. In the accompanying illustration the third or fourth of these bas-reliefs appear, whilst between them stands an image of the Blessed Virgin. The smaller bas-reliefs at the base are the work of Alfonso Lombardi, that to the extreme right representing the vision beheld by Blessed Guala of the

*Scala Cæli.* Below this (not represented in the illustration)
is the actual altar, the frontal of which, by a later artist,
represents the translation of the saint's body.

The wonderful beauty of this celebrated tomb, both as
a whole and in the perfection of every detail, is universally
acknowledged. It stands alone and without a rival among
sepulchral monuments. "You feel as you behold it," to use
the words of Père Lacordaire, "that the hand of the artist
must have been divinely guided to express the sanctity of
him whose dust it covers."

Since the erection of this shrine the actual coffin of
St. Dominic has never been opened, or even exposed to
view. But in 1784, a portion of the skull was taken from
the other reliquary in which the head is preserved, at the
request of Ferdinand, first Duke of Parma, who obtained
possession of this treasure through the intervention of Pope
Pius VI. At a later period, however, it passed into the
hands of Sister Hyacintha de Bourbon, who, when she
took the habit of religion in the convent of SS. Domenico
e Sisto, brought it to the convent, where it is still devoutly
preserved. Other portions of the holy body are to be found
in various places, of which we will only name an entire bone,
about the length and thickness of a finger, which is preserved
at the Carmelite convent of Chichester.

No original portrait of St. Dominic now remains, that
shown at Santa Sabina being comparatively of modern
date. Two so-called portraits are shown at Bologna, one
of which formerly occupied the refectory, and has been
engraved by the Bollandists; the other, also ancient, was
painted in fresco on the wall near his tomb. When the
church was undergoing repairs, the portion of wall on which
this latter picture was painted was removed to another
chapel, and as no name had been inscribed below it, a
certain man named Machiavelli though fit to give it the
name of St. Thomas, though it was well known to have
been intended as a representation of St. Dominic. Although
it has probably no more claims than the others to be
regarded as a real portrait, yet the bent position of the head,

THE CHASUBLE OF ST. DOMINIC.

[To face p. 473.

and the general character of recollection and humility, agree very well with what is told us of this appearance of the saint. This portrait has been engraved as a frontispiece to the French translation of the Life by Theodoric of Apoldia. The numerous and beautiful representations of the saint by Fra Angelico are all works of the imagination only.

Passing to relics of a different description, there is one of great interest and value and undoubted authenticity preserved in the convent of SS. Domenico e Sisto at Rome, namely, the breviary commonly used by the saint, which from certain abbreviations which appear in it, seems to have been intended for the purpose of being more conveniently carried on a journey.

It is written on fine parchment and well preserved, the writing evidently of the thirteenth century, with the rubrics in red, and the whole perfectly legible. This priceless treasure, the book so often held in the hands of our holy Father, and watered, it may be, with his pious tears, is contained in a handsome reliquary which stands on an altar within the choir of the religious; a fitting resting-place among the descendants of the saint's Roman daughters, for this monument of his daily prayers.

Of his crucifix preserved in the church of St. Sernin at Toulouse, we have already spoken. Another crucifix used by him was saved with a few other relics formerly preserved in the ancient convent of Prouille, and is now in possession of the community established in the restored convent at that place. In the church of St. Sernin is also shown the superb chasuble, called the chasuble of St. Dominic, from the fact of its having been worn by him; for its exceeding richness renders it doubtful whether it can really have belonged to him or to any of his convents, in which the sacred vestments were, as we know, of the plainest description. This chasuble displays the ample proportions of the ancient form. On a silken ground thickly embroidered with flowers and foliage, appear eagles and peacocks, with their names written on their wings. On a pillar in front and on the back appear figures of saints, each standing under a Gothic niche. This magnificent relic is also in good preservation and is considered as unique even as a mere object of ecclesiastical art.

The cell in which St. Dominic expired was after his death converted into a chapel, and was so preserved with loving reverence up to the day when the friars were driven out of their convent. In the hope of saving the spot from profanation, they took the precaution of walling up the door. But the military authorities who occupied the convent and used it as a barrack, desiring to enlarge a passage for their greater convenience, ruthlessly destroyed the room to which attached so precious a memory. His cell at Santa Sabina has hitherto escaped a similar fate.

Three festivals have been consecrated to the memory of St. Dominic: the 4th of August, on which his death is celebrated; the 25th of May,[2] in memory of the translation of his relics; and lastly, the 15th of September, in honour of the miraculous picture of Suriano. This picture first appeared in the convent of Suriano in Calabria, in the year 1530, and did not attract much popular regard until the beginning of the following century, when the miracles and conversions wrought at Suriano made it a place of pilgrimage to the whole world. After a number of briefs granted by successive Pontiffs, and a severe examination of the facts, Benedict XIII. at length appointed the 15th of September to be observed through the whole Order, in commemoration of the almost innumerable graces received before this remarkable picture.

"We should have wished," says Polidori, in the concluding chapter of his Life, "to have been able to put before the eyes of our readers all that St. Dominic ever wrote in defence of the Catholic religion, for the instruction of his disciples, in order that they might collect from these writings yet greater and more copious illustrations of his virtues. But

---

[2] The feast of the translation has been recently removed from the 24th to the 25th of May; the 24th being now set apart for the Office of Our Lady Help of Christians.

there remains to us nothing except the Constitutions of his
Order (added to the Rule of St. Austin), the sentence of
reconciliation to the Church of Ponce Roger, and the faculty
granted to Raymond William de Hauterive Pelaganira to
entertain the heretic William Huguecion in his house. It
is, however, certain that he wrote many letters to his
brethren, especially exhorting them to the study of the
Sacred Scriptures, but none of these now remain; that
addressed to the Polish friars, and bearing his name, not
being genuine."

Father Andrea Rovetta of Brescia, in his *Bibliotheca
Chronologica* of the province of Lombardy, gives a list of the
works supposed to have been composed by the saint. They
are as follows: two books against the Heresies of the Albigenses; a Paraphrase on St. Paul's Epistles; a Paraphrase
on the other Canonical Epistles; a Commentary on the
Psalter of David; a Commentary on St. Matthew's Gospel;
another Commentary on the passage in the ninth chapter
of St. Matthew's Gospel, beginning *Ascendente Jesu in navi-
culam;* Pious Salutations to the Blessed Virgin; Sermons on
the Angelic Salutation; other Sermons in Praise of the
Blessed Virgin; a Treatise on the Psalter of the Blessed
Virgin Mary, or Rosary; a Method of Meditating on the
same; and lastly, a Treatise on the Most Holy Body of our
Lord Jesus Christ.

Father Anthony of Siena, who died in 1363, in his
*Bibliotheca Dominicana*, speaks of his Commentaries on the
Gospel of St. Matthew and the Epistles of St. Paul, as
existing in his day; but if so, they have since been lost, and,
with the exceptions above noted, none of his writings now
remain to us. The first works on Father Andrea's list
would indeed have a peculiar interest could they be restored
to us, as they would naturally be identified with the treatise
the mention of which occurs in one of the most striking
passages of the saint's Life. We refer of course to the book
written by St. Dominic in confutation of the Albigensian
heresies, and which, thrice cast into the fire, remained
uninjured, aud was even flung out of the burning heap by

the flames which refused to touch it. Although this book is lost to us, together with his other writings, there exists a tradition concerning its contents which we will give, without passing any judgment as to its authenticity, as it is to be found alluded to by several writers. The following extract is from a letter of Father Alessandro Santo Canalo, of the Society of Jesus, published in a collection of letters on the Immaculate Conception, at Palermo, in the year 1742. He says, " All the regular Orders, following the inclination of the Holy Church their mother, have always shown a courageous zeal in defence of the Immaculate Conception. And I say *all;* because one of the most earnest in favour of the Immaculate Conception has been the most learned and most holy Dominican Order, even from its very first beginning—I mean even from the time of the great patriarch St. Dominic, in the dispute which he held with the Albigenses at Toulouse, with so much glory to the Church and to himself. Almost from the time of St. Dominic down to the present day, there has been preserved in the public archives of Barcelona a very ancient tablet, whereon is described the famous dispute of the saint with the Albigenses, and the triumph of the truth, confirmed by the miracle of the fire, into which, at the request of the heretics, the saint having thrown his book, when that of the Albigenses was destroyed, his remained uninjured. Of which book this inscription thus speaks: ' Against these errors St. Dominic wrote a book on the Flesh of Christ. And the Albigenses, rising up furiously against the said blessed Dominic, said that the Virgin was conceived in original sin. And the blessed Dominic replied, even as it is contained in his book, that what they said was not true: because the Virgin Mary was she of whom the Holy Ghost says by Solomon, "Thou art all fair, My beloved, and there is no stain in thee." ' In this book of St. Dominic's on the Flesh of Christ, chap. xvii., there are, among other passages, the following words, quoted from the Acts of St. Andrew: ' Even as the first Adam was made of virgin earth, which had never been cursed, so also was it fitting for the second

Adam to be made in like manner.'" It would seem, therefore, that the book was still extant at the time of this inscription, and that the above passages were quoted from it.

This tradition is accepted as authentic by many authorities, both ancient and modern. "According to credible opinion," says Monseigneur Parisis, "St. Dominic professed in very express terms his belief in the Immaculate Conception. It is even said that he committed it to writing in a certain book, which the heretics required him to cast into the flames. It contained (it is said) in the following terms the precious text of the Acts of the Martyrdom of St. Andrew." And he proceeds to quote the words given above.[3] The same tradition is referred to by the Blessed Peter Canisius,[4] by Suarez,[5] and by other authors who have written in defence of the Immaculate Conception. Nor is there anything improbable in the supposition that St. Dominic, educated in the schools of Palencia, should have been the firm defender of a doctrine which was held and taught by all Spanish theologians.

In closing the history of this glorious saint, what fitting words can be found in which to sum up his life and character? The greatest of Christian poets has drawn his portrait in some of the noblest lines that ever flowed even from his inspired pen. "There," he says, "where the gentle breeze whispers among the young flowers that blossom over the fields of Europe, not far from that shore where break the waves behind which the big sun sinks at eventide, is the fortunate Calaroga; and there was born the loyal lover of the Christian faith, the holy athlete, gentle to his friends, and terrible only to the enemies of truth. They called him Dominic. He was the ambassador and the friend of Christ;[6] and his first love was for the first counsel that Jesus gave. His nurse found him often lying on the ground, as though he had said, 'It was for this that I came.' It was because of his

---

[3] *Demonstration de l'Immaculée Conception de la B.Vierge Marie, Mère de Dieu.*
[4] *De B. Maria,* lib. i. cap. 7.
[5] Suarez, tom. 2, in 3, S. Thomas, disp. 3, sect. 5.
[6] *Messo e famigliar* di Christo.

love for the Divine truth, and not for the world, that he
became a great doctor in a short time; and he came before
the throne of Peter, not to seek dispensations, or tithes, or
the best benefices, or the patrimony of the poor, but only
for freedom to combat against the errors of the world by the
Word of God. Then, armed with his doctrine and his mighty
will, he went forth to his apostolic ministry, even as some
mountain torrent precipitates itself from a rocky height.
And the impetuosity of that great flood, throwing itself on
the heresies that stemmed its way, flowed on far and wide,
and broke into many a stream that watered the garden of the
Church."[7]

But there is another writer whose words have a better
right to be heard on this subject than even the greatest of
poets. St. Catherine of Siena, one of the glories of the
Dominican Order, and the devout client of him whose life
and virtues it was her constant desire to imitate, when (in
the person of the Eternal Father) she declares the excellence
of the various religious Orders established in the Church, and
the spirit of their respective founders, she speaks thus of the
Order of Preachers, and of its illustrious patriarch:[8]

·"If you look at the ship of your Father Dominic, My
beloved son, you will see with what perfect order he governed
it, desiring that his children should devote themselves solely
to My honour and the salvation of souls, by the light of
science. Not indeed that he despised voluntary poverty, . . .
but he chose as his special object the light of science to
extirpate the errors which had then arisen in the world.
He took on him the office of My Son, the only-begotten
Word. He appeared in the world as an apostle, sowing the
seed of My Word, scattering darkness, and bringing light.
He was indeed a shining light whom I gave to the world
through the hands of Mary, and whom I placed in the mystical
body of the Church, to root out heresy. For it was from
the hands of Mary that he received the habit, that office
having been committed to her by My goodness. On what
table did he and his sons feed by the light of science? At

[7] Dante, *Par.* canto xii. 46—105.   [8] *Dial.* c. 158.

the table of the Cross, where full of holy desires they fed on souls in My honour. For Dominic desired that his sons should attend to no other thing than this, to seek the praise and glory of My Name by the salvation of souls. It was to enable them to do this that he delivered them from temporal cares by the vow of poverty. And when the faith of some failed, fearing lest they should be in want of necessary things, his confidence never failed, but with firm hope he trusted in My Providence. He willed also that they should observe obedience and chastity, that the eye of their under-standing might never be darkened. . . . For the light of science may be darkened by pride, and where pride is there can never be true obedience. For, as I have before declared, a man is humble in proportion as he is obedient, and he is obedient in proportion as he is humble, and it rarely happens that any one transgresses the vow of obedience without failing in the other vows also. Thus then did Dominic govern the ship of his Order, bound by the three cables of obedience, chastity, and poverty. And he made it a royal Order, wherein none were bound under mortal sin, . . . for enlightened by Me the true Light, he willed not the death of the sinner, but that all should be converted and should live. Therefore is his Order large and joyous, and odoriferous as a delightful garden."

With St. Catherine's magnificent words we close these pages. That which St. Dominic chose to be the one work and object of his Order demands now as ever to be accom-plished by his children, to labour, namely, for "the glory and praise of God's holy Name by the salvation of souls." Nor does he leave them without promise of assistance, for the words spoken on his dying bed are their everlasting inheritance. "Oh, wonderful hope which thou gavest to those who wept for thee in the hour of thy death, promising after thy departure to be helpful to thy children; fulfil, O Father, what thou hast said, and assist us by thy prayers.'

FINIS.

# INDEX.

## A

ADORATION, heretical rite of, 27, 43
Agnes, St., monastery of, Cologne, 128
Alan de la Roche, 123, 127, 129, 131
—Lanvalay, 329
Albert, Franciscan lay-brother, 273
Albigenses, their origin, 23
—doctrines, 24, 25
—practices, 26, 28
—power finally broken, 188
Alexander of Toulouse, 152
—of Scotland, 329
Al Sicari, 90
Amadour, St., 303
Amizo of Milan, 338
Amy, Sister, 223
Angelic Salutation, 125, 127
Angelus the Carmelite, St., 161
Angels, visit of, at Rome, 202, 211
—at Faenza, 274
—at Bologna, 277
—St. Dominic led by, 243
—defend the convent of Bologna, 375
Anthony Sers, will of, 133, 296
Appearance of St. Dominic, 270
Ark of St. Dominic, 471
Arnold of Citeaux, 35, 39, 63, 78
—of Lyons, 301
Assassination of Peter of Castlenau, 70
Aventine, the, 225
Avignon, St. Dominic at, 335
Austin, Rule of St., 163

## B

BACON and Fishacre, 442, 443
Barcelona, St. Dominic at, 297
—Foundation at, 377
Bees swarm on lips of St. Dominic, 5
—at Bosquet, 98
—at Brives, 328
Beguinage of Ghent, 129

Bell at Rocamadour, 305
Benedicta, conversion of, 380
Bergamo, St. Dominic at, 337, 417
Bertrand of Garrigua, 97, 101
—at Rocamadour, 308
Beziers, massacre at, 478
Biblical Concordance, the first, 450
Bishoprics refused by St. Dominic, 94, note
Blackfriars, London, 446
Blanche of Castile, 325
Boatman, paid, the, 97
Bologna, brethren sent to, 204
—Reginald at, 342
—St. Dominic at, 352
—he heals the feuds of, 365
—made citizen of, 431
Bonviso of Placentia, 366, 381
Book of Charity, the, 120
Books lost and found, 96

## C

CALAROGA, St. Dominic born at, 2
—convent of, 296
Canons Regular, 12, 13
Canonical penances 123, 124
Canonization of St. Dominic, 468
Carcassonne, St. Dominic resides at, 89
Cardinal Ugolino, 20, 173, 275, 460
—James de Vitry, 387
—Capocci, 97, 411
Castres, St. Dominic at, 130, 140
Castelnau, Peter of, 41
—his murder, 70
Cassian's Conferences, 13, 415
Castelnaudry, 83
Catacombs, St. Dominic in the, 212
Catherine, St., her vision of St. Dominic, 271
—on the Order, 473
—of Rome, story of, 383
Cecilia and Catherine, SS., appear, 240
Cecilia, Sister, 221

FF

Cells at St. Romain, 168, 178
Champ des, Épis, 42
Chapter General, first, 391
—second, 429
—at Oxford, 446
—at London, 446
Chapter-house at St. Sixtus, 207
—at Paris, 323
Charity, the book of, 120
Chasuble of St. Dominic, 473
Cistercians, 268
Citeaux, St. Dominic at, 20, 21
Clare, Brother, 276, 345
Claret, William de, 56
—leaves the Order, 165
Cock restored to life, 291
Como, convent of, 416
Conferences at Servian, 40
—Montreal, 43
—Fanjeaux 45
Confidence in God, 267
Confirmation of the Rule, 170
Confraternity of the Rosary, 133, 201
Conrad of Germany, 404
—of Porto, 373
Consolamentum, the, 26
Constitutions, the, 163, 164
Conversion of Carino, 434
Cotteraux, the, 32
Cremona, convent of, 419
—Roland of, 345
Crucifix of St. Dominic, 146
—in cells, 392
Crusade, the, 73
Cuna, the, 2
Cypress tree at Bologna, 403

D

DANIEL, ST., hermitage of, 192
Dartford, Kent, convent of, 451
Death of Diego, 62
—of Peter of Aragon, 145
—De Montfort, 186
—Reginald, 359
—Everard, 432
Demon, malice of the, 235, 238, 385, 386
Demoniacs delivered, 222, 348
Desertion of the brethren, 292
Diana d'Andalo, 275, 351
—her troubles, 401
Diego of Azevedo, 12, 17, 38, 62
Dispersion of the brethren, 182
Doge of Venice, 192
Dominic, St., birth and baptism, 24
—education, 7
—university life, 8
—during famine, 10
—Canon Regular, 13
—mission to Marches, 16

Dominic, St., first visit to Rome, 19
—in Languedoc, 36
—disputes with heretics, 41
—book not burnt, 41, 46
—founds Prouille, 50
—is left alone, 63
—disperses tempest, 99
—Inquisitor, 106 et seq.
—institutes the Rosary, 122
—at Castres, 140
—at Muret, 146
—founds the Order, 150
—second visit to Rome, 154
—meets St. Francis, 160
—chooses Rule, 163
—third visit to Rome, 168
—vision of Apostles, 169
—profession, 175
—rule of life, 179
—disperses brethren, 183
—at Venice, 192
—manner of travelling, 193
—at St. Sixtus, 200
—raises two persons to life, 207
—multiplies bread, 214, 277
—and wine, 211, 242, 277
—raises Napoleon to life, 219, 220
—delivers possessed, 222
—at Santa Sabina, 226
—Master of the Sacred Palace, 230
—reforms nuns, 216, 235
—is led by an angel, 243
—founds Third Order, 243
—portrait of, 254
—friend of Jesus Christ, 257
—goes to Spain, 281
—letter to nuns of Madrid, 289
—at Saragossa, 294
—at Barcelona, 297
—at Toulouse, 300
—at Rocamadour, 308
—speaks German, 310
—at Paris, 311
—preaches in Notre Dame, 330
—at Avignon, 335
—returns to Bologna, 352
—life there, 371
—fifth visit to Rome, 379
—brings spoons to nuns, 382
—holds first Chapter, 390
—gains Master Conrad, 404
—progress through Lombardy, 412
—illness at Milan, 415
—at Como, 416
—his seal, 427
—cures nuns, 418
—made citizen of Bologna, 431
—last illness, 456
—and death, 459
—obsequies, 460
—translation, 464

Dominic, St., canonization, 468
—office and feast, 470
—ark, 471
—relics, 472
—writings, 475
—Dominic the little, 166
—of Segovia, *ibid*.
Drought at Segovia, 282
Dumb, a woman struck, 279


E

EELS, 334
England, Order in, 441
English Concordance, 450
English pilgrims saved, 95, 96
Eustorgio, St., 415
Everard, death of, 432
Ezzelino, 422


F

FAENZA, St. Dominic at, 274
—pulpit at, *ibid*.
Fanjeaux, 45,
—miracle of, 46,
—St. Dominic, parish priest of, 51, 82
Fever, Sisters cured of, 428
Florence, brethren sent to, 376
—St. Dominic at, 379
Francis, St., meeting with, 160, 386, 419
Friars of Mary, 398
"Friend of Jesus Christ," St. Dominic the, 257, 285
Fulk of Toulouse, 64
—munificence to the Order, 55, 153
—last meeting with St. Dominic, 427


G

GERARD DE FRACHET, 326
German pilgrims massacred, 82
—St. Dominic speaks, 310
Gilbert de Fresnoy, 441
Gilbertines and St. Sixtus, 200
Gilles, church of St., 74
Gormas, nuns of, 296
Government of the Order, 429
Gregory IX. canonizes St. Dominic, 468
Grotto at Carcassonne, 104
—at Segovia, 284
Guala of Brescia, 420, 421
—his vision, 462
Guerric of Metz, 313
—of St. Quentin, 314
Gumiel d'Izan, 6, 7
Guzman, family of, 2

H

HABIT of the Order shown to Reginald, 250
—Theodoric on, 251
Healing of feuds, 365
Henry of Moravia, 229
—of Marburgh, 318
—of Cologne, 357, 361
—of Rome, 213
Hereford, convent of, 447
Heretics, Dominic disputes with, 41, 43
—attempt his life, 90
—their malice, 91
Holy Name, 363
Honorius III., elected, 169
—confirms the Order, 171
—gives St. Sixtus to St. Dominic, 200
—and Sta. Sabina, 217
Horses to shoe, 399
Hugh de St. Cher, 317, 449
Humbert de Romans, his vocation, 316
Hungary, brethren sent to, 431
Hyacinth, St., vocation of, 228


I

Immaculate Conception, St. Dominic on the, 476
Incarnation, Albigenses denied the, 24, 127
Innocence of the brethren, 184, 185
Innocent III., accession, 34
—letter to Count Raymond, 68
—his vision, 157
—death, 168
Inquisitor, St. Dominic the first, 106
Ireland, Order in, 452
Isnard, Brother, 418


J

JAMES, ST., convent of, 190, 311
Jews, Dominicans of London protect, 450
John of Navarre, 184
—lay-brother, 336
—of Salerno, 368
—of Vicenza,
—the Teutonic, 398, 399
John and Paul, SS., convent of, 192
Jordan of Saxony, 331
—his vocation, 357


L

LANDUCCI, Chiaro, 410
Languedoc, St. Dominic's first visit, 18
—Apostle of, 87
Lateran, third Council of, 33
—fourth, 155, 159
*Laudare, benedicere, prædicare*, 373

Laughter and tears of St. Dominic, 403
Lawrence, Brother, 96, 166
—goes to Paris, 190
—at Rome, 212
Legends, 237
Letter to Poland, 446
—to nuns of Madrid, 289
Likeness to our Lord, 270
Limoges, convent of, 327
London, convent of, 446
Louis, St., 188, 325
Love of children, St. Dominic's, 94
—of souls, 256
Lymborch, Philip de, on the Inquisition, 112

M

MADRID, St. Dominic at, 287
—nuns of, 289, 290
Manes Guzman, 3, 167, 288
Matthew of France, 140
—Abbot, 183
—sent to Paris, 182
—his troubles there, 324
Mercy, the house of, 350
Metz, St. Dominic at, 191
Milan, St. Dominic at, 191, 337, 339, 412
Militia of Jesus Christ, 243
Miracles, 42, 46, 95, 207, 209, 220, 242, 298
Moneta, vocation of, 344
Montferrat, W. de, 173, 331
Montfort, de, character of, 79
—elected chief, 80
—friendship with St. Dominic, 82
—his death, 186
Muret, battle of, 143, 144
Murate, 172, 209

N.

NAPOLEON ORSINI raised to life, 219, 220
Nicholas, St., Convent of, 275, under Reginald, 347, under St. Dominic,
—Palea, 368, 370
—the Englishman, 463, 466
Nine methods of prayer, 258
Noel, Brother, 56, is drowned, 165
Norbert, St., Rule of, 163
Nuns of Prouille, 54, 55, of Trastavere, 216, of St. Sixtus, 235, of Madrid, 287, 288, of Dartford, 451

O.

ODERIC, first lay-brother, 167
Order, foundation of the, 149

Orange-tree, 227
Orvieto, 380
Osma, 12
Our Father, St. Dominic's love of the, 9, 261
Oxford, 442, 444

P.

PALACE, Master of the Sacred, 230
Palencia, St. Dominic at, 8, 296
Pamiers, Conference at, 61, 64, 188
Paris, brethren sent to, 182, 190, Dominic's first visit to, 189, second, 311, University of, 357
Paul, St., Epistles of, 15, 170, 230, of Hungary, 368, of Venice, 393
Peacemakers, the friars, 367
Penafiel, 11
Penance, of Count Raymund VI. 74, VII. 188, inflicted by Reginald, 349, by Dominic, 374
Perfect and believers, the, 26, 85, 114, 115
Perugia, foundation at, 370
Peter and Paul, SS. vision of, 169, de Castelnau, 35, 41, 66, 70, Peter Cellani, 150, 325, 328, of Aragon, 83, his death, 145
Peter Martyr, St., 433, Peter of Saragossa, conversion of, 293, 294
Picture of our Lady at St. Sisto, 216, of St. Dominic at Santa Sabina, 226, 271, at Bologna, 472, Suriano, 474
Ponce Roger, 109, 111
Poverty, of St. Dominic, 178, 267, his love of, 393, 425, rule of explained, 394, 396
Prayer used by St. Dominic, 194, nine methods of, 258
Preachers, title of, 159, anecdotes of, 435
Preaching, St. Dominic's style of, 266
— yard at Hereford, 441
Profession of St. Dominic, 175, of first brethren, 182
Prouille, foundation of, 53, 54, assembly at, 181
Pulpit at Fanjeaux, 51, at Faenza, 274
Puy, St. Dominic at, 189

R.

RAYMUND, V. 30, VI. 35
—VII., does penance, 188
—St., of Pennafort, 377, 378
Raoul, 385, his vision, 462
Recaldo, conversion of, 315
Reginald of Orleans, 347, at Bologna, 341, at Paris, 356, death of, 359
Relics of St. Dominic, 472

Rhuddlan, tombstone near, 448
Robaldo of Milan, 413
Rocamadour, St. Dominic at, 308
Robert Kilwardby, 311
Rodolph of Faenza, 275
Roland the Paladin, 306, 307, of Cremona, 345
Romain, St., convent of, 167, 177
Rome, St. Dominic's first visit to, second, 155, third, 168, fourth, 189, fifth, 379, last, 426
Romeo of Livia, 185, 301
Rosary, Confraternities of, 133, instructions on the, 384
Rule, Confirmation of, 170, 171
Rule of life, Dominic's, 179

S.

SACRISTAN penanced, 374
Salve Regina, 239
Santa Sabina, 225, 227
Schools, Dominic in the, 152
Scholars, anecdotes of, 314
Seal, of St. Dominic, 427, of Norwich, 447
Segnadou, the, 51
Segovia, Dominic at, 282, grotto of, 285
Serenity of St. Dominic, 255, 256
Servian, Conference at, 40
Sickness of St. Dominic, 381, 415, his last, 456
Siena, St. Dominic at, 162, convent of, 408
Silence, St. Dominic's, 180, observance of, 348
Silvos, 3
Song of the Crusade, 65, note, its continuation, 159, note
Spain, St. Dominic in, 281
Spoons from Spain, 382
Staff of St. Dominic, 170, he gives one to Reginald, 252
St. Sixtus, 200
Stephen of Paris, vocation of, 366, 367
Studies, sacred, 320
Suero Gomez, 165, 183, 205

T.

TABLE of St. Dominic, 278
Tancred of Germany, 204, of Siena, 409

Tenderness of St. Dominic, 264
Teresa, St., at Segovia, 285
Testament, priest and, 372, of St. Dominic, 457
Toulouse, St. Dominic spends Lent at, 92, surrender of, 148
Training of novices, 331, 371
Translation of St. Dominic, 464
Travelling, mode of, 193
Trees, orange and peach, at Rome, 227, cypress of Agosta, 252, of Bologna, 403, Juniper at Brescia, 420
Truce of God, 67, Raymund breaks it, 69, 75

U.

UGOLINO, Cardinal, 173, 215, 249, 386, 400, 414
University of Toulouse, 188, of Paris, 312, of Bologna, 364, of Oxford, 442.

V.

VENICE, St. Dominic at, 192, 455
Verona, 421
Vicenza, John of, 422
Vincent de Beauvais, 311
Virgin, the Blessed, visions of, 122, 239, 250, Order under her mantle, 240, 241, note
Viterbo, 381, 411
Vocation, stories of, 314

W.

WALTER MALCLERK, 442, 444
William, abbot of St. Paul's, 103, 104, de Montferrat, 173, 370
Wine increased, 242, 277, 297
Word the, St. Dominic represents, 255
Writings of St. Dominic, 475

X.

Xuron of Milan, 339

Z.

Zaccheus, 303
Zacharias, horses of, 399
Zamora, 286